Lecture Notes in Computer Science 2071
Edited by G. Goos, J. Hartmanis and J. van Leeuwen

Springer
Berlin
Heidelberg
New York
Barcelona
Hong Kong
London
Milan
Paris
Singapore
Tokyo

Robert Harper (Ed.)

Types in Compilation

Third International Workshop, TIC 2000
Montreal, Canada, September 21, 2000
Revised Selected Papers

Springer

Series Editors

Gerhard Goos, Karlsruhe University, Germany
Juris Hartmanis, Cornell University, NY, USA
Jan van Leeuwen, Utrecht University, The Netherlands

Volume Editor

Robert Harper
Carnegie Mellon University
School of Computer Science
5000 Forbes Avenue, Pittsburgh, PA 15213-3891, USA
E-mail: rwh@cs.cmu.edu

Cataloging-in-Publication Data applied for

Die Deutsche Bibliothek - CIP-Einheitsaufnahme

Types in compilation : third international workshop ; revised selected papers / TIC 2000, Montreal, Canada, September 21, 2000. Robert Harper (ed.). - Berlin ; Heidelberg ; New York ; Barcelona ; Hong Kong ; London ; Milan ; Paris ; Singapore ; Tokyo : Springer, 2001
(Lecture notes in computer science ; Vol. 2071)
ISBN 3-540-42196-3

CR Subject Classification (1998): D.3, F.3, F.4,

ISSN 0302-9743
ISBN 3-540-42196-3 Springer-Verlag Berlin Heidelberg New York

Springer-Verlag Berlin Heidelberg New York
a member of BertelsmannSpringer Science+Business Media GmbH

http://www.springer.de

Printed in Germany

Typesetting: Camera-ready by author, data conversion by PTP Berlin, Stefan Sossna
Printed on acid-free paper SPIN 10781674 06/3142 5 4 3 2 1 0

Preface

The importance of typed languages for building robust software systems is, by now, an undisputed fact. Years of research have led to languages with richly expressive, yet easy to use, type systems for high-level programming languages. Types provide not only a conceptual framework for language designers, but also afford positive benefits to the programmer, principally the ability to express and enforce levels of abstraction within a program.

Early compilers for typed languages followed closely the methods used for their untyped counterparts. The role of types was limited to the earliest stages of compilation, and they were thereafter ignored during the remainder of the translation process. More recently, however, implementors have come to recognize the importance of types during compilation and even for object code. Several advantages of types in compilation have been noted to date:

- They support self-checking by the compiler. By tracking types during compilation it is possible for an internal type checker to detect translation errors at an early stage, greatly facilitating compiler development.
- They support certification of object code. By extending types to the generated object code, it becomes possible for a code user to ensure the basic integrity of that code by checking its type consistency before execution.
- They support optimized data representations and calling conventions, even in the presence of modularity. By passing types at compile-, link-, and even run-time, it is possible to avoid compromises of data representation imposed by untyped compilation techniques.
- They support checked integration of program components. By attaching type information to modules, a linker can ensure the integrity of a composite system by checking compliance with interface requirements.

Types in Compilation (TIC) is a recurring workshop devoted to the application of types in the implementation of programming languages. This volume consists of a selection of papers from the TIC 2000 Workshop held in Montreal, Canada in September 2000. The papers published herein were chosen from submissions solicited after the meeting by a rigorous refereeing process comparable in depth and scope to the selection criteria for an archival journal. Each paper was reviewed by at least three referees chosen from the TIC 2000 program committee (named below), with final publication decisions made by the program chair. This volume represents the result of that review and revision process.

March 2001 — Robert Harper

Organization

TIC 2000 was held in cooperation with ACM SIGPLAN in Montreal, Canada on September 21, 2000 as part of the Colloquium on Principles, Logics, and Implementations of High-Level Programming Languages (PLI 2000). The TIC organizers are grateful to ACM SIGPLAN and to PLI for their assistance and support.

Organizing Committee

Craig Chambers, University of Washington
Karl Crary (chair), Carnegie Mellon University
Robert Harper, Carnegie Mellon University
Xavier Leroy, INRIA Rocquencourt
Robert Muller, Boston College
Atsushi Ohori, Kyoto University
Simon Peyton Jones, Microsoft Corporation

Program Committee

Dominic Duggan, Stevens Institute of Technology
Robert Harper (chair), Carnegie Mellon University
Trevor Jim, AT&T
Andrew Kennedy, Microsoft Corporation
Atsushi Ohori, Kyoto University
Franklyn Turbak, Wellesley College

Table of Contents

Types in Compilation

Sound and Complete Elimination of Singleton Kinds

Karl Crary

Carnegie Mellon University

Abstract. Singleton kinds provide an elegant device for expressing type equality information resulting from modern module languages, but they can complicate the metatheory of languages in which they appear. I present a translation from a language with singleton kinds to one without, and prove that translation to be sound and complete. This translation is useful for type-preserving compilers generating typed target languages. The proof of soundness and completeness is done by normalizing type equivalence derivations using Stone and Harper's type equivalence decision procedure.

1 Introduction

Type-preserving compilation, compilation using statically typed intermediate languages, offers many compelling advantages over conventional untyped compilation. A typed compiler can utilize type information to enable optimizations that would otherwise be prohibitively difficult or impossible. Internal type checking can be used to help debug a compiler by catching errors introduced into programs in optimization or transformation stages. Finally, if preserved through the compiler to its ultimate output, types can be used to certify that executables are *safe*, that is, free of certain fatal errors or malicious behavior [16].

For typed compilation to be practical, we require elegant yet expressive type theories for use in the compiler: expressive because they must support the full expressive power of a real source language, and elegant because they must be practical for a compiler to manipulate. One important issue arising in the design of such type theories for compiling Standard ML, Objective CAML, and similar languages is how to account for type abbreviations and sharing constraints in the module language. For example, consider the following SML signature:

```
signature SIG =
  sig
    type t = int
    val x : t
    val f : t -> t
  end
```

If `S` is a structure having signature `SIG`, the type theory must ensure that `S.t` is interchangeable with `int` in any code having access to `S`.

R. Harper (Ed.): TIC 2000, LNCS 2071, pp. 1–25, 2001.

The standard account of sharing in type theory was developed independently by Harper and Lillibridge, under the name translucent sums [6,13], and by Leroy, under the name manifest types [10] (and extended in Leroy [11]). These type theories provide a facility for stating type abbreviations in signatures and (importantly) ensure the correct propagation of type information resulting from those abbreviations. (Exactly what is meant by correct propagation is discussed in Section 2.1.) Translucent sums are employed in the type-theoretic definition of Standard ML given by Harper and Stone [9] (currently the only formal account of an entire practical programming language in type theory), and manifest types are similarly employed (somewhat less formally) by Leroy [12] for Objective CAML.

In this paper I consider a type theory based on *singleton kinds* [21], a variant of the translucent sum/manifest type formalism. The singleton kind calculus differs from the standard accounts in that it separates the module system from the mechanisms for type abbreviations and focuses on the latter. This separation is appropriate, first, because the two issues are orthogonal (although they typically arise together in practice), but more importantly, because type abbreviations persevere even after the compiler eliminates modules [7]. Furthermore, separating modules from the issue of type propagation makes it unnecessary to compare types by name (as in the module-based accounts), which makes it possible to propagate more type information. (An example of this is given in Section 2.1.)

Singleton kinds provide a very elegant and uniform type-theoretic mechanism for ensuring the propagation of type information. Kinds are used in type theories containing higher-order type constructors to classify type constructors just as types classify ordinary terms. Using singleton kinds, in the above example `S.t` is given the kind $S(\texttt{int})$, the kind containing only the type `int` (and types equal to it). Propagation of type information is then obtained by augmenting the typechecker with the rule that if τ has kind $S(\tau')$, then $\tau = \tau'$.

When using singleton kinds in practice, the question arises of how singleton kinds affect typechecking, given that they provide a new (and conceivably difficult to discover) way to show types to be equal. In fact, Harper and Stone [21] show that there exists a very simple algorithm for deciding equality of types in the presence of singleton kinds. Indeed, the algorithm is very nearly identical to the usual algorithm employed in the absence of singletons in practice (as opposed to the less-efficient algorithms often considered in theory). In this sense, singleton kinds complicate the compiler very little.

Nevertheless, there are some good reasons why one may want to compile away singleton kinds: Although the decision algorithm discussed above is simple, its proof of correctness is quite complex, and may be difficult to extend to more complicated type systems. (The complexity of this proof is probably the source of the common misconception that singleton kinds make typechecking difficult.) The latter phases of a type-preserving compiler may involve some very complicated type systems indeed [15,3,4,20]. Extending Stone and Harper's proof to these type systems, some of which already have nontrivial decidability proofs, is a daunting prospect. Moreover, there already exist a variety of tools for manipulating low-level typed languages that, by and large, do not support singleton kinds.

In this paper, I present such a strategy for compiling away singleton kinds. To implement the source language correctly, this elimination strategy should be sound and complete relative to the singleton calculus, that is, two types should be equal in the singleton calculus if and only if they are equal after singleton elimination. This means that the elimination process does not cause any programs to cease to typecheck, nor does it allow any programs to typecheck that would not have before.[1]

The compilation process is based on the natural idea of substituting definitions for any appearances of variables having singleton kinds. However, how to do this in a sound and complete manner is not obvious because, as discussed below in Section 3.1, in the presence of internal bindings, it is difficult to determine whether or not a variable has a singleton kind. Although I show this issue can be handled elegantly, as with Stone and Harper, the correctness proof is not obvious. This proof is the central technical contribution of the paper.

The existence of a sound and complete compilation strategy does not imply that singleton kinds are useless. They provide an extremely elegant and succinct account of ML's type sharing that (with modules taken out of the picture) is essentially equivalent to the standard type-theoretic accounts employed to explain practical source languages. To exploit this result and remove singletons from consideration entirely (in the absence of some alternative) would require programmers to eliminate type abbreviations by hand, resulting in verbose, unreadable code (to no particular benefit). Moreover, singleton kinds may also be useful for some other purposes such as compression of type information, or polymorphic closure conversion [14].

What this result does mean is using translucent sums, manifest types or singleton kinds to express sharing in the source language need not constrain the compilation strategy. One may use singleton kinds through as many compilation phases as desired, and then compile them away and proceed without them. For example, a reasonable architecture is to use singleton kinds in the compiler's front end (which performs ML-specific optimizations and transformations), but not in the back end (which may use complicated type systems for code generation and low-level transformations).

This paper is organized as follows: In Section 2, I formalize the singleton kind calculus and discuss some of its subtleties that make it complicated to work with. In Section 3, I present the singleton elimination strategy and state its correctness theorem. Section 4 is dedicated to the proof of the correctness theorem, and concluding remarks appear in Section 5.

---

[1] It may be argued that only the former property is essential to implement the source language correctly, that it is acceptable to allow more programs to typecheck provided that the post-translation type system is still sound. Nevertheless, the latter is still a desirable property.

$$
\begin{array}{lll}
\text{kinds} & K ::= T \mid S(c) \mid \Pi\alpha{:}K_1.K_2 \mid \Sigma\alpha{:}K_1.K_2 \\
\text{constructors} & c ::= \alpha \mid b \mid \lambda\alpha{:}K.c \mid c_1 c_2 \mid \langle c_1, c_2 \rangle \mid \\
& \qquad \pi_1 c \mid \pi_2 c \\
\text{assignments} & \Gamma ::= \epsilon \mid \Gamma, \alpha{:}K
\end{array}
$$

Fig. 1. Syntax

This paper assumes familiarity with type systems with higher-order type constructors and dependent types. The correctness proof draws from the work of Stone and Harper [21] showing decidability of type equivalence in the presence of singleton kinds, but we will use their results almost entirely "off the shelf," so familiarity with their paper is not required.

2 A Singleton Kind Calculus

We begin by formalizing the singleton calculus that is the subject of this paper. The syntax of the singleton calculus is given in Figure 1. It consists of a class of type constructors (usually referred to as "constructors" for brevity) and a class of kinds, which classify constructors. The class of constructors contains variables (ranged over by α), a collection of base types (ranged over by b), and the usual introduction and elimination forms for functions and pairs over constructors. We could also add a collection of primitive type operators (such as `list` or `->`) without difficulty, but have not done so in the interest of simplicity.

The kind structure is the novelty of the singleton calculus. The base kinds include T, the kind of all types, and $S(c)$, the kind of all types definitionally equal to c. Thus, $S(c)$ represents a singleton set, up to definitional equality. The constructor c in $S(c)$ is permitted to be open, and consequently kinds may contain free constructor variables, which makes it useful to have *dependent* kinds. The kind $\Pi\alpha{:}K_1.K_2$ contains functions from K_1 to K_2, where α refers to the function's argument and may appear free in K_2. Analogously, the kind $\Sigma\alpha{:}K_1.K_2$ contains pairs of constructors from K_1 and K_2, where α refers to the left-hand member and may appear free in K_2. As usual, when α does not appear free in K_2, we write $\Pi\alpha{:}K_1.K_2$ as $K_1 \rightarrow K_2$ and $\Sigma\alpha{:}K_1.K_2$ as $K_1 \times K_2$.

In addition, the syntax provides a class of *assignments*, which assign kinds to free constructor variables, for use in the calculus's static semantics. In a practical application, the language would be extended with an additional class of terms, but for our purposes (which deal with constructor equality) we need not be concerned with terms, so they are omitted.

As usual, alpha-equivalent expressions (written $E \equiv E'$) are taken to be identical. The capture-avoiding substitution of c for α in E (where E is a kind, constructor or assignment) is written $E\{c/\alpha\}$. We also will often desire to define substitutions independent of a particular place of use, so when σ is a substitution, we denote the application of σ to the expression E by $E\{\sigma\}$. Separately defined

```
signature SIG2 =
  sig
    type s
    type t = int
    type u = s * t
    ... value fields ...
  end

funsig FSIG (S : sig
                   type s
                   ... value fields ...
                 end) =
  sig
    type t
    type u = S.s * t
    ... value fields ...
  end
```

Fig. 2. Sample Signatures

substitutions will usually be written in the form $\{c_1/\alpha_1\} \cdots \{c_n/\alpha_n\}$, denoting a sequential substitution with the leftmost substitution taking place first.

As discussed in the introduction, the principal intended use of singleton kinds is in conjunction with module systems. For example, the type portion of signature `SIG2` in Figure 2 is translated to the kind:

$$\Sigma\alpha{:}T.\, \Sigma\beta{:}S(\mathtt{int}).\, S(\alpha{*}\beta)$$

Note the essential use of dependent sums in this kind. Dependent products arise from the phase splitting [7] of functors, in which the static portion of a functor (*i.e.*, its action on types) is separated from the dynamic portion. For example, after phase-splitting, the type portion of the functor signature `FSIG` in Figure 2 (given in the syntax of Standard ML of New Jersey version 110) is translated to the kind:

$$\Pi\alpha{:}T.\, (\Sigma\beta{:}T.\, S(\alpha{*}\beta))$$

2.1 Judgements

The inference rules defining the static semantics of the singleton calculus are given in Appendix A. For the reader's convenience, the rules are given in the same order and essentially the same form as in Stone and Harper [21]. A summary of the judgements that these rules define, and their interpretations, are given in Figure 3. The context and kind equality judgements are auxiliary judgements used in theorems but not by any of the other judgements. For the most part, the static semantics consists of the usual rules for a dependently typed lambda

Judgement	Interpretation
$\Gamma \vdash \mathrm{ok}$	Γ is a valid assignment
$\vdash \Gamma_1 = \Gamma_2$	Γ_1 and Γ_2 are equivalent assignments
$\Gamma \vdash K$	K is a valid kind
$\Gamma \vdash K_1 \leq K_2$	K_1 is a subkind of K_2
$\Gamma \vdash K_1 = K_2$	K_1 and K_2 are equivalent kinds
$\Gamma \vdash c : K$	c is a valid constructor with kind K
$\Gamma \vdash c_1 = c_2 : K$	c_1 and c_2 are equivalent as members of kind K

Fig. 3. Judgement Forms

calculus with products and sums (but lifted to the constructor level). Again, the novelty lies with the singleton kinds. Singleton kinds have two introduction rules (one for kind assignment and one for equivalence),

$$\frac{\Gamma \vdash c : T}{\Gamma \vdash c : S(c)} \qquad \frac{\Gamma \vdash c = c' : T}{\Gamma \vdash c = c' : S(c)}$$

and one elimination rule:

$$\frac{\Gamma \vdash c : S(c')}{\Gamma \vdash c = c' : T}$$

These rules capture the intuition of singleton kinds: The first says that any type belongs to its own singleton kind. The second says that equivalent types are also considered equivalent as members of their singleton kind. The third says that if one type belongs to another's singleton kind, then those types are equivalent.

The complexity of the singleton calculus arises from the above rules in conjunction with the subkinding relation generated by the following two rules:

$$\frac{\Gamma \vdash c : T}{\Gamma \vdash S(c) \leq T} \qquad \frac{\Gamma \vdash c_1 = c_2 : T}{\Gamma \vdash S(c_1) \leq S(c_2)}$$

These rules are essential for singleton kinds to serve their intended purpose in a modern module system. The first allows a signature to match a supersignature obtained by removing equality specifications. For example, structures having the signature `SIG` from the introduction should also match the signature obtained by replacing the specification "`type t = int`" (which we might write `type t` : $S(\texttt{int})$) with simply "`type t`" (which we might write `type t` : T). The second allows a signature to match another signature obtained by replacing equality specifications with different but equivalent ones.

The presence of subkinding makes the usual context-insensitive methods of dealing with equivalence impossible. Consider the identity function, $\lambda\alpha{:}T.\alpha$, and the constant `int` function, $\lambda\alpha{:}T.\texttt{int}$. These functions are clearly inequivalent as members of $T \to T$; that is, the judgement $\vdash \lambda\alpha{:}T.\alpha = \lambda\alpha{:}T.\texttt{int} : T \to T$ is not derivable. However, since $T \to T$ is a subkind of $S(\texttt{int}) \to T$, these two functions can also be compared as members of $S(\texttt{int}) \to T$ and in that kind they *are* equivalent. This is because the bodies α and `int` are compared under the assignment $\alpha{:}S(\texttt{int})$, under which α and `int` are equivalent by the singleton elimination rule. This example makes it clear that to deal with constructor equivalence in the singleton calculus, one must take into account the contexts in which the constructors appear.

The determination of equivalence is further complicated by the fact that the classifying kind may be given *implicitly*. For example, the classifying kind may be imposed by a function on its argument. Consider the constructors $\beta(\lambda\alpha{:}T.\alpha)$ and $\beta(\lambda\alpha{:}T.\texttt{int})$. These are well-formed under an assignment giving β the kind $(T \rightarrow T) \rightarrow T$ and also under one giving β the kind $(S(\texttt{int}) \rightarrow T) \rightarrow T$. However, for the same reason as above, the two constructors are equivalent under the second assignment but not the first.[2] The classifying kind can then be made even further remote by making β a function's formal argument instead of a free variable, and so on.

2.2 A Singleton-Free System

To formalize our results, we also require a singleton-free target language into which to translate expressions from the singleton calculus. We will define the singleton-free system in terms of its differences from the singleton calculus.

We will say that a constructor c (not necessarily well-formed) syntactically belongs to the singleton-free calculus provided that c contains no singleton kinds. Note that as a consequence of containing no singleton kinds, all product and sum kinds may be written in non-dependent form. Also, all kinds in the singleton-free calculus are well-formed.

The inference rules for the singleton-free system are obtained by removing from the singleton calculus all the rules dealing with subkinding (Rules 9–13, 28 and 45) and all the rules dealing with singleton kinds (Rules 6, 15, 25, 34 and 35). Note that derivable judgements in the singleton-free system must be built using only expressions syntactically belonging to the singleton-free calculus. When a judgement is derivable in the singleton-free system, we will note this fact by marking the turnstile $\vdash_{sf}$.

3 Elimination of Singleton Kinds

The critical rule in the static semantics of the singleton calculus is the singleton elimination rule (Rule 34). The main aim of the singleton kind elimination

[2] As an aside, in the module-based accounts [6,13,10,11] it is impossible to discover that the module analogues of these types are equal because comparisons can be made only on expressions in named form. Naming the expressions $\lambda\alpha{:}T.\alpha$ and $\lambda\alpha{:}T.\texttt{int}$ obscures the possible connection between them, which depends essentially on their actual code. (In the first-class account of Harper and Lillibridge [6,13] this is essential because the equality may not hold—in addition to being impossible to discover—since a functor can inspect the store before deciding what type to return.) This is an example of when the singleton kind account can propagate more type information than the module-based accounts.

$$T^\circ \stackrel{\text{def}}{=} T$$
$$S(c)^\circ \stackrel{\text{def}}{=} T$$
$$(\Pi\alpha{:}K_1.K_2)^\circ \stackrel{\text{def}}{=} {K_1}^\circ \rightarrow {K_2}^\circ$$
$$(\Sigma\alpha{:}K_1.K_2)^\circ \stackrel{\text{def}}{=} {K_1}^\circ \times {K_2}^\circ$$

Fig. 4. Singleton Erasure

process is to rewrite constructors so that any equivalences that hold for those constructors may be derived without using that rule. If this aim is achieved, any singleton kinds remaining within the constructors are not used (in any essential way) and can simply be erased, resulting in valid constructors and derivations in the singleton-free system.

This erasure process is made precise in Figure 4, which defines a mapping $(-)^\circ$ from singleton calculus kinds to singleton-free kinds that replaces all singleton kinds by T. The erasure mapping is lifted to constructors and assignments in the obvious manner. If $\Gamma \vdash c_1 = c_2 : K$ is derivable without using singleton elimination, then $\Gamma^\circ \vdash_{sf} {c_1}^\circ = {c_2}^\circ : K^\circ$ is derivable in the singleton-free system. A slightly stronger version of this fact is formalized as Lemma 5 in Section 4.3.

Thus, our goal is to rewrite constructors in such a manner that the singleton elimination rule is not necessary. As mentioned in the introduction, this rewriting is done by substituting definitions for variables whenever singleton kinds provide such definitions. This works out quite simply in first-order cases, but higher-order cases raise some subtle issues. We will explore these issues by considering a number of examples before defining the fully general elimination process.

Example 1. Suppose we are working under the assignment $\alpha{:}S(\texttt{int}), \beta{:}S(\texttt{bool})$. Naturally, we replace all free appearances of α in the constructor in question by `int`, and replace all free appearances of β by `bool`. This is done simply by performing the substitution $\{\texttt{bool}/\beta\}\{\texttt{int}/\alpha\}$ on the constructor in question.

In this example, we refer to `int` as the *expansion* of α, and likewise `bool` is the expansion of β. In general, the elimination process will have the same gross structure as in this example. For an assignment $\Gamma = \alpha_1{:}K_1, \ldots, \alpha_n{:}K_n$ we will define a substitution $R(\Gamma)$ of the form $\{c_n/\alpha_n\} \cdots \{c_1/\alpha_1\}$ where each c_i is the expansion of α_i.

Example 2. Suppose we are working under the assignment $\Gamma = \alpha{:}S(\texttt{int}), \beta{:}S(\alpha)$. In this case, analogously to the previous example, $R(\Gamma)$ is $\{\alpha/\beta\}\{\texttt{int}/\alpha\}$. Note that since this is a sequential substitution, it is equivalent to the substitution $\{\texttt{int}/\beta\}\{\texttt{int}/\alpha\}$, as one would expect.

Example 3. Suppose α is assigned the kind $S(\texttt{int}) \times S(\texttt{bool})$. In this case, $\pi_1\alpha$ is equal to `int` and $\pi_2\alpha$ is equal to `bool`. We can write these equalities into a constructor by substituting for α with the pair $\langle\texttt{int}, \texttt{bool}\rangle$.

Example 4. In the previous examples, the expansion of a variable α did not contain α, but this is not true in general. Suppose α is assigned the kind $T \times S(\mathtt{int})$. In this case, $\pi_2\alpha$ is equal to $\mathtt{int}$, but $\pi_1\alpha$ is not given a definition and should not be changed. We handle this by substituting for α with the pair $\langle \pi_1\alpha, \mathtt{int}\rangle$.

As this example illustrates, a good way to understand expansions is to view them as eta-long forms[3] of constructors. This interpretation is precisely correct, provided we view the replacement of a constructor by its singleton definition as an eta-expansion. In fact, the ultimate definition of expansions will eta-expand constructors uniformly, so, for example, if α has kind $T \times T$, its expansion will be $\langle \pi_1\alpha, \pi_2\alpha\rangle$ (instead of just α). This uniformity will make the correctness proof simpler, but a practical implementation would probably optimize such cases.

Example 5. Suppose α is assigned the kind $\Sigma\beta{:}T.S(\beta)$. Then $\pi_2\alpha$ is known to be equal to $\pi_1\alpha$ (although its precise value is unknown). In this case the expansion of α is $\langle \pi_1\alpha, \pi_1\alpha\rangle$.

Example 6. Suppose α is assigned the kind $\Sigma\beta{:}S(\mathtt{int}).S(\beta)$. In this case $\pi_1\alpha$ and $\pi_2\alpha$ are equal to $\mathtt{int}$ and the expansion is $\langle \mathtt{int}, \mathtt{int}\rangle$.

Generally, if α has the kind $\Sigma\beta{:}K_1.K_2$, the expansion of α will be the pair $\langle c_1, c_2\rangle$ where c_1 is the expansion of $\pi_1\alpha$, and c_2 is the expansion of $\pi_2\alpha$ *with the additional information* that β refers to $\pi_1\alpha$ and has kind K_1. We may generalize all the examples so far with the following definition, where $R(c, K)$ is the expansion of c assuming c is known to have kind K:

$$
\begin{aligned}
R(c, T) &\stackrel{\text{def}}{=} c \\
R(c, S(c')) &\stackrel{\text{def}}{=} c' \\
R(c, \Sigma\alpha{:}K_1.K_2) &\stackrel{\text{def}}{=} \langle R(\pi_1 c, K_1), \\
&\qquad R(\pi_2 c, K_2\{R(\pi_1 c, K_1)/\alpha\}\rangle
\end{aligned}
$$

Example 7. Suppose α is assigned the kind $\Pi\beta{:}T.S(\mathtt{list}\,\beta)$ (where $\mathtt{list} : T \to T$). Then for any argument c, the application $\alpha\, c$ is equal to $\mathtt{list}\, c$. Thus, the appropriate expansion of α is $\lambda\beta{:}T.\mathtt{list}\,\beta$. Note that this is the eta-long form of $\mathtt{list}$.

Example 8. Suppose α is assigned the kind $\Pi\beta{:}T.\,(T \times S(\beta))$. In this case, for any argument c, $\pi_2(\alpha\, c)$ is known to be equal to c, but no definition is given for $\pi_1(\alpha\, c)$. Thus, the expansion of α is $\lambda\beta{:}T.\langle \pi_1(\alpha\,\beta), \beta\rangle$.

These last two examples suggest the following generalization for product kinds:

$$R(c, \Pi\alpha{:}K_1.K_2) = \lambda\alpha{:}K_1.\, R(c\alpha, K_2) \qquad \text{(wrong)}$$

This is close to the right generalization, but, as we will see in the next section, it is not quite satisfactory due to the need to account for bound variables. Nevertheless, it provides good intuition on the process of expansion over product kinds.

[3] That is, beta-normal forms such that no eta-expansions can be performed without creating beta-redices.

3.1 Bound Variables

Thus far we have exclusively considered rewriting constructors to account for the kinds of their free variables. To be sure that no uses of the singleton elimination rule are necessary, we must also consider bound variables. For example, it would seem as though the constructor $\lambda\alpha{:}S(\texttt{int}).\alpha$ should be rewritten to something like $\lambda\alpha{:}S(\texttt{int}).\texttt{int}$.

A naive approach would be to traverse the constructor in question and replace every bound variable with its expansion resulting from the kind in its binding occurrence. For example, in $\lambda\alpha{:}S(\texttt{int}).\alpha$, the binding occurrence of α gives it kind $S(\texttt{int})$, so the α in the abstraction's body would be replaced by $R(\alpha, S(\texttt{int})) \equiv \texttt{int}$. However this traversal is not sufficient to account for all bound variables, nor in fact is it even necessary.

To see why a traversal is insufficient, suppose β has kind $(S(\texttt{int}) \to T) \to T$ and consider the constructors $\beta(\lambda\alpha{:}T.\alpha)$ and $\beta(\lambda\alpha{:}T.\texttt{int})$. (Recall Section 2.1.) In the former constructor, the binding occurrence of α gives it kind T, and consequently the hypothetical traversal would not replace it. However, as we saw in Section 2.1, the two constructors should be equal, and for this to happen without the singleton elimination rule, α must be replaced by int in the former constructor. What this illustrates is that when an abstraction appears in an argument position, the abstraction's domain kind can sometimes be strengthened (in this case from T to $S(\texttt{int})$). This means that the kind given in a variable's binding occurrence cannot be relied upon.

One possibility for dealing with this would be to perform a much more complicated traversal that attempts to determine the "true" kind for every bound variable. Fortunately, we may deal with this in a much simpler way by shifting the responsibility for expanding a bound variable from the abstraction where that variable is bound to all constructors that might consume that abstraction.

In the above example, β changes the effective domain of its arguments to $S(\texttt{int})$; in other words, it promises only to call them with int. The expansion process for product kinds makes this explicit. In this case, the expansion of β is $\lambda\gamma{:}(S(\texttt{int}) \to T).\, \beta(\lambda\alpha{:}S(\texttt{int}).\gamma\,\texttt{int})$. After substituting this expansion for β, each of the constructors above normalizes to $\beta(\lambda\alpha{:}S(\texttt{int}).\texttt{int})$. This can again be seen as an eta-long form for β where replacement of a variable by its definition is considered an eta-expansion.

In general, the expansion that achieves this is:

$$R(c, \Pi\alpha{:}K_1.K_2) \stackrel{\text{def}}{=} \lambda\alpha{:}K_1.\, R(c\alpha, K_2)\{R(\alpha, K_1)/\alpha\}$$

Making this expansion part of the substitution for free variables accounts for all cases in which the kind of an abstraction (and therefore its domain kind) is given by some other constructor to which the abstraction is passed as an argument. The only other way a kind may be imposed on an abstraction is at the top level. Again recall Section 2.1 and consider the constructors $\lambda\alpha{:}T.\alpha$ and $\lambda\alpha{:}T.\texttt{int}$. These constructors should be considered equivalent when compared as members of kind $S(\texttt{int}) \to T$, but not as members of $T \to T$. Thus, the

$$
\begin{aligned}
R(c, T) &\stackrel{\text{def}}{=} c \\
R(c, S(c')) &\stackrel{\text{def}}{=} c' \\
R(c, \Pi\alpha{:}K_1.K_2) &\stackrel{\text{def}}{=} \lambda\alpha{:}K_1.\, R(c\, R(\alpha, K_1), K_2\{R(\alpha, K_1)/\alpha\}) \\
&\qquad \text{(where } \alpha \text{ is not free in } c \text{ or } K_1\text{)} \\
R(c, \Sigma\alpha{:}K_1.K_2) &\stackrel{\text{def}}{=} \langle R(\pi_1 c, K_1), R(\pi_2 c, K_2\{R(\pi_1 c, K_1)/\alpha\}\rangle
\end{aligned}
$$

$$
R(\alpha_1{:}K_1, \ldots, \alpha_n{:}K_n) \stackrel{\text{def}}{=} \{R(\alpha_n, K_n)/\alpha_n\} \cdots \{R(\alpha_1, K_1)/\alpha_1\}
$$

Fig. 5. Expansions

elimination process must be affected by the kinds in which a constructor is considered to lie.

This is neatly dealt with by (in addition to substituting expansions for free variables) expanding the entire constructor using the kind to which it belongs. Thus, when considered as members of $S(\texttt{int}) \to T$, the two constructors above become $\lambda\alpha{:}S(\texttt{int}).((\lambda\alpha{:}T.\alpha)\texttt{int})$ and $\lambda\alpha{:}S(\texttt{int}).((\lambda\alpha{:}T.\texttt{int})\texttt{int})$; each of which normalize to $\lambda\alpha{:}S(\texttt{int}).\texttt{int}$. However, when considered as members of $T \to T$, the two become $\lambda\alpha{:}T.((\lambda\alpha{:}T.\alpha)\alpha)$ and $\lambda\alpha{:}T.((\lambda\alpha{:}T.\texttt{int})\alpha)$; each of which normalizes to its original form.

It is worth noting that the required top-level expansion adds very little complexity to the use of singleton elimination in practice. In this paper we have largely ignored the term-level constructs of the intermediate language in question, but, in fact, constructors lie within surrounding terms, and elimination of singleton kinds in constructors is part of an overall transformation on terms. Typically, constructors appearing within terms are simply types (the domain of a lambda, for example), and in such cases the top-level expansion has no effect at all (since $R(c, T) = c$). In other cases constructors may by considered to lie in more interesting kinds (such as with the argument to a constructor abstraction), but in all such cases the intended kind is clearly given by context and the top-level expansion is still easy to perform.

3.2 The Elimination Process

The full definition of the expansion constructors[4] and substitutions is given in Figure 5. Using expansion, the singleton kind elimination proceeds in three steps: Given a constructor c considered to have kind K under assignment Γ, we first expand c, resulting in $R(c, K)$. Second, we substitute expansions for all free variables, resulting in $R(c, K)\{R(\Gamma)\}$. Third, we erase any remaining singleton kinds, resulting in $(R(c, K)\{R(\Gamma)\})^\circ$. This elimination process is easily seen to be terminating, since R is defined by induction over the structure of kinds.

[4] Expansion of constructors is shown to be well-defined by induction on the structure of the kind, ignoring the contents of singleton kinds.

We may state the following correctness theorem for the elimination process, which states that rewritten constructors will be equivalent if and only if the original constructors were equivalent:

Theorem 1. *Suppose $\Gamma \vdash c_1 : K$ and $\Gamma \vdash c_2 : K$. Then $\Gamma \vdash c_1 = c_2 : K$ if and only if $\Gamma^\circ \vdash_{sf} (R(c_1, K)\{R(\Gamma)\})^\circ = (R(c_2, K)\{R(\Gamma)\})^\circ : K^\circ$.*

The proof of the correctness theorem is the subject of the next section.

4 Correctness Proof

The previous section's informal discussion motivates why we might expect the elimination process to be correct. Unfortunately, Theorem 1 defies direct proof, because there are too many ways that a judgement might be derived, and those derivations have no particular structure in common. We may see a reason why the proof is difficult by considering the theorem's implications. Since it is easy to determine equality of constructors in the singleton-free system, the theorem provides a simple test for equality: translate constructors into the singleton-free system and check that they are equal there. The theorem states that such a test is sound and complete. However, this also indicates that proving the theorem is at least as difficult as proving decidability of constructor equality in the full system.

The decidability of constructor equality has recently been shown by Stone and Harper [21]. They provide an algorithm for deciding constructor equality and prove that algorithm sound and complete using a Kripke-style logical relation. In addition to settling the decidability question, they provide a tool with which we may prove Theorem 1. One approach would be to follow Stone and Harper and prove the theorem directly using a logical relation. This approach is not attractive, due to the substantial complexity of the arguments involved. However, we may still take advantage of their result.

The proof works essentially by using Stone and Harper's algorithm to normalize the derivations of equality judgements. Given a derivable equality judgement, we use completeness of the algorithm to deduce the existence of a derivation in the *algorithmic system*. That derivation can have only one form, making it much easier to reason about.

Due to space limitations, we do not present the entire proof here, and instead only present the key lemmas and definitions. The full details may be found in the companion technical report [2].

The only-if portion of the proof (the difficult part, as it turns out) is structured as follows:

1. Suppose $\Gamma \vdash c_1 = c_2 : K$.
2. Prove that constructors are equal to their expansions; that is, $\Gamma \vdash c_1 = R(c_1, K)\{R(\Gamma)\} : K$ and $\Gamma \vdash c_2 = R(c_2, K)\{R(\Gamma)\} : K$. By symmetry and transitivity it follows that the expansions are equal: $\Gamma \vdash R(c_1, K)\{R(\Gamma)\} = R(c_2, K)\{R(\Gamma)\} : K$.

3. By algorithmic completeness, deduce that there exists a derivation of the algorithmic judgement $\Gamma \vdash R(c_1, K)\{R(\Gamma)\} : K \Leftrightarrow \Gamma \vdash R(c_2, K)\{R(\Gamma)\} : K$.
4. Prove that singleton reduction (the algorithmic counterpart of the singleton elimination rule) is not used in the algorithmic derivation. This step is the heart of the proof.
5. By algorithmic soundness, deduce that there exists a derivation of $\Gamma \vdash R(c_1, K)\{R(\Gamma)\} = R(c_2, K)\{R(\Gamma)\} : K$ in which the singleton elimination rule (Rule 34) is not used (except within subderivations for kinding or subkinding judgements).
6. Prove that therefore there exists a derivation of $\Gamma^\circ \vdash_{sf} (R(c_1, K)\{R(\Gamma)\})^\circ = (R(c_2, K)\{R(\Gamma)\})^\circ : K^\circ$.

Once the only-if portion is proved, the converse is easily established. The converse's proof is discussed in Section 4.3.

We begin by stating two lemmas that establish that well-formed constructors are equal to their expansions. These are each proven by straightforward inductions. It then follows by transitivity that when constructors are equal, so are their expansions.

Lemma 1. *If* $\Gamma \vdash c : K$ *then* $\Gamma \vdash c = R(c, K) : K$.

Lemma 2. *If* $\Gamma \vdash c : K$ *then* $\Gamma \vdash c = R(c, K)\{R(\Gamma)\} : K$.

Corollary 1. *If* $\Gamma \vdash c_1 = c_2 : K$ *then* $\Gamma \vdash R(c_1, K)\{R(\Gamma)\} = R(c_2, K)\{R(\Gamma)\} : K$

4.1 The Decision Algorithm

Stone and Harper's decision algorithm for constructor equivalence is given in Figure 6. This algorithm is unusual in that it is a *six-place* algorithm; it maintains two assignments and two kinds. This allows the two halves of the algorithm to operate independently, which is critical to Stone and Harper's proof and to this one.[5] In common usage, the two assignments and the two kinds are equivalent (but often not identical). The critical singleton reduction rule appears as the ninth clause.

The algorithm works as follows:

1. The algorithm is presented with a query of the form[6] $\Gamma \vdash c : K \Leftrightarrow \Gamma' \vdash c' : K'$. When $\vdash \Gamma = \Gamma'$ and $\Gamma \vdash K = K'$, this determines whether $\Gamma \vdash c = c' : K$ is derivable.

[5] Stone and Harper also prove their six-place algorithm equivalent to a conventional four-place algorithm employing judgements of the form $\Gamma \vdash c_1 \Leftrightarrow c_2 : K$, which is preferable in practice.

[6] It is awkward to render six-place judgements in spoken language. My preferred rendering of the algorithmic judgement is "In assignments Γ and Γ', c and c' are related at kinds K and K'."

2. The constructor equivalence rules add appropriate elimination forms (applications or projections) to the constructors being compared in order to drive them down to kind T or a singleton kind. Then those constructors are reduced to weak head normal form.
3. Elimination contexts (E) are defined in the usual manner, as shown below. A constructor of the form $E[\alpha]$ is referred to as a *path,* and α is called the *head* of the path. We will often use the metavariable p to range over paths.

$$E ::= [\,] \mid Ec \mid \pi_1 E \mid \pi_2 E$$

   A constructor is reduced to weak head normal form by alternating beta reductions and singleton reductions. Beta reduction of a constructor c is performed by placing it in the form $E[c]$ where c is a beta redex, and reducing to $E[c']$ where c' is the corresponding contractum. Repetition of this will ultimately result in a path (if the constructor is well-formed, which is assumed).
4. Singleton reduction of a path p is performed by determining its *natural kind*, and replacing p with c whenever p's natural kind is some singleton kind $S(c)$. (Formally, the algorithm adds an elimination context, reducing $E[p]$ to $E[c]$ when p has natural kind c, but E will be empty when $E[p]$ is well-formed.) Note that the natural kind of a path is *not* a principal kind. For example, if $\Gamma(\alpha) = T$ then the natural kind of α is T, but α has principal kind $S(\alpha)$.
5. When no more beta or singleton reductions apply, the algorithm compares the two paths, checking that they have the same head variable and the same series of eliminations. When checking that two applications are the same, the main algorithm is reinvoked to determine whether the arguments are equal.

We may state the following correctness theorem for the algorithm:

Theorem 2 (Stone-Harper).

1. **(Completeness)** *If* $\Gamma \vdash c_1 = c_2 : K$ *then* $\Gamma \vdash c_1 : K \Leftrightarrow \Gamma \vdash c_2 : K$.
2. **(Soundness)** *Suppose* $\vdash \Gamma = \Gamma'$, $\Gamma \vdash K = K'$, $\Gamma \vdash c_1 : K$ *and* $\Gamma' \vdash c_2 : K'$. *Then if* $\Gamma \vdash c_1 : K \Leftrightarrow \Gamma' \vdash c_2 : K'$ *then* $\Gamma \vdash c_1 = c_2 : K$.

Corollary 2. *If* $\Gamma \vdash c_1 = c_2 : K$ *then* $\Gamma \vdash R(c_1, K)\{R(\Gamma)\} : K \Leftrightarrow \Gamma \vdash R(c_2, K)\{R(\Gamma)\} : K$.

There is one minor difference between this algorithm and the one presented in Stone and Harper. When checking constructor equivalence at a singleton kind, Stone and Harper's algorithm immediately succeeds, while the algorithm here behaves the same as when comparing at kind T. However, Stone and Harper's proof goes through in almost exactly the same way, with only a change to one subcase of their "Main Lemma." Their algorithm is more efficient, since it terminates early in some cases, but for our purposes we are not concerned with efficiency. The advantage of this version of the algorithm is that we may obtain the stronger version of soundness given in Theorem 4:

Natural kind extraction

$\Gamma \vdash \alpha \uparrow \Gamma(\alpha)$
$\Gamma \vdash b \uparrow T$
$\Gamma \vdash \pi_1 p \uparrow K_1$ if $\Gamma \vdash p \uparrow \Sigma\alpha{:}K_1.K_2$
$\Gamma \vdash \pi_2 p \uparrow K_2\{\pi_1 p/\alpha\}$ if $\Gamma \vdash p \uparrow \Sigma\alpha{:}K_1.K_2$
$\Gamma \vdash p\,c \uparrow K_2\{c/\alpha\}$ if $\Gamma \vdash p \uparrow \Pi\alpha{:}K_1.K_2$

Weak head reduction

$\Gamma \vdash E[(\lambda\alpha{:}K.c)c'] \longrightarrow E[c\{c'/\alpha\}]$
$\Gamma \vdash E[\pi_1\langle c_1, c_2\rangle] \longrightarrow E[c_1]$
$\Gamma \vdash E[\pi_2\langle c_1, c_2\rangle] \longrightarrow E[c_2]$
$\Gamma \vdash E[p] \longrightarrow E[c]$ if $\Gamma \vdash p \uparrow S(c)$ **(singleton reduction)**

Weak head normalization

$\Gamma \vdash c \Downarrow c'$ if $\Gamma \vdash c \longrightarrow c''$ and $\Gamma \vdash c'' \Downarrow c'$
$\Gamma \vdash c \Downarrow c$ otherwise

Algorithmic constructor equivalence

$\Gamma_1 \vdash c_1 : T \Leftrightarrow \Gamma_2 \vdash c_2 : T$ if $\Gamma_1 \vdash c_1 \Downarrow p_1$ and $\Gamma_2 \vdash c_2 \Downarrow p_2$ and $\Gamma_1 \vdash p_1 \uparrow T \leftrightarrow \Gamma_2 \vdash p_2 \uparrow T$
$\Gamma_1 \vdash c_1 : S(c_1') \Leftrightarrow \Gamma_2 \vdash c_2 : S(c_2')$ if $\Gamma_1 \vdash c_1 \Downarrow p_1$ and $\Gamma_2 \vdash c_2 \Downarrow p_2$ and $\Gamma_1 \vdash p_1 \uparrow T \leftrightarrow \Gamma_2 \vdash p_2 \uparrow T$
$\Gamma_1 \vdash c_1 : \Pi\alpha{:}K_1.K_1' \Leftrightarrow \Gamma_2 \vdash c_2 : \Pi\alpha{:}K_2.K_2'$ if $\Gamma_1, \alpha{:}K_1 \vdash c_1\alpha : K_1' \Leftrightarrow \Gamma_2, \alpha{:}K_2 \vdash c_2\alpha : K_2'$
$\Gamma_1 \vdash c_1 : \Sigma\alpha{:}K_1.K_1' \Leftrightarrow \Gamma_2 \vdash c_2 : \Sigma\alpha{:}K_2.K_2'$ if $\Gamma_1 \vdash \pi_1 c_1 : K_1 \Leftrightarrow \Gamma_2 \vdash \pi_1 c_2 : K_2$ and $\Gamma_1 \vdash \pi_2 c_1 : K_1'\{\pi_1 c_1/\alpha\} \Leftrightarrow \Gamma_2 \vdash \pi_2 c_2 : K_2'\{\pi_2 c_2/\alpha\}$

Algorithmic path equivalence

$\Gamma_1 \vdash \alpha \uparrow \Gamma_1(\alpha) \leftrightarrow \Gamma_2 \vdash \alpha \uparrow \Gamma_2(\alpha)$
$\Gamma_1 \vdash b_1 \uparrow T \leftrightarrow \Gamma_2 \vdash b_2 \uparrow T$ if $b_1 \equiv b_2$
$\Gamma_1 \vdash p_1 c_1 \uparrow K_1'\{c_1/\alpha\} \leftrightarrow \Gamma_2 \vdash p_2 c_2 \uparrow K_2'\{c_2/\alpha\}$ if $\Gamma_1 \vdash p_1 \uparrow \Pi\alpha{:}K_1.K_1' \leftrightarrow \Gamma_2 \vdash p_2 \uparrow \Pi\alpha{:}K_2.K_2'$ and $\Gamma_1 \vdash c_1 : K_1 \Leftrightarrow \Gamma_2 \vdash c_2 : K_2$
$\Gamma_1 \vdash \pi_1 p_1 \uparrow K_1 \leftrightarrow \Gamma_2 \vdash \pi_1 p_2 \uparrow K_2$ if $\Gamma_1 \vdash p_1 \uparrow \Sigma\alpha{:}K_1.K_1' \leftrightarrow \Gamma_2 \vdash p_2 \uparrow \Sigma\alpha{:}K_2.K_2'$
$\Gamma_1 \vdash \pi_2 p_1 \uparrow K_1'\{\pi_1 p_1/\alpha\} \leftrightarrow \Gamma_2 \vdash \pi_2 p_2 \uparrow K_2'\{\pi_1 p_2/\alpha\}$ if $\Gamma_1 \vdash p_1 \uparrow \Sigma\alpha{:}K_1.K_1' \leftrightarrow \Gamma_2 \vdash p_2 \uparrow \Sigma\alpha{:}K_2.K_2'$

Fig. 6. Constructor Equivalence Algorithm (Six-Place Version)

Definition 3. *A derivation is* mostly free of singleton elimination *if every use of singleton elimination (Rule 34) in that derivation lies within a subderivation whose root is a constructor formation or subkinding judgement.*

Theorem 4 (Singleton-free soundness). *Suppose* $\vdash \Gamma = \Gamma'$, $\Gamma \vdash K = K'$, $\Gamma \vdash c_1 : K$ *and* $\Gamma' \vdash c_2 : K'$. *Then if* $\Gamma \vdash c_1 : K \Leftrightarrow \Gamma' \vdash c_2 : K'$ *without* *using singleton reduction then there exists a derivation of $\Gamma \vdash c_1 = c_2 : K$ that is mostly free of singleton elimination.*

Proof. By inspection of Stone and Harper's proof.

Theorem 4 fails with the more efficient version of the algorithm because when $\Gamma_1 \vdash c_1 : S(c_1') \Leftrightarrow \Gamma_2 \vdash c_2 : S(c_2')$, the soundness proof must use singleton elimination to show that c_1 and c_1' are equal and that c_2 and c_2' are equal, in the course of showing that c_1 and c_2 are equal.

In the next section we will show that the algorithmic derivation shown to exist by Corollary 2 is free of singleton reduction. Then Theorem 4 will permit us to conclude that the corresponding derivation in the declarative system is mostly free of singleton elimination. A derivation mostly free of singleton elimination uses singleton elimination in no significant manner; any residual uses (within constructor formation or subkinding) will be removed by singleton erasure in Section 4.3.

4.2 Absence of Singleton Reduction

The heart of the proof is to show that singleton reduction will not be used in a derivation of algorithmic equivalence of expanded constructors. It is here that we really show that expansion works to eliminate singleton kinds: if the algorithm is able to deduce that the two expanded terms are equal without using singleton reduction, then we have obviated the need for singleton kinds.

The proof works by defining a condition, called *protectedness,* that is satisfied by expanded constructors, that rules out any need for singleton reduction, and that is preserved by the algorithm. First we make some preliminary definitions:

Definition 5.

- *Two kinds K and K' are* similar *(written $K \approx K'$) if they are the same modulo the contents of singleton kinds. That is, similarity is the least congruence such that $S(c) \approx S(c')$ for any constructors c and c'.*
- *Two assignments Γ and Γ' are* similar *(written $\Gamma \approx \Gamma'$) if they bind the same variables in the same order, and if $\Gamma(\alpha) \approx \Gamma'(\alpha)$ for all $\alpha \in \mathrm{Dom}(\Gamma)$.*

Note that a well-formed kind can be similar to an ill-formed kind, and likewise for assignments. When two kinds or two assignments are similar, they are said to have the same shape. For the proof of the absence of singleton reductions, we will be able to disregard the actual kinds and assignments being used and consider only their shapes; this will simplify the proof considerably. This works because the contents of singleton kinds are only pertinent to singleton reduction, which we are showing never takes place.

We also define *contexts* (C) as shown below. Note that contexts are defined to have exactly one hole, and note also that elimination contexts are a subclass of contexts. As we are not concerned with the contents of singleton kinds, there is no need for contexts to account for constructors appearing within the domain kind of a lambda abstraction. Instantiation of a context is defined in the usual manner; in particular, it is permissible for instantiation to capture free variables.

$$C ::= [\,] \mid \lambda\alpha{:}K.C \mid C\,c \mid c\,C \mid \langle C, c\rangle \mid \langle c, C\rangle \mid \pi_1 C \mid \pi_2 C$$

Finally, we define weak head reduction without an assignment[7] in the usual manner (that is, $E[(\lambda\alpha{:}K.c)c'] \longrightarrow E[c\{c'/\alpha\}]$ and $E[\pi_i\langle c_1, c_2\rangle] \longrightarrow E[c_i]$). Note that if $c_1 \longrightarrow c_2$ then $\Gamma \vdash c_1 \longrightarrow c_2$ (recall algorithmic weak head reduction).

We are now ready to define the protectedness property. The intuition is that a constructor is protected if every variable in that constructor appears in an elimination context that drives it down to kind T (*i.e.*, that performs elimination operations on it resulting in a constructor of kind T). By implication, this means that no variable appears in an elimination context driving it down to a singleton kind. In other words, no path within the constructor will have a singleton natural kind and consequently singleton reduction will not take place. In order to ensure that protectedness is preserved by the algorithm, we strengthen the condition so that the elimination context that drives a variable to kind T must be *appropriate.* An elimination context is appropriate if, for every application appearing in that context, the argument constructor is protected (and, moreover, is still protected when driven to kind T and weak head normalized).

Definition 6. *Suppose Γ is an assignment and K is a kind. The relations Γ-*protected, K-Γ-appropriate, *and* K-Γ-protected *are the least relations such that:*

1. **Protectedness**
   - *A constructor c is Γ-protected if whenever $c \equiv C[\alpha]$ (where $\alpha \in \mathrm{Dom}(\Gamma)$ and C does not capture α), there exist C' and E such that $C[\,] \equiv C'[E[\,]]$, and $E[\alpha]$ is T-Γ-appropriate.*
2. **Appropriateness**
   - *A path α is K-Γ-appropriate if $\Gamma(\alpha) \approx K$.*
   - *A path $p\,c$ is K_2-Γ-appropriate if p is $(\Pi\alpha{:}K_1.K_2)$-Γ-appropriate and c is K_1-Γ-protected.*
   - *A path $\pi_1 p$ is K_1-Γ-appropriate if p is $(\Sigma\alpha{:}K_1.K_2)$-Γ-appropriate.*
   - *A path $\pi_2 p$ is K_2-Γ-appropriate if p is $(\Sigma\alpha{:}K_1.K_2)$-Γ-appropriate.*
3. **Protectedness relative to a kind**
   - *A constructor c is T-Γ-protected if c is Γ-protected.*
   - *A constructor c is $S(c'')$-Γ-protected if c is Γ-protected.*
   - *A lambda abstraction $\lambda\alpha{:}K_1'.c$ is $(\Pi\alpha{:}K_1.K_2)$-Γ-protected if c is K_2-$(\Gamma, \alpha{:}K_1)$-protected.*
   - *A pair $\langle c_1, c_2\rangle$ is $(\Sigma\alpha{:}K_1.K_2)$-Γ-protected if c_1 is K_1-Γ-protected and c_2 is K_2-Γ-protected.*

---

[7] As opposed to the algorithm's judgement $\Gamma \vdash c_1 \longrightarrow c_2$ for weak head reduction within an assignment Γ.

Note that the relations being defined appear only positively above, so Definition 6 is a valid inductive definition. Also, note that these definitions are concerned with kinds only up to similarity, and for this reason the definition can safely ignore the presence of free variables in kinds and assignments.

We are now ready to prove the main lemma:

Lemma 3 (Main Lemma).

1. *If $\Gamma_1 \vdash c_1 : K_1 \Leftrightarrow \Gamma_2 \vdash c_2 : K_2$ is derivable, $c_1 \longrightarrow^* c_1'$, $c_2 \longrightarrow^* c_2'$, c_1' is K_1-Γ_1-protected, and c_2' is K_2-Γ_2-protected, then the derivation does not use singleton reduction.*
2. *If $\Gamma_1 \vdash p_1 \uparrow K_1 \leftrightarrow \Gamma_2 \vdash p_2 \uparrow K_2$ is derivable, c_1 is K_1-Γ_1-appropriate, and c_2 is K_2-Γ_2-appropriate, then the derivation does not use singleton reduction.*

Proof. By induction on the algorithmic derivation, using a substitution lemma to establish that protectedness is preserved by the weak head reduction.

It remains to show that expanded constructors are protected. In the following lemma, protectedness is lifted to kinds in the obvious manner.

Lemma 4.

1. *If p is K-Γ-appropriate and K is Γ-protected then $R(p, K)$ is Γ-protected.*
2. *If c and K are Γ-protected then $R(c, K)$ is K-Γ-protected.*

Corollary 3. *If $\Gamma \vdash \mathrm{ok}$ then $R(c, K)\{R(\Gamma)\}$ is K-Γ-protected.*

Corollary 4. *If $\Gamma \vdash c_1 = c_2 : K$ then there exists a derivation of $\Gamma \vdash R(c_1, K)\{R(\Gamma)\} = R(c_2, K)\{R(\Gamma)\} : K$ that is mostly free of singleton elimination.*

4.3 Wrapping Up

To complete the first half of the proof, we need only the fact that singleton erasure preserves derivability of judgements with mostly singleton free derivations.

Lemma 5.

1. *If $\Gamma \vdash c_1 = c_2 : K$ has a derivation mostly free of singleton elimination, then $\Gamma^\circ \vdash_{sf} {c_1}^\circ = {c_2}^\circ : K^\circ$.*
2. *If $\Gamma \vdash c : K$ then $\Gamma^\circ \vdash_{sf} c^\circ : K^\circ$.*
3. *If $\Gamma \vdash K_1 \leq K_2$ then ${K_1}^\circ \equiv {K_2}^\circ$.*
4. *If $\Gamma \vdash \mathrm{ok}$ then $\Gamma^\circ \vdash_{sf} \mathrm{ok}$.*

Corollary 5. *If $\Gamma \vdash c_1 = c_2 : K$ then $\Gamma^\circ \vdash_{sf} (R(c_1, K)\{R(\Gamma)\})^\circ = (R(c_2, K)\{R(\Gamma)\})^\circ : K^\circ$.*

For the converse, we already have most of the facts we need at our disposal. We require two more lemmas. One states that the algorithm is symmetric and transitive. It is here that the use of a six-place algorithm is critical. For the six-place algorithm it is easy to show that symmetry and transitivity hold. For a four-place algorithm, on the other hand, it is a deep fact depending on soundness and completeness that symmetry and transitivity hold for well-formed instances, and for ill-formed instances it is not known to hold at all.

Lemma 6.

1. *If* $\Gamma_1 \vdash c_1 : K_1 \Leftrightarrow \Gamma_2 \vdash c_2 : K_2$ *then* $\Gamma_2 \vdash c_2 : K_2 \Leftrightarrow \Gamma_1 \vdash c_1 : K_1$.
2. *If* $\Gamma_1 \vdash c_1 : K_1 \Leftrightarrow \Gamma_2 \vdash c_2 : K_2$ *and* $\Gamma_2 \vdash c_2 : K_2 \Leftrightarrow \Gamma_3 \vdash c_3 : K_3$ *then* $\Gamma_1 \vdash c_1 : K_1 \Leftrightarrow \Gamma_3 \vdash c_3 : K_3$.

The other lemma states that if singleton reduction is not employed in the algorithm, then whatever singleton kinds appear are not relevant and may be erased. Moreover, since the two halves of the algorithm operate independently (here again the six-place algorithm is critical), we may erase them from either half of the algorithm.

Lemma 7.

1. *If* $\Gamma_1 \vdash c_1 : K_1 \Leftrightarrow \Gamma_2 \vdash c_2 : K_2$ *without using singleton reduction, then* $\Gamma_1 \vdash c_1 : K_1 \Leftrightarrow {\Gamma_2}^\circ \vdash {c_2}^\circ : {K_2}^\circ$
2. *If* $\Gamma_1 \vdash p_1 \uparrow K_1 \leftrightarrow \Gamma_2 \vdash p_2 \uparrow K_2$ *without using singleton reduction, then* $\Gamma_1 \vdash p_1 \uparrow K_1 \leftrightarrow {\Gamma_2}^\circ \vdash {p_2}^\circ \uparrow {K_2}^\circ$.

It is worth noting that the algorithmic judgement in Lemma 7 is quite peculiar, in that Γ is ordinarily not equal to Γ° and K is ordinarily not equal to K°. Although there is a valid derivation of this algorithmic judgement, the soundness theorem does not apply, so it does not correspond to any derivation in the declarative system. When we apply this lemma below we will use transitivity to bring the assignments and kinds back into agreement before invoking soundness.

Lemma 8. *If* $\Gamma \vdash c_1 : K$, $\Gamma \vdash c_2 : K$, *and* $\Gamma^\circ \vdash_{sf} (R(c_1, K)\{R(\Gamma)\})^\circ = (R(c_2, K)\{R(\Gamma)\})^\circ : K^\circ$ *then* $\Gamma \vdash c_1 = c_2 : K$.

Proof. By Lemma 2, $\Gamma \vdash c_1 = R(c_1, K)\{R(\Gamma)\} : K$. By algorithmic completeness, $\Gamma \vdash c_1 : K \Leftrightarrow \Gamma \vdash R(c_1, K)\{R(\Gamma)\} : K$. By symmetry and transitivity of the algorithm, $\Gamma \vdash R(c_1, K)\{R(\Gamma)\} : K \Leftrightarrow \Gamma \vdash R(c_1, K)\{R(\Gamma)\} : K$. Then, by Corollary 3 and Lemmas 3 and 7, $\Gamma \vdash R(c_1, K)\{R(\Gamma)\} : K \Leftrightarrow \Gamma^\circ \vdash (R(c_1, K)\{R(\Gamma)\})^\circ : K^\circ$. By transitivity, $\Gamma \vdash c_1 : K \Leftrightarrow \Gamma^\circ \vdash (R(c_1, K)\{R(\Gamma)\})^\circ : K^\circ$. Similarly, $\Gamma \vdash c_2 : K \Leftrightarrow \Gamma^\circ \vdash (R(c_2, K)\{R(\Gamma)\})^\circ : K^\circ$.

Since the singleton-free system is a subsystem of the full system, we have by algorithmic completeness that $\Gamma^\circ \vdash (R(c_1, K)\{R(\Gamma)\})^\circ : K^\circ \Leftrightarrow \Gamma^\circ \vdash (R(c_2, K)\{R(\Gamma)\})^\circ : K^\circ$. Hence, by symmetry and transitivity, $\Gamma \vdash c_1 : K \Leftrightarrow \Gamma \vdash c_2 : K$. (Note that by applying transitivity, we have swept away the peculiarity noted above.) Therefore $\Gamma \vdash c_1 = c_2 : K$ by algorithmic soundness.

This completes the proof.

5 Related Work and Conclusions

The primary purpose of this work is to allow the reification of type equality information in a type-preserving compiler for a language like Standard ML, thereby eliminating the need to complicate the metatheory of the latter phases of the compiler with singleton kinds. Within this architecture, equality (or "sharing") information would initially be expressed using singleton kinds, but at some point singleton kind elimination would be exploited to eliminate them. Thereafter, with singleton kinds no longer available, type information would be propagated by substitution, as in Harper *et al.* [7].

Shao [18] proposes a different approach for dealing with type equality in module languages. Shao's approach resembles the approach in this paper, in that it substitutes definitions for variables. However, it does so less thoroughly than the approach here, since, in keeping with the module-based accounts, less type information is to be propagated than in the singleton account, as mentioned in Section 2.1. In effect, Shao's substitution does not account for the issue of internal bindings discussed here in Section 3.1.

Another alternative is given in an earlier paper by Shao [17]. In his earlier approach, equality specifications are taken as mere abbreviations and deleted from signatures. The main work arises in ensuring that the appropriate subsignature relationships hold: a signature containing a type abbreviation must be considered a subsignature of a similar one that contains that type but not the abbreviation (as required by Standard ML and the standard type-theoretic accounts). To accomplish this, when a structure matching a signature with a deleted field is used in a context where that deleted field is required, the translation coerces the structure to reinsert the deleted field. Thus, Shao's earlier approach differs from the one here in two main ways: it interprets the subsignature relation by coercion, whereas this paper's approach interprets it by inclusion; and (as with the later approach) it does not account for indirect equalities resulting from internal bindings—abbreviation occurs only where equality specifications appear syntactically.

Aspinall [1] studies in detail a related type system with singleton types. The difference between singleton kinds and his singleton types is entirely cosmetic (this work could just as easily be presented as singleton type elimination), but various other technical differences between his system and this one make it unclear whether the same elimination process would apply to his system as well. Stone and Harper [21] compare this system to Aspinall's in greater detail.

An implementation of this paper's singleton kind elimination procedure in the context of the TILT compiler is planned, but has not yet been done. The main challenge we anticipate in this implementation, is that singleton kinds, in addition to expressing type equality information from the module language, are also very useful for expressing type information compactly. The elimination of singleton kinds could thus substantially increase the space taken up by type information. (In the limit, a particularly naive implementation could result in exponential blowup of type information by breaking DAGs into trees.) This issue could arise in two ways; first, type information could take up more space in the compiler, resulting in slower compilation, and, second, if types are constructed and passed at run time [8], inefficient type representation could result in poor performance at run time. Shao *et al.* [19] discuss a number of ways to deal with the former issue, such as hash-consing and using explicit substitutions. The latter issue can be addressed by making the construction and passing of type information explicit [5] and doing so before performing singleton elimination; then singleton elimination will have no effect on the run-time version of type information.

References

1. David Aspinall. Subtyping with singleton types. In *Eighth International Workshop on Computer Science Logic*, volume 933 of *Lecture Notes in Computer Science*, pages 1–15, Kazimierz, Poland, September 1994. Springer-Verlag.
2. Karl Crary. Sound and complete elimination of singleton kinds. Technical Report CMU-CS-00-104, Carnegie Mellon University, School of Computer Science, January 2000.
3. Karl Crary, David Walker, and Greg Morrisett. Typed memory management in a calculus of capabilities. In *Twenty-Sixth ACM Symposium on Principles of Programming Languages*, pages 262–275, San Antonio, Texas, January 1999.
4. Karl Crary and Stephanie Weirich. Flexible type analysis. In *1999 ACM International Conference on Functional Programming*, pages 233–248, Paris, September 1999.
5. Karl Crary, Stephanie Weirich, and Greg Morrisett. Intensional polymorphism in type-erasure semantics. In *1998 ACM International Conference on Functional Programming*, pages 301–312, Baltimore, September 1998. Extended version published as Cornell University technical report TR98-1721.
6. Robert Harper and Mark Lillibridge. A type-theoretic approach to higher-order modules with sharing. In *Twenty-First ACM Symposium on Principles of Programming Languages*, pages 123–137, Portland, Oregon, January 1994.
7. Robert Harper, John C. Mitchell, and Eugenio Moggi. Higher-order modules and the phase distinction. In *Seventeenth ACM Symposium on Principles of Programming Languages*, pages 341–354, San Francisco, January 1990.
8. Robert Harper and Greg Morrisett. Compiling polymorphism using intensional type analysis. In *Twenty-Second ACM Symposium on Principles of Programming Languages*, pages 130–141, San Francisco, January 1995.
9. Robert Harper and Chris Stone. A type-theoretic interpretation of Standard ML. In *Proof, Language and Interaction: Essays in Honour of Robin Milner*. The MIT Press, 2000. Extended version published as CMU technical report CMU-CS-97-147.
10. Xavier Leroy. Manifest types, modules and separate compilation. In *Twenty-First ACM Symposium on Principles of Programming Languages*, pages 109–122, Portland, Oregon, January 1994.
11. Xavier Leroy. Applicative functors and fully transparent higher-order modules. In *Twenty-Second ACM Symposium on Principles of Programming Languages*, San Francisco, January 1995.
12. Xavier Leroy. A modular module system. *Journal of Functional Programming*, 2000. To appear.

13. Mark Lillibridge. *Translucent Sums: A Foundation for Higher-Order Module Systems.* PhD thesis, Carnegie Mellon University, School of Computer Science, Pittsburgh, Pennsylvania, May 1997.
14. Yasuhiko Minamide, Greg Morrisett, and Robert Harper. Typed closure conversion. In *Twenty-Third ACM Symposium on Principles of Programming Languages*, pages 271–283, St. Petersburg, Florida, January 1996.
15. Greg Morrisett, Karl Crary, Neal Glew, and David Walker. Stack-based typed assembly language. In *Second Workshop on Types in Compilation*, volume 1473 of *Lecture Notes in Computer Science*, pages 28–52. Springer-Verlag, March 1998. Extended version published as CMU technical report CMU-CS-98-178.
16. Greg Morrisett, David Walker, Karl Crary, and Neal Glew. From System F to typed assembly language. *ACM Transactions on Programming Languages and Systems*, 21(3):527–568, May 1999. An earlier version appeared in the 1998 Symposium on Principles of Programming Languages.
17. Zhong Shao. Typed cross-module compilation. In *1998 ACM International Conference on Functional Programming*, pages 141–152, Baltimore, Maryland, September 1998.
18. Zhong Shao. Transparent modules with fully syntactic signatures. In *1999 ACM International Conference on Functional Programming*, pages 220–232, Paris, September 1999.
19. Zhong Shao, Christopher League, and Stefan Monnier. Implementing typed intermediate languages. In *1998 ACM International Conference on Functional Programming*, pages 313–323, Baltimore, Maryland, September 1998.
20. Frederick Smith, David Walker, and Greg Morrisett. Alias types. In *European Symposium on Programming*, Berlin, Germany, March 2000.
21. Christopher A. Stone and Robert Harper. Deciding type equivalence in a language with singleton kinds. In *Twenty-Seventh ACM Symposium on Principles of Programming Languages*, Boston, January 2000. Extended version published as CMU technical report CMU-CS-99-155.

A Inference Rules

Well-Formed Context $\boxed{\Gamma \vdash \mathrm{ok}}$

$$\frac{}{\epsilon \vdash \mathrm{ok}} \tag{1}$$

$$\frac{\Gamma \vdash K \qquad \alpha \notin \mathrm{Dom}(\Gamma)}{\Gamma, \alpha{:}K \vdash \mathrm{ok}} \tag{2}$$

Context Equivalence $\boxed{\vdash \Gamma_1 = \Gamma_2}$

$$\frac{}{\vdash \epsilon = \epsilon} \tag{3}$$

$$\frac{\vdash \Gamma_1 = \Gamma_2 \qquad \Gamma_1 \vdash K_1 = K_2 \qquad \alpha \notin \mathrm{Dom}(\Gamma_1)}{\vdash \Gamma_1, \alpha{:}K_1 = \Gamma_2, \alpha{:}K_2} \tag{4}$$

Well-Formed Kind $\boxed{\Gamma \vdash K}$

$$\frac{\Gamma \vdash \mathrm{ok}}{\Gamma \vdash T} \tag{5}$$

$$\frac{\Gamma \vdash c : T}{\Gamma \vdash S(c)} \tag{6}$$

$$\frac{\Gamma, \alpha{:}K' \vdash K''}{\Gamma \vdash \Pi\alpha{:}K'.K''} \tag{7}$$

$$\frac{\Gamma, \alpha{:}K' \vdash K''}{\Gamma \vdash \Sigma\alpha{:}K'.K''} \tag{8}$$

Subkinding $\boxed{\Gamma \vdash K \leq K'}$

$$\frac{\Gamma \vdash c : T}{\Gamma \vdash S(c) \leq T} \tag{9}$$

$$\frac{\Gamma \vdash \mathrm{ok}}{\Gamma \vdash T \leq T} \tag{10}$$

$$\frac{\Gamma \vdash c_1 = c_2 : T}{\Gamma \vdash S(c_1) \leq S(c_2)} \tag{11}$$

$$\frac{\begin{array}{c}\Gamma \vdash \Pi\alpha{:}K_1'.K_1'' \\ \Gamma \vdash K_2' \leq K_1' \qquad \Gamma, \alpha{:}K_2' \vdash K_1'' \leq K_2''\end{array}}{\Gamma \vdash \Pi\alpha{:}K_1'.K_1'' \leq \Pi\alpha{:}K_2'.K_2''} \tag{12}$$

$$\frac{\begin{array}{c}\Gamma \vdash \Sigma\alpha{:}K_2'.K_2'' \\ \Gamma \vdash K_1' \leq K_2' \qquad \Gamma, \alpha{:}K_1' \vdash K_1'' \leq K_2''\end{array}}{\Gamma \vdash \Sigma\alpha{:}K_1'.K_1'' \leq \Sigma\alpha{:}K_2'.K_2''} \tag{13}$$

Kind Equivalence $\boxed{\Gamma \vdash K_1 = K_2}$

$$\frac{\Gamma \vdash \mathrm{ok}}{\Gamma \vdash T = T} \tag{14}$$

$$\frac{\Gamma \vdash c_1 = c_2 : T}{\Gamma \vdash S(c_1) = S(c_2)} \tag{15}$$

$$\frac{\Gamma \vdash K_2' = K_1' \qquad \Gamma, \alpha{:}K_1' \vdash K_1'' = K_2''}{\Gamma \vdash \Pi\alpha{:}K_1'.K_1'' = \Pi\alpha{:}K_2'.K_2''} \tag{16}$$

$$\frac{\Gamma \vdash K_1' = K_2' \qquad \Gamma, \alpha{:}K_1' \vdash K_1'' = K_2''}{\Gamma \vdash \Sigma\alpha{:}K_1'.K_1'' = \Sigma\alpha{:}K_2'.K_2''} \tag{17}$$

Well-Formed Constructor $\boxed{\Gamma \vdash c : K}$

$$\frac{\Gamma \vdash \mathrm{ok}}{\Gamma \vdash b : T} \tag{18}$$

$$\frac{\Gamma \vdash \text{ok}}{\Gamma \vdash \alpha : \Gamma(\alpha)} \tag{19}$$

$$\frac{\Gamma, \alpha{:}K' \vdash c : K''}{\Gamma \vdash \lambda\alpha{:}K'.c : \Pi\alpha{:}K'.K''} \tag{20}$$

$$\frac{\Gamma \vdash c : \Pi\alpha{:}K'.K'' \qquad \Gamma \vdash c' : K'}{\Gamma \vdash cc' : K''\{c'/\alpha\}} \tag{21}$$

$$\frac{\Gamma \vdash c : \Sigma\alpha{:}K'.K''}{\Gamma \vdash \pi_1 c : K'} \tag{22}$$

$$\frac{\Gamma \vdash c : \Sigma\alpha{:}K'.K''}{\Gamma \vdash \pi_2 c : K''\{\pi_1 c/\alpha\}} \tag{23}$$

$$\frac{\begin{array}{c}\Gamma \vdash \Sigma\alpha{:}K'.K'' \\ \Gamma \vdash c_1 : K' \\ \Gamma \vdash c_2 : K''\{c_1/\alpha\}\end{array}}{\Gamma \vdash \langle c_1, c_2\rangle : \Sigma\alpha{:}K'.K''} \tag{24}$$

$$\frac{\Gamma \vdash c : T}{\Gamma \vdash c : S(c)} \tag{25}$$

$$\frac{\begin{array}{c}\Gamma \vdash \Sigma\alpha{:}K'.K'' \\ \Gamma \vdash \pi_1 c : K' \\ \Gamma \vdash \pi_2 c : K''\{\pi_1 c/\alpha\}\end{array}}{\Gamma \vdash c : \Sigma\alpha{:}K'.K''} \tag{26}$$

$$\frac{\begin{array}{c}\Gamma \vdash c : \Pi\alpha{:}K'.K_1'' \\ \Gamma, \alpha{:}K' \vdash c\alpha : K''\end{array}}{\Gamma \vdash c : \Pi\alpha{:}K'.K''} \tag{27}$$

$$\frac{\Gamma \vdash c : K_1 \qquad \Gamma \vdash K_1 \leq K_2}{\Gamma \vdash c : K_2} \tag{28}$$

Constructor Equivalence $\boxed{\Gamma \vdash c = c' : K}$

$$\frac{\Gamma, \alpha{:}K' \vdash c_1 = c_2 : K'' \qquad \Gamma \vdash c_1' = c_2' : K'}{\Gamma \vdash (\lambda\alpha{:}K'.c_1)c_1' = c_2\{c_2'/\alpha\} : K''\{c_1'/\alpha\}} \tag{29}$$

$$\frac{\begin{array}{c}\Gamma \vdash c_1 : \Pi\alpha{:}K'.K_1'' \\ \Gamma \vdash c_2 : \Pi\alpha{:}K'.K_2'' \\ \Gamma, \alpha{:}K' \vdash c_1\alpha = c_2\alpha : K''\end{array}}{\Gamma \vdash c_1 = c_2 : \Pi\alpha{:}K'.K''} \tag{30}$$

$$\frac{\begin{array}{c}\Gamma \vdash \Sigma\alpha{:}K'.K'' \\ \Gamma \vdash \pi_1 c_1 = \pi_1 c_2 : K' \\ \Gamma \vdash \pi_2 c_1 = \pi_2 c_2 : K''\{\pi_1 c_1/\alpha\}\end{array}}{\Gamma \vdash c_1 = c_2 : \Sigma\alpha{:}K'.K''} \tag{31}$$

$$\frac{\Gamma \vdash c_1 = c_1' : K_1 \qquad \Gamma \vdash c_2 : K_2}{\Gamma \vdash \pi_1\langle c_1, c_2\rangle = c_1' : K_1} \tag{32}$$

$$\frac{\Gamma \vdash c_1 : K_1 \qquad \Gamma \vdash c_2 = c_2' : K_2}{\Gamma \vdash \pi_2\langle c_1, c_2\rangle = c_2' : K_2} \tag{33}$$

$$\frac{\Gamma \vdash c : S(c')}{\Gamma \vdash c = c' : T} \tag{34}$$

$$\frac{\Gamma \vdash c = c' : T}{\Gamma \vdash c = c' : S(c)} \tag{35}$$

$$\frac{\Gamma \vdash c' = c : K}{\Gamma \vdash c = c' : K} \tag{36}$$

$$\frac{\Gamma \vdash c = c' : K \qquad \Gamma \vdash c' = c'' : K}{\Gamma \vdash c = c'' : K} \tag{37}$$

$$\frac{\Gamma \vdash \mathrm{ok}}{\Gamma \vdash b = b : T} \tag{38}$$

$$\frac{\Gamma \vdash \mathrm{ok}}{\Gamma \vdash \alpha = \alpha : \Gamma(\alpha)} \tag{39}$$

$$\frac{\Gamma \vdash K_1' = K_2' \qquad \Gamma, \alpha{:}K_1' \vdash c_1 = c_2 : K''}{\Gamma \vdash \lambda\alpha{:}K_1'.c_1 = \lambda\alpha{:}K_2'.c_2 : \Pi\alpha{:}K'.K''} \tag{40}$$

$$\frac{\Gamma \vdash c = c' : \Pi\alpha{:}K_1.K_2 \qquad \Gamma \vdash c_1 = c_1' : K_1}{\Gamma \vdash cc_1 = c'c_1' : K_2\{c_1/\alpha\}} \tag{41}$$

$$\frac{\Gamma \vdash c_1 = c_2 : \Sigma\alpha{:}K'.K''}{\Gamma \vdash \pi_1 c_1 = \pi_1 c_2 : K'} \tag{42}$$

$$\frac{\Gamma \vdash c_1 = c_2 : \Sigma\alpha{:}K'.K''}{\Gamma \vdash \pi_2 c_1 = \pi_2 c_2 : K''\{\pi_1 c_1/\alpha\}} \tag{43}$$

$$\frac{\begin{array}{c}\Gamma \vdash \Sigma\alpha{:}K'.K'' \\ \Gamma \vdash c_1' = c_2' : K' \\ \Gamma \vdash c_1'' = c_2'' : K''\{c_1'/\alpha\}\end{array}}{\Gamma \vdash \langle c_1', c_1''\rangle = \langle c_2', c_2''\rangle : \Sigma\alpha{:}K'.K''} \tag{44}$$

$$\frac{\Gamma \vdash c_1 = c_2 : K \qquad \Gamma \vdash K \leq K'}{\Gamma \vdash c_1 = c_2 : K'} \tag{45}$$

Program Representation Size in an Intermediate Language with Intersection and Union Types

Allyn Dimock[1,*,†], Ian Westmacott[2,*,†], Robert Muller[3,‡,†,§], Franklyn Turbak[4,‡,†], J.B. Wells[5,*,‡,†,¶], and Jeffrey Considine[2,†,¶]

[1] Harvard University
[2] Boston University
[3] Boston College
[4] Wellesley College
[5] Heriot-Watt University

Abstract. The CIL compiler for core Standard ML compiles whole programs using a novel typed intermediate language (TIL) with intersection and union types and flow labels on both terms and types. The CIL term representation duplicates portions of the program where intersection types are introduced and union types are eliminated. This duplication makes it easier to represent type information and to introduce customized data representations. However, duplication incurs compile-time space costs that are potentially much greater than are incurred in TILs employing type-level abstraction or quantification. In this paper, we present empirical data on the compile-time space costs of using CIL as an intermediate language. The data shows that these costs can be made tractable by using sufficiently fine-grained flow analyses together with standard hash-consing techniques. The data also suggests that non-duplicating formulations of intersection (and union) types would not achieve significantly better space complexity.

1 Introduction

1.1 The Compile-Time Space Costs of Typed Intermediate Languages

Recent research has demonstrated the benefits of compiling with an explicitly typed intermediate language (TIL) [Mor95,PJ96,TMC+96,PJM97,JS98,BKR98, TO98,FKR+99,CJW00,MWCG99,WDMT0X]. One benefit is that explicit types can be used in compiler passes to guide program transformations and select efficient data representations. Another advantage of using a TIL is that the

* Partially supported by NSF grant CCR–9417382.
† Partially supported by Sun grant EDUD-7826-990410-US.
‡ Partially supported by NSF CISE/CCR ESS grant 9806747.
§ Partially supported by a Faculty Fellowship of the Carroll School of Management, Boston College.
¶ Partially supported by EPSRC grants GR/L 36963 and GR/L 15685.

R. Harper (Ed.): TIC 2000, LNCS 2071, pp. 27–52, 2001.

compiler can invoke its type checker after every transformation, greatly reducing the possibility of introducing errors. If strongly typed intermediate languages are used all the way through the compiler to the assembly level (something we do not yet do), the resulting object code is certifiably type safe [Nec97, MWCG99]. Furthermore, types that survive through the back end can be used to support run-time operations such as garbage collection [Tol94] and run-time type dispatch [Mor95].

The benefits of using a TIL are not achieved without costs. These costs include the space needed to represent the types at compile-time, the time to manipulate the types at compile-time, and the added complications of transforming types along with terms. This report focuses on the compile-time space cost.

Using a naive type representation can incur huge space costs, even if types are only used in the compiler front end for initial type checking. In the worst case, the tree representation of types in Standard ML (SML) programs can have size doubly exponential in the program size, and the DAG representation can be exponential in the program size [Mit96]. Although we are mainly concerned with ordinary programs where the worst case space complexity is not encountered, these ordinary programs often have types with impractically large tree representations but acceptable DAG representations. So in practice, DAG representations of types and other techniques are necessary to engineer types of tractable size. For example, the SML/NJ compiler's FLINT intermediate language uses hash-consing, memoization, explicit substitutions, and de Bruijn indices to achieve space-efficient implementation of types [SLM98]. The TIL compiler achieves type sharing by binding all types to type variables, and then performing dead code elimination, hoisting and common subexpression elimination on the types [Tar96, pp. 217–219]. The compiler must then preserve type bindings across transformations, or else repeat the type-sharing transformations. Tarditi reports that the representation size increase imposed by using types in TIL averages 5.15 times without this sharing scheme, but only 1.93 times with sharing.

We have constructed a whole-program compiler for core SML based on a typed intermediate language we call CIL[1]. Unlike FLINT and TIL, CIL has three features that make compile-time space issues potentially more challenging to address than in other typed intermediate languages:

1. **Listing-based types:** The CIL type system can encode polyvariant flow analyses using *polyvariant flow types* where labels on type constructors provide flow information and intersection and union types provide polyvariant analysis. Intersection and union types can be viewed as finitary (listing-based) versions of infinitary (schema-based) universal and existential types.

[1] "CIL" is an acronym for "Church Intermediate Language." The authors are members of of the Church Project (`http://types.bu.edu`), which is investigating applications of sophisticated type systems in the efficient and reliable implementation of higher-order typed programming languages.

For example, CIL uses the intersection type

$$\tau_{\text{id}} \equiv \bigwedge\{p_1 : \text{int} \rightarrow \text{int},\ p_2 : \text{real} \rightarrow \text{real}\}$$

to represent an occurrence of the universal type $\forall\alpha.\alpha \rightarrow \alpha$ that is instantiated only at types int and real. The intersection type τ_{id} is similar in structure to the CIL product (record) type

$$\tau_{\text{funs}} \equiv \times\{p_1 : \text{int} \rightarrow \text{int},\ p_2 : \text{real} \rightarrow \text{real}\}.$$

The difference is that a value of type τ_{funs} is a pair of two possibly distinct functions having the respective component types while a value of type τ_{id} is a single function having *both* component types. CIL union types (introduced via $\bigvee$) are the dual of intersection types; they are listing-based versions of existential types that are similar in structure to CIL sum (variant) types (introduced via $+$).
Encoding polyvariant analyses, which analyze a function multiple times relative to different contexts of use, can introduce components of intersection and union types that differ only by flow information. For instance, when encoding polyvariance, an innocuous type like int $\rightarrow$ int might expand into

$$\bigvee\{q_1 : \text{int} \xrightarrow[\{3,4\}]{\{1\}} \text{int},\ q_2 : \bigwedge\{r_1 : \text{int} \xrightarrow[\{3\}]{\{2\}} \text{int},\ r_2 : \text{int} \xrightarrow[\{4\}]{\{2\}} \text{int}\}\}.$$

In the function type notation $\sigma \xrightarrow[\psi]{\phi} \tau$, the annotation $\genfrac{}{}{0pt}{}{\phi}{\psi}$ is a *flow bundle* in which ϕ (resp. ψ) conservatively approximates the sites in a program that can be sources, or introduction points (resp. sinks, or elimination points) for the function values having this type. In this paper, we only show flow bundles annotating function types, but CIL supports such annotations on almost all types.
Intersection and union types have several advantages over universal and existential types as a means of expressing polymorphism [WDMT0X]: (1) by making usage contexts apparent, they support flow-based customizations in a type-safe way; (2) finitary polymorphism can type some terms not typable using infinitary polymorphism, thus potentially allowing some program transformations to be typable which would not be allowable in a TIL based on infinitary polymorphism; and (3) the listing-based nature of finitary polymorphic types can avoid some complications of bound variables in representing and manipulating quantified types (see Sec. 2.2). There is a space cost for these benefits: the listing-based nature of finitary polymorphic types, in combination with flow annotations encoding finer grained types, can lead to CIL types that are much larger than those expressed via infinitary polymorphic types.
Assuming whole-program compilation, the finitary polymorphism afforded by flow types is sufficient to compile SML programs. In this respect, the CIL SML compiler is similar to monomorphizing whole-program compilers [TO98,BKR98,CJW00].

2. **Duplicating term representations:** CIL represents the introduction of intersection types by a *virtual record* — a term that explicitly lists multiple copies of the same component term that differ only in their flow type annotations. For example, here is a CIL term that has the type τ_{id} defined above:

$$\wedge(p_1 = \lambda x^{\mathrm{int}}.x,\ p_2 = \lambda x^{\mathrm{real}}.x).$$

   Virtual record components are extracted via *virtual projections*. Similarly, values of union type (virtual variants) are introduced via *virtual injections* and are eliminated by a *virtual case expressions* — terms whose branches explicitly list multiple type-annotated versions of the same untyped branch. Virtual terms that persist until code generation are eliminated at that time. Code is generated for only one component of a virtual record and for one branch of a virtual case expression, and virtual projections and injections disappear entirely. Thus, these virtual term constructs have a compile-time space cost but no run-time space (or time) cost.
   Because it makes copies of terms that differ only in type annotations, we call CIL a *duplicating* representation. An advantage of the duplicating approach is that type information for guiding customization decisions is locally accessible in each copy of a duplicated term. An obvious disadvantage of this representation is the duplicated term structure, which is potentially much larger than the more compact introduction and elimination forms used for universal and existential types. Duplication arises in the CIL compiler whenever intersection or union types are used. The Type/Flow Inference and Flow Separation compiler stages discussed in Sec. 2.3 both introduce additional uses of intersection and union types.
3. **Closure types exposing free variable types:** CIL does not have universal or existential types because they hide important information about contexts of use and encourage uniform data representations rather than customized ones [WDMT0X]. However, existential types are particularly useful for abstracting over differences in free variables that are exposed in typed closure representations for functions of the same source type [MMH96,MWCG99, CWM98]. In the CIL compiler, these differences are reconciled by injecting the types of closures into a union type and performing a virtual case dispatch at the application site [DMTW97]. In a type-erasure semantics, these injections do not give rise to any run-time code. However, they can potentially cause a blowup in compile-time space when many functions with different free variables flow together.
   Our approach to closure conversion is similar to that used by TIL-based compilers that remove higher-order functions via defunctionalization [TO98, CJW00]. As in the CIL compiler, these compilers use flow analysis to customize the closure representation for particular application sites. However, these flow analyses are not integrated into the type system. These defunctionalizing compilers maintain type correctness during closure conversion by injecting closures with different free variables that flow to the same application site into a sum type, and performing a case dispatch on the constructed

value at the application site. The difference here is that in CIL this can be done with a mix of virtual and real sum types while in the defunctionalizing compilers all of the sum types must be real and hence require run-time analysis. Some defunctionalizing compilers avoid this run-time cost by using the appropriate code pointer as a "tag" in the generated object code and replacing the case dispatch by a jump, but their type systems do not support this as a well typed operation and hence this must be done in the code generator after types are dropped. In contrast, in CIL the combination of a virtual sum (i.e., union) type with real closure types makes this approach well typed.

1.2 Contributions

Taken together, listing-based types, duplicating term representations, and closure types that expose free variable types raise the specter of compile-time space explosion at both the term and the type level. However, preliminary experiments with a small benchmark suite indicate that standard hash-consing techniques are able to keep the size of CIL types and terms tractable.

The main contributions of this paper are the following two observations:

1. **Duplicating term representations are practical:** Our experiments show that, for the flow analyses that we have investigated, the space required for CIL terms in our benchmarks is always within a factor of 2.1 of (and usually significantly closer to) our estimate of a minimal size for a non-duplicating TIL. This result is surprising, since we and many others expected the duplicating term representation to have a significantly higher space cost. Before we obtained these results, we expected that it would be essential to develop a *non-duplicating* term representation in which a single term schema somehow contains multiple flow type annotations. For example, using the notation of [Pie91], τ_{id} could be expressed as something like: **for** $\alpha \in \{\mathrm{int}, \mathrm{real}\}.\lambda x^{\alpha}.x$. Although this notation is more compact, it makes type information less accessible and can be tricky to adapt to more complex situations [WDMT0X]. We have made preliminary investigations into other representations, e.g., one based on the skeletons and substitutions of [KW99]. Based on the empirical results presented here, we believe that developing a non-duplicating representation of CIL may be not critical (though it may still be worthwhile). However, only one of the flow analyses we have experimented with to date expresses a non-trivial form of polyvariance, so it remains to be seen whether these results hold up in the presence of more polyvariant flow analyses.
2. **Finer-grained flow analyses yield smaller types and terms:** Our experiments indicate that, for some classes of flow analyses, increasing the precision of flow analysis can significantly reduce the size of program representations in CIL. Benchmarks require the most compile-time space for the least precise type-respecting flow analysis (one that assumes that any function with a given monomorphic type can flow to any call site applying

a function with this type). This imprecision leads to union types for closures that are much larger than necessary. More precise flow analyses can substantially reduce the size of these closure types.
Flow analysis has similarly been used to reduce the size of closure types in monomorphizing and defunctionalizing TIL compilers [TO98,CJW00]. However, previous work has neither quantified the benefits of using flow analysis in this context nor studied the effects of different flow analyses on compile-time space. We believe that we are the first to present a detailed empirical study of the effects of a variety of flow analyses on program representation size.

1.3 Representation Pollution

In addition to our results about the tractability of compile-time space in the CIL compiler, we have preliminary evidence that the compiler may be able to achieve one of its main design goals: avoiding *representation pollution* when choosing customized data representations. Representation pollution occurs when a source form is constrained to have an inefficient representation because it shares a sink with other source forms using the inefficient represention. A complementary phenomenon occurs with pollution of sink representations.

As an example of representation pollution, as well as some other issues that arise in a compiler based on CIL, we will consider the compilation of the untyped CIL source term in Fig. 1.[2] The term contains two abstractions, two applications (denoted by the @ symbol), and a tuple introduction form (introduced via $\times$[3]). The abstraction $(\lambda x.x * 2)$ flows to both application sites while the abstraction $(\lambda y.y + a)$ flows only to the rightmost application site.

$$
\begin{array}{l}
\textbf{let } f = (\lambda x.x * 2) \\
\textbf{in let } g = (\lambda y.y + a) \\
\quad \textbf{in } \times(f \mathbin{@} 5, (\textbf{if } b \textbf{ then } f \textbf{ else } g) \mathbin{@} 7)
\end{array}
$$

Fig. 1. An untyped CIL term

The diagram in Fig. 2 gives an abstract depiction of a CIL compiler intermediate representation of the code in Fig. 1 that might emerge from the Type

[2] We introduce and explain elements of the CIL language on an "as needed" basis in the context of our examples; readers interested in the details of the language and its type system should consult the appendix of the companion technical report [DWM+01].

[3] In CIL, as in ML, a *tuple* is a record with implicit positional labels. In general, the term notation $P(M_1, \ldots, M_n)$ is a shorthand for $P(\mathrm{f}_1 = M_1, \ldots, \mathrm{f}_n = M_n)$, where P ranges over $\times$ and $\wedge$, and $\mathrm{f}_1, \mathrm{f}_2, \ldots,$ is some fixed infinite sequence of distinct field names. Similarly, the type notation $Q[\tau_1, \ldots, \tau_n]$ is shorthand for $Q\{\mathrm{f}_1 : \tau_1, \ldots, \mathrm{f}_n : \tau_n\}$, where Q ranges over $\times$, $+$, $\wedge$, and $\vee$.

Inference/Flow Analysis (TI/FA) stage of the compiler. The TI/FA stage (described in more detail in Sec. 2.3) computes an approximation of the flow of values between sources and sinks in the input term and represents the analysis in the output typing. In this case, the CIL representation of the source term $(\lambda x^{\text{int}}.x * 2)$ has been *split* into the virtual tuple

$$\bigwedge\!\left(\lambda^1_{\{3\}} x^{\text{int}}.x * 2,\; \lambda^1_{\{4\}} x^{\text{int}}.x * 2\right),$$

which contains one copy of the function for each of the application sites to which it flows. The notation λ^ℓ_ψ denotes an abstraction labelled ℓ that may flow to the sinks whose labels are in the set ψ, while $@^\phi_k$ denotes a sink labelled k to which abstractions whose labels are in the set ϕ may flow. Free variables and λ-bound variables are superscripted with their type. Terms of the form $(\pi^\wedge_i \square)$ are *virtual tuple projections* that select the ith component of a virtual tuple.

The typing rules of CIL (not detailed here) guarantee that the flow annotations appearing in CIL types are sound. That is, an abstraction may only be applied at sites listed in its sink set, and only the abstractions appearing in the source set of an application site may be applied at that site. In Fig. 2, the type of the first component of the virtual tuple $(\text{int} \xrightarrow[\{3\}]{\{1\}} \text{int})$ is the type required for the function position of the application site $@^{\{1\}}_3$ to which the function flows. The type on the second component of the virtual tuple $(\tau_1 = \text{int} \xrightarrow[\{4\}]{\{1\}} \text{int})$ does not match the type $(\tau_3 = \text{int} \xrightarrow[\{4\}]{\{1,2\}} \text{int})$ required at its application site $@^{\{1,2\}}_3$, so this component value must be coerced to the correct type somewhere along the flow path to the application site. A subtype coercion from a term M of type σ to a supertype τ of σ is witnessed by an explicit term of the form $\mathbf{coerce}\,(\sigma, \tau)\, M$.

where $\tau_1 = \text{int} \xrightarrow[\{4\}]{\{1\}} \text{int}$, $\tau_2 = \text{int} \xrightarrow[\{4\}]{\{2\}} \text{int}$, and $\tau_3 = \text{int} \xrightarrow[\{4\}]{\{1,2\}} \text{int}$

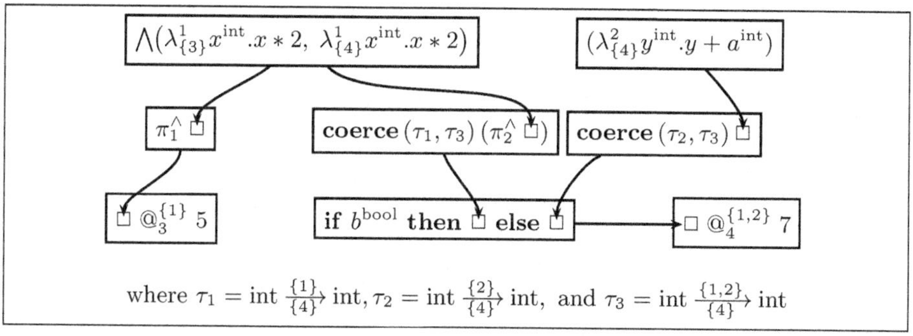

Fig. 2. A possible result of Type Inference/Flow Analysis

The typing rules also require that the type erasures of all the components of a virtual record and all the branches of a virtual case expression must be the same. The *type erasure* of a term is the untyped terms that result from eliminating all types, labels, and virtual forms (virtual records, virtual projections, virtual injections, virtual case expressions, and coercions) from the term. This type erasure constraint guarantees that virtual record components and virtual case expression branches are just different typings of the same untyped term and can therefore share the same run-time representation if the virtual forms survive to the code generation phase. If the compiler elects to customize the representations of the components of a virtual record, the virtual record will be *reified* into a real record (by changing $\wedge$ to $\times$ in terms and types) that is explicitly represented in the run-time code. Similarly, by changing $\vee$ to $+$, the compiler can reify a virtual case expression to be a real case expression that performs a dispatch on a real variant at run-time. The compiler is designed so that reifying virtual forms in this manner is type-safe.

As representation decisions are made during subsequent stages of compilation, further duplication may occur. Fig. 3 depicts a possible output of the Flow Separation stage. This stage (described in more detail in Sec. 2.3) introduces new virtual forms to guarantee that the output of the later Representation Transformation stage will be well-typed. In Fig. 3, the Flow Separation stage has split the application site $@_4^{\{1,2\}}$ into two applications sites $@_4^{\{1\}}$ and $@_4^{\{2\}}$. These applications occur within a virtual case expression, which has the form

$$\mathbf{case}^{\vee}\, M_{\text{disc}}\ \mathbf{bind}\ x\ \mathbf{in}\ \tau_1 \Rightarrow M_1 \ldots \tau_n \Rightarrow M_n.$$

A virtual case expression dispatches to the branch $\tau_k \Rightarrow M_k$ based on the positional tag k of the of the discriminant M_{disc}, which must have type $\vee[\tau_1, \ldots \tau_n]$. Within the chosen branch, the variable x of type τ_k is bound to the value of M_{disc}. In Fig. 3, the functions formerly flowing to the single application site $@_4^{\{1,2\}}$ are now injected into virtual variants (values of union type τ) via $(\iota_i^{\vee}\ \square)^{\tau}$, where i in $\{1, 2\}$ is the positional tag of the variant. These virtual variants both flow to the discriminant position of the virtual case expression, which chooses one of the two type-annotated versions of the application $h\ @\ 7$. Splitting $h\ @\ 7$ in this manner gives the compiler the option to use different representations for the closed abstraction $\lambda^1_{\{4\}}$ and the open abstraction $\lambda^2_{\{4\}}$.

As with source splitting, this kind of sink duplication increases the size of the compile-time representation of the program, but the object code size and run-time space costs increase only if some of the virtual variants and virtual case expressions are reified in a subsequent compilation stage. Observe that the sink duplication introduced by Flow Separation in this example has eliminated the need for both of the coercions present in Fig. 2 and will usually reduce the sizes of flow sets. In general, there are many trade-offs between the amount of virtual duplication and subtype coercion. The trade-offs are very sensitive to the granularity of the flow analysis and to the representation customization strategy.

We have developed several strategies for reducing (and in some cases completely eliminating) representation pollution in the case of function representations (see Sec. 2.3). More work is necessary to evaluate the run-time aspects of the customization capabilities of the CIL SML compiler. In a future report we will present a detailed study of the run-time consequences of compiling with polyvariant flow types.

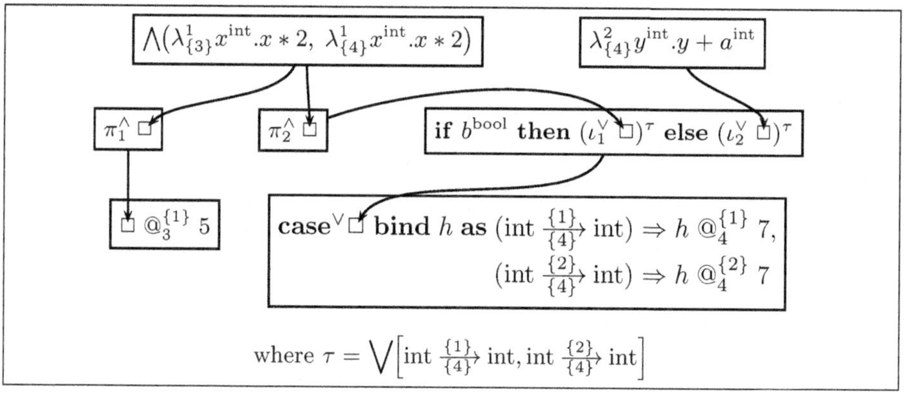

Fig. 3. A possible result of Flow Separation

1.4 Outline

The remainder of this paper is organized as follows. Sec. 2 provides an overview of the CIL compiler for SML. Sec. 3 presents space-related measurements for several standard benchmark programs at various phases of compilation. Sec. 4 summarizes our conclusions and describes future work.

2 An Overview of the CIL Compiler

2.1 The Intermediate Language

To implement the features of core SML, CIL extends the purely functional λ^{CIL}-calculus [WDMT0X] with primitive datatypes, references, arrays, and exceptions. For details of the the syntax and typing rules of CIL, see the companion technical report [DWM+01]. Although CIL is based on the λ^{CIL}-calculus, CIL itself is not a calculus. We have implemented a semantics for CIL, but we have not written its formal counterpart. While we have proven formal properties like standardization, subject reduction, and type soundness for the λ^{CIL}-calculus, we have not yet established any of these properties for CIL.

2.2 Type and Term Representations

To keep the sizes of types tractable, the CIL compiler uses hash-consing to represent types as compact directed acyclic graphs instead of as trees. This is similar to the type representation in the SML/NJ compiler's implementation of its FLINT intermediate language [SLM98]. One important issue faced in FLINT is not an issue for CIL. FLINT types have higher-order features such as abstractions and applications, i.e., a λ-calculus inside the types. Because FLINT types are identified modulo β-conversion, and because eager β-normalization of types can lose sharing and do excess work, the hash-consing scheme for FLINT types uses explicit substitutions [KR95] and memoization of substitution propagation steps. Unlike FLINT, the CIL types do not have such higher-order features, so the CIL hash-consing of types is simpler.

Sets of flow labels are often used by many types and/or terms. A single copy of each set is shared by all uses. Using the duplicating representation for terms, two CIL term occurrences are rarely structurally equivalent, so we do not use hash-consing for terms. However, the types and flow sets annotating terms are hash-consed, as described above. Strings, used for record field names and constructor names, are also shared by all uses and lists of strings are hash-consed.

2.3 Compiler Architecture

The architecture of the CIL compiler [DMTW97] is summarized in Fig. 4. This section briefly describes the compilation stages depicted in the figure.

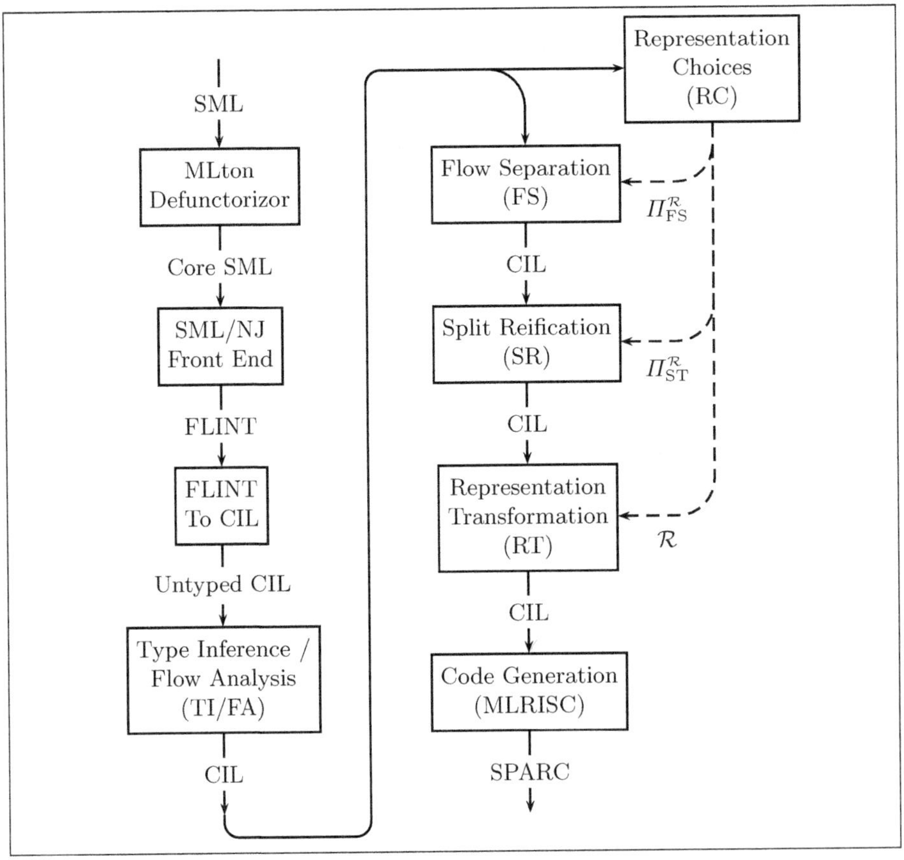

Fig. 4. Compiler Architecture

Defunctorizing, Parsing, Elaboration. Our compiler implementation takes advantage of existing tools and other freely available SML compilers. The CIL compiler uses the MLton source-to-source defunctorizer [CJW00] as a prepass to convert SML into Core SML. It then uses the front end of the SML/NJ 110.03 compiler (somewhat modified) to produce FLINT code. The FLINT code is translated to untyped CIL code, keeping datatype information on the side to avoid reinference of recursive types.

Type Inference/Flow Analysis(TI/FA). This stage accepts an untyped CIL term (plus some of the FLINT type information) as input and returns a typed CIL term as output. The typed term encodes a flow analysis that is a conservative approximation of the run-time flow. The TI/FA module is parameterized over a choice of flow analysis. We currently support five different flow analyses, which vary with respect to the precision of the approximation. In this paper, we present data from two of these:

1. The *typed source split* analysis is a variant of Banerjee's [Ban97] modified for shallow subtyping [WDMT0X]; the use of shallow subtyping makes it slightly less precise than the combination of monomorphization and 0CFA analysis. It introduces virtual tuples and virtual projections but neither virtual variants nor virtual case forms.
2. The *min type respecting* analysis is the least precise flow analysis that is still type-correct (cf. [JWW97]). It conflates the flow information on all values of the same flow erased type. For example, an abstraction of type **int** $\rightarrow$ **int** will be assumed to flow to every application site whose rator has this type. This analysis models a monomorphizing compiler in which types carry no useful flow information.

We have also implemented a finer analysis that splits some **let** and **letrec** definitions based on variable occurrences. Both *typed source split* and this *limited let split* analysis may be implemented either with shallow subtyping constraints, or with equality constraints. Unless specifically stated, we will use these terms to refer to the analysis with shallow subtyping constraints.

The granularity of the flow analysis can greatly affect program size. A coarser grained flow analysis will generally show more functions flowing to a given call site than will a finer analysis. This can lead to larger union types and more branches in virtual case expressions.

The precision of flow analysis also affects which variables are considered to be free, and thus affects the size of environments. The CIL compiler currently implements a *known function* optimization in which an invocation of a function whose identity is known at compile time (as determined by flow analysis) compiles to a direct jump. The name of such a known function is not considered to be a free variable. A coarser grained analysis will find that fewer functions are known, leading to larger environment types.[4]

[4] The numbers presented in this paper were taken before the known function optimization was implemented. This optimization further widens the space gap between coarse grained analyses like *min type respecting* and finer grained ones like *typed source split*.

Representation Choices (RC). This module selects representations for a function that are adequate for each of the application sites to which it flows. Seven different function representation choice strategies have been implemented. The *uniform* strategy represents all functions with closure records having the type

$$\times\{\text{code} : \{\text{arg} : \tau_{\text{arg}}, \text{env} : \tau_{\text{env}}\} \rightarrow \tau_{\text{body}}, \text{env} : \tau_{\text{env}}\},$$

where the *code* field contains a closed function and the *env* field contains a record of the values of the free variables of the function. A closure data structure is applied to an argument by projecting both fields from the closure record and applying the function from the code field to an argument record consisting of (the closure conversion of) the actual argument packaged together with the projected environment.

The other three representation strategies generate specialized representations based on various conditions detected in the term structure. Wand and Steckler [WS94] coined the term "selective" representation to refer to representations of functions that do not include an environment component. A selective representation is adequate for a closed function if the function flows only to call sites with compatible application protocols. In [WS94], selective representations were disabled in the presence of representation pollution — i.e., when a closed function shared a call site with some number of open functions. In contrast, the CIL compiler can still use selective representations in such situations removing the pollution via a *splitting strategy.*

The *selective sink splitting* strategy implemented in the CIL compiler generates a selective representation when the function has no free variables. This representation is called "sink splitting" because if the function shares call sites with open functions, the transformation framework will inject the function representations into a sum type and the application site will be split into multiple sites governed by a case dispatch. The transformation of the program depicted in Fig. 2 to the one depicted in Fig. 3 is a sample application of the selective sink splitting strategy. It is also possible that selective sink splitting will cause virtual records created by TI/FA to be reified into normal records if, e.g. a selective representation is chosen for a call site in one element of the virtual record, and a closure representation is chosen for the corresponding call site in a different element of the virtual record.

The *selective source splitting* strategy generates a selective representation for a closed function flowing to call sites that are not shared with open functions. Under this strategy, if a closed function shares some application sites with other closed functions but shares other application sites with open functions, then the framework will "split the source" by generating a record containing several copies of the function. The appropriate representations are projected from the record somewhere along the flow path to the respective call sites.

Other strategies implemented in the CIL compiler include an inlining strategy, defunctionalization, and a strategy which disables selective representations in the presence of representation pollution.

The selective sink splitting generates more duplication than the the other strategies for selective closure representation, and is thus of more interest in this paper.

Flow Separation (FS). This stage accepts as input a typed program and a flow-path partitioning function ($\Pi^{\mathcal{R}}_{\mathrm{FS}}$) supplied by RC. It specifies which flow paths can coexist in the same flow bundles. For flow paths that cannot coexist in the same bundle, the FS phase will introduce whatever coercions and virtual forms (i.e., virtual variant injections, virtual case expressions, virtual tuples, or virtual tuple projections) are required to ensure that the result of the later Representation Transformation stage will be well-typed.

Split Reification (SR). This stage accepts as input a typed term and a flow-path-partitioning function ($\Pi^{\mathcal{R}}_{\mathrm{ST}}$) supplied by RC. This phase reifies whatever virtual forms are required to remove representation pollution. We refer to the reification process as *splitting* because it causes the code generator to generate multiple copies of a term in situations where only one copy would have been generated without reification. In general, the current simple algorithm may split more than is necessary[DMTW97]. Specifying and implementing a more efficient splitting algorithm remains for future work.

Representation Transformation (RT). This stage accepts as input a typed term and a representation map ($\mathcal{R}$) provided by RC. It walks the term and installs the function representations specified by the map. The FS stage only introduces virtual forms, and the SR stage only reifies virtual forms. The RT stage performs the actual work of changing the code for specialized representations. For instance, in the case of selective closure conversion, it is RT which changes some functions to closures, and some call sites to calls to closures.

An interesting aspect of the transformation is that the result of the transformation may have a recursive type even though the source of the transformation has no recursion in either terms or types: recursion through flow labels in the source term may be enough to cause the transformed term to have a recursive type.

Code Generation. The CIL compiler back end transforms typed CIL programs into assembly code for the SPARC processor. It does not currently add any type annotations, or assertions, to the assembly code, although this is planned for future work. The produced assembly code is linked with a runtime library providing the environment in which CIL programs are executed. The back end is based on MLRISC, a framework for building portable optimizing code generators [Geo97]. CIL programs are translated into the MLRISC intermediate language, and the framework is specialized with CIL conventions for each target architecture.[5] MLRISC handles language-independent issues such as register allocation and code emission.

The runtime library is written in C and provides memory management, exception handling, basis functions and a foreign function interface for CIL programs at runtime. The runtime library currently manages memory using the Boehm-Demers-Weiser conservative garbage collector for C [Boe93]. CIL programs use stack-allocated activation records, which have a layout similar to C stack frames. Basis functions are called through the foreign function interface, which provides data and activation record conversions between CIL and foreign languages. The code generator does not yet optimize tail recursion.

CIL data representations are straightforward. Records, arrays, references, and strings are heap-allocated and include size headers[6]. Exception identifiers and all other constants are immediate. Injections may either be immediate or heap allocated, depending on the number and type of summands in their type.

Recursive bindings are restricted to CIL values – terms that cannot diverge, affect the store, or raise exceptions. The CIL notion of value is more liberal than that of SML; in particular, CIL allows recursive bindings that specify cyclic data structures, whereas SML does not. Although input programs must adhere to SML restrictions on recursive definitions (because we use the SML/NJ elaborator), compiler transformations may (and do) create recursive specifications of cyclic data structures. The CIL value restriction allows the code generator to use a two phase algorithm for recursive bindings: the first phase allocates memory for the values, while the second phase fills them in.

3 Representation Measurements

The main purpose of this paper is to determine whether CIL has acceptable compile-time space costs and to evaluate how flow analysis and representation strategy combinations affect these costs. This section presents data indicating that CIL is tractable as a compiler intermediate language when used with a reasonably fine-grained flow analysis.

3.1 Space Profiles

We have tested the CIL SML compiler for most combinations of flow analyses and function representation strategies on 22 kernels and small benchmarks taken from the O'Caml, TIL and SML/NJ benchmark suites. Figures 5 and 6 present space profiles for a geometric weighted average of all our benchmarks, and profiles for five individual benchmarks for two flow analyses and two function representation strategies. We show data for the *uniform* function representation

[5] Although an advantage of the MLRISC framework is its portability, it still requires substantial work to port a code generator based on MLRISC. For this reason we have concentrated only on the SPARC architecture to date.

[6] Such headers are currently unnecessary since we use conservative GC. But it is expected that in the future we will develop customized memory management.

strategy to indicate the amount of data needed to correctly closure convert functions without customizing representations. We show the *selective sink splitting* strategy as an example of a strategy that customizes function representations. The *typed source splitting* flow analysis is currently our most accurate analysis that does not split on variable occurrences. The *min type respecting* flow analysis is included to show size bloat that can occur when flow analysis provides no information beyond the type.

Each space profile shows intermediate representation size information at various CIL compiler stages. The legend in Fig. 5 explains how to interpret the data. Of particular importance is the position of the horizontal tick mark found in each bar of a profile. The portion of the entire bar below the tick mark is our conservative estimate of the space that might be required for a hypothetical non-duplicating representation of the term (including the space for type and flow information in such a term). The position of the horizontal tick mark is computed as the term size ignoring all but the leftmost branches of virtual records and virtual case expressions. Ignoring all but the leftmost branches approximates the size of a non-duplicating "skeleton" that could be instantiated to the full duplicating type representation. Since we do not include any information about the non-leftmost branches, we assume that our approximation underestimates the true size of the a non-duplicating representation. Virtual record nodes and virtual case nodes are included in the count because they serve as markers for intersection type introduction and union type elimination points. We assume that such markers would be required in any non-duplicating representation. Virtual projection and virtual injection nodes are included to approximate (resp.) the markers required for intersection type elimination and union type introduction forms. Finally, the count also includes coercion nodes.[7]

The size information was gathered by adding a function to the SML/NJ runtime system which runs the *mark* stage of the SML/NJ garbage collector using a particular object as the root. The function reports the size of all marked objects that are reachable from the root object. We present all size information in bytes rather than in type or term constructor nodes. We find that the average size of our type nodes and of our term nodes for a given benchmark is generally in the range of 10 to 12 times the size of a machine word.

3.2 Interpretation of the Space Profiles

Interpreting the size of the untyped term. When compiling small programs, the untyped CIL code, **U**, is smaller than the typed FLINT code, **F**. For benchmark programs of any reasonable size, the untyped CIL code is slightly larger than the typed FLINT code. This is due in part to the fact that the CIL representation carries more information about records and datatypes than does the FLINT representation. Of the profiles shown in this paper, only **quad** shows less space for untyped CIL than for FLINT; in all other cases that we

[7] An even more conservative approximation of the space required for a nonduplicating representation would be the size of the type-erased term. We believe that this is unrealistically small.

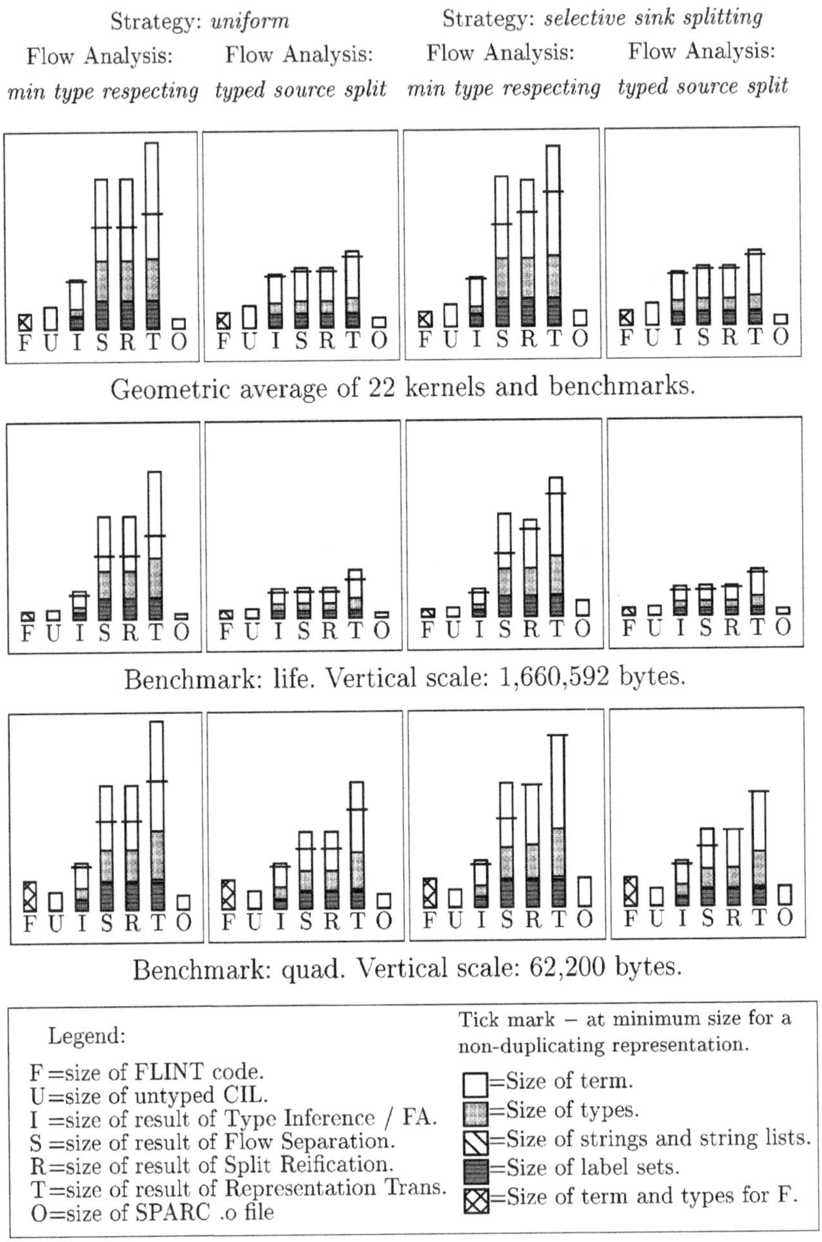
Strategy: *uniform*
Strategy: *selective sink splitting*
Flow Analysis: *min type respecting*
Flow Analysis: *typed source split*
Flow Analysis: *min type respecting*
Flow Analysis: *typed source split*
F U I S R T O
Geometric average of 22 kernels and benchmarks.
Benchmark: life. Vertical scale: 1,660,592 bytes.
Benchmark: quad. Vertical scale: 62,200 bytes.
Legend:
F=size of FLINT code.
U=size of untyped CIL.
I =size of result of Type Inference / FA.
S =size of result of Flow Separation.
R=size of result of Split Reification.
T=size of result of Representation Trans.
O=size of SPARC .o file
Tick mark – at minimum size for a non-duplicating representation.
=Size of term.
=Size of types.
=Size of strings and string lists.
=Size of label sets.
=Size of term and types for F.

Fig. 5. Sizes of benchmark phases by strategy and flow analysis I

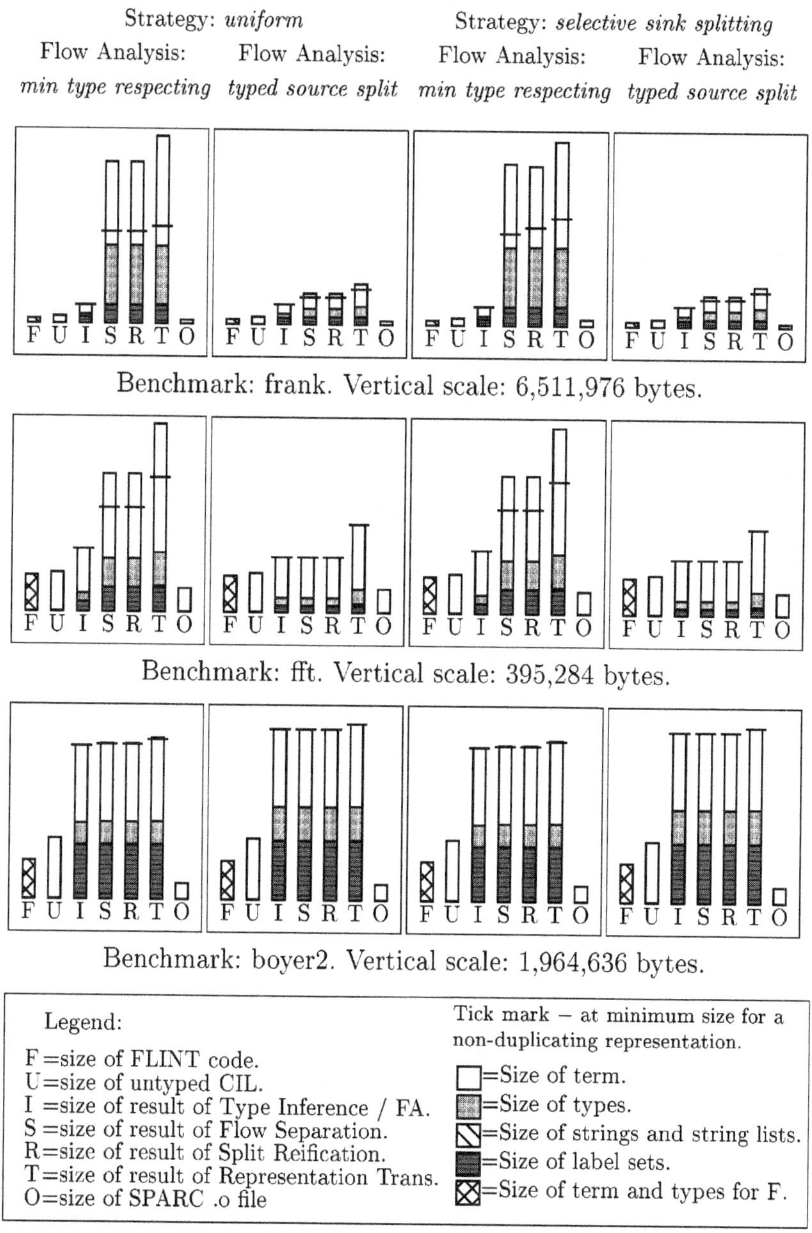

Fig. 6. Sizes of benchmark phases by strategy and flow analysis II

show, the untyped CIL code is larger than the FLINT code. While other small benchmarks are smaller in untyped CIL than in FLINT, the weighted average shows that untyped CIL is usually the bulkier representation.

The **F** and **U** columns are not quite comparable for several reasons. The **F** column overestimates the size of the FLINT code in the sense that it includes the size of FLINT type information. FLINT and CIL also differ in terms of which basis functions are compiled with the program and which are pre-compiled in the run-time system.

Columns **F** and **U** are independent of the flow analysis or the function representation strategy, but are repeated in each profile as reference points.

Interpreting the output of the Type Inference/Flow Analysis stage. Column **I** shows the size of the typed and flowed term output from the TI/FA stage. As illustrated by the representative space profiles, the TI/FA pass can expand the size of the term by introducing virtual nodes. In monomorphic benchmarks, (e.g., **boyer2**, **fft**, and **frank**), term size is only increased by the addition of **coerce** forms that indicate where subtyping is used. In benchmarks with polymorphic functions (e.g., **life**, and **quad**), the TI/FA stage makes one virtual copy (using $\wedge$) of each polymorphic function at each flow-erased type at which the function is used.

In the two flow analyses shown, the distance of the tick mark from the top of the **I** bar reflects the amount of type polymorphism in the benchmark. In general, the tick mark indicates the amount of *polyvariance* of the analysis, which, for some analyses, may be substantial even for monomorphic code.

Interpreting the output of the Flow Separation stage. Column **S** shows the size of the output from the FS stage. The FS stage introduces whatever new virtual constructs are required to ensure that the result of the (later) RT stage will be well-typed. For example, abstractions that share a call site may have the same type, up to flow information, after the TI/FA stage, but may differ from each other in the number, name and types of free variables. The FS stage must create types that differ in structure as well as in flow information for these different terms.

Under the uniform strategy, the growth in size from **I** to **S** is due only to differences in the environment component of closures – differences that will not be reflected in the object code. In other strategies, some of the growth may be due to function representations that require different object code.

The growth in size from **I** to **S** depends on the accuracy of the flow analysis. In the *min type respecting* flow analysis, the labels for all abstractions of a given (flow erased) type appear in the source label set for each application site for that type. This requires the flow separator to introduce larger intersection and union types, and to perform more virtual term duplication than would be required for a finer flow analysis. This is seen consistently throughout the data, with **frank** being the most dramatic example, and **boyer2** being the least dramatic. The **frank** benchmark is a combination of human written code for a Warren Abstract Machine using some curried and higher-order functions, and machine generated code to play a solitaire game on the WAM. The machine-generated code contains many different anonymous functions of the same few types but with different free variables. The *min type respecting* flow analysis causes these calls to be conflated. The **boyer2** benchmark is a tautology checker which has been written in closed, uncurried, first-order style. In **boyer2**, all abstractions are closed up to names of known functions[8], so there are few free variables requiring separation.

Interpreting the output of the Split Reification stage. Column **R** shows the size of the output from the SR stage, which reifies some virtual constructs — splitting them to pave the way for different representations that will be installed by the Representation Transformation stage. The number of term and type nodes remains the same because the transformation is merely changing virtual entities to real ones.[9] However, reifying type and term nodes causes the the position of the tick mark on the bar graph to rise, giving an indication of how much reification is performed.

Under the *uniform* strategy, the **S** and **R** columns show identical tick mark positions. This is expected because we implement only a single function calling convention for the uniform strategy, and so splits are never necessary. Under the *selective sink splitting* strategy, the position of the tick mark may change upwards due to reification of virtual constructions: this is what we expect from splittings introduced to circumvent representation pollution and to insert customized data representations. This is shown most dramatically in **quad** (a kernel repeatedly applying a doubling function), in which all virtual constructs are reified. In contrast, the **fft** (Fast Fourier Transform) benchmark shows no pollution of function representations when compiled with the *selective sink splitting* strategy. Most functions in **fft** are open, but the control flow structure of **fft** is quite simple: just nested loops, so open functions and closed functions never flow together.

If we see even a little reification for a strategy, we know that some part of the transformed program will use a simpler representation. If this change is in an inner loop, then a single reification may dramatically affect program performance. To determine the effectiveness of a strategy, we need to show data about the performance of the transformed programs — something outside the scope of this paper.

Our current SR stage is quite simple: if it encounters two different representations in a single virtual construct, then it converts the virtual construct into the equivalent real construct. Our current splitting algorithm can oversplit because it reifies a virtual form whenever it contains components that require different representations. But given an n-way virtual form whose components require $m < n$ different representations, the virtual form could be replaced with

[8] For this paper, known function names are treated as free variables. Enabling the known function optimization creates slightly smaller representations. The size decrease depends on the accuracy of the flow analysis (circa a 5% decrease when using the *typed source split* analysis).

[9] The size of the term component decreases slightly in some profiles due to assymetries between virtual and real injections in the current implementation (e.g., **life**, with strategy = *selective sink splitting* and flow analysis = *min type respecting*).

a real form containing m virtual forms. Oversplitting will result in unnecessary duplicated code in the object file. Oversplitting impacts the performance of the generated code when the m-way real form could be more efficiently compiled than the n-way form. We have neither measured the amount of oversplitting arising from the current algorithm nor have we experimented with other splitting algorithms.

Interpreting the output of the Representation Transformation stage. The type information in a closure-converted term is larger than in the pre-converted term. This is visible in the profiles for all the benchmarks. Part of this growth is in the creation of types for the required closure and argument records. Part of this growth is the creation of types for environments. In our framework, programs with more open terms will experience more growth in types.

The introduction of closure and argument records and the storage of free variable values in environments causes an increase in term size. In our implementation of closure conversion, the major increase in term size is from projections from the environment: our implementation puts in a projection from the environment wherever a free variable occurs.[10] The creation and destructuring of closure and argument records will show different percentage effects in different benchmarks depending on the relation of the number of abstractions and applications to other term constructors.

The **boyer2** benchmark has the highest ratio of closed to open terms, so its term size grows, essentially, only by introduction of closure and (mostly empty) argument records; there are few projections. For this reason, the growth in size is relatively small. In contrast, **fft** has a high percentage growth. Transforming the nested looping functions of **fft** creates closures having large environment records and code containing numerous environment projections.

The change in the position of the tick mark relative to the height of the bar from **R** to **T** indicates how much expansion occurs in virtual terms relative to real terms. The relative position of the tick mark decreases when there is a high ratio of virtual to real terms, but can increase when the total growth in the size of real terms is larger than that for virtual terms.

Duplicating vs. nonduplicating intermediate representations. Columns **I**, **S**, **R** and **T** have tick marks showing our estimated lower bound on the size of a typed and flowed term in a non-duplicating TIL. The position of the tick mark shows that in the benchmark programs presented (and so far in all benchmarks that we have tried), for the flow analyses presented, the space used in CIL's duplicating term representation is never more than about twice our estimate for a non-duplicating representation. This is both surprising and encouraging. However, it remains to be seen whether these results hold up in the presence of more polyvariant flow analyses.

[10] In the time since the measurements reported here were taken, we have modified the compiler to project each environment variable only once per function body.

Coarse vs. fine flow analysis. We have shown that the choice of flow analysis can greatly influence the growth in term size needed to produce well-typed function representations. The most dramatic example occurring in the benchmark **frank**, where, for the *uniform* function representation strategy the *min type respecting* analysis resulted in a size after Flow Separation 5.2 times the size of that produced using the *typed source split* analysis. At the other extreme, the benchmark **boyer2** shows a slight decrease in overall size from *typed source split* analysis to *min type respecting* analysis. The *min type respecting* flow analysis yields a smaller number of flow types for the number of underlying flow erased types than the *typed source split* analysis. In the case of **boyer2**, the slightly larger term size using *min type respecting* analysis is offset by the significantly smaller size of the flow types.

We have accumulated some data so far for the version of *typed source split* using only equality constraints. This analysis can be thought of as performing Henglein's "simple" flow analysis [Hen92] over monomorphized code, and is the flow analysis used in the RML compiler [TO98]. As expected, profiles generated using this analysis generate somewhat larger code in many cases, than profiles generated with the usual *typed source split*, but are much closer to the profiles for *typed source split* than they are to the profiles for *min type respecting*.

We have also implemented an analysis, *limited let split*, which causes some **let** and **letrec** bound definitions to be duplicated per occurrence of the bound variable, rather than just once per type. In this analysis, benchmarks **life** after the RT stage, and **simple** after TI/FA stage (but not subsequently), show a ratio of CIL code size to non-duplicating TIL code size of 2.1. The code size ratios are less than 2 for all other compiler phases and benchmarks in our benchmark suite. A study of aggressive nested cloning in a lazy functional language [Fax01] shows code size increases of a factor of up to 3 for some benchmarks of up to 800 lines of code. That study also shows that, when identical clones are merged after transformation, the code size increase is only a factor of 1.2.

The cost of accurate closure types. The profiles give us some idea as to the compile-time space cost of accurately representing closure types. With *uniform* function representation and *typed source split* analysis the growth in size from the output of Type Inference/Flow Analysis stage to the output of the Representation Transformation stage shows the space needed for closure types and for virtual cases where multiple closures flow together. This growth ranges from the size of RT output 1.03 times the size of TI/FA output for **boyer2** to 2.76 times for **quad**. The ratio of the types sizes is 1.02 for **boyer2** and 3.11 for **quad**. **quad** is atypical, being a very small program constructed to have relativly large types.

4 Conclusions and Future Work

We have shown that the amount of space used in compiling SML with CIL terms and types is practical on our benchmarks for the more precise flow analyses that we have investigated. Most importantly, the term sizes in our straightforward duplicating representation are never more than about twice our underestimate of term sizes using a non-duplicating representation. Transformations that use type and flow information on virtual terms to generate customized data representations would be more difficult to engineer in a non-duplicating representation. A factor of less than two in space is acceptable to avoid further complicating the transformations.

This is the kind of result that requires benchmarking to determine, as it depends on the style in which programs are written. It appears to be the case that for the human written and machine generated programs which we have been able to test that (1) the bulk of the program code is not used in a highly polymorphic manner so that a whole program analysis finding actual polymorphism rather than potential polymorphism need not perform too much duplication – this limits the number of virtual records created in type inference; (2) A reasonable flow analysis will find that a large percentage of calls in most programs are direct calls – this limits the number of virtual cases created in the Flow Separation phase for correctness of typed closure conversion, and for pollution removal in the selective sink splitting strategy.

The typical non-trivial growth in size from the result of TI/FA to the result of RT is obviously undesirable, and might be smaller in an intermediate representation that could hide environment types with an existential quantifier. This raises the question of whether the more precise type information maintained in CIL after closure conversion without the $\exists$ type quantifier is useful in terms of transforming a program for better run-time performance. If not, we should extend CIL with existential types.

Although the standard technique for hash-consing types sketched earlier is the one used to generate the statistics for this paper, we have almost finished changing to a new type hash-consing scheme, which we expect to give much better performance. The motivation for the new scheme is due to the combination of (1) the pervasive use of recursive types in CIL and (2) the fact that the CIL type system identifies recursive types with the infinite trees that result from unwinding them infinitely. The new scheme represents types as directed graphs and implements recursion using cycles. The use of cycles to represent recursion automatically causes α-equivalent types to be shared — the variable names are no longer present leaving only the structure of the recursive type to be stored in this representation. It will also avoid the need to have type manipulation special-case the type recursion form (which can currently appear anywhere). The new scheme uses a method of incremental DFA minimization to maintain the invariant that each possible type is represented by at most one node in the graph. This will allow constant-time type equality checking, which our current hash-consing scheme does not support due to the possibility of differing representations of the same recursive type.

Our new method of incremental DFA minimization to represent all types in the same graph is similar to a method suggested by Mauborgne [Mau00], but was developed completely independently. Our method needs $O(n \log n)$ space to store the types, while Mauborgne's needs $O(n^2 \log n)$ space, where n is the number of distinct types and some upper-bound on the arity of type constructors is assumed. Also, even in cases where Mauborgne's method approaches linear space complexity, ours will typically use half as much space.

Encoding more flow analyses in CIL remains an important area for future work. Recent work has shown that many standard flow analyses, such as k-CFA [Shi91,JW95,NN97] and the cartesian product argument-based analysis [Age95] can be encoded into a type system with intersection and union types and flow labels [PP0X,AT00]. However, unlike CIL, these type systems have deep subtyping. We are exploring a translation between deep and shallow subtyping that will allow us to employ these recent theoretical results in the CIL compiler. We are eager to see how highly polyvariant flow analyses affect our results regarding the duplicating term representation.

There are many areas for improvement in the CIL compiler as a whole. The compiler can benefit from many standard optimizations not yet implemented (e.g., tuple flattening and loop optimizations) as well as some important non-standard optimizations (e.g., the complete removal of polymorphic equality). Several existing algorithms can be more efficiently implemented, such as the algorithm used in Split Reification. There are also many opportunities for improvement in the representation of the intermediate language.

We have designed and implemented a general framework for generating customized data representations, but work remains to be done in optimizing those representations and developing heuristics for choosing between allowable representations. In terms of function representations, we are currently investigating function representations that do not close over variables whose values are available on the stack (the so-called *lightweight* closure conversion of [SW97]), higher-order uncurrying [HH98], removing manipulation of records with known components (along the lines of the *fictitious data* elimination in [Sis99]), and register allocation and calling conventions informed by flow information. We have yet to explore customized representations for other kinds of data, but CIL is rich enough to support flow-directed representation transformations for all types of data.

Finally, we emphasize that this report has focused only on compile-time space issues. In the future, we will report on compile-time time complexity as well as run-time space- and time-complexity.

Acknowledgments. This paper, and the CIL compiler project in general, have benefited greatly from the advice and support of other members of the Church Project. We especially acknowledge the contributions of Santiago Pericas-Geersten and and Glenn Holloway to early versions of the CIL compiler. We also thank the anonymous TIC workshop referees for their helpful feedback.

References

[Age95] O. Agesen. The Cartesian product algorithm. In *Proceedings of ECOOP'95, Seventh European Conference on Object-Oriented Programming*, vol. 952, pp. 2–26. Springer-Verlag, 1995.

[AT00] T. Amtoft and F. Turbak. Faithful translations between polyvariant flows and polymorphic types. In ESOP '00 [ESOP00], pp. 26–40.

[Ban97] A. Banerjee. A modular, polyvariant, and type-based closure analysis. In ICFP '97 [ICFP97].

[BKR98] N. Benton, A. Kennedy, and G. Russell. Compiling Standard ML to Java bytecodes. In ICFP '98 [ICFP98].

[Boe93] H.-J. Boehm. Space efficient conservative garbage collection. In *Proc. ACM SIGPLAN '93 Conf. Prog. Lang. Design & Impl.*, pp. 197–206, 1993.

[CJW00] H. Cejtin, S. Jagannathan, and S. Weeks. Flow-directed closure conversion for typed languages. In ESOP '00 [ESOP00], pp. 56–71.

[CWM98] K. Crary, S. Weirich, and G. Morrisett. Intensional polymorphism in type erasure semantics. In ICFP '98 [ICFP98], pp. 301–312.

[DMTW97] A. Dimock, R. Muller, F. Turbak, and J. B. Wells. Strongly typed flow-directed representation transformations. In ICFP '97 [ICFP97], pp. 11–24.

[DWM+01] A. Dimock, I. Westmacott, R. Muller, F. Turbak, J. B. Wells, and J. Considine. Program representation size in an intermediate language with intersection and union types. Technical Report BUCS-TR-2001-02, Comp. Sci. Dept., Boston Univ., Mar. 2001.

[ESOP00] *Programming Languages & Systems, 9th European Symp. Programming*, vol. 1782 of *LNCS*. Springer-Verlag, 2000.

[Fax01] K.-F. Faxén. The costs and benefits of cloning in a lazy functional language. In *Trends in Functional Programming, Volume 2*. Intellect, 2001.

[FKR+99] R. Fitzgerald, T. Knoblock, E. Ruf, B. Steensgaard, and D. Tarditi. Marmot: An optimizing compiler for Java. Technical Report 99-33, Microsoft Research, 1999.

[Geo97] L. George. MLRISC: Customizable and reusable code generators. Technical report, Bell Labs, 1997.

[Hen92] F. Henglein. Simple closure analysis. Technical Report D-193, DIKU, Mar. 1992.

[HH98] J. Hannan and P. Hicks. Higher-order uncurrying. In POPL '98 [POPL98], pp. 1–11.

[ICFP97] *Proc. 1997 Int'l Conf. Functional Programming.* ACM Press, 1997.

[ICFP98] *Proc. 1998 Int'l Conf. Functional Programming.* ACM Press, 1998.

[JS98] S. L. P. Jones and A. L. M. Santos. A transformation-based optimiser for Haskell. *Sci. Comput. Programming*, 32(1–3):3–47, Sept. 1998.

[JW95] S. Jagannathan and S. Weeks. A unified treatment of flow analysis in higher-order languages. In *Conf. Rec. 22nd Ann. ACM Symp. Princ. of Prog. Langs.*, pp. 393–407, 1995.

[JWW97] S. Jagannathan, S. Weeks, and A. Wright. Type-directed flow analysis for typed intermediate languages. In *Proc. 4th Int'l Static Analysis Symp.*, vol. 1302 of *LNCS*. Springer-Verlag, 1997.

[KR95] F. Kamareddine and A. Ríos. A λ-calculus à la de Bruijn with explicit substitution. In *7th Int'l Symp. Prog. Lang.: Implem., Logics & Programs, PLILP '95*, vol. 982 of *LNCS*, pp. 45–62. Springer-Verlag, 1995.

[KW99] A. J. Kfoury and J. B. Wells. Principality and decidable type inference for finite-rank intersection types. In *Conf. Rec. POPL '99: 26th ACM Symp. Princ. of Prog. Langs.*, pp. 161–174, 1999.

[Mau00] L. Mauborgne. Improving the representation of infinite trees to deal with sets of trees. In ESOP '00 [ESOP00], pp. 275–289.

[Mit96] J. C. Mitchell. *Foundations for Programming Languages.* MIT Press, 1996.

[MMH96] Y. Minamide, G. Morrisett, and R. Harper. Typed closure conversion. In *Conf. Rec. POPL '96: 23rd ACM Symp. Princ. of Prog. Langs.*, 1996.

[Mor95] G. Morrisett. *Compiling with Types.* Ph.D. thesis, Carnegie Mellon University, 1995.

[MWCG99] G. Morrisett, D. Walker, K. Crary, and N. Glew. From System F to typed assembly language. *ACM Trans. on Prog. Langs. & Systs.*, 21(3):528–569, May 1999.

[Nec97] G. C. Necula. Proof-carrying code. In POPL '97 [POPL97], pp. 106–119.

[NN97] F. Nielson and H. R. Nielson. Infinitary control flow analysis: A collecting semantics for closure analysis. In POPL '97 [POPL97], pp. 332–345.

[Pie91] B. C. Pierce. Programming with intersection types, union types, and polymorphism. Technical Report CMU-CS-91-106, Carnegie Mellon University, Feb. 1991.

[PJ96] S. L. Peyton Jones. Compiling Haskell by program transformation: A report from the trenches. In *Proc. European Symp. on Programming*, 1996.

[PJM97] S. L. Peyton Jones and E. Meijer. Henk: A typed intermediate language. In TIC '97 [TIC97].

[POPL97] *Conf. Rec. POPL '97: 24th ACM Symp. Princ. of Prog. Langs.*, 1997.

[POPL98] *Conf. Rec. POPL '98: 25th ACM Symp. Princ. of Prog. Langs.*, 1998.

[PP0X] J. Palsberg and C. Pavlopoulou. From polyvariant flow information to intersection and union types. *J. Funct. Programming*, 200X. To appear.

[Shi91] O. Shivers. *Control Flow Analysis of Higher Order Languages.* Ph.D. thesis, Carnegie Mellon University, 1991.

[Sis99] J. M. Siskind. Flow-directed lightweight closure conversion. Technical Report 99-190R, NEC Research Institute, Inc., Dec. 1999.

[SLM98] Z. Shao, C. League, and S. Monnier. Implementing typed intermediate languages. In ICFP '98 [ICFP98], pp. 313–323.

[SW97] P. Steckler and M. Wand. Lightweight closure conversion. *ACM Trans. on Prog. Langs. & Systs.*, 19(1):48–86, Jan. 1997.

[Tar96] D. Tarditi. *Design and Implementation of Code Optimizations for a Type-Directed Compiler for Standard ML.* Ph.D. thesis, Carnegie Mellon University, Dec. 1996.

[TIC97] *Proc. First Int'l Workshop on Types in Compilation*, June 1997. The printed TIC '97 proceedings is Boston Coll. Comp. Sci. Dept. Tech. Rep. BCCS-97-03. The individual papers are available at http://www.cs.bc.edu/~muller/TIC97/ or http://oak.bc.edu/~muller/TIC97/.

[TMC+96] D. Tarditi, G. Morrisett, P. Cheng, C. Stone, R. Harper, and P. Lee. TIL: A type-directed optimizing compiler for ML. In *Proc. ACM SIGPLAN '96 Conf. Prog. Lang. Design & Impl.*, 1996.

[TO98] A. P. Tolmach and D. Oliva. From ML to Ada: Strongly-typed language interoperability via source translation. *J. Funct. Programming*, 8(4):367–412, 1998.

[Tol94] A. Tolmach. Tag-free garbage collection using explict type parameters. In *Proc. 1994 ACM Conf. LISP Funct. Program.*, pp. 1–11, 1994.

[WDMT97] J. B. Wells, A. Dimock, R. Muller, and F. Turbak. A typed intermediate language for flow-directed compilation. In *Proc. 7th Int'l Joint Conf. Theory & Practice of Software Development*, pp. 757–771, 1997. Superseded by [WDMT0X].

[WDMT0X] J. B. Wells, A. Dimock, R. Muller, and F. Turbak. A calculus with polymorphic and polyvariant flow types. *J. Funct. Programming*, 200X. To appear. Supersedes [WDMT97].

[WS94] M. Wand and P. Steckler. Selective and lightweight closure conversion. In *Conf. Rec. 21st Ann. ACM Symp. Princ. of Prog. Langs.*, pp. 435–445, 1994.

An Abstract Model of Java Dynamic Linking and Loading

Sophia Drossopoulou*

Department of Computing, Imperial College

Abstract. We suggest a model for dynamic loading and linking as in Java. We distinguish five components in a Java implementation: evaluation, resolution, loading, verification, and preparation – with their associated checks. We demonstrate how these five together guarantee type soundness.
We take an abstract view, and base our model on a language nearer to Java source than to bytecode. We consider the following features of Java: classes, subclasses, fields and hiding, methods and inheritance, and interfaces.

1 Introduction

Java's recent spectacular success is partly due to its novel approach to code deployment. Rather than compiling and linking a fixed piece of code for a target machine, Java is compiled to bytecode[21], that can be executed on several platforms, and can link further code on demand. The security of Java greatly depends on type safety [4]. Type safety is ensured by the bytecode verifier, which checks that loaded bytecode conforms to the rules of the Java source language, and by the verifier's interplay with the other components of the Java abstract machine.

The bytecode verifier was formalized as a type inference system [25,13,12, 22], where stack locations have types on a per-instruction basis. [24] reported security flaws due to inconsistencies between loaders, which were rectified in later releases, as described in [19]. An operational semantics for multiple loaders is given in [17]. Thus, various components of Java and the virtual machine have been studied at considerable depth in isolation, but, except for this work and [23,27] their interplay has not yet been formalized.

We attempt a synthesis, and consider the complete process, consisting of five components: evaluation, loading, verification, preparation and resolution. We base our model on a language that is nearer to Java source, than to bytecode as in [23,27] .

Our model is therefore useful for source language programmers: Even if they do not program in bytecode, and do not download unverified bytecode, they may become aware of these issues, and may trigger verification, resolution or load

* This work was partly supported by EPSRC, Grant ref: GR/L 76709

R. Harper (Ed.): TIC 2000, LNCS 2071, pp. 53–84, 2001.

errors.[1] Furthermore, a clear understanding of these checks and their interplay at a level independent of the bytecode is crucial for the design of new binary formats for Java. In fact, while most Java implementations use the class format [21], any format satisfying the properties outlined in ch. 13.1 of [14] may be used instead. Last, because our model is at a high level, and independent of Java reflection, it demonstrates clearly, through the format of the judgments, how components depend on each other.

We distinguish the checks performed by verification and resolution, and demonstrate their dependencies: Resolution checks do not guarantee consistency unless applied on verified code, nor are verification checks sufficient unless later supported by resolution checks. Our model clarifies which situation will throw which exceptions, a question that is not unambiguously answered in [14,21], and demonstrates how execution of unverified code may corrupt the store.

1.1 Overview of Java Dynamic Linking and Loading, and of Our Formalization

In traditional programming languages, *e.g.,* Ada, Modula-2, the compiler checks all type-related requirements, and produces code which does not contain type information. If the various components of the program code have been compiled in an order consistent with their dependencies (dependencies through imports or inheritance) then execution is expected to be be sound with respect to types. Before execution, the code is linked eagerly, and all external references are resolved and type-checked. Execution therefore has the form

$$\mathsf{e}, \sigma, \mathsf{Code} \rightsquigarrow \mathsf{e}', \sigma', \mathsf{Code}$$

i.e., takes place in the context of fixed Code, and modifies the expression and the store.

Java on the other hand, does not require the complete program to have been linked before execution. During execution, a type (*i.e.,* class or interface) may be needed which is not in the current code. If bytecode for the type can be found and verified, then the code is enriched with the new type. Furthermore, Code consists of a verified, prepared part P, and a loaded part L, which was loaded in order to support verification of P. We consider language $\mathcal{L}$, which stands for *loaded* binary programs, and $\mathcal{P}$, which stands for verified and *prepared* binary programs.

Therefore, we describe execution in terms of expressions e, states σ, verified code P, and loaded but not verified code L. It has the general form

$$\mathsf{e}, \sigma, \mathsf{P}, \mathsf{L}_1\mathsf{L}_2 \rightsquigarrow \mathsf{e}', \sigma', \mathsf{P}\mathsf{P}_1, \mathsf{L}_2\mathsf{L}_3$$

thus describing that the expression may be rewritten, the state may be modified, code may be loaded, and some of the loaded code may be verified and prepared – the terms $\mathsf{L}_1\mathsf{L}_2$, PP_1, and $\mathsf{L}_2\mathsf{L}_3$ indicate concatenation of $\mathcal{L}$ or $\mathcal{P}$ code.

[1] By compiling modified Java classes without recompiling all importing classes one may obtain bytecode that does not verify. Also, execution sometimes does not attempt to verify local classes.

We classify execution into the following five components:

- *evaluation* corresponds to execution as in most programming languages,
- *resolution* is the process of resolving references to fields and methods,
- *loading* is the process of loading types required for further execution,
- *verification* is the process of verifying $\mathcal{L}$ code,
- *preparation* turns verified $\mathcal{L}$ code into $\mathcal{P}$ code.

Evaluation is the execution that is unaffected by the dynamic linking nature of Java, *e.g.,* assignment to variables, loops, conditionals, parameter passing, *etc.* Resolution applies the offsets of the static type stored in field access or method calls to an object or to the dynamic class of the receiver.

Loading loads types (*i.e.,* class bodies or interface descriptors) necessary for the verification of further classes, or for the resolution of field access and method calls. A loader exception is thrown if the type cannot be found. Verification checks that the subtype relations required in some expressions are satisfied, but does *not* check the presence of fields or methods referred to in some piece of code. This is checked only when and if the method or field is accessed; if these cannot be found, then a resolution exception is thrown. A verification exception is thrown if verification is not successful. Preparation determines the object and method lookup table layout for classes, ensuring that the offsets for inherited fields and methods coincide with those of the superclasses.

In Java literature, the term *linking* describes resolution, verification and preparation. Java resolution is particularly interesting: It takes place at run-time, but has both a static and a dynamic part: it depends on the particular (dynamically loaded) classes or interfaces mentioned in the corresponding signature, *and* on the particular object which appears as receiver in the corresponding expression – more later.

An example. We demonstrate these components in terms of an example, which is also outlined in figure 1. We also use some of our notation, which we will introduce formally in later chapters.

Consider the following high level view of bytecode method call:

$$\textbf{new}\ \mathsf{A}[\mathsf{A}, \textbf{int}, \textbf{void}].\mathsf{m}(\ 3)$$

which stands for the call of a method m, with receiver **new** A, and argument 3. The signature [A, **int**, **void**] indicates that m is defined in class A, takes an **int** parameter, and returns **void**[2].

We start with configuration (1), *i.e.,* the prepared code is P, the loaded code is L, and the store is σ. Assume that the above expression had been verified, but that class A was not defined in L, nor in P. Since an object of class A has to be created, class A needs to be loaded and verified. If A cannot be found, a loader error, LoadErr, is thrown. Otherwise, A is loaded, and L is extended by L_A. Assume also that class A had a unique method

$$\textbf{void}\ \mathsf{m}(\textbf{int}\ \mathsf{x})\{\ \mathsf{B}\ \mathsf{aB};\ \ \mathsf{aB} = \textbf{new}\ \textbf{C};\ \mathsf{aB}[\mathsf{B}, \textbf{int}].\mathsf{f} = \mathsf{x}\ \}.$$

Note that the term aB[B, **int**].f indicates selection from aB of a field f defined in class B with type **int**.

[2] Method calls in Java bytecode contain the signature of the method.

(1) $\textbf{new}\ \mathsf{A}[\mathsf{A},\textbf{int},\textbf{void}].\mathsf{m}(3), \sigma, \mathsf{P}, \mathsf{L}$
load A, found?
NO, then $\leadsto$ LoadErr
YES; assume $\mathsf{L}_\mathsf{A} = ld(\mathsf{A}, \mathsf{P}, \mathsf{L})$
and assume that class A contains unique method
void m(**int** x)**{** B aB = **new C**; aB[B, **int**].f = x **} }**

$\leadsto$

(2) $\textbf{new}\ \mathsf{A}[\mathsf{A},\textbf{int},\textbf{void}].\mathsf{m}(3), \sigma, \mathsf{P}, \mathsf{L}\mathsf{L}_\mathsf{A}$
attempt to verify A
attempt to establish C subtype B
load C and superclasses
found? NO, then $\leadsto$ LoadErr
YES
C subtype B?
NO, then $\leadsto$ VerifErr
YES, assume C direct subclass of B, *i.e.,* $\mathsf{L}_\mathsf{B}\mathsf{L}_\mathsf{C} = ld(\mathsf{C}, \mathsf{P}, \mathsf{L})$
then established $\mathsf{P}, \mathsf{L} \vdash_v \mathsf{C} \leq \mathsf{B} \ \overleftarrow{\scriptstyle loads}\ \mathsf{L}_\mathsf{B}\mathsf{L}_\mathsf{C}$
thus verified A, *i.e.,* $\mathsf{P}, \mathsf{L} \vdash_v \mathsf{L}_\mathsf{A} \diamond \ \overleftarrow{\scriptstyle loads}\ \mathsf{L}_\mathsf{B}\mathsf{L}_\mathsf{C}$
thus can prepare A, thus $\mathsf{P}_\mathsf{A} = pr(\mathsf{L}_\mathsf{A}, \mathsf{P})$

$\leadsto$

(3) $\textbf{new}\ \mathsf{A}[\mathsf{A},\textbf{int},\textbf{void}].\mathsf{m}(3), \sigma, \mathsf{P}\mathsf{P}_\mathsf{A}, \mathsf{L}\mathsf{L}_\mathsf{B}\mathsf{L}_\mathsf{C}$
create an A object, $\sigma' = \sigma[\alpha \mapsto \mathsf{A}...]$, α new in σ

$\leadsto$

(4) $\alpha[\mathsf{A},\textbf{int},\textbf{void}].\mathsf{m}(3), \sigma', \mathsf{P}\mathsf{P}_\mathsf{A}, \mathsf{L}\mathsf{L}_\mathsf{B}\mathsf{L}_\mathsf{C}$

$\leadsto$

(5) $\mathsf{aB} = \textbf{new}\ \mathsf{C}; \mathsf{aB}[\mathsf{B}, \textbf{int}].\mathsf{f} = \mathsf{x}, \sigma'', \mathsf{P}\mathsf{P}_\mathsf{A}, \mathsf{L}\mathsf{L}_\mathsf{B}\mathsf{L}_\mathsf{C}$
attempt to verify C
success? NO, then $\leadsto$ VerifErr
YES, assume $\mathsf{P}\mathsf{P}_\mathsf{A}, \mathsf{L} \vdash_v \mathsf{L}_\mathsf{B}\mathsf{L}_\mathsf{C} \diamond \ \overleftarrow{\scriptstyle loads}\ \mathsf{L}_\emptyset$
assume $\mathsf{P}_\mathsf{B}\mathsf{P}_\mathsf{C} = pr(\mathsf{L}_\mathsf{B}\mathsf{L}_\mathsf{C}, \mathsf{P}\mathsf{P}_\mathsf{A})$

$\leadsto$

(6) $\mathsf{aB} = \textbf{new}\ \mathsf{C}; \mathsf{aB}[\mathsf{B}, \textbf{int}].\mathsf{f} = \mathsf{x}, \sigma'', \mathsf{P}\mathsf{P}_\mathsf{A}\mathsf{P}_\mathsf{B}\mathsf{P}_\mathsf{C}, \mathsf{L}$

$\leadsto$

...

$\leadsto$

(7) $\alpha'[\mathsf{B}, \textbf{int}].\mathsf{f} = 3, \sigma''', \mathsf{P}\mathsf{P}_\mathsf{A}\mathsf{P}_\mathsf{B}\mathsf{P}_\mathsf{C}, \mathsf{L}$
find offset of field **int** f in class B
found? NO $\leadsto$ NoFldErr
YES, assume $\phi = \mathcal{F}\!\!f(\mathsf{f}, \mathsf{B}, \textbf{int}, \mathsf{P}\mathsf{P}_\mathsf{A}\mathsf{P}_\mathsf{B}\mathsf{P}_\mathsf{C})$
store 3 at $\alpha' + \phi$, *i.e.,* $\sigma'''' = \sigma'''[(\alpha' + \phi) \mapsto 3]$

$\leadsto$

(8) $3, \sigma'''', \mathsf{P}\mathsf{P}_\mathsf{A}\mathsf{P}_\mathsf{B}\mathsf{P}_\mathsf{C}, \mathsf{L}$

Fig. 1. Example of loading, verification, resolution, evaluation, and preparation

We now have configuration (2). Class A needs to be verified, and so all method bodies, and all superclasses of A will be verified, and all required subtype relationships will be checked. In our example, verification of the method body in A requires class C to be a subtype of B. Assume that C has not been loaded yet. Then, either a loader error will be thrown (LoadErr) or C will get loaded together with all its superclasses. Assume that the superclasses of C only include B. So, we have established that C is a subtype of B, while loading L_B and L_C. In terms of our formalism, we have established $P, L \vdash_v C \leq B \underset{loads}{\leftharpoonup} L_B L_C$. This gives successful verification while loading L_B and L_C. In terms of our formalism, $P, L \vdash_v L_A \diamond \underset{loads}{\leftharpoonup} L_B L_C$. Note that L_B and L_C are loaded but *not verified.* Then prepare A, obtaining $P_A = pr(L_A, P)$, which contains the information from L_A extended by offset information. We replace L_A by P_A, and load L_B and L_C.

We arrive at configuration (3). Then we create the A object. The new state, σ', contains the new object at address α, whose first cell indicates its class, namely A.

We obtain configuration (4). We then execute the method call. This requires resolution *i.e.,* looking up the offset of the method in class A stored in the signature, and application of this offset to the method lookup table of the class of the object stored at α. In this example, the two classes coincide. The method body is aB $=$ **new** C; aB[B, **int**].f $=$ x }.

This leads to configuration (5). Execution of the expression **new** C requires verification and preparation of the classes B and C. If verification fails, then a verification error is thrown. Otherwise, assume that verification did not require loading of any further classes, *i.e.,* $P, L L_A \vdash_v L_B L_C \diamond \underset{loads}{\leftharpoonup} L_\emptyset$, and that preparation of C and B gives $P_C P_B$, *i.e.,* $P_C P_B = pr(L_C L_B, P)$.

This leads to configuration (6). We then create a new C object at the new address α' and obtain store σ'''.

After some steps, we obtain configuration (7) – assuming that x in σ''' contains the value 3. For the assignment α'[B, **int**].f $=$ 3, the field access α'[B, **int**].f has to be resolved. If class B does not have a field f of type **int**, then the resolution exception NoFldErr is thrown. Otherwise, resolution returns ϕ, the offset of **int** f from class B. This offset is used to access the field in the object at α'. The object at α' happens to belong to class C, which is different from B. But because C is a subclass of B, and because preparation guarantees that the object layout of a class conforms to that of a superclass, class C will have inherited the field at the same offset as in B. And so, the assignment will not break the consistency of the object.

This brings us to configuration (8).

If however, the method body had not been verified and C was not a subclass of B, or if resolution did not read the offsets properly, or if preparation did not preserve the object layout from superclasses, then the integrity of the object could be violated – more on that in section 3.1.

term	meaning	definition
$\mathsf{L} \in \mathcal{L}$	loaded code	def 1
$\mathsf{P} \in \mathcal{P}$	prepared code	def 2
e	a term (identical in $\mathcal{L}$ and $\mathcal{P}$)	fig 3
σ	a store, mapping identifiers and addresses to identifiers or integers	sect. 5.1
$\mathcal{T}(\mathsf{t},\mathsf{P})$, $\mathcal{T}(\mathsf{t},\mathsf{L})$	the superclasses/superinterfaces of t in L, P	defs 1, 2
$\mathcal{M}(\mathsf{m},\mathsf{c},\mathsf{t}_2,\mathsf{t}_1,\mathsf{L})$	the body of method m, with argument type t_2, and result type t_1 in class c	def 1
$\mathcal{F}_{\mathit{ff}}(\mathsf{f},\mathsf{c},\mathsf{t},\mathsf{P})$	the offset of field f with type t in class c	def 2
$\mathcal{F}s(\mathsf{c},\mathsf{P})$	all fields with types and offsets, defined or inherited in class c	def 2
$\mathcal{M}_{\mathit{ff}}(\mathsf{m},\mathsf{c},\mathsf{t}_2,\mathsf{t}_1,\mathsf{P})$	the offset of method m with argument type t_2, and result type t_1 in class c	def 2
$\mathcal{M}_e(\phi,\mathsf{c},\mathsf{P})$	the method body at offset ϕ in class c	def 2
$\mathcal{M}^{\mathsf{i}}_{\mathit{ff}}(\mathsf{m},\mathsf{i},\mathsf{t}_2,\mathsf{t}_1,\mathsf{P})$	the offset of method m with argument type t_2, and result type t_1 in interface i	def 2
$\mathsf{e},\sigma,\mathsf{P},\mathsf{L}_1\mathsf{L}_2 \leadsto \mathsf{e}',\sigma',\mathsf{PP}_1,\mathsf{L}_2\mathsf{L}_3$	e rewrites to e', and σ rewrites to σ', prepared code augmented by P_1, new code L_3 loaded	fig 4
$\sqsubset\cdot\sqsupset^{exp}$	expression context, propagates to sub-expression	fig 5
$\sqsubset\cdot\sqsupset^{nll}$	null context, may throw exception	fig 5
$\sqsubset\cdot\sqsupset^{typ}$	type context, may cause loading and verification	fig 5
$\mathsf{P},\mathsf{L}\vdash\mathsf{c}\ \leq_{clss}\ \mathsf{c}'$	c is a subclass of c' in context of P, L	fig 6
$\mathsf{P},\mathsf{L}\vdash\mathsf{c}\ \leq_{impl}\ \mathsf{i}$	c implements i in context of P, L	fig 6
$\mathsf{P},\mathsf{L}\vdash\mathsf{i}\ \leq_{intf}\ \mathsf{i}'$	i is a subinterface of i' in context of P, L	fig 6
$\vdash\ \mathsf{P},\mathsf{L}\ \diamond_a$	the subclass/subinterface relationship in P, L is acyclic	fig 6
$\vdash\ \mathsf{P},\mathsf{L}\diamond_{sups}$	P, L contain all supertypes of types defined in PL	fig 6
$\mathsf{P},\mathsf{L}\vdash_v\mathsf{L}'\diamond\ \underset{loads}{\leftharpoondown}\ \mathsf{L}''$	verifier checks that L' is well formed in context P, L, and loads L''	fig 7
$\mathsf{P},\mathsf{L}\vdash_v\mathsf{t}\ \leq\ \mathsf{t}'\ \underset{loads}{\leftharpoondown}\ \mathsf{L}'$	verifier checks that t widens to t' in context P, L, and loads L'	fig 7
$\mathsf{P},\mathsf{L},\mathsf{E}\vdash_v\mathsf{e}\ :\ \mathsf{t}\ \underset{loads}{\leftharpoondown}\ \mathsf{L}'$	verifier checks that e has type t in context P, L, while loading L'	fig 7
E	environment for the declaration of variables	fig 8
$\mathsf{P},\mathsf{L}\vdash\mathsf{t}\ \leq\ \mathsf{t}'$	t widens to t' in the context of prepared P, and loaded L	fig 3.6
$\mathsf{P},\mathsf{L},\mathsf{E}\vdash\mathsf{e}\ :\ \mathsf{t}$	e has type t in the context of prepared P, and environment E	fig 3.6
$\mathsf{P},\mathsf{L}\vdash\mathsf{P}'\diamond$	P' is well-formed in the context of P and L	fig 3.6
$\mathsf{L}\vdash\mathsf{P}\diamond$	P is well-formed in the context of L	fig 3.6
$\sigma,\mathsf{P}\vdash_w\beta:\mathsf{t}$	value β conforms weakly to type t in context of P	fig 10
$\sigma,\mathsf{P}\vdash_c\alpha\ \diamond$	the object stored at α in σ is well-formed (conforms strongly)	fig 10
$\mathsf{P},\mathsf{E}\vdash_c\sigma\ \diamond$	all objects in σ are well-formed, and agree to their declarations in E	fig 10
$\mathsf{P},\mathsf{L},\mathsf{E}\vdash_r\sigma,\mathsf{e}\ :\ \mathsf{t}$	runtime expression e has type t in store σ in the context of P, L, E	fig 10
$ld(\mathsf{t},\mathsf{P},\mathsf{L})$	loading	def 4
$pr(\mathsf{L},\mathsf{P})$	preparation	def 5

Fig. 2. Concepts defined in this paper

Thus, the above example demonstrates

- classes may be loaded without being verified[3],
- execution of verified code may throw loader, resolution or verification errors[4],
- verification checks subtype relationships, and does not guarantee the presence of methods or fields,
- resolution checks the presence of methods and fields,
- verification and resolution checks complement each other.

The treatment of interfaces. In order to establish that required subtype relationships are satisfied, verification looks up the appropriate classes. However, if the required subtype relationships involve interfaces, then these relationships are automatically assumed to hold and are *not* checked!

> Apparently overawed by the multiplicity of parents possible in a Java interface hierarchy, the implementors of Sun's verifier ... abdicated responsibility for type checking involving the use of interfaces. Instead, ..., the burden of checking for compatibility, ... passed implicitly to the runtime system.
>
> Philipp Yelland [29]

Thus, at runtime these subtype requirements need to be checked, and execution of interface method calls will check the satisfaction of the associated subtype relationship. Again, we see that checks from two different JVM components complement each other, and in slightly different ways for classes than for interfaces.

An example is given in the appendix.

Organization of this paper. In figure 2 we list all judgments and functions defined in the paper, with a brief description of their intention, and the place of their definition. In section 2 we introduce $\mathcal{L}$ and $\mathcal{P}$ for the description of loaded or prepared code. In section 3 we describe an operational semantics, and distinguish the five components. In section 4 we define consistency of states with prepared code, and types for runtime expressions, and we state subject reduction and progress lemmas. In section 5 we give a summary and outline alternatives, and in section 6 we draw conclusions, compare with other work, and introduce some open questions.

Hand-written proofs are available at http : //www.doc.ic.ac.uk/ ~ scd/proofs.

[3] In the particular example, all loaded classes are eventually verified, but it would take a slight modification (*e.g.*, put the creation of the C object in a conditional), for this not to be the case.

[4] The latter while attempting to verify further classes.

2 The Languages $\mathcal{L}$ and $\mathcal{P}$

The languages $\mathcal{L}$ and $\mathcal{P}$ present an abstract view of the Java bytecode. For the sake of simplicity, we only consider classes, subclasses, interfaces, subinterfaces, assignment, method overloading and inheritance, field inheritance and hiding.[5] We chose these features, because inheritance with fields allows for an interesting notion of consistent state, inheritance with method calls and fields demonstrates the interplay between resolution and verification, and interfaces pose the same requirement as classes, but are treated differently. We do not model super. Even though our examples use sequential statements, we have not included them in the $\mathcal{L}$- and $\mathcal{P}$-syntax, as they can be easily encoded by extra methods. Also, all methods have one argument – multiple arguments can be encoded through objects.

Expressions. Figure 3 contains the syntax of expressions in $\mathcal{L}$ or in $\mathcal{P}$ programs.

Field accesses and instance or class method calls[6] are annotated by signatures. Field access has the form $\mathsf{e_1[t_1,t_2].f}$, where $\mathsf{t_1}$ is the class containing the field definition, and $\mathsf{t_2}$ the type of that field. Instance method calls have the form $\mathsf{e_1[t_1,t_2,t_3].m(e_2)}$, where $\mathsf{t_1}$ is the class containing the method definition, $\mathsf{t_2}$ is the type of the method's argument, and $\mathsf{t_3}$ is the result type. Similarly, interface method calls have the form $\mathsf{e[t_1,t_2,t_3]^i.m(e_2)}$, where $\mathsf{t_1}$ is the interface containing the method header, $\mathsf{t_2}$ is the argument type, and $\mathsf{t_3}$ is the result type.

The only types we consider are classes, interfaces, and **int**; these demonstrate several interesting properties of the Java system. Interfaces introduce multiple subtyping. More interestingly, subtyping introduced through interfaces is dealt with differently from subtyping introduced through subclassing: as we shall see, the verifier assumes an interface to be a supertype of *any* type, whereas it considers a class to be a supertype of its loaded subclasses only; conversely, at runtime subclasses are not checked for instance method calls, but subtypes are checked for interface method calls. Also, the type **int** and the address calculations during execution open the possibility of pitfalls, which, as we shall demonstrate, are averted by verification and the resolution checks.

Values are either integers, or addresses of objects. Addresses are represented by positive numbers and are denoted by α, α' *etc*; the null pointer is denoted by **0**. Values, whether they stand for addresses or for integers, are denoted by β, β' *etc.*

Contrary to Java source language rules [14], $\mathcal{L}$- and $\mathcal{P}$-methods may have the same identifier and argument type but *different* result type as a method from a superclass. Such binaries may be created, *e.g.*, through compilation of a class and its subclass, subsequent addition of a method in the superclass, and recompilation of the superclass without recompilation of the subclass. The method

[5] $\mathcal{L}$ is a similar language to language Javacito[18] or the Java subset from [10]; it is larger than [16] because it considers imperative features, overloading and interfaces; and, though at a different abstraction level than [23], it is larger because it studies interfaces.

[6] corresponding to bytecode instructions getfield, putfield, invokevirtual and invokeinterface.

$e \in$ Expr	::=	$e[t,t,t].m\ (e)$	method call
	—	$e[t,t,t]^{\mathrm{i}}.m\ (e)$	interface method call
	—	$v = e$	assignment
	—	**new** c — **this**	object creation, receiver
	—	v — β	variable, integer value
	—	NllPErr — LoadErr	null-pointer err., load err.
	—	VerifErr — ClssChngErr	verification err., class change err.
	—	NoFldErr — NoMethErr	field not found, method not found
v	::=	$e[t,t].f$	field access
	—	z	parameter
$t \in$ Typ	::=	c — i — **int**	class, interface or integer
$\phi \in$ Offs	::=	**1** — **2** — ...	offsets
$\chi \in$ErrOffs	::=	**−1**	member undefined
	—	**−2**	type of wrong kind
	—	**−3**	type undefined
$\alpha \in$ Addr	::=	**0** — ϕ	address
$\beta \in$ Val	::=	α — **−1** — **−2** — ...	value
c, i $\in$Id			c class names, i interface names
m, f, $z$$\in$Id			m method names, f field names

Fig. 3. The syntax of expressions

calls will then be dis-ambiguated through the result type of the signature. For example, $\mathsf{x}[\mathsf{c}_1,\mathsf{t}_2\mathsf{t}_3].\mathsf{m}_2(...)$ selects from class c_1 the method with parameter type t_2 and result type t_3, whereas $\mathsf{x}[\mathsf{c}_1,\mathsf{t}_2,\mathsf{t}_4].\mathsf{m}_2(...)$ selects from class c_1 the method with parameter type t_2 and result type t_4.

Language for loaded code, $\mathcal{L}$. Rather than give the syntax of $\mathcal{L}$ and $\mathcal{P}$ programs, we describe these, as in [10], through functions that lookup the superclasses, superinterfaces, fields and methods of a class or interface. $\mathbb{P}(\mathcal{A})$ denotes the powerset of $\mathcal{A}$.

Definition 1 *The tuple* $(\mathcal{L}, \mathcal{T}, \mathcal{M}, \mathsf{L}_\emptyset)$ *is a* language for loaded code, *iff*

- $\mathcal{L}$ *is a set.*
- $\mathcal{T}$ *is a function,* $\mathcal{T}: \ \mathsf{Id} \times \mathcal{L} \longrightarrow (\mathsf{Id} \times \mathbb{P}(\mathsf{Id})) \cup (\mathbb{P}(\mathsf{Id})) \cup \{\epsilon\}$.
- $\mathcal{M}$ *is a function,* $\mathcal{M}\ :\ \mathsf{Id} \times \mathsf{Id} \times \mathsf{Typ} \times \mathsf{Typ} \times \mathcal{L} \longrightarrow \mathsf{Expr} \cup \{\epsilon\}$.
- $\mathsf{L}_\emptyset \in \mathcal{L}$, $\forall \mathsf{t} \in \mathsf{Id}$: $\mathcal{T}(\mathsf{t}, \mathsf{L}_\emptyset) = \epsilon$.
- *for any* $\mathsf{L}_1, \mathsf{L}_2 \in \mathcal{L}$, *their concatenation,* $\mathsf{L}_1\mathsf{L}_2$, *gives a further element of* $\mathcal{L}$, *with:*
  - $\mathcal{T}(\mathsf{t}, \mathsf{L}_1\mathsf{L}_2) \ = \ \mathcal{T}(\mathsf{t}, \mathsf{L}_1)$ *if* $\mathcal{T}(\mathsf{t}, \mathsf{L}_1) \neq \epsilon$, $\ \mathcal{T}(\mathsf{t}, \mathsf{L}_2)$ *otherwise.*
  - $\mathcal{M}(\mathsf{m}, \mathsf{c}, \mathsf{t}_2, \mathsf{t}_3, \mathsf{L}_1\mathsf{L}_2) \ = \ \mathcal{M}(\mathsf{m}, \mathsf{c}, \mathsf{t}_2, \mathsf{t}_3, \mathsf{L}_1)$ *if* $\mathcal{T}(\mathsf{c}, \mathsf{L}_1) \neq \epsilon$,
    $\mathcal{M}(\mathsf{m}, \mathsf{c}, \mathsf{t}_2, \mathsf{t}_3, \mathsf{L}_2)$ *otherwise.*

In the above, $\mathsf{L}_\emptyset$ indicates the empty program in $\mathcal{L}$, and ϵ indicates lookup of a non-existing entity. $\mathcal{T}(\mathsf{t}, \mathsf{L})$ is intended to return the direct superclass of t and the (possibly empty) set of its direct superinterfaces, if t is declared as a class in L; or, return the (possibly empty) set of the direct superinterfaces, if t is declared as an interface in L; and ϵ otherwise. $\mathcal{M}(\mathsf{m}, \mathsf{c}, \mathsf{t}_2, \mathsf{t}_1, \mathsf{L})$ is intended to return the body of method m defined in class c, with result type t_1 and argument type t_2, or ϵ if no such method is found. Note, that we have no functions looking up the fields, nor any functions looking up entities in interfaces – this is so, because these are not used for verification, and so, in our setting can be considered as non-existing in $\mathcal{L}$ code.

For example, assume classes B and C, class B has fields **int** f_1, and C f_2, and method **int** m(D x){4 + 44}, where C extends class B, implements interfaces I2 and I4 and has field **int** f_1, and method **int** m(D x){777}. It would be represented through L_{BC}, whith $\mathcal{T}(\mathsf{B}, \mathsf{L}_{\mathsf{BC}})=$ Object, { }, $\mathcal{T}(\mathsf{C}, \mathsf{L}_{\mathsf{BC}})=$ B, {I2, I4}, and for method lookup: $\mathcal{M}(\mathsf{m}, \mathsf{B}, \mathsf{D}, \mathbf{int}, \mathsf{L}_{\mathsf{BC}}) = 4 + 44$, $\mathcal{M}(\mathsf{m}, \mathsf{C}, \mathsf{D}, \mathbf{int}, \mathsf{L}_{\mathsf{BC}}) = 777$.

In [5] we gave the syntax of a language for which we defined by construction functions corresponding to $\mathcal{T}$and $\mathcal{M}$. Therefore, the definition 1 is well-formed. From now on, we expect $(\mathcal{L}, \mathcal{T}, \mathcal{M}, \mathsf{L}_\emptyset)$ to stand for a fixed language for loaded code.

Language for prepared code, $\mathcal{P}$. The language $\mathcal{P}$ describes code after preparation; the programs are extended by method and field lookup tables. We model this by offsets, which are positive numbers, denoted by ϕ, ϕ'∈Offs, while χ∈ErrOffs indicate non-existing entities, or entities of the wrong kind.

Definition 2 *A tuple* $(\mathcal{P}, \mathcal{T}, \mathcal{M}_{\mathit{ff}}, \mathcal{F}_{\mathit{ff}}, \mathcal{M}_e, \mathcal{M}^{\mathsf{i}}_{\mathit{ff}})$ *is a* language for prepared code *iff*

- $\mathcal{P}$ *is a set.*
- $\mathcal{T}$ *is a function,* $\mathcal{T}: \mathsf{Id} \times \mathcal{P} \longrightarrow (\mathsf{Id} \times \mathbb{P}(\mathsf{Id})) \cup (\mathbb{P}(\mathsf{Id})) \cup \{\epsilon\}$.
- $\mathcal{M}_{\mathit{ff}}$ *is a function,* $\mathcal{M}_{\mathit{ff}}: \mathsf{Id} \times \mathsf{Id} \times \mathsf{Typ} \times \mathsf{Typ} \times \mathcal{P} \longrightarrow \mathsf{Offs} \cup \mathsf{ErrOffs}$.
- $\mathcal{F}_{\mathit{ff}}$ *is a function,* $\mathcal{F}_{\mathit{ff}}: \mathsf{Id} \times \mathsf{Id} \times \mathsf{Typ} \times \mathcal{P} \longrightarrow \mathsf{Offs} \cup \mathsf{ErrOffs}$.
- $\mathcal{M}_e$ *is a function,* $\mathcal{M}_e: \mathsf{Offs} \times \mathsf{Id} \times \mathcal{P} \longrightarrow \mathsf{Expr} \cup \{\epsilon\}$.
- $\mathcal{M}^{\mathsf{i}}_{\mathit{ff}}$ *is a function,* $\mathcal{M}^{\mathsf{i}}_{\mathit{ff}}: \mathsf{Id} \times \mathsf{Id} \times \mathsf{Typ} \times \mathsf{Typ} \times \mathcal{P} \longrightarrow \{\mathbf{0}\} \cup \mathsf{ErrOffs}$.
- $\forall$ c, c′, m, t, t′,P: $\mathcal{T}(\mathsf{c}, \mathsf{P}) = \mathsf{c}', \{...\} \Rightarrow \mathcal{M}^{\mathsf{i}}_{\mathit{ff}}(\mathsf{m}, \mathsf{c}, \mathsf{t}, \mathsf{t}', \mathsf{P}) = \mathbf{-2}$.
- $\forall$ i, m, f, t, t′,P: $\mathcal{T}(\mathsf{i}, \mathsf{P}) = \{...\} \Rightarrow \mathcal{F}_{\mathit{ff}}(\mathsf{f}, \mathsf{i}, \mathsf{t}, \mathsf{P}) = \mathbf{-2}$, $\mathcal{M}_{\mathit{ff}}(\mathsf{m}, \mathsf{i}, \mathsf{t}, \mathsf{t}', \mathsf{P}) = \mathbf{-2}$.
- $\forall$ t, m, f, t_1, t_2,P: $\mathcal{M}_{\mathit{ff}}(\mathsf{m}, \mathsf{t}, \mathsf{t}_1, \mathsf{t}_2, \mathsf{P}) = \mathbf{-3} \Leftrightarrow \mathcal{F}_{\mathit{ff}}(\mathsf{f}, \mathsf{t}, \mathsf{t}_1, \mathsf{P}) = \mathbf{-3} \Leftrightarrow$
  $\mathcal{M}^{\mathsf{i}}_{\mathit{ff}}(\mathsf{m}, \mathsf{t}, \mathsf{t}_1, \mathsf{t}_2, \mathsf{P}) = \mathbf{-3} \Leftrightarrow \mathcal{T}(\mathsf{t}, \mathsf{P}) = \epsilon$.
- $\mathsf{P}_\emptyset \in \mathcal{P}$, $\forall \mathsf{t} \in \mathsf{Id} : \mathcal{T}(\mathsf{t}, \mathsf{P}_\emptyset) = \epsilon$.
- *For any* $\mathsf{P}_1, \mathsf{P}_2 \in \mathcal{P}$, *their concatenation,* $\mathsf{P}_1\mathsf{P}_2$, *gives a further element of* $\mathcal{P}$, *with*
  - $\mathcal{T}(\mathsf{t}, \mathsf{P}_1\mathsf{P}_2) = \mathcal{T}(\mathsf{t}, \mathsf{P}_1)$ *if* $\mathcal{T}(\mathsf{t}, \mathsf{P}_1) \neq \epsilon$, $\mathcal{T}(\mathsf{t}, \mathsf{P}_2)$ *otherwise.*
  - $\mathcal{M}_{\mathit{ff}}(\mathsf{m}, \mathsf{c}, \mathsf{t}_2, \mathsf{t}_3, \mathsf{P}_1\mathsf{P}_2) = \mathcal{M}_{\mathit{ff}}(\mathsf{m}, \mathsf{c}, \mathsf{t}_2, \mathsf{t}_3, \mathsf{P}_1)$ *if* $\mathcal{T}(\mathsf{c}, \mathsf{P}_1) \neq \epsilon$,
    $\mathcal{M}_{\mathit{ff}}(\mathsf{m}, \mathsf{c}, \mathsf{t}_2, \mathsf{t}_3, \mathsf{P}_2)$ *otherwise.*
  - $\mathcal{M}_e(\phi, \mathsf{c}, \mathsf{P}_1\mathsf{P}_2) = \mathcal{M}_e(\phi, \mathsf{c}, \mathsf{P}_1)$ *if* $\mathcal{T}(\mathsf{c}, \mathsf{P}_1) \neq \epsilon$, $\mathcal{M}_e(\phi, \mathsf{c}, \mathsf{P}_2)$ *otherwise.*

- $\mathcal{F}_{ff}(\mathsf{f},\mathsf{c},\mathsf{t},\mathsf{P}_1\mathsf{P}_2) = \mathcal{F}_{ff}(\mathsf{f},\mathsf{c},\mathsf{t},\mathsf{P}_1)$ *if* $\mathcal{T}(\mathsf{c},\mathsf{P}_1)\neq\epsilon$, $\mathcal{F}_{ff}(\mathsf{f},\mathsf{c},\mathsf{t},\mathsf{P}_2)$ *otherwise.*
- $\mathcal{M}^{\mathbf{i}}_{ff}(\mathsf{m},\mathsf{i},\mathsf{t}_2,\mathsf{t}_3,\mathsf{P}_1) = \mathcal{M}^{\mathbf{i}}_{ff}(\mathsf{m},\mathsf{i},\mathsf{t}_2,\mathsf{t}_3,\mathsf{P}_1\mathsf{P}_2)$ *if* $\mathcal{T}(\mathsf{i},\mathsf{P}_1)\neq\epsilon$, $\mathcal{M}^{\mathbf{i}}_{ff}(\mathsf{m},\mathsf{i},\mathsf{t}_2,\mathsf{t}_3,\mathsf{P}_2)$ *otherwise.*

The function $\mathcal{T}$ has the same intention as in def. 1. The functions $\mathcal{M}_{ff}(\mathsf{m},\mathsf{c},\mathsf{t}_2,\mathsf{t}_1,\mathsf{P})$, or $\mathcal{F}_{ff}(\mathsf{f},\mathsf{c},\mathsf{t},\mathsf{P})$ are intended to return the offset of method m defined in class c with argument type t_2 and return type t_1, or the offset of field f defined in class c with type t; if c does not contain m or f, then they should return $-\mathbf{1}$, if c is the name of an interface, they should return $-\mathbf{2}$; and if P does not define any type for c they should return $-\mathbf{3}$. The function $\mathcal{M}_e(\phi,\mathsf{c},\mathsf{P})$ looks up the method body in class c using offset ϕ, while $\mathcal{M}^{\mathbf{i}}_{ff}(\mathsf{m},\mathsf{i},\mathsf{t}_2,\mathsf{t}_1,\mathsf{P})$, used for interface method call, indicates whether the method m with argument type t_2 and result type t_1 is defined in interface i; it should return $\mathbf{0}$ if i defines such a method, $-\mathbf{1}$ if i does not define such a method, $-\mathbf{2}$ if i is the name of a class, and $-\mathbf{3}$ if P does not define any type for i.

For the program L_{BC} from before a possible corresponding $\mathcal{P}$ program is P_{BC} where, for all t∈Typ: $\mathcal{T}(\mathsf{t},\mathsf{P}_{\mathsf{BC}}) = \mathcal{T}(\mathsf{t},\mathsf{L}_{\mathsf{BC}})$, and $\mathcal{F}_{ff}(\mathsf{f}_1,\mathsf{B},\mathbf{int},\mathsf{P}_{\mathsf{BC}}) = 3$, $\mathcal{F}_{ff}(\mathsf{f}_2,\mathsf{B},\mathsf{C},\mathsf{P}_{\mathsf{BC}}) = 5$, $\mathcal{M}_{ff}(\mathsf{m},\mathsf{B},\mathsf{D},\mathbf{int},\mathsf{P}_{\mathsf{BC}}) = 2$, $\mathcal{M}_e(2,\mathsf{B},\mathsf{P}_{\mathsf{BC}}) = 4+44$, and for class C, we would have $\mathcal{F}_{ff}(\mathsf{f}_1,\mathsf{C},\mathbf{int},\mathsf{P}_{\mathsf{BC}}) = 6$, $\mathcal{M}_{ff}(\mathsf{m},\mathsf{C},\mathsf{D},\mathbf{int},\mathsf{P}_{\mathsf{BC}}) = 2$, $\mathcal{M}_e(2,\mathsf{C},\mathsf{P}_{\mathsf{BC}}) = 777$.

In [5] we gave the syntax of a language for which we defined constructively functions corresponding to $\mathcal{T}$, $\mathcal{M}_{ff}$, $\mathcal{F}_{ff}$, $\mathcal{M}_e$, and $\mathcal{M}^{\mathbf{i}}_{ff}$. Thus, the definition 2 is well-formed. From now on, we assume $(\mathcal{P},\mathcal{T},\mathcal{M}_{ff},\mathcal{F}_{ff},\mathcal{M}_e,\mathcal{M}^{\mathbf{i}}_{ff})$ to be a given language for prepared code.

Combined $\mathcal{L}$ and $\mathcal{P}$ code. We define functions to collect all types declared in $\mathcal{L}$, or $\mathcal{P}$, or combined code, and to collect all fields and all methods in such code.

Definition 3 *For* $\mathsf{L}\in\mathcal{L}$, $\mathsf{P}\in\mathcal{P}$, $\mathsf{c}\in\mathsf{Id}$ *with* $\mathcal{T}(\mathsf{c},\mathsf{P}) = \mathsf{c}', \{...\}$, *we define:*

- $\mathcal{T}(\mathsf{t},\mathsf{P},\mathsf{L}) = \mathcal{T}(\mathsf{t},\mathsf{P})$ *if* $\mathcal{T}(\mathsf{t},\mathsf{P})\neq\epsilon$, $\mathcal{T}(\mathsf{t},\mathsf{L})$ *otherwise.*
- $\mathcal{T}s(\mathsf{L}) = \{\ \mathsf{t} \mid \mathcal{T}(\mathsf{t},\mathsf{L})\neq\epsilon\ \}$, $\mathcal{T}s(\mathsf{P}) = \{\ \mathsf{t} \mid \mathcal{T}(\mathsf{t},\mathsf{P})\neq\epsilon\ \}$,
  $\mathcal{T}s(\mathsf{P},\mathsf{L}) = \{\ \mathsf{t} \mid \mathcal{T}(\mathsf{t},\mathsf{P})\neq\epsilon\ \mathit{or}\ \mathcal{T}(\mathsf{t},\mathsf{L})\neq\epsilon\ \}$.
- $\mathcal{M}s(\mathsf{c},\mathsf{L}) = \{\ \mathsf{t}_1\ \mathsf{m}(\mathsf{t}_2\ \mathsf{x})\{\mathsf{e}\} \mid \mathsf{e} = \mathcal{M}(\mathsf{m},\mathsf{c},\mathsf{t}_1,\mathsf{t}_2,\mathsf{L})\neq\epsilon\ \}$.
- $\mathcal{F}s(\mathsf{c},\mathsf{P}) = \{\ (\mathsf{t},\mathsf{f},\phi) \mid \mathcal{F}_{ff}(\mathsf{f},\mathsf{c},\mathsf{t},\mathsf{P}) = \phi^7\ \} \cup \mathcal{F}s(\mathsf{c}',\mathsf{P})$, $\mathcal{F}s(\mathsf{Object},\mathsf{P}) = \emptyset$.

Thus, $\mathcal{T}s(\mathsf{L}_{\mathsf{BC}}) = \{\mathsf{B},\mathsf{C}\}$, and $\mathcal{M}s(\mathsf{B},\mathsf{L}_{\mathsf{BC}}) = \{\mathbf{int}\ \mathsf{m}(\mathsf{D}\ \mathsf{x})\{777\}\}$, and $\mathcal{F}s(\mathsf{C},\mathsf{P}_{\mathsf{BC}}) = \{\ (\mathbf{int},\mathsf{f}_1,3),\ (\mathsf{C},\mathsf{f}_2,5),\ (\mathbf{int},\mathsf{f}_1,6)\ \}$.

Lemma 1 *For programs* $\mathsf{L},\mathsf{L}_1,\mathsf{L}_2,\in\mathcal{L}$, *and* $\mathsf{P},\mathsf{P}_1,\mathsf{P}_2,\in\mathcal{P}$*:*

- $\mathcal{T}s(\mathsf{L}_1)\cap\mathcal{T}s(\mathsf{L}_2) = \emptyset \Rightarrow \mathsf{L}_1\ \mathsf{L}_2 = \mathsf{L}_2\ \mathsf{L}_1$.
- $\mathcal{T}s(\mathsf{P}_1)\cap\mathcal{T}s(\mathsf{P}_2) = \emptyset \Rightarrow \mathsf{P}_1\ \mathsf{P}_2 = \mathsf{P}_2\ \mathsf{P}_1$.
- $\mathcal{T}s(\mathsf{L}_2)\subseteq\mathcal{T}s(\mathsf{L}_1) \Rightarrow \mathsf{L}_1\ \mathsf{L}_2 = \mathsf{L}_1$.
- $\mathcal{T}s(\mathsf{P}_2)\subseteq\mathcal{T}s(\mathsf{P}_1) \Rightarrow \mathsf{P}_1\ \mathsf{P}_2 = \mathsf{P}_1$.
- $\mathcal{T}s(\mathsf{P},\mathsf{L}) = \mathcal{T}s(\mathsf{P})\cup\mathcal{T}s(\mathsf{L})$.

[7] Remember, that $\phi > 0$, by definition.

3 Execution

Execution, described in fig. 4, is defined in terms of a rewriting relationship on *configurations*, consisting of expression e, store σ, prepared code P, and loaded binary L. The expression and store may be modified, more code may be prepared, and further code may be loaded. Thus, execution has the form $\mathsf{e}, \sigma, \mathsf{P}, \mathsf{L_1 L_2} \leadsto \mathsf{e}', \sigma', \mathsf{PP_1}, \mathsf{L_2 L_3}$.

In order to give a more concise description of the rewrite semantics, and also, in order to distinguish between routine rewrite rules, and those particular to Java implementation, in fig. 5 we introduce three kinds of contexts. Expression contexts, $\sqsubset \cdot \sqsupset^{exp}$, are filled with a sub-expression; their execution propagates execution to this sub-expression, as in rule PROPAGATE. Null-contexts, $\sqsubset \cdot \sqsupset^{nll}$, when filled with **0**, raise an exception when executed as in rule NULLPOINTERR. Type contexts, $\sqsubset \cdot \sqsupset^{typ}$, are filled with a type name; their execution causes the type to be loaded and prepared if the type is not part of the loaded or the prepared code, as in rules LOAD, LOADERR, VERIF, VERIFERR and VERIFANDPREP[8].

We call an expression *ground*, if it is a value β[9], and *l-ground*, if it is an identifier, or has the form $\alpha[\mathsf{t_1},\mathsf{t_2}].\mathsf{f}$.

3.1 The Runtime Model

States represent stacks and heaps, and contain values for identifiers and addresses, Addresses point to objects. An object consists of its class (an identifier) and values for its fields. These are either **int** values (Val), or addresses (Addr). As Addr is the set of positive numbers, Addr $\subset$ Val. The symbol ϵ means undefined. The sets Val, Id, and $\{\epsilon\}$ are disjoint. Stores thus have the form:

$$\sigma : [\ \mathsf{Id} \rightarrow (\ \mathsf{Val}\ \cup \{\epsilon\}\ )]\ \cup\ [\ \mathsf{Addr} \rightarrow (\ \mathsf{Val}\ \cup\ \mathsf{Id}\ \cup \{\epsilon\}\ )].$$

The store lookup $\sigma(\mathsf{z})$ or $\sigma(\alpha)$ describes the value of variable z, or address α in σ; if $\sigma(\alpha) = \mathsf{c} \in \mathsf{Id}$ then α points to an object of class c. The fields of the object stored at address α are stored at some offset from α.

We say that an address α is *new* in σ iff $\forall \beta \geq 0 :\ \sigma(\alpha + \beta) = \epsilon$.

Our model of the store is therefore at a lower level than those found in studies of the verifier [25,12,23], where objects are indivisible entities, and where there are no address calculations. This lower level model allows us to describe the potential damage when executing unverified code; as in the following example.

On the other hand, our definition of states requires the distinction of the sets Addr, Id and $\{\epsilon\}$, and so it is at a higher level than plain bitstrings. Even though "real" memory contains such plain bitstrings, a faithful modeling of this aspect would not have promoted the study of Java dynamic linking[10].

---

[8] Observe, that type contexts do not include the argument or result type of a method; thus, an unverified expression $\mathsf{e_1}[\mathsf{t_1},\mathsf{t_2},\mathsf{t_3}].\mathsf{m}(\mathsf{e_2})$ could be executed without ever loading $\mathsf{t_2}$ or $\mathsf{t_3}$.

[9] and thus, implicitly, also if it is an address α.

[10] We could have represented the distinction between Val, Id, and $\{\epsilon\}$ through a tagged union, but this would have cluttered the presentation.

Evaluation

PROPAGATE
$$\frac{\mathsf{e},\sigma,\mathsf{P},\mathsf{L} \leadsto \mathsf{e}',\sigma',\mathsf{P}',\mathsf{L}'}{\sqsubset\mathsf{e}\sqsupset^{exp},\sigma,\mathsf{P},\mathsf{L} \leadsto \sqsubset\mathsf{e}'\sqsupset^{exp},\sigma',\mathsf{P}',\mathsf{L}'}$$

NULLPOINTERR
$$\frac{}{\sqsubset\mathbf{0}\sqsupset^{nll},\sigma,\mathsf{P},\mathsf{L} \leadsto \mathsf{NllPErr},\sigma,\mathsf{P},\mathsf{L}}$$

ACC
$$\frac{\mathsf{z} \text{ a variable}}{\mathsf{z},\sigma,\mathsf{P},\mathsf{L} \leadsto \sigma(\mathsf{z}),\sigma,\mathsf{P},\mathsf{L}}$$

NEW
$$\frac{\begin{array}{l}\mathsf{c} \in \mathcal{T}s(\mathsf{P})\\ \alpha \text{ new in } \sigma\\ \mathcal{F}s(\mathsf{c},\mathsf{P}) = \{(\mathsf{t}_1\ \mathsf{f}_1\ \phi_1),\ldots(\mathsf{t}_n\ \mathsf{f}_n\ \phi_n)\}\\ \sigma' = \sigma[\alpha \mapsto \mathsf{c}, \alpha+\phi_1 \mapsto \mathbf{0},\ \ldots\ , \alpha+\phi_n \mapsto \mathbf{0}]\end{array}}{\mathbf{new}\ \mathsf{c},\sigma,\mathsf{P},\mathsf{L} \leadsto \alpha,\sigma',\mathsf{P},\mathsf{L}}$$

VARASS
$$\frac{}{\mathsf{z} = \beta,\sigma,\mathsf{P},\mathsf{L} \leadsto \beta,\sigma[\mathsf{z}\mapsto\beta],\mathsf{P},\mathsf{L}}$$

Resolution

FLDACC1
$$\frac{\mathcal{F}_{\!ff}(\mathsf{f},\mathsf{t}_1,\mathsf{t}_2,\mathsf{P}) = \phi}{\begin{array}{l}\alpha[\mathsf{t}_1,\mathsf{t}_2].\mathsf{f},\sigma,\mathsf{P},\mathsf{L} \leadsto \sigma(\alpha+\phi),\sigma,\mathsf{P},\mathsf{L}\\ \alpha[\mathsf{t}_1,\mathsf{t}_2].\mathsf{f} = \beta,\sigma,\mathsf{P},\mathsf{L} \leadsto \beta,\sigma[\alpha+\phi\mapsto\beta],\mathsf{P},\mathsf{L}\end{array}}$$

FLDACC2
$$\frac{\mathcal{F}_{\!ff}(\mathsf{f},\mathsf{t}_1,\mathsf{t}_2,\mathsf{P}) = \mathbf{-1}}{\begin{array}{l}\alpha[\mathsf{t}_1,\mathsf{t}_2].\mathsf{f},\sigma,\mathsf{P},\mathsf{L} \leadsto \mathsf{NoFldErr},\sigma,\mathsf{P},\mathsf{L}\\ \alpha[\mathsf{t}_1,\mathsf{t}_2].\mathsf{f} = \beta,\sigma,\mathsf{P},\mathsf{L} \leadsto \mathsf{NoFldErr},\sigma,\mathsf{P},\mathsf{L}\end{array}}$$

FLDACC3
$$\frac{\mathcal{F}_{\!ff}(\mathsf{f},\mathsf{t}_1,\mathsf{t}_2,\mathsf{P}) = \mathbf{-2}}{\begin{array}{l}\alpha[\mathsf{t}_1,\mathsf{t}_2].\mathsf{f},\sigma,\mathsf{P},\mathsf{L} \leadsto \mathsf{ClssChngErr},\sigma,\mathsf{P},\mathsf{L}\\ \alpha[\mathsf{t}_1,\mathsf{t}_2].\mathsf{f} = \beta,\sigma,\mathsf{P},\mathsf{L} \leadsto \mathsf{ClssChngErr},\sigma,\mathsf{P},\mathsf{L}\end{array}}$$

METHCALL1
$$\frac{\begin{array}{l}\mathcal{M}_{ff}(\mathsf{m},\mathsf{t}_1,\mathsf{t}_2,\mathsf{t}_3,\mathsf{P}) = \phi\\ \mathcal{M}_e(\phi,\sigma(\alpha),\mathsf{P}) = \mathsf{e}\\ \mathsf{y}_1,\mathsf{y}_2 \text{ are fresh variables in } \sigma\\ \mathsf{e}' = \mathsf{e}[\mathsf{y}_1/\mathsf{x},\mathsf{y}_2/\mathbf{this}]\\ \sigma' = \sigma[\mathsf{y}_1\mapsto\beta,\mathsf{y}_2\mapsto\alpha]\end{array}}{\alpha[\mathsf{t}_1,\mathsf{t}_2,\mathsf{t}_3].\mathsf{m}(\beta),\sigma,\mathsf{P},\mathsf{L} \leadsto \mathsf{e}',\sigma',\mathsf{P},\mathsf{L}}$$

METHCALL2
$$\frac{\mathcal{M}_{ff}(\mathsf{m},\mathsf{t}_1,\mathsf{t}_2,\mathsf{t}_3,\mathsf{P}) = \mathbf{-1}}{\alpha[\mathsf{t}_1,\mathsf{t}_2,\mathsf{t}_3].\mathsf{m}(\beta),\sigma,\mathsf{P},\mathsf{L} \leadsto \mathsf{NoMethErr},\sigma,\mathsf{P},\mathsf{L}}$$

METHCALL3
$$\frac{\mathcal{M}_{ff}(\mathsf{m},\mathsf{t}_1,\mathsf{t}_2,\mathsf{t}_3,\mathsf{P}) = \mathbf{-2}}{\alpha[\mathsf{t}_1,\mathsf{t}_2,\mathsf{t}_3].\mathsf{m}(\beta),\sigma,\mathsf{P},\mathsf{L} \leadsto \mathsf{ClssChngErr},\sigma,\mathsf{P},\mathsf{L}}$$

INTFMETHCALL1
$$\frac{\begin{array}{l}\mathsf{P},\mathsf{L} \vdash \sigma(\alpha)\ \leq_{impl}\ \mathsf{t}_1\\ \mathcal{M}^{\mathsf{i}}_{ff}(\mathsf{m},\mathsf{t}_1,\mathsf{t}_2,\mathsf{t}_3,\mathsf{P}) = \mathbf{0}\end{array}}{\begin{array}{l}\alpha[\mathsf{t}_1,\mathsf{t}_2,\mathsf{t}_3]^{\mathsf{i}}.\mathsf{m}(\beta),\sigma,\mathsf{P},\mathsf{L} \leadsto\\ \qquad\qquad \alpha[\sigma(\alpha),\mathsf{t}_2,\mathsf{t}_3].\mathsf{m}(\beta),\sigma,\mathsf{P},\mathsf{L}\end{array}}$$

INTFMETHCALL2
$$\frac{\mathcal{M}^{\mathsf{i}}_{ff}(\mathsf{m},\mathsf{t}_1,\mathsf{t}_2,\mathsf{t}_3,\mathsf{P}) = \mathbf{-1}}{\alpha[\mathsf{t}_1,\mathsf{t}_2,\mathsf{t}_3]^{\mathsf{i}}.\mathsf{m}(\beta),\sigma,\mathsf{P},\mathsf{L} \leadsto \mathsf{NoMethErr},\sigma,\mathsf{P},\mathsf{L}}$$

INTFMETHCALL4
$$\frac{\mathsf{P},\mathsf{L} \not\vdash \sigma(\alpha)\ \leq_{impl}\ \mathsf{t}_1}{\alpha[\mathsf{t}_1,\mathsf{t}_2,\mathsf{t}_3]^{\mathsf{i}}.\mathsf{m}(\beta),\sigma,\mathsf{P},\mathsf{L} \leadsto \mathsf{ClssChngErr},\sigma,\mathsf{P},\mathsf{L}}$$

INTFMETHCALL3
$$\frac{\mathcal{M}^{\mathsf{i}}_{ff}(\mathsf{m},\mathsf{t}_1,\mathsf{t}_2,\mathsf{t}_3,\mathsf{P}) = \mathbf{-2}}{\alpha[\mathsf{t}_1,\mathsf{t}_2,\mathsf{t}_3]^{\mathsf{i}}.\mathsf{m}(\beta),\sigma,\mathsf{P},\mathsf{L} \leadsto \mathsf{ClssChngErr},\sigma,\mathsf{P},\mathsf{L}}$$

Loading

LOADERR
$$\frac{\mathsf{t} \notin \mathcal{T}\mathsf{s}(\mathsf{P},\mathsf{L})}{\sqsubset\mathsf{t}\sqsupset^{typ},\sigma,\mathsf{P},\mathsf{L} \leadsto \mathsf{LoadErr},\sigma,\mathsf{P},\mathsf{L}}$$

LOAD
$$\frac{\begin{array}{l}\mathsf{e} = \sqsubset\mathsf{t}\sqsupset^{typ}\\ \mathsf{t} \notin \mathcal{T}\mathsf{s}(\mathsf{P},\mathsf{L})\\ ld(\mathsf{t},\mathsf{P},\mathsf{L}) = \mathsf{L}' \neq \mathsf{L}_\emptyset, \quad \text{for a loader } ld\end{array}}{\mathsf{e},\sigma,\mathsf{P},\mathsf{L} \leadsto \mathsf{e},\sigma,\mathsf{P},\mathsf{L}\mathsf{L}'}$$

Verification

VERIFERR
$$\frac{\mathsf{t} \in \mathcal{T}\mathsf{s}(\mathsf{L}) \setminus \mathcal{T}\mathsf{s}(\mathsf{P})}{\sqsubset\mathsf{t}\sqsupset^{typ},\sigma,\mathsf{P},\mathsf{L} \leadsto \mathsf{VerifErr},\sigma,\mathsf{P},\mathsf{L}}$$

Preparation

VERIFANDPREP
$$\frac{\begin{array}{l}\mathsf{e} = \sqsubset\mathsf{t}\sqsupset^{typ}\\ \mathsf{t} \in \mathcal{T}\mathsf{s}(\mathsf{L}_1) \setminus \mathcal{T}\mathsf{s}(\mathsf{P}), \quad \vdash \mathsf{P},\mathsf{L}_1 \diamond_{\mathsf{sups}}\\ \mathsf{P},\mathsf{L}_1\mathsf{L}_2 \vdash_{\!v} \mathsf{L}_1 \diamond \xleftarrow[loads]{} \mathsf{L}'\\ \mathsf{P}_1 = pr(\mathsf{L}_1,\mathsf{P}), \quad \text{for a preparation } pr\end{array}}{\mathsf{e},\sigma,\mathsf{P},\mathsf{L}_1\mathsf{L}_2 \leadsto \mathsf{e},\sigma,\mathsf{P}\mathsf{P}_1,\mathsf{L}_2\mathsf{L}'}$$

Fig. 4. Execution

$$
\begin{array}{lll}
\sqsubset\cdot\sqsupset^{exp} & ::= \sqsubset\cdot\sqsupset[t,t,t].m\,(e) \mid \alpha\,[t,t,t].m\,(\sqsubset\cdot\sqsupset) & \\
& \mid\ \sqsubset\cdot\sqsupset[t,t,t]^{\mathbf{i}}.m\,(e) \mid \alpha\,[t,t,t]^{\mathbf{i}}.m\,(\sqsubset\cdot\sqsupset) & \\
& \mid\ \sqsubset\cdot\sqsupset[t,t].f & \\
& \mid\ \sqsubset\cdot\sqsupset = e & \text{if } \sqsubset\cdot\sqsupset \text{ non-l-ground variable} \\
& \mid\ v = \sqsubset\cdot\sqsupset & \text{if } v \text{ l-ground variable} \\
\sqsubset\cdot\sqsupset^{nll} & ::= \sqsubset\cdot\sqsupset[t,t,t].m\,(e) \mid \sqsubset\cdot\sqsupset[t,t,t]^{\mathbf{i}}.m\,(e) & \\
& \mid\ \sqsubset\cdot\sqsupset[t,t].f \mid \sqsubset\cdot\sqsupset[t,t].f = \beta & \\
\sqsubset\cdot\sqsupset^{typ} & ::= \alpha\,[\sqsubset\cdot\sqsupset,t,t].m\,(\beta) \mid \alpha\,[\sqsubset\cdot\sqsupset,t,t]^{\mathbf{i}}.m\,(\beta) & \\
& \mid\ \alpha\,[\sqsubset\cdot\sqsupset,t].f \mid \mathbf{new}\ \sqsubset\cdot\sqsupset &
\end{array}
$$

Fig. 5. Contexts

An example. For the program P_{BC} from section 2, and a class A subclass of Object and without any fields, the following store σ_0 maps identifier anA to an object of class A, and aB to an object of class B:

$\sigma_0(\mathsf{anA})$	$= 2$	address of object	$\sigma_0(2)$	$=$	A	object of class A
$\sigma_0(\mathsf{aB})$	$= 5$	address of object	$\sigma_0(5)$	$=$	B	object of class B
$\sigma_0(8)$	$= 45$	field **int** f_1 from B	$\sigma_0(10)$	$=$	11	field C f_2 from B
$\sigma_0(11)$	$=$ C	object of class C	$\sigma_0(14)$	$=$	55	field **int** f_1 from B
$\sigma_0(16)$	$=$ **0**	field C f_2 from B	$\sigma_0(17)$	$=$	65	field **int** f_1 from C
$\sigma_0(\mathsf{y})$	$= \epsilon$	for the other y's				

Thus, 18 is new in σ_0, but 15 is not, even though $\sigma_0(15)=\epsilon$.

Consider the expression $\mathsf{e}_3 \equiv \mathsf{anA}[\mathsf{B},\mathbf{int}].\mathsf{f}_1 = 12$ [11]. Because A is not a subclass of B, expression e_3 does not verify. But if we either switched the verifier off or managed to fool the verifier, and executed $\mathsf{e}_3, \sigma_0, \mathsf{P}_{\mathsf{ABC}}, \mathsf{L}_\emptyset$, we would obtain $12, \sigma_1, \mathsf{P}_{\mathsf{ABC}}, \mathsf{L}_\emptyset$, where $\sigma_1 = \sigma_0[5 \mapsto 12]$. In the new store, σ_1, the class of the object at address 5 has been overwritten by an integer; the consistency of the store has been destroyed! Thus, resolution checks alone do not ensure "well-behavedness" either.

In the appendix we give an example which demonstrates the treatment of interfaces based on the one given by Buechi[2].

We now study the five components of execution. Note, that the five components are "disjoint", in the sense that for any configuration, if a rule from one components is applicable, then no rule from another component is applicable.

3.2 Evaluation

Evaluation is the part of execution that is not affected by dynamic linking and verification. It is described in the first section of fig. 4, and it comprises:

[11] The expression e_3 could be the result of compilation of expression $\mathsf{e}_4 \equiv \mathsf{anA}.\mathsf{f}_1 = 12$ in a context where anA had type A, and A was a subclass of B; then class A was modified so that it no longer was a subclass of B, A was recompiled, and e_4 was not recompiled.

$$\frac{\mathcal{T}(\mathsf{c},\mathsf{P},\mathsf{L}) = \mathsf{c}', \{\mathsf{i}_1 \ldots \mathsf{i}_n\} \qquad n \geq 0}{\begin{array}{l}\mathsf{P},\mathsf{L} \vdash \mathsf{c} \leq_{clss} \mathsf{c} \\ \mathsf{P},\mathsf{L} \vdash \mathsf{c} \leq_{clss} \mathsf{c}' \\ \mathsf{P},\mathsf{L} \vdash \mathsf{c} \leq_{impl} \mathsf{i}_j \qquad \forall j \in 1 \ldots n\end{array}}$$

$$\frac{\mathcal{T}(\mathsf{i},\mathsf{P},\mathsf{L}) = \{\mathsf{i}_1 \ldots \mathsf{i}_n\} \qquad n \geq 0}{\begin{array}{l}\mathsf{P},\mathsf{L} \vdash \mathsf{i} \leq_{intf} \mathsf{i} \\ \mathsf{P},\mathsf{L} \vdash \mathsf{i} \leq_{intf} \mathsf{i}_j \qquad \forall j \in 1 \ldots n\end{array}}$$

$$\frac{\begin{array}{l}\mathsf{P},\mathsf{L} \vdash \mathsf{c} \leq_{clss} \mathsf{c}'' \\ \mathsf{P},\mathsf{L} \vdash \mathsf{c}'' \leq_{clss} \mathsf{c}'\end{array}}{\mathsf{P},\mathsf{L} \vdash \mathsf{c} \leq_{clss} \mathsf{c}'}$$

$$\frac{}{\mathsf{P},\mathsf{L} \vdash \mathsf{Object} \leq_{clss} \mathsf{Object}}$$

$$\frac{\begin{array}{l}\mathsf{P},\mathsf{L} \vdash \mathsf{i} \leq_{intf} \mathsf{i}' \\ \mathsf{P},\mathsf{L} \vdash \mathsf{c} \leq_{impl} \mathsf{i} \\ \mathsf{P},\mathsf{L} \vdash \mathsf{c}' \leq_{clss} \mathsf{c}\end{array}}{\mathsf{P},\mathsf{L} \vdash \mathsf{c}' \leq_{impl} \mathsf{i}'}$$

$$\frac{\begin{array}{lcl}\mathsf{P},\mathsf{L} \vdash \mathsf{c} \leq_{clss} \mathsf{c}' & \Rightarrow & \\ \quad \mathsf{c}' = \mathsf{Object}, & \text{or} & \mathcal{T}(\mathsf{c}',\mathsf{P},\mathsf{L}) \neq \epsilon \\ \mathsf{P},\mathsf{L} \vdash \mathsf{i} \leq_{intf} \mathsf{i}' & \Rightarrow & \mathcal{T}(\mathsf{i}',\mathsf{P},\mathsf{L}) \neq \epsilon \\ \mathsf{P},\mathsf{L} \vdash \mathsf{c} \leq_{impl} \mathsf{i} & \Rightarrow & \mathcal{T}(\mathsf{i},\mathsf{P},\mathsf{L}) \neq \epsilon\end{array}}{\vdash \mathsf{P},\mathsf{L} \diamond_{sups}}$$

$$\frac{\begin{array}{l}\vdash \mathsf{P},\mathsf{L} \diamond_{sups} \\ \mathsf{P},\mathsf{L} \vdash \mathsf{c} \leq_{clss} \mathsf{c}', \quad \mathsf{P},\mathsf{L} \vdash \mathsf{c}' \leq_{clss} \mathsf{c} \\ \qquad \Rightarrow \quad \mathsf{c} = \mathsf{c}' \\ \mathsf{P},\mathsf{L} \vdash \mathsf{i} \leq_{intf} \mathsf{i}', \quad \mathsf{P},\mathsf{L} \vdash \mathsf{i}' \leq_{intf} \mathsf{i} \\ \qquad \Rightarrow \quad \mathsf{i} = \mathsf{i}'\end{array}}{\vdash \mathsf{P},\mathsf{L} \diamond_a}$$

Fig. 6. Subclasses, acyclic programs, programs with complete superclasses

- propagation, *i.e.*, propagate execution at the receiver and then the argument of a method call, at the receiver of a field access and to the left hand and right hand sides of an assignment (Propagate) [12],
- throwing the NllPErr exception when attempting to call a method, access a field, or assign to a field of **0** (NullPointErr),
- accessing variables or addresses (Acc), and assigning to variables (VarAss),
- creating new objects (New) of already prepared class c ($\mathsf{c} \in \mathcal{T}s(\mathsf{P})$), initializing the fields with **0** at the offsets prescribed in P. Note that $\mathcal{F}s(\mathsf{c},\mathsf{P})$ from def. 2 returns types and offsets for all fields declared in class c or in any of c's superclasses.

3.3 Resolution

Resolution describes the process of resolving references to fields or methods. It corresponds to the bytecode instructions getfield, putfield, invokeinterface and invokevirtual.

We describe these instructions in more detail, and at a lower level than they are described in [21]: We describe what happens if the instruction attempts to access fields or methods from a class which is not a subtype of the type stored in the signature, and thus the offset obtained bears no relation to the runtime object. This situation is not described in [21], although it may happen if unverified code is executed[13].

[12] We did not supply rules for the propagation of exceptions; these would have been standard.

[13] It was, however, discussed to some extent in [20].

Java is probably unique, in that resolution happens at runtime, but has both a static part, *i.e.*, calculation of offsets in terms of the statically determined offsets, and a dynamic part, *i.e.*, application of these offsets to the different objects. Thus, the effect of resolution depends on the particular classes or interfaces mentioned in the corresponding signature, *and* on the particular object which appears as receiver in the particular expression. In Java implementations these two parts may take place at different times. In fact, the static part need only take place once and store the calculated offset, whereas the dynamic part has to be applied as often as the instruction is executed. For reasons of simplicity, we do not describe this in our model.

Field Resolution. Field access has the form $\alpha[\mathsf{t}_1,\mathsf{t}_2].\mathsf{f}$. The offset of that field is determined using $\mathcal{F}_{\mathit{ff}}(\mathsf{f},\mathsf{t}_1,\mathsf{t}_2,\mathsf{P})$, and if found, *i.e.*, if $\mathcal{F}_{\mathit{ff}}(\mathsf{f},\mathsf{t}_1,\mathsf{t}_2,\mathsf{P})=\phi$, then it is used to calculate the address of that field, *i.e.*, $\alpha+\phi$ (FLDACC1). Thus, our model describes address calculations – it that sense it is at a lower-level than those in [12,23,22].

Note that the offset calculation $\mathcal{F}_{\mathit{ff}}(\mathsf{f},\mathsf{t}_1,\mathsf{t}_2,\mathsf{P})$ is in terms of the stored, *static* type t_1, and not the actual, *dynamic* class of the object in α. This offset is then applied to the address α, which may, but need not contain an object of class t_1.[14] This combination of static with dynamic information is safe, if applied to a verified expression, to well-formed prepared code, and a well-formed state. Namely, as we shall see, verification of an expression $\mathsf{e}[\mathsf{t}_1,\mathsf{t}_2].\mathsf{f}$ guarantees that execution of e will return an object of class t_1 or a subclass; well-formed prepared code guarantees that object layout of a class conforms to object layout of a superclass, and well-formed states guarantee that all objects in the store are organized according to the object layout for their class.

The rules FLDACC2,FLDACC3 describe the erroneous situations: If t_1 is defined, but does not have a field f of type t_2, *i.e.*, $\mathcal{F}_{\mathit{ff}}(\mathsf{f},\mathsf{t}_1,\mathsf{t}_2,\mathsf{P})=\mathbf{-1}$, or if t_1 is an interface, *i.e.*, $\mathcal{F}_{\mathit{ff}}(\mathsf{f},\mathsf{t}_1,\mathsf{t}_2,\mathsf{P})=\mathbf{-2}$, then exceptions are thrown. The case where $\mathcal{F}_{\mathit{ff}}(\mathsf{f},\mathsf{t}_1,\mathsf{t}_2,\mathsf{P})=\mathbf{-3}$ need not be treated here, as it corresponds to the case where t_1 has not been prepared yet (*c.f.* def. 5 and fig. 3.6), which is treated by the rules for loading, verification and preparation, ie LOADDERR, VERIFERR, LOADPREPVERIF.

Instance Method Call Resolution. These calls have the form $\alpha[\mathsf{t}_1,\mathsf{t}_2,\mathsf{t}_3].\mathsf{m}(\beta)$. The offset is determined using $\mathcal{M}_{\mathit{ff}}(\mathsf{m},\mathsf{t}_1,\mathsf{t}_2,\mathsf{t}_3,\mathsf{P})$, which considers m, the name of the method, t_1, the class containing the method, t_2, the type of the argument, and t_3, the result. The latter two are necessary for overloading resolution.

As for fields, the *actual class* of the receiver, *i.e.*, the class of α, is *not* considered in $\mathcal{M}_{\mathit{ff}}(\mathsf{m},\mathsf{t}_1,\mathsf{t}_2,\mathsf{t}_3,\mathsf{P})$. If a method is found, *i.e.*, if $\mathcal{M}_{\mathit{ff}}(\mathsf{m},\mathsf{t}_1,\mathsf{t}_2,\mathsf{t}_3,\mathsf{P})=\phi$ for some ϕ, then ϕ is used to select the method body from the lookup table of the class of α through $\mathcal{M}_e(\phi,\sigma(\alpha),\mathsf{P})$ in METHCALL1 – here the actual class of the receiver *is* used. This combination of static with dynamic information is safe, if

[14] This is why the configuration $\mathsf{e}_3,\sigma_0,\mathsf{P}_{\mathsf{ABC}},\mathsf{L}_\emptyset$ leads to the unsafe configuration described earlier: namely $\mathcal{F}_{\mathit{ff}}(\mathsf{f}_1,\mathsf{B},\mathbf{int},\mathsf{P}_{\mathsf{ABC}})=3$.

applied to a verified expression, and to well-formed prepared code. Verification of $\mathsf{e}[\mathsf{t}_1,\mathsf{t}_2,\mathsf{t}_3].\mathsf{m}(\mathsf{e}')$guarantees that execution of e will return an object of class t_1 or a subclass, well-formed prepared code guarantees that the method lookup table of a class is a prefix of the method lookup table of any subclass.

The erroneous situations are described by METHCALL2 and METHCALL3. If t_1 is an interface, then $\mathcal{M}_{\mathit{ff}}(\mathsf{m},\mathsf{t}_1,\mathsf{t}_2,\mathsf{t}_3,\mathsf{P})= \mathbf{-2}$, and the exception ClssChngErr is thrown[15]. If class t_1 exists, but no such method can be found in t_1, the exception NoMethErr is thrown. The case where t_1 has not been prepared yet, *i.e.*, $\mathcal{M}_{\mathit{ff}}(\mathsf{m},\mathsf{t}_1,\mathsf{t}_2,\mathsf{t}_3,\mathsf{P})= \mathbf{-3}$, is taken care of by the loading, verification and preparation rules.

Interface Method Call Resolution. These calls have the form $\alpha[\mathsf{t}_1,\mathsf{t}_2,\mathsf{t}_3]^{\mathsf{i}}.\mathsf{m}(\beta)$. The method is first looked up in the interface through $\mathcal{M}^{\mathsf{i}}_{\mathit{ff}}(\mathsf{m},\mathsf{t}_1,\mathsf{t}_2,\mathsf{t}_3,\mathsf{P})$. If t_1 is a class[16] or if the class of the receiver, denoted by $\sigma(\alpha)$, does not implement t_1[17], then the exception ClssChngErr is thrown. If interface t_1 exists, but does not contain nor inherit an appropriate method declaration[18], then the exception NoMethErr is thrown. Otherwise, the interface method call proceeds as an instance method call (INTFMETHCALL1).

If we compare instance method calls and interface method calls, we notice that the latter require an extra check, which ascertains that the receiver implements t_1. Such a check is not necessary for method calls, $\mathsf{e}'_1[\mathsf{t}'_1,\mathsf{t}'_2,\mathsf{t}'_3].\mathsf{m}(\mathsf{e}'_2)$, because verification guarantees that e'_1 will evaluate to an object of a subtype of t'_1. However, the verifier is more lenient with interface method calls, and verification of $\mathsf{e}_1[\mathsf{t}_1,\mathsf{t}_2,\mathsf{t}_3]^{\mathsf{i}}.\mathsf{m}(\mathsf{e}_2)$ does not guarantee that e_1 will evaluate to an object of a subtype of t_1; therefore this needs to be checked at the time of execution of the method call.

The case where t_1 has not been prepared yet, *i.e.*, where $\mathcal{M}^{\mathsf{i}}_{\mathit{ff}}(\mathsf{m},\mathsf{t}_1,\mathsf{t}_2,\mathsf{t}_3,\mathsf{P}) = \mathbf{-3}$, is taken care of by the loading, verification and preparation rules.

3.4 Loading

Loading is required when a type context, $\sqsubset \mathsf{t} \sqsupset^{typ}$, is executed for a type t which has not been loaded yet. That is, when a new object of class t is created, or a when a field of class t is accessed, or when a method from class or interface t is called.

---

15 This can happen, if one compiles t_1 as a class, then compiles the class containing the method call, then recompiles t_1 as an interface, without further recompilations.

16 This can happen, if one compiles t_1 as an interface, then compiles the class containing the method call, then recompiles t_1 as a class, without further recompilations.

17 This can happen, if one compiles a class c' which is a superclass of $\sigma(\alpha)$ and which implements the interface t_1, then compiles the class containing the method call, then recompiles making sure that none of the superclasses of $\sigma(\alpha)$ implement the interface t_1, without further recompilations.

18 This can happen, if one compiles t_1 with the method declaration, then compiles the method call, then removes from t_1 the method declaration, and recompiles t_1, without further recompilations.

If loading is successful, *i.e.*, $ld(\mathsf{t},\mathsf{P},\mathsf{L}) = \mathsf{L}' \neq \mathsf{L}_\emptyset$, then execution continues with the loaded code augmented by L' (LOAD), otherwise an exception is thrown (LOADERR).Our operational semantics is non-deterministic with respect to loading: it allows a load exception to be thrown in all type-contexts, without even attempting to load the types. This simplifies our system considerably, and does not diminish the applicability of the soundness property.

A *loader* function $ld(\mathsf{t},\mathsf{P},\mathsf{L})$ returns class or interface definitions for t and all its superclasses and superinterfaces except for those already defined in P or L, provided that no class or interface circularity was encountered; otherwise it returns $\mathsf{L}_\emptyset$. Any function satisfying these requirements is a loader. A "real" loader would lookup type definitions in the filesystem or a database; these can be modified from outside the Java program, and so different calls of the loader for the same type can return different bytecode. In order to simplify the model, rather than providing a filesystem/database parameter, we allow for different loader functions to be called, thus obtaining the same effect.

Definition 4 *A function* $ld : \mathsf{Id} \times \mathcal{P} \times \mathcal{L} \to \mathcal{L}$ *is a* loader *iff:*

$ld(\mathsf{t},\mathsf{P},\mathsf{L}) = \mathsf{L}' \neq \mathsf{L}_\emptyset \quad \Rightarrow$

- $\mathsf{t} \in \mathcal{T}s(\mathsf{L}') \setminus \mathcal{T}s(\mathsf{PL})$.
- $\vdash \mathsf{P},\mathsf{L} \ \Diamond_a \quad \Rightarrow \quad \vdash \mathsf{P},\mathsf{LL}' \ \Diamond_a$.

3.5 Verification

Verification is required when executing a type context, $\sqsubset \mathsf{t} \sqsupset^{typ}$, and t has been loaded but not yet prepared, *i.e.*, $\mathsf{t} \in \mathcal{T}\mathsf{s}(\mathsf{L}_1) \setminus \mathcal{T}\mathsf{s}(\mathsf{P})$. The loaded code consists of L_1 and L_2, where L_1 contains the definition of t and its supertypes, except for those already defined in P, *i.e.*, $\vdash \mathsf{P},\mathsf{L}_1 \Diamond_{sups}$. Then L_1 is verified. If verification succeeds and requires the loading of L', then L_1 is prepared, and execution continues with the augmented prepared code P_1, and additional loaded code L', *c.f.* VERIFANDPREP. If verification fails, an exception is thrown, *c.f.* VERIFERR. As for loading, our operational semantics is highly nondeterministic with respect to verification: it allows a verification error to be thrown in all contexts which require verification, without requiring the verification to have been attempted and failed. This allows for a simpler model, and simpler proofs, and does not diminish the applicability of the soundness property.

Verification in our paper is described in fig. 7. It corresponds to the third pass of the "real" verifier as in ch. 4.9.1 of [21], and is expressed through the judgment

$$\mathsf{P},\mathsf{L} \vdash_{v} \mathsf{L}'' \Diamond \ \underset{loads}{\leftharpoondown} \ \mathsf{L}'$$

meaning that the binary L'' could be verified in the context of the prepared code P, and the loaded but not yet prepared code L, and caused L' to be loaded (but not verified). Thus, this judgment has the "side-effect" of loading L'.

Verification of classes is defined in terms of verification of expressions, with the judgment

$$\mathsf{P}, \mathsf{L}, \mathsf{E} \vdash_{\bar{v}} \mathsf{e} : \mathsf{t} \underset{loads}{\leftharpoondown} \mathsf{L}'$$

meaning that the expression e could be verified as having type t, in the context of P, L, and the environment E, and caused L′ to be loaded (but not verified).

Establishing the above sometimes requires a judgment

$$\mathsf{P}, \mathsf{L} \vdash_{\bar{v}} \mathsf{t} \leq \mathsf{t}' \underset{loads}{\leftharpoondown} \mathsf{L}'$$

meaning that type t could be verified as widening to type t′ in the context of P and L, and caused further classes/interfaces L′ to be loaded (but not verified). Classes or interfaces may be loaded when trying to establish whether a t undefined in P or L is a subtype of t′, as in rules (5) and (6) of fig. 7.

For example, verification of

$e_{\mathsf{bake}} \equiv$ **new** Pear[Food, Spice, **void**].bake(**new** Spice)

requires establishing that Pear widens to Food, which, in its turn, if Pear is not loaded, requires loading Pear and all its superclasses. Therefore, if

$ld(\mathsf{Pear}, \mathsf{P}_\emptyset, \mathsf{L}_\emptyset) = \mathsf{L}_{\mathsf{Pear}}\mathsf{L}_{\mathsf{Food}}$,

and the superclass of Pear is Food, then:

$\mathsf{P}_\emptyset, \mathsf{L}_\emptyset \vdash_{\bar{v}} \mathsf{Pear} \leq \mathsf{Food} \underset{loads}{\leftharpoondown} \mathsf{L}_{\mathsf{Pear}}\mathsf{L}_{\mathsf{Food}}$.

The difference between (5) and (6) is, that in (5) class c and all its superclasses are loaded, whereas in (6) only interface i and its superinterfaces are loaded.

The assertion $\mathsf{P}, \mathsf{L} \vdash_{\bar{v}} \mathsf{t} \leq \mathsf{t} \underset{loads}{\leftharpoondown} \mathsf{L}_\emptyset$ holds for any t, *c.f.* rule (1). Thus, verification assumes *any* identifier to stand for a class, or interface and so to widen to itself. Therefore,

$\mathsf{P}_\emptyset, \mathsf{L}_\emptyset \vdash_{\bar{v}} \mathsf{Spice} \leq \mathsf{Spice} \underset{loads}{\leftharpoondown} \mathsf{L}_\emptyset$.

Also, the assertion $\mathsf{P}, \mathsf{L} \vdash_{\bar{v}} \mathsf{t} \leq \mathsf{i} \underset{loads}{\leftharpoondown} \mathsf{L}_\emptyset$ holds for any interface i, *c.f.* rules (3) and (6). Thus verification assumes *any* identifier to widen to i, provided that i stands for an already loaded or prepared interface.

Verification is "optimistic" with respect to method calls and field accesses (rules (10) and (11)), and more liberal than the Java source checks. For field access, $\mathsf{e}_1[\mathsf{t}_1,\mathsf{t}_2].\mathsf{f}$, verification only checks that the type of e_1 widens to t_1, the static type in the signature, and gives to the whole expression the type t_2 – it does *not* attempt to check the existence of a field with type t_2, but leaves this to the resolution checks. Similarly for method calls. Therefore, verification of e_{bake} will load Food and Pear, and not Spice, and will not verify either of these classes, *i.e.*,

$\mathsf{P}_\emptyset, \mathsf{L}_\emptyset, \epsilon \vdash_{\bar{v}} e_{\mathsf{bake}} : \mathbf{void} \underset{loads}{\leftharpoondown} \mathsf{L}_{\mathsf{Pear}}\mathsf{L}_{\mathsf{Food}}$

Verification of a class (rule (13)) does not imply verification of all classes used: If $\mathsf{L}_{\mathsf{Cook}}$ contained a unique method

void boil(Spoon x){ x = **new** Spoon; e_{bake} }

then, even though the classes Pear, Food, Spice and Spoon are mentioned, the verification of $\mathsf{L}_{\mathsf{Cook}}$ only requires class Pear and all its superclasses to be loaded. Thus,

$\mathsf{P}_\emptyset, \mathsf{L}_\emptyset \vdash_{\bar{v}} \mathsf{L}_{\mathsf{Cook}} \diamond \underset{loads}{\leftharpoondown} \mathsf{L}_{\mathsf{Food}}\mathsf{L}_{\mathsf{Pear}}$.

Finally, if an order can be found to verify classes and/or interfaces t_i, then verification is successful, *c.f.* rule (15). Note, that judgment $\mathsf{P}, \mathsf{L} \vdash \mathsf{c} \leq_{clss} \mathsf{c}$ means that c is the name of a class, whereas $\mathsf{P}, \mathsf{L} \vdash \mathsf{i} \leq_{intf} \mathsf{i}$ means that i is the name of an interface.

$$\frac{t \in Id}{P, L \vdash_v t \le t \underset{loads}{\leftarrow} L_\emptyset} \quad (1)$$

$$\frac{P, L \vdash c \le_{clss} c'}{P, L \vdash_v c \le c' \underset{loads}{\leftarrow} L_\emptyset} \quad (2)$$

$$\frac{\begin{array}{l} t \in Id \\ P, L \vdash i \le_{intf} i \end{array}}{P, L \vdash_v t \le i \underset{loads}{\leftarrow} L_\emptyset} \quad (3)$$

$$\frac{}{P, L \vdash_v \mathbf{int} \le \mathbf{int} \underset{loads}{\leftarrow} L_\emptyset} \quad (4)$$

$$\frac{\begin{array}{l} \mathcal{T}(c, PL) = \epsilon \\ ld(c, P, L) = L' \\ P, LL' \vdash c \le_{clss} c' \end{array}}{P, L \vdash_v c \le c' \underset{loads}{\leftarrow} L'} \quad (5)$$

$$\frac{\begin{array}{l} \mathcal{T}(PL, i) = \epsilon \\ ld(i, P, L) = L' \\ P, LL' \vdash i \le_{intf} i \end{array}}{P, L \vdash_v t \le i \underset{loads}{\leftarrow} L'} \quad (6)$$

$$\frac{}{\begin{array}{l} P, L, E \vdash_v \beta : int \underset{loads}{\leftarrow} L_\emptyset \\ P, L, E \vdash_v \mathbf{0} : c \underset{loads}{\leftarrow} L_\emptyset \\ P, L, E \vdash_v \mathbf{new}\ c : c \underset{loads}{\leftarrow} L_\emptyset \end{array}} \quad (7)$$

$$\frac{E(y) = t}{P, L, E \vdash_v y : t \underset{loads}{\leftarrow} L_\emptyset} \quad (8)$$

$$\frac{\begin{array}{l} P, L, E \vdash_v v : t \underset{loads}{\leftarrow} L' \\ P, LL', E \vdash_v e : t' \underset{loads}{\leftarrow} L'' \\ P, LL'L'' \vdash_v t' \le t \underset{loads}{\leftarrow} L''' \end{array}}{P, L, E \vdash_v v = e : t' \underset{loads}{\leftarrow} L'L''L'''} \quad (9)$$

$$\frac{\begin{array}{l} P, L, E \vdash_v e_1 : t'_1 \underset{loads}{\leftarrow} L'_1 \\ P, LL'_1, E \vdash_v e_2 : t'_2 \underset{loads}{\leftarrow} L'_2 \\ P, LL'_1L'_2 \vdash_v t'_1 \le t_1 \underset{loads}{\leftarrow} L'_3 \\ P, LL'_1L'_2L'_3 \vdash_v t'_2 \le t_2 \underset{loads}{\leftarrow} L'_4 \end{array}}{P, L, E \vdash_v e_1[t_1, t_2, t_3].m(e_2) : t_3 \underset{loads}{\leftarrow} L'_1L'_2L'_3L'_4} \quad (10)$$

$$\frac{\begin{array}{l} P, L, E \vdash_v e : t \underset{loads}{\leftarrow} L' \\ P, LL' \vdash_v t \le t_1 \underset{loads}{\leftarrow} L'' \end{array}}{P, L, E \vdash_v e[t_1, t_2].f : t_2 \underset{loads}{\leftarrow} L'L''} \quad (11)$$

$$\frac{\begin{array}{l} P, L, E \vdash_v e_1 : t'_1 \underset{loads}{\leftarrow} L'_1 \\ P, LL'_1, E \vdash_v e_2 : t'_2 \underset{loads}{\leftarrow} L'_2 \\ P, LL'_1L'_2 \vdash_v t'_2 \le t_2 \underset{loads}{\leftarrow} L'_4 \end{array}}{P, L, E \vdash_v e_1[t_1, t_2, t_3]^{i}.m(e_2) : t_3 \underset{loads}{\leftarrow} L'_1L'_2L'_4} \quad (12)$$

$$\frac{\begin{array}{ll} \mathcal{T}(c, L) = c', \{i_1 ... i_n\} & n \ge 0 \\ P, L \vdash c' \le_{clss} c' & \\ P, L \vdash i_j \le_{intf} i_j & \forall j \in 1...n \\ \mathcal{M}s(c, L) = \{\ t_{11}\ m_1(t_{12}\ x)\{e_1\}, \ldots, t_{k1}\ m_k(t_{k2}\ x)\{e_k\}\ \} & \\ P, LL'_1 ... L'_{2(i-1)}, (t_{i2}\ x, c\ \mathbf{this}) \vdash_v e_i : t'_{i1} \underset{loads}{\leftarrow} L'_{2i-1} & \forall i \in 1...k \\ P, LL'_1 ... L'_{2i-1} \vdash_v t'_{i1} \le t_{i1} \underset{loads}{\leftarrow} L'_{2i} & \forall i \in 1...k \end{array}}{P, L \vdash_v c \diamond \underset{loads}{\leftarrow} L'_1 \ldots L'_{2k}} \quad (13)$$

$$\frac{\begin{array}{ll} \mathcal{T}(i, L) = \{i_1 ... i_n\} & n \ge 0 \\ P, L \vdash i_j \le_{intf} i_j & \forall j \in 1...n \end{array}}{P, L \vdash_v i \diamond \underset{loads}{\leftarrow} L_\emptyset} \quad (14)$$

$$\frac{\begin{array}{ll} \vdash P, L \diamond_a & \\ \{t_1, \ldots t_n\} = \mathcal{T}s(L') & \\ P, LL'_1 \ldots L'_{i-1} \vdash_v t_i \diamond \underset{loads}{\leftarrow} L'_i & \forall i \in 1...n \end{array}}{P, L \vdash_v L' \diamond \underset{loads}{\leftarrow} L'_1 \ldots L'_n} \quad (15)$$

Fig. 7. Verification

$Env ::= \epsilon$ — $Env, t\ z$ — Env, t **this**

$$\frac{\mathsf{E(z)} \neq \epsilon \quad \Rightarrow \quad \mathsf{E'(z)} = \mathsf{E(z)}}{\vdash \mathsf{E'} \leq \mathsf{E}}$$

Fig. 8. Environments

Verification requires type assignments, expressed through *environments*, E. Environments are sequences of declarations of the form $\mathsf{t_i}$ $\mathsf{var_i}$; they are described in fig. 8. They should contain unique declarations, as expressed by the judgment $\vdash \mathsf{E}\ \diamond_u$, and allow looking up the type of variable z through E(z) .[19] We do *not* require the $\mathsf{t_i}$ to indicate types declared in P or L. So, an environment may use identifiers as types which have no corresponding definition in P or L.

3.6 Preparation

If verification is successful, code is prepared using the function $pr: \mathcal{P} \times \mathcal{L} \longrightarrow \mathcal{P}$, which maps L to $pr(\mathsf{L}, \mathsf{P})$. Preparation determines the object layout (*i.e.*, assigns offsets to fields), and creates method lookup tables (*i.e.*, assigns offsets to methods, and method bodies to offsets).

Rather than prescribe the exact strategy for offset determination, we give requirements in definition 5, *i.e.*, a mapping is a *preparation function* if (1) it maps all types from L onto corresponding types in P′ with same superclasses and superinterfaces, (2a) allocates distinct offsets to fields, (2b) preserves field offsets from superclasses 2c) preserves method offsets from superclasses, (2d) all valid offsets lead to a method body either defined for that class in L, or inherited from a superclass.

Definition 5 *A function* $pr: \mathcal{L} \times \mathcal{P} \rightarrow \mathcal{P}$ *is a* preparation *function iff:*

$\vdash \mathsf{P,L}\ \diamond_a, \quad pr(\mathsf{L,P}) = \mathsf{P'} \quad \Rightarrow$

1. $\forall\ \mathsf{t}: \quad \mathcal{T}(\mathsf{t,L}) = \mathcal{T}(\mathsf{t,P'})$.
2. $\mathcal{T}(\mathsf{c,L}) = \mathsf{c'}, \{\mathsf{i_1,...i_n}\}, \mathsf{t} \in \mathcal{T}s(\mathsf{L}) \quad \Rightarrow$
   $\forall\ \mathsf{f,f',t,t',t_1,t_2,m}:$
   a) $\mathcal{F}_{\!f\!f}(\mathsf{f,c,t,P'}) = \mathcal{F}_{\!f\!f}(\mathsf{f',c,t',P'}) > 0 \quad \Rightarrow \quad \mathsf{f = f', t = t'}$.
   b) $\mathcal{F}_{\!f\!f}(\mathsf{f,c',t,PP'}) > 0 \quad \Rightarrow \quad \mathcal{F}_{\!f\!f}(\mathsf{f,c',t,PP'}) = \mathcal{F}_{\!f\!f}(\mathsf{f,c,t,P'})$.
   c) $\mathcal{M}_{\!f\!f}(\mathsf{m,c',t_2,t_1,PP'})$ *¿ 0* $\Rightarrow$
   $\mathcal{M}_{\!f\!f}(\mathsf{m,c',t_2,t_1,PP'}) = \mathcal{M}_{\!f\!f}(\mathsf{m,c,t_2,t_1,P'})$.
   d) $\mathcal{M}_{\!f\!f}(\mathsf{m,c,t_2,t_1,P'}) = \phi \quad \Rightarrow$
   $\mathcal{M}_e(\phi,\mathsf{c,P'}) = \mathcal{M}(\mathsf{m,c,t_2,t_1,L}) \neq \epsilon, \quad or \quad \mathcal{M}_{\!f\!f}(\mathsf{m,c',t_2,t_1,PP'}) = \phi$.

In [5] we gave a constructive definition of such a preparation function. In general, many different results may come from a preparation function, because there may be many different offset allocation strategies.

[19] We do not define $\vdash \mathsf{E}\ \diamond_u$, nor E(z) , because they are standard.

$$\frac{\mathsf{t} \in \mathsf{Id}}{\mathsf{P},\mathsf{L} \vdash \mathsf{t} \le \mathsf{t}}\ (1) \qquad \frac{}{\mathsf{P},\mathsf{L} \vdash \mathbf{int} \le \mathbf{int}}\ (4) \qquad \frac{\mathsf{P},\mathsf{L} \vdash \mathsf{c} \le_{clss} \mathsf{c}'}{\mathsf{P},\mathsf{L} \vdash \mathsf{c} \le \mathsf{c}'}\ (2,5) \qquad \frac{\begin{array}{l}\mathsf{t} \in \mathsf{Id} \\ \mathsf{P},\mathsf{L} \vdash \mathsf{i} \le_{intf} \mathsf{i}\end{array}}{\mathsf{P},\mathsf{L} \vdash \mathsf{t} \le \mathsf{i}}\ (3,6)$$

$$\frac{}{\begin{array}{l}\mathsf{P},\mathsf{L},\mathsf{E} \vdash \beta : \mathsf{int} \\ \mathsf{P},\mathsf{L},\mathsf{E} \vdash \mathbf{0} : \mathsf{c} \\ \mathsf{P},\mathsf{L},\mathsf{E} \vdash \mathbf{new}\, \mathsf{c} : \mathsf{c}\end{array}}\ (7) \qquad \frac{\mathsf{E}(\mathsf{y}) = \mathsf{t}}{\mathsf{P},\mathsf{L},\mathsf{E} \vdash \mathsf{y} : \mathsf{t}}\ (8)$$

$$\frac{\begin{array}{l}\mathsf{P},\mathsf{L},\mathsf{E} \vdash \mathsf{v} : \mathsf{t} \\ \mathsf{P},\mathsf{L},\mathsf{E} \vdash \mathsf{e} : \mathsf{t}' \\ \mathsf{P},\mathsf{L} \vdash \mathsf{t}' \le \mathsf{t}\end{array}}{\mathsf{P},\mathsf{L},\mathsf{E} \vdash \mathsf{v} = \mathsf{e} : \mathsf{t}'}\ (9) \qquad \frac{\begin{array}{l}\mathsf{P},\mathsf{L},\mathsf{E} \vdash \mathsf{e}_1 : \mathsf{t}_1' \\ \mathsf{P},\mathsf{L},\mathsf{E} \vdash \mathsf{e}_2 : \mathsf{t}_2' \\ \mathsf{P},\mathsf{L} \vdash \mathsf{t}_1' \le \mathsf{t}_1 \\ \mathsf{P},\mathsf{L} \vdash \mathsf{t}_2' \le \mathsf{t}_2\end{array}}{\mathsf{P},\mathsf{L},\mathsf{E} \vdash \mathsf{e}_1[\mathsf{t}_1,\mathsf{t}_2,\mathsf{t}_3].\mathsf{m}(\mathsf{e}_2) : \mathsf{t}_3}\ (10)$$

$$\frac{\begin{array}{l}\mathsf{P},\mathsf{L},\mathsf{E} \vdash \mathsf{e} : \mathsf{t} \\ \mathsf{P},\mathsf{L} \vdash \mathsf{t} \le \mathsf{t}_1\end{array}}{\mathsf{P},\mathsf{L},\mathsf{E} \vdash \mathsf{e}[\mathsf{t}_1,\mathsf{t}_2].\mathsf{f} : \mathsf{t}_2}\ (11) \qquad \frac{\begin{array}{l}\mathsf{P},\mathsf{L},\mathsf{E} \vdash \mathsf{e}_1 : \mathsf{t}_1' \\ \mathsf{P},\mathsf{L},\mathsf{E} \vdash \mathsf{e}_2 : \mathsf{t}_2' \\ \mathsf{P},\mathsf{L} \vdash \mathsf{t}_2' \le \mathsf{t}_2\end{array}}{\mathsf{P},\mathsf{L},\mathsf{E} \vdash \mathsf{e}_1[\mathsf{t}_1,\mathsf{t}_2,\mathsf{t}_3]^{\mathsf{i}}.\mathsf{m}(\mathsf{e}_2) : \mathsf{t}_3}\ (12)$$

$$\frac{\begin{array}{lll}\mathcal{T}(\mathsf{c},\mathsf{P}) = \mathsf{c}', \{\mathsf{i}_1, \ldots \mathsf{i}_n\} & \mathsf{n} \ge 0 & \\ \mathsf{P},\mathsf{L} \vdash \mathsf{c}' \le_{clss} \mathsf{c}' & & \\ \mathsf{P},\mathsf{L} \vdash \mathsf{i}_j \le_{intf} \mathsf{i}_j & \forall \mathsf{j} \in 1 \ldots \mathsf{n} & \\ \mathcal{F}_{ff}(\mathsf{f},\mathsf{c}',\mathsf{t},\mathsf{P}) > 0 \quad \Rightarrow & \mathcal{F}_{ff}(\mathsf{f},\mathsf{c}',\mathsf{t},\mathsf{P}) = \mathcal{F}_{ff}(\mathsf{f},\mathsf{c},\mathsf{t},\mathsf{P}) & \forall\, \mathsf{f},\mathsf{t} \\ \mathcal{F}_{ff}(\mathsf{f},\mathsf{c},\mathsf{t},\mathsf{P}) = \mathcal{F}_{ff}(\mathsf{f}',\mathsf{c},\mathsf{t}',\mathsf{P}) > 0 \quad \Rightarrow & \mathsf{f} = \mathsf{f}', \mathsf{t} = \mathsf{t}' & \forall\, \mathsf{f},\mathsf{f}',\mathsf{t},\mathsf{t}' \\ \mathcal{M}_{ff}(\mathsf{m},\mathsf{c}',\mathsf{t},\mathsf{t}',\mathsf{P}) > 0 \quad \Rightarrow & \mathcal{M}_{ff}(\mathsf{m},\mathsf{c},\mathsf{t},\mathsf{t}',\mathsf{P}) = \mathcal{M}_{ff}(\mathsf{m},\mathsf{c}',\mathsf{t},\mathsf{t}',\mathsf{P}) & \forall \mathsf{m},\mathsf{t},\mathsf{t}' \\ \mathcal{M}_{ff}(\mathsf{m},\mathsf{c},\mathsf{t},\mathsf{t}',\mathsf{P}) = \phi \quad \Rightarrow & & \\ \quad \mathcal{M}_e(\phi,\mathsf{c},\mathsf{P}) = \mathsf{e}, & \mathsf{P},\mathsf{L},(\mathsf{t}\,\mathsf{x}, \mathsf{c}\,\mathbf{this}) \vdash \mathsf{e} : \mathsf{t}_1', \quad \mathsf{P},\mathsf{L} \vdash \mathsf{t}_1' \le \mathsf{t}_1 & \forall \mathsf{m},\mathsf{t},\mathsf{t}'\end{array}}{\mathsf{P},\mathsf{L} \vdash \mathsf{c}\,\diamond}\ (13)$$

$$\frac{\begin{array}{ll}\mathcal{T}(\mathsf{i},\mathsf{P}) = \{\mathsf{i}_1, \ldots \mathsf{i}_n\} & \mathsf{n} \ge 0 \\ \mathsf{P},\mathsf{L} \vdash \mathsf{i}_j \le_{intf} \mathsf{i}_j & \forall \mathsf{j} \in 1 \ldots \mathsf{n}\end{array}}{\mathsf{P},\mathsf{L} \vdash \mathsf{i}\,\diamond}\ (14)$$

$$\frac{\begin{array}{l}\vdash \mathsf{P},\mathsf{L}\ \diamond_a \\ \forall \mathsf{t} \in \mathcal{T}\mathsf{s}(\mathsf{P}) : \quad \mathsf{P},\mathsf{L} \vdash \mathsf{t}\,\diamond\end{array}}{\mathsf{L} \vdash \mathsf{P}\,\diamond}\ (15)$$

Fig. 9. Well-formed prepared code – rule numbering consistent with that for verification

The code $\mathsf{P_{BC}}$ from section 2 is the result of the application of a preparation function on $\mathsf{L_{BC}}$.

Interestingly, definition 5 does not pose any requirements on interfaces. It does not require inheritance of methods from superinterfaces (*i.e.*, that $\mathcal{T}(\mathsf{i}, \mathsf{P}')$ $= \{...\mathsf{i}'...\}$ and $\mathcal{M}\!\!\dot{f\!f}(\mathsf{m}, \mathsf{i}', \mathsf{t}_2, \mathsf{t}_3, \mathsf{PP}') = \mathbf{0}$ implies that $\mathcal{M}\!\!\dot{f\!f}(\mathsf{m}, \mathsf{i}, \mathsf{t}_2, \mathsf{t}_3, \mathsf{P}') =$ $\mathbf{0}$), even though this is a property of Java implementations, and even though it is an integral part of soundness of the Java source language, it is not required for soundness at this level (namely, at the level of $\mathcal{L}$ or $\mathcal{P}$ expressions, the types are largely determined by the signatures). This reflects how weak the notion of interfaces is. Note also, that fields were not reflected in $\mathcal{L}$ code, but they are in $\mathcal{P}$ code.

4 Soundness

4.1 Well Formed Prepared Code

The judgment $\mathsf{L} \vdash \mathsf{P} \diamond$, defined in fig. 3.6, guarantees that the prepared code P is well formed in the context of loaded code L. Well-formedness is a similar requirement to verification, in the sense that the types of expressions are checked, and subtype relationships implied through the type annotations need to be established. For this reason we organized fig. 3.6 in a similar way to fig. 7.

As in verification, well-formedness of prepared code does not guarantee the existence of fields or methods required in method bodies. In contrast to verification, well-formedness of prepared code does not cause loading of further binaries. Also, while judgment $\mathsf{P}, \mathsf{L} \vdash_{v} \mathsf{L}' \diamond \underset{loads}{\leftharpoondown} \mathsf{L}''$ represents checks that are performed by Java implementations, the judgment $\mathsf{L} \vdash \mathsf{P} \diamond$ is only a vehicle for proving soundness.

The main requirements for well-formedness of prepared code are:

- all classes/interfaces defined in P have their superclasses/superinterfaces in P,
- identifiers mentioned as superclasses belong to classes,
- identifiers mentioned as superinterfaces belong to interfaces,
- fields have distinct offsets,
- fields defined in a superclass c' have the same offsets in a subclass c,
- methods defined in a class c' have the same offsets in a subclass c,
- method bodies are well-formed and respect their signatures.

As for preparation, the requirements posed on interfaces are very weak.

4.2 Conformance and Runtime Types

The judgments $\sigma, \mathsf{P} \vdash_{c} \beta \diamond$, and $\mathsf{P}, \mathsf{E} \vdash_{c} \sigma \diamond$, defined in rules (1)-(5) of fig. 10, express conformance of values to types, and of states to programs and environments.

The judgment $\sigma, \mathsf{P} \vdash_{c} \alpha \diamond$ in rule (4) expresses that the object stored at α conforms to its class. The class of the object, c, is stored at the beginning of the object. For all fields of c, the object must contain appropriate values at the corresponding offsets. In order to obtain a well-founded relation, we defined conformance in terms of the auxiliary *weak conformance* judgment $\sigma, \mathsf{P} \vdash_{w} \beta : \mathsf{t}$.

(1)
$$\frac{}{\sigma, \mathsf{P} \vdash_{w} \beta : \mathbf{int}}$$

(2)
$$\frac{\sigma(\alpha) = \mathsf{c}' \in \mathsf{Id} \qquad \mathsf{P}, \mathsf{L}_{\emptyset} \vdash \mathsf{c}' \ \leq_{clss} \ \mathsf{c}}{\sigma, \mathsf{P} \vdash_{w} \alpha : \mathsf{c} \qquad \sigma, \mathsf{P} \vdash_{w} \mathbf{0} : \mathsf{c}}$$

(3)
$$\frac{\sigma(\alpha) = \mathsf{c} \qquad \mathsf{P}, \mathsf{L}_{\emptyset} \vdash \mathsf{c} \ \leq_{clss} \ \mathsf{c} \qquad \mathsf{P}, \mathsf{L}_{\emptyset} \vdash \mathsf{i} \ \leq_{intf} \ \mathsf{i}}{\sigma, \mathsf{P} \vdash_{w} \alpha : \mathsf{i}}$$

(4)
$$\frac{\begin{array}{l} \sigma(\alpha) = \mathsf{c} \in \mathsf{Id} \\ \mathsf{P}, \mathsf{L}_{\emptyset} \vdash \mathsf{c} \ \leq_{clss} \ \mathsf{c} \\ \forall \mathsf{f}, \mathsf{t}: \quad \mathcal{F}_{\!ff}(\mathsf{f}, \mathsf{c}, \mathsf{t}, \mathsf{P}) = \phi \ \Rightarrow \ \sigma, \mathsf{P} \vdash_{w} \sigma(\alpha + \phi) : \mathsf{t}, \ \text{and} \ \forall \phi' \leq \phi\text{:} \ \sigma(\alpha + \phi') \notin \mathsf{Id} \end{array}}{\sigma, \mathsf{P} \vdash_{c} \alpha \diamond}$$

(5)
$$\frac{\begin{array}{l} \sigma(\alpha) \in \mathsf{Id} \ \Rightarrow \ \sigma, \mathsf{P} \vdash_{c} \alpha \diamond \\ \mathsf{E}(\mathsf{z}) \neq \epsilon \ \Rightarrow \ \sigma, \mathsf{P} \vdash_{w} \sigma(\mathsf{z}) : \mathsf{E}(\mathsf{z}) \end{array}}{\mathsf{P}, \mathsf{E} \vdash_{c} \sigma \diamond}$$

(6)
$$\frac{\mathsf{P}, \mathsf{E} \vdash_{c} \sigma \diamond}{\begin{array}{l} \mathsf{P}, \mathsf{L}, \mathsf{E} \vdash_{r} \sigma, \beta \ : \ \mathbf{int} \\ \mathsf{P}, \mathsf{L}, \mathsf{E} \vdash_{r} \sigma, \mathbf{0} \ : \ \mathsf{c} \\ \mathsf{P}, \mathsf{L}, \mathsf{E} \vdash_{r} \sigma, \mathbf{new}\ \mathsf{c} \ : \ \mathsf{c} \end{array}}$$

(7)
$$\frac{\mathsf{P}, \mathsf{E} \vdash_{c} \sigma \diamond \qquad \sigma(\alpha) = \mathsf{c} \qquad \mathsf{P}, \mathsf{L}_{\emptyset} \vdash \mathsf{c} \ \leq_{clss} \ \mathsf{c}}{\mathsf{P}, \mathsf{L}, \mathsf{E} \vdash_{r} \sigma, \alpha \ : \ \mathsf{c}}$$

(8)
$$\frac{\mathsf{P}, \mathsf{E} \vdash_{c} \sigma \diamond \qquad \mathsf{E}(\mathsf{y}) = \mathsf{t}}{\mathsf{P}, \mathsf{L}, \mathsf{E} \vdash_{r} \sigma, \mathsf{y} \ : \ \mathsf{t}}$$

(9)
$$\frac{\mathsf{P}, \mathsf{L}, \mathsf{E} \vdash_{r} \sigma, \mathsf{v} \ : \ \mathsf{t} \qquad \mathsf{P}, \mathsf{L}, \mathsf{E} \vdash_{r} \sigma, \mathsf{e} \ : \ \mathsf{t}' \qquad \mathsf{P}, \mathsf{L} \vdash \mathsf{t}' \ \leq \ \mathsf{t}}{\mathsf{P}, \mathsf{L}, \mathsf{E} \vdash_{r} \sigma, \mathsf{v} = \mathsf{e} \ : \ \mathsf{t}'}$$

(10)
$$\frac{\begin{array}{l} \mathsf{P}, \mathsf{L}, \mathsf{E} \vdash_{r} \sigma, \mathsf{e}_1 \ : \ \mathsf{t}_1' \\ \mathsf{P}, \mathsf{L}, \mathsf{E} \vdash_{r} \sigma, \mathsf{e}_2 \ : \ \mathsf{t}_2' \\ \mathsf{P}, \mathsf{L} \vdash \mathsf{t}_1' \ \leq \ \mathsf{t}_1 \\ \mathsf{P}, \mathsf{L} \vdash \mathsf{t}_2' \ \leq \ \mathsf{t}_2 \end{array}}{\mathsf{P}, \mathsf{L}, \mathsf{E} \vdash_{r} \sigma, \mathsf{e}_1[\mathsf{t}_1, \mathsf{t}_2, \mathsf{t}_3].\mathsf{m}(\mathsf{e}_2) \ : \ \mathsf{t}_3}$$

(11)
$$\frac{\mathsf{P}, \mathsf{L}, \mathsf{E} \vdash_{r} \sigma, \mathsf{e} \ : \ \mathsf{t} \qquad \mathsf{P}, \mathsf{L} \vdash \mathsf{t} \ \leq \ \mathsf{t}_1}{\mathsf{P}, \mathsf{L}, \mathsf{E} \vdash_{r} \sigma, \mathsf{e}[\mathsf{t}_1, \mathsf{t}_2].\mathsf{f} \ : \ \mathsf{t}_2}$$

(12)
$$\frac{\begin{array}{l} \mathsf{P}, \mathsf{L}, \mathsf{E} \vdash_{r} \sigma, \mathsf{e}_1 \ : \ \mathsf{t}_1' \\ \mathsf{P}, \mathsf{L}, \mathsf{E} \vdash_{r} \sigma, \mathsf{e}_2 \ : \ \mathsf{t}_2' \\ \mathsf{P}, \mathsf{L} \vdash \mathsf{t}_2' \ \leq \ \mathsf{t}_2 \end{array}}{\mathsf{P}, \mathsf{L}, \mathsf{E} \vdash_{r} \sigma, \mathsf{e}_1[\mathsf{t}_1, \mathsf{t}_2, \mathsf{t}_3]^{\mathsf{i}}.\mathsf{m}(\mathsf{e}_2) \ : \ \mathsf{t}_3}$$

Fig. 10. Conformance, and types of runtime expressions

Notice, that a positive value β may conform to both **int** and a class type, and to *any* interface type. For example, $\sigma_0, \mathsf{P}_{\mathsf{ABC}} \vdash_w 5 : \mathbf{int}$, and $\sigma_0, \mathsf{P}_{\mathsf{ABC}} \vdash_w 5 : \mathsf{B}$, but $\sigma_0, \mathsf{P}_{\mathsf{ABC}} \not\vdash_w 5 : \mathsf{A}$. Also, if $\mathsf{P}_{\mathsf{Intf1}}$ contains the declaration of an interface $\mathsf{Intf1}$, then $\sigma_0, \mathsf{P}_{\mathsf{Intf1}}\mathsf{P}_{\mathsf{ABC}} \vdash_w 5 : \mathsf{Intf1}$, and $\sigma_0, \mathsf{P}_{\mathsf{Intf1}}\mathsf{P}_{\mathsf{ABC}} \not\vdash_w 6 : \mathsf{Intf1}$. Finally, the requirement $\forall \phi' \leq \phi$: $\sigma(\alpha + \phi') \notin \mathsf{Id}$ ensures that no object is stored "inside" another object, and is used to prove that execution does not affect the type of expressions (lemma 4).

The judgment $\mathsf{P}, \mathsf{E} \vdash_c \sigma \diamond$, defined in rule (5), expresses that the store σ *conforms* to prepared program P and to variable declarations in E, and requires that:

- all classes/interfaces defined in P have their superclasses/superinterfaces in P,
- the classes of all objects stored in σ are defined in P,
- all objects stored in σ conform to their class,
- all variables defined in E have in σ values appropriate to their types,

Notice, that store conformance does not take the loaded, not yet verified code L into account. This can be seen from the form of the judgments. Also, $\mathbf{0}$ conforms to any class, allowing objects with a field initialized to $\mathbf{0}$, belonging to a yet undefined class.

Types for runtime expressions are given by the judgment $\mathsf{P}, \mathsf{L}, \mathsf{E} \vdash_r \sigma, \mathsf{e} : \mathsf{t}$, defined in rules (6)-(12) in fig. 10. The rules are similar to well-formedness, with the difference that for runtime expressions the store σ is taken into account.

4.3 Locality and Preservation of Judgments

In general, one expects properties established in a certain context to hold for larger contexts as well. Locality properties were proven in [6], used in [4], and explored in our model of binary compatibility [7].

We prove that judgments in the context of P and $\mathsf{L}_1\mathsf{L}_2$ are preserved, if loaded code is replaced by prepared code which has the same subclass/subinterface information (*i.e.*, replace L_1 by P_1, where $\mathcal{T}(\mathsf{t}'', \mathsf{P}_1) = \mathcal{T}(\mathsf{t}'', \mathsf{L}_1)$ for all t''), the loaded code is augmented by P_3, and the environment E is extended to E':

Lemma 2 *For all* P, P_1, L, L_1, L_2, L_3, e, t, t', σ, E, E', *if* $\mathcal{T}(\mathsf{t}'', \mathsf{P}_1) = \mathcal{T}(\mathsf{t}'', \mathsf{L}_1)$ *for all* t'', *and* $\vdash \mathsf{E}' \leq \mathsf{E}$ *then:*

- $\mathcal{T}(\mathsf{t}, \mathsf{P}, \mathsf{L}_1\mathsf{L}_2) \neq \epsilon \quad \Rightarrow \quad \mathcal{T}(\mathsf{t}, \mathsf{P}, \mathsf{L}_1\mathsf{L}_2) = \mathcal{T}(\mathsf{t}, \mathsf{PP}_1, \mathsf{L}_2\mathsf{L}_3)$.
- $\mathsf{P}, \mathsf{L}_1\mathsf{L}_2 \vdash \mathsf{t} \leq \mathsf{t}' \quad \Rightarrow \quad \mathsf{PP}_1, \mathsf{L}_2\mathsf{L}_3 \vdash \mathsf{t} \leq \mathsf{t}'$.
- $\mathsf{P}, \mathsf{L}_1\mathsf{L}_2, \mathsf{E} \vdash \mathsf{e} : \mathsf{t} \quad \Rightarrow \quad \mathsf{PP}_1, \mathsf{L}_2\mathsf{L}_3, \mathsf{E}' \vdash \mathsf{e} : \mathsf{t}$.
- $\mathsf{P}, \mathsf{L}_1\mathsf{L}_2, \mathsf{E} \vdash_r \sigma, \mathsf{e} : \mathsf{t} \quad \Rightarrow \quad \mathsf{PP}_1, \mathsf{L}_2\mathsf{L}_3, \mathsf{E}' \vdash_r \sigma, \mathsf{e} : \mathsf{t}$.

Verification of classes implies verification of the bodies of their methods:

Lemma 3 *For any* P, L, L', L'', c, *if*
$\mathsf{P}, \mathsf{L} \vdash_v \mathsf{L}'' \diamond \underset{loads}{\leftharpoondown} \mathsf{L}'$, *and* $\mathcal{M}(\mathsf{m}, \mathsf{c}, \mathsf{t}_1, \mathsf{t}_2, \mathsf{L}'') = \mathsf{e}$,
then, there exist t_1', L_1', L_2', L_3' *and* L_4' *such that* $\mathsf{L}' = \mathsf{L}_1'\mathsf{L}_2'\mathsf{L}_3'\mathsf{L}_4'$, *and*
$\mathsf{P}, \mathsf{LL}_1', (\mathsf{t}_2\ \mathsf{x}, \mathsf{c}\ \mathbf{this}) \vdash_v \mathsf{e} : \mathsf{t}_1' \underset{loads}{\leftharpoondown} \mathsf{L}_2'$, *and* $\mathsf{P}, \mathsf{LL}_1'\mathsf{L}_2' \vdash_v \mathsf{t}_1' \leq \mathsf{t}_1 \underset{loads}{\leftharpoondown} \mathsf{L}_3'$.

Preparation of verified code preserves judgments:

Lemma 4 *For any* P, P_1, L_1, L_2, L_3, e, t, E, σ, *where* $\mathsf{P}, \mathsf{L}_1\mathsf{L}_2 \vdash_{v} \mathsf{L}_1 \diamond \;\; \underset{loads}{\leftarrow} \mathsf{L}_3$, *if* $\mathsf{P}_1 = pr(\mathsf{L}_1, \mathsf{P})$, *then* :

- $\mathsf{P}, \mathsf{L}_1\mathsf{L}_2 \vdash \mathsf{t} \le \mathsf{t}' \quad \Rightarrow \quad \mathsf{PP}_1, \mathsf{L}_2\mathsf{L}_3 \vdash \mathsf{t} \le \mathsf{t}'$.
- $\mathsf{P}, \mathsf{L}_1\mathsf{L}_2, \mathsf{E} \vdash \mathsf{e} : \mathsf{t} \quad \Rightarrow \quad \mathsf{PP}_1, \mathsf{L}_2\mathsf{L}_3, \mathsf{E} \vdash \mathsf{e} : \mathsf{t}$.
- $\mathsf{L}_1\mathsf{L}_2 \vdash \mathsf{P} \diamond \quad \Rightarrow \quad \mathsf{L}_2\mathsf{L}_3 \vdash \mathsf{PP}_1 \diamond$.
- $\mathsf{P}, \mathsf{E} \vdash_{c} \sigma \diamond \quad \Rightarrow \quad \mathsf{PP}_1, \mathsf{E} \vdash_{c} \sigma \diamond$.
- $\mathsf{P}, \mathsf{L}_1\mathsf{L}_2, \mathsf{E} \vdash_{r} \sigma, \mathsf{e} : \mathsf{t} \quad \Rightarrow \quad \mathsf{PP}_1, \mathsf{L}_2\mathsf{L}_3, \mathsf{E} \vdash_{r} \sigma, \mathsf{e} : \mathsf{t}$.

4.4 Subject Reduction and Progress

Execution of a well-typed expression e does not overwrite objects, creates new objects in the free space, and does *not* affect the type of any expression e'' – even if e'' were a subexpression of e! Such a property is required for type soundness in imperative object oriented languages, and was proven, *e.g.*, , in [6,26]. In the current work this property holds only when *well-typed* expressions are executed.

Lemma 5 *For* P, L, E, σ, *non-ground* e, t, $\mathsf{c} \in \mathsf{Id}$, *if*
- $\mathsf{L} \vdash \mathsf{P} \diamond$, *and*
- $\mathsf{P}, \mathsf{L}, \mathsf{E} \vdash_{r} \sigma, \mathsf{e} : \mathsf{t}$, *and*
- $\mathsf{e}, \sigma, \mathsf{P}, \mathsf{L} \leadsto \mathsf{e}', \sigma', \mathsf{P}', \mathsf{L}'$,

then
- $\sigma(\alpha) = \mathsf{c} \quad \Rightarrow \quad \sigma'(\alpha) = \mathsf{c}$,
- $\sigma'(\alpha) = \mathsf{c} \quad \Rightarrow \quad \sigma(\alpha) = \mathsf{c}$ *or* α *new in* σ,
- $\mathsf{P}, \mathsf{E} \vdash_{c} \sigma \diamond \quad \Rightarrow \quad \mathsf{P}, \mathsf{E} \vdash_{c} \sigma' \diamond$,
- $\mathsf{P}, \mathsf{L}, \mathsf{E} \vdash_{r} \sigma, \mathsf{e}'' : \mathsf{t}'' \quad \Rightarrow \quad \mathsf{P}', \mathsf{L}', \mathsf{E} \vdash_{r} \sigma', \mathsf{e}'' : \mathsf{t}''$.

Proof by structural induction over the derivation $\leadsto$, and for the fourth part of the lemma, in the cases of VarAss or FldAcc1 by structural induction over the typing of e'', using the store conformance requirement whereby no object is stored within another object.

Lemma 6 (Progress) *For any* P, L, E, σ, t, *non-ground* e, *if* e *does not contain an exception, then there exist* P', L', σ', e', *such that* $\mathsf{e}, \sigma, \mathsf{P}, \mathsf{L} \leadsto \mathsf{e}', \sigma', \mathsf{P}', \mathsf{L}'$.

Theorem 1 (Subject reduction) *For any* P, L, t, E, e, e', σ, *if*

- $\mathsf{L} \vdash \mathsf{P} \diamond$, *and*
- $\mathsf{P}, \mathsf{L}, \mathsf{E} \vdash_{r} \sigma, \mathsf{e} : \mathsf{t}$, *and*
- $\mathsf{e}, \sigma, \mathsf{P}, \mathsf{L} \leadsto \mathsf{e}', \sigma', \mathsf{P}', \mathsf{L}'$,

then

- $\mathsf{L}' \vdash \mathsf{P}' \diamond$, *and*
  - $\mathsf{P}', \mathsf{L}', \mathsf{E}' \vdash_{r} \sigma', \mathsf{e}' : \mathsf{t}'$, *and* $\mathsf{P}', \mathsf{L}' \vdash \mathsf{t}' \le \mathsf{t}$, *for appropriate* E', t', *and*
    $\mathsf{t} = \mathsf{t}'$ *if* e *is a non-l-ground variable,*
    or
  - e' *contains and exception.*

Proof by structural induction over typing $\mathsf{P}, \mathsf{L}, \mathsf{E} \vdash_{r} \sigma, \mathsf{e} : \mathsf{t}$.

Thus, the new, possibly augmented, prepared code, P', preserves its well-formedness, and the store σ' preserves conformance. Uninitialized parts of the store, where $\sigma(\alpha) = \epsilon$, are never dereferenced. Finally, execution never gets stuck.

5 Summary and Alternatives

Verification of class c requires verification of all methods in c and all its (not yet prepared) superclasses. Verification of terms requires establishing subtype relations between types t and t'. If t has not been loaded yet, then it will be loaded with all its superclasses, except if t and t' are identical, or t' is an interface. Verification does not ensure the presence of fields or methods, it only ensures that all methods in a verified class respect their signatures. Resolution checks for the presence of fields and methods of given signatures. Thus the verifier relies on resolution to detect some of the possible errors, and resolution is safe only on code previously checked by the verifier.

The system does not guard against link-time errors (*i.e.,* LoadErr, or VerifErr, or NoMethErr, or NoFldErr, or ClssChngErr), but it does guarantee the integrity of the store. On the other hand, execution of unverified code may overwrite *any* part of the memory, and execute *any* methods.

Our model is independent of Java reflection: We represented prepared and loaded code as separate entities of the configuration, rather than as objects of class Class in the store σ. This abstraction from "real" implementations allows us to demonstrate in the format of the judgments how the various components depend on each other. Namely:

- $\mathcal{F}\!\mathit{ff}(\mathsf{f},\mathsf{c},\mathsf{t},\mathsf{P})$, $\mathcal{M}\!\mathit{ff}(\mathsf{m},\mathsf{c},\mathsf{t}_2,\mathsf{t}_1,\mathsf{P})$, and $\mathcal{M}\!\mathit{ff}^{\mathit{i}}(\mathsf{m},\mathsf{i},\mathsf{t}_2,\mathsf{t}_1,\mathsf{P})$ show that offsets are looked up in the prepared code only, and the operational semantics rules show that they depend on the types t_2 and t_1 stored in signatures, and not the runtime types of the objects.
- $\mathsf{e},\sigma,\mathsf{P},\mathsf{L}_1\mathsf{L}_2 \leadsto \mathsf{e}',\sigma',\mathsf{PP}_1,\mathsf{L}_2\mathsf{L}_3$ shows which components may be affected by execution.
- $\mathsf{P},\mathsf{L} \vdash_v \mathsf{L}' \diamond \ \overleftarrow{\scriptstyle loads}\ \mathsf{L}''$ shows that verification takes the prepared and the loaded code into account, does not take the store into account, and that may load further code.
- $\mathsf{P},\mathsf{L} \vdash \mathsf{P}' \diamond$ shows that well-formedness of prepared code takes the prepared and the loaded code into account, but does *not* load further code.
- $\mathsf{P},\mathsf{E} \vdash_c \sigma \diamond$ shows that conformance of a store depends on the prepared code and *not* on the loaded code; in particular, any objects in σ must belong to prepared classes.
- $\mathsf{P},\mathsf{L},\mathsf{E} \vdash_r \sigma,\mathsf{e} : \mathsf{t}$ shows that types of runtime expressions depend on the prepared code, but also on the store and on the loaded code (the latter because of the arguments to method calls).
- $\mathit{pr}(\mathsf{L},\mathsf{P})$ shows that preparation depends on the code already prepared, and on the loaded code to be prepared, but does *not* depend on the remaining loaded code.
- The role of the loaded code L in checking is limited; the only information extracted from L is which class/interface extends/implements which other class/interface, but the contents of the classes/interfaces is ignored.

Link-time errors can occur also when running code that was produced by a compiler, as shown in the various footnotes. However, link-time errors will not occur, if one re-complies all importing classes/interfaces and all suclasses/subinterfaces after recompiling a class or interface – we have not demonstrated this yet.

It is interesting that interfaces are treated by verification more leniently than classes, and thus require more runtime checks. It would have been possible to treat classes as leniently, or to treat interfaces more strictly.

In current implementations the boundary of decomposition is at classes or interfaces. That is, we load several classes or interfaces together, and we verify several classes or interfaces together. Is it possible to consider other levels of decomposition? A probably less attractive, more lazy alternative would put the boundary of decomposition at methods, and would verify method bodies only before they are first called. This would make the judgment $\mathsf{L} \vdash \mathsf{P} \diamond$ even weaker, and would extend the operational semantics to verify method bodies on a per call basis, and check for previous verification.

Another lazy alternative, as suggested in in [11,23] and formalized in [23], instead of immediately establishing that $\mathtt{t}$ is a subtype of $\mathtt{t}'$ would post a constraint requiring $\mathtt{t}$ to be a subtype of $\mathtt{t}'$, to be validated only when $\mathtt{t}$ is loaded. This would treat L's as constraints, and the judgment $\mathsf{P}, \mathsf{L}, \vdash_{v} \mathtt{e} : \mathtt{t} \;\underset{loads}{\leftharpoondown}\; \mathsf{L}'$ to mean that the verifier established $\mathtt{e}$ to have type $\mathtt{t}$, while posting L'.

It is easy to modify our model to express the above alternatives. More challenging would be a unified framework that would allow to characterize all such alternatives.

6 Conclusions, Discussion, and Further Work

We have given a model for the five execution components, and have demonstrated how the corresponding checks together ensure type soundness. Our model describes is at a high level, and distinguishes the components and the time of the associated checks. Thus, our account is useful for source language programmers, designers of new binary formats for Java, and designers of alternative distributions of the checks among the four components. The format of the judgments reflects the dependencies of the components. We do not yet treat multiple loaders.

Formal treatments of linking were suggested in [3], albeit in a static setting. Dynamic linking at a fundamental level has been studied in [9,1,28], allowing for modules as first class values, usually untyped, concentrating on confluence and optimization issues. Recently, [15], discuss dynamic linking of native code as an extension of Typed Assembly Language without expanding the trusted computing base, while [8] takes a higher-level view and suggests extensions of Typed Assembly Language to support type safe dynamic linking of modules and sharing. The above works are based on structural type equivalence, higher order types, and linking as a one-phase transformation which binds free references; Java however, has name type equivalence, first order types, and its resolution is a multiple phase activity.

Recent work on Java linking [23,27] complements ours. They both uncovered errors in current verifiers, in that insufficient constraints were posted for the arguments of inherited methods, or the arguments of a class implementing an interface. [23] suggest a model of Java evaluation, preparation, verification and loading at the bytecode level, without interfaces, but with multiple loaders. Their approach is lazier than that of SUN implementations, and verification posts constraints as opposed to loading classes. [27] provide a model of Java evaluation, preparation, verification and multiple loaders, describing interfaces, but only treating method calls. Both approaches adopt a higher level runtime model than ours, and thus do not demonstrate how unverified code can destroy the consistency of the store. Furthermore, the above works consider a couple of bytecode instructions, do not describe complete classes or interfaces, do not distinguish crlearly between loading and verification.

The current paper is an improvement over the work presented at TIC [5]. The adoption of non-deterministic operational semantics, and the use of the look-up functions $\mathcal{T}$, $\mathcal{M}_{\mathit{ff}}$, $\mathcal{F}_{\mathit{ff}}$, $\mathcal{M}_e$, $\mathcal{M}_{\mathit{ff}}^{i}$ as opposed to complete program code, allowed a more concise, abstract account.

Further work includes refining the model to allow multiple class loaders, extending the model to describe the source language and the compilation process, extending languages $\mathcal{L}$ and $\mathcal{P}$ with more Java features, considering different levels of decomposition, applying the model to reconsider the meaning of binary compatibility [7].

Finally, though Java is novel in its approach to verification and dynamic linking, similar components and associated checks could be defined for any language that supports some concept of modularity. The generalization of such ideas to other programming languages is an open issue.

Acknowledgments. I am deeply indebted to the TIC referees for extensive and very useful feedback. One of the referees, in particular, provided many insightful remarks and valuable suggestions that have improved this work considerably. Earlier versions of this paper have benefited from input from David Wragg, Tatyana Valkevych, Susan Eisenbach, Mark Skipper, Elena Zucca, and Eugenio Moggi.

References

1. Davide Ancona and Elena Zucca. A Primitive calculus for module systems. In *PPDP Proceedings*, September 1999.
2. Martin Buechi. Type soundness Issues in Java, May 1999. Types mailing list, at http : //www.cis.upenn.edu/ bcpierce/types/archives and then /current/msg00140.html.
3. Luca Cardelli. Program Fragments, Linking, and Modularization. In *POPL'97 Proceedings*, January 1997.
4. Drew Dean. The Security of Static Typing with Dynamic Linking. In *Fourth ACM Conference on Computer and Communication Security*, 1997.
5. Sophia Drossopoulou. Towards an Abstract model of Java dynami linking and verification. In *Preliminary Proceedings of the Third Workshop on Types in Compilation (TIC 2000)*. Carnegie Mellon, CMU-CS-00-161, 2000.
6. Sophia Drossopoulou, Susan Eisenbach, and Sarfraz Khurshid. Is Java Sound? *Theory and Practice of Object Systems*, 5(1), January 1999.

7. Sophia Drossopoulou, Susan Eisenbach, and David Wragg. A Fragment Calculus - towards a model of Separate Compilation, Linking and Binary Compatibility. In *LICS Proceedings*, 1999.
8. Dominic Duggan. Saring in Typed Module Assembly Language. In *Preliminary Proceedings of the Third Workshop on Types in Compilation (TIC 2000)*. Carnegie Mellon, CMU-CS-00-161, 2000.
9. Kathleen Fisher, John Reppy, and Jon Riecke. A Calculus for Compiling and Linking Classes. In *ESOP Proceedings*, March 2000.
10. Matthew Flatt, Shiram Khrishnamurthi, and Matthias Felleisen. Classes and Mixins. In *POPL Proceedings*, January 1998.
11. Philip W. L. Fong and Robert D. Cameron. Proof linking: An architecture for modular verification of dynamically-linked mobile code. In *ACM SIGSOFT Sixth International Symposium on the Foundations of Software Engineering (FSE'98)*, November 1998.
12. Stephen N. Freund and J. C. Mitchell. A Formal Framework for the Java Bytecode Language and Verifier. In *OOPSLA Proceeedings*, November 1999.
13. Stephen N. Freund and J. C. Mitchell. A Type System for Object Initialization in the Java Bytecode Language. In *OOPSLA Proceeedings*, October 1998.
14. James Gosling, Bill Joy, and Guy Steele. *The Java Language Specification.* Addison-Wesley, August 1996.
15. Michael Hicks, Stephanie Weirich, and Karl Crary. Safe and Flexible Dynamic Linking of Native Code. In *Preliminary Proceedings of the Third Workshop on Types in Compilation (TIC 2000)*. Carnegie Mellon, CMU-CS-00-161, 2000.
16. Atsushi Igarashi, Benjamin Pierce, and Philip Wadler. Featherweight Java: A minimal core calculus for Java and GJ. In *OOPSLA Proceedings*, November 1999.
17. Thomas Jensen, Daniel Le Metyayer, and Tommy Thorn. A Formalization of Visibility and Dynamic Loading in Java. In *IEEE ICCL*, 1998.
18. Christopher League, Zhong Shao, and Valery Trifonov. Representing Java Classes in a Typed Intermediate language. In *ICFP Proceedings*, September 1999.
19. Sheng Liang and Gilad Bracha. Dynamic Class Loading in the Java^{TM} Virtual Machine. In *OOPSLA Proceedings*, October 1998.
20. Tim Lindholm and Frank Yellin. *The Java Virtual Machine.* Addison-Wesley, 1997.
21. Tim Lindholm and Frank Yellin. *The Java Virtual Machine.* Addison-Wesley, 1999.
22. Zhenyu Qian. Least Types for Memory Locations in Java Bytecode. In *FOOL 6.* http: //www.cs.williams.edu/ kim/FOOL/sched6.html, 1999.
23. Zhenyu Qian, Allen Goldberg, and Alessandro Coglio. A Formal Specification of Java^{TM} Class Loading. In *OOPSLA'2000*, November 2000.
24. Vijay Saraswat. Java is not type-safe. Technical report, AT&T Rresearch, 1997. http://www.research. att.comp/ vj/bug.html.
25. Raymie Stata and Martin Abadi. A Type System For Java Bytecode Subroutines. In *POPL'98 Proceedings*, January 1998.
26. Donald Syme. Proving Java Type Sound. In Jim Alves-Foss, editor, *Formal Syntax and Semantics of Java*, volume 1523 of *LNCS*. Springer, 1999.
27. Akihiko Tozawa and Masami Hagiya. Careful Analysis of Type Spoofing. In *Java Informationstage*. Springer Verlag, 1999.

28. Joe Wells and Rene Vestergaard. Confluent Equational Reasoning for Linking with First-Class Primitive Modules. In *ESOP Proceedings*, March 2000.
29. Phillip Yelland. Re: Type soundness Issues in Java, May 1999. Types mailing list, at http : //www.cis.upenn.edu/ bcpierce/types/archives and then /current/msg00145.html.

An Example Demonstrating Interfaces

The following example demonstrates the verifier's and run-time system's treatment of interfaces. It is an adaptation of the example which was posted by Martin Buechi [2] in the types mailing list, and was then discussed at some length.

We start with an interface Thinker implemented by class Man, and the class Main with method main:

```
interface Thinker { void be(); }

class Man  impl  Thinker {
   void be(){ System.out.println("be") ; }
}

class Main  {
   public static void main (String args[] ) }
       Thinker descartes;
       Man john = new Man();
       System.out.println("a Man object created");
       if  ( john instanceof  Thinker)
          System.out.println("john is aThinker");
       else
          System.out.println("john is NOT a Thinker");
       descartes = new Man();
       System.out.println("a Man assigned to a Thinker") ;
       john.be();
}
```

We compile Thinker, Man and Main, and we then modify class Man, so that it does not implement Thinker, *i.e.*,

```
class Man { void be(){ System.out.println("be") ; } }
```

We compile Man, without re-compiling Main. When we execute Main, we obtain the output:

```
a Man object created
john is NOT a Thinker
a Man assigned to a Thinker
IncompatibleClassChangeError :        class Man does not implement Thinker
```

The above behavior is described by our model, namely:

- Verification of method main considers the assignment descartes = **new** Man(); as type correct, because the verifier is "liberal" with respect to interfaces
- Verification of the interface method call john.be() requires loading of the interface Thinker.
- Verification of method main does not need to load class Man.
- The assignment descartes = **new** Man(); is executed without any checks, and therefore without errors.
- The interface method call john.be() is compiled to a bytecode term which corresponds to $\text{john[Thinker,void,void]}^{\text{i}}.()$. Execution of that term requires a run-time check according to rule IntfMethCall3. This check fails, and gives the error message IncompatibleClassChangeError : class Man does not implement Thinker.

Sharing in Typed Module Assembly Language

Dominic Duggan

Department of Computer Science
Stevens Institute of Technology
Hoboken, NJ 07030.
dduggan@cs.stevens-tech.edu

Abstract. There is a growing need to provide low-overhead software-based protection mechanisms to protect against malicious or untrusted code. Type-based approaches such as proof-carrying code and typed assembly language provide this protection by relying on untrusted compilers to certify the safety properties of machine language programs. Typed Module Assembly Language (TMAL) is an extension of typed assembly language with support for the type-safe manipulation of dynamically linked libraries. A particularly important aspect of TMAL is its support for shared libraries.

1 Introduction

Protection of programs from other programs is an old and venerable problem, given new urgency with the growing use of applets, plug-ins, shareware software programs and ActiveX controls (and just plain buggy commercial code). Historically the conventional approach to providing this protection has been based on hardware support for isolating the address spaces of different running programs, from each other and from the operating system. The OS kernel and its data structures sit in a protected region of memory, and machine instructions are provided to "trap" into the kernel in a safe way to execute kernel code.

While this approach to protection is widely popularized by operating systems such as Windows 2000 and Linux, there is a growing desire to find alternatives. The problem is that this technique is a fairly heavyweight mechanism for providing protection, relying on expensive context switching between modes and between address spaces. Although application designers have learned to program around this expensive context switching (for example, buffering I/O in application space), this approach breaks down very quickly in software systems composed of separately authored subsystems that do not place much trust in each other, and where context switches may occur much more frequently than in an OS/application scenario [36].

In the OS research community, investigation of alternatives has been motivated by the demands of modular micro-kernel operating systems, where OS modules outside the kernel might not be trusted. Software fault isolation (where the loader inserts software sandboxing checks into machine code [35]) and the SPIN project (where type-safe OS modules are compiled by a trusted compiler

R. Harper (Ed.): TIC 2000, LNCS 2071, pp. 85–116, 2001.

[5]) are examples of approaches to providing protection in software rather than hardware. Sandboxing in Java VMs has also been motivated by the expense of hardware-based memory protection for applets [36]. The commercial world is seeing an explosion in the use of component technology, exemplified by Java Beans and ActiveX controls. This use of component technology again motivates the need to find some relatively lightweight software-based approach to protection in running programs.

Proof-carrying code [30,29] and typed assembly language [28,27] are approaches to providing this protection at low run-time cost. These approaches are examples of *self-certifying code*. A compiler produces a certificate that a program satisfies some property of interest, for example, that the program is well-typed. The user of a compiled program can check that the certificate supplied with a program is valid for that program. If the check succeeds, the program can be run without run-time checks for the safety properties verified by the certificate. This approach has the advantage of moving the compiler out of the trusted computing base, while reducing the need for run-time checks in the code.

Typed assembly language (TAL) enforces a type discipline at the assembly language level, ensuring that malicious or carelessly written components cannot use "tricks" such as buffer overflows or pointer arithmetic to corrupt the data structures in a running program. Unlike the typed machine language underlying the JVM, TAL is not tied to a particular language's type system or interpreter architecture. Instead the type system is a moderately generic high-level type system with procedures, records and parametric polymorphism, while the target assembly language is any modern RISC or CISC assembly language. The type system is designed to be rich enough that it can serve as a target for compilers for many different languages, while at the same time having as much freedom as possible in its choice of code optimizations, parameter-passing conventions, and data and environment representations [10].

Given the importance of component technology as a motivating factor for TAL, it is clear that there should be support for manipulating components in a type-safe but flexible manner. Modular Typed Assembly Language (MTAL) extends TAL to typed object files and type-safe linking [14]. However this is limited by the assumption that all of a program is linked together before the program is run, with linking happening outside of the program itself. Dynamic linking may be used to avoid loading an entire library when only a small part of the library will be needed. For example, the Linux kernel uses dynamic linking to load in kernel modules on an as-needed basis. While static linkers do a good job of only linking those parts of a library that a program references, they cannot predict in advance what of the referenced modules a program might actually use. Dynamic linking is also useful for shared libraries, allowing several processes to share a commonly used library in memory. Indeed one can consider the operating system itself as a shared library, one that is made available in a protected region of memory to all running programs.

Our interest is in extending TAL with support for dynamic linking and shared libraries. Glew and Morrisett [14] consider some alternative approaches to extending MTAL with dynamic linking[1], but this consideration is only informal. One issue that they do not consider, which is central to our work, is what model dynamic linking should use for software components and for linking components.

An obvious candidate is the ML module system [26], which provides fairly sophisticated support for type-safe linking as a language construct [23,6]. Indeed this is the philosophy underlying MTAL, which relies on a phase-splitting transformation to translate ML modules to TAL object files. However the problem with this approach is that it leads to two different models of linking:

1. At the source language level, linking is based on applying parameterized modules. Higher-order parameterized modules may be useful for separate compilation [16,15,18,24,19], but there are still problems with supporting recursive modules [8] (as are found in Java and C).
2. At the assembly language level, linking is based on a type-safe version of the Unix `ld` command. Circular imports present no problem at this level, but much of the sophistication of the type system for ML modules is lost. This is unfortunate, since there are many lessons to be learned from ML that could fruitfully be applied to develop rich linking operations for languages such as Java.

This article describes Typed Module Assembly Language (TMAL), an extension of TAL with run-time support for loading, linking and running modules. Work on dynamic linking has focussed on class loading in the Java virtual machine [21]. Java has the problem of a weak MIL. On the other hand, ML has a powerful MIL but no support for dynamic linking. The current work was originally motivated by the desire to bridge this gap. TMAL pursues a model of linking that is closer to the MTAL approach than the ML approach, because it is closer to the form of linking used by popular languages such as Java. TMAL enriches the MTAL approach in several ways, drawing lessons from the ML experience, but also limiting the ML approach in some ways that are not limiting for Java applications, but do avoid problems with extending ML modules to support Java.

We make the following contributions to TAL:

1. We enrich TAL with coercive interface matching, which allows a module to be coerced to an expected type that makes some fields of the module "private." This is present in for example the ML module system, but not in MTAL. On the other hand, ML does not provide the same linking primitives as MTAL.
2. We enrich TAL with support for shared libraries. This is supported in the ML module language but not in MTAL. On the other hand, ML does not

[1] Glew and Morrisett refer to "dynamic linking" as the process of linking an executable with libraries when it is first invoked, while they refer to "dynamic loading" as the linking and loading of libraries at an arbitrary point during execution. Our use of the generic term *dynamic linking* is meant in the latter sense. We provide separate operations for "loading" a module (reflecting it from the core language to the module language) and for "linking" (linking together two modules).

support recursive modules, which are present in MTAL and which complicate the definition of shared libraries.
3. We extend TAL with primitives for type-safe dynamic linking. Our approach resolves some open problems with dynamic linking and abstract data types. In particular, because types exported by modules are named but opaque (wholly or partially), it is not possible for run-time type checking to discern the underlying representation type for an abstract type.

TMAL arises out of work on a high-level module language, incorporating ideas from ML but with application to languages such as Java, including support for recursive DLLs and shared libraries [12]. It can be viewed as a demonstration of how the semantics of that module language can be incorporated into typed assembly language. A central aspect of this scheme is the proper treatment of shared libraries, an important issue that is addressed in the ML module language but not in more low-level typed module languages [7,14]. A related issue is a *phase distinction* in module languages[2], between the link-time phase of a module and the run-time phase of a module. The link-time phase is characterized by the application of linking operations to combine a library with other libraries. The run-time phase is initiated by the execution of the initialization code for a library, during or after which the definitions in the library are available to a running client. In static linking the client is always another software component with which the library is linked. With dynamic linking, the client is the running program that loads and initializes the library. This issue is not often explicitly acknowledged in the literature. In TMAL it is recognized by an explicit initialization operation, `dlopen`, that provides the demarcation point between these two phases in the lifetime of a module.

In Sect. 2 we give a brief review of TAL and MTAL. In Sect. 3 we reconsider the approach used in MTAL to represent abstract types that are exported by typed object files, and in particular how type equality and type definitions are handled. In Sect. 4 we give an overview of TMAL. The next four sections describe the operations of TMAL in more detail. In Sect. 5 we describe TMAL's support for coercive interface matching. In Sect. 6 we describe how types and values can be dynamically obtained from a module in TMAL. In Sect. 7 we describe how shared libraries can be constructed in TMAL. In Sect. 8 we describe how DLLs are loaded in a type-safe manner in TMAL. Finally Sect. 10 provides our conclusions.

For reasons of space, we are unable to provide a comprehensive discussion of the various issues in module type systems that motivate some of the design choices presented here. The reader desirous of more contextual discussion than that presented here, is invited to consult [12]. The TMAL type system is based on the linking calculus λ^{link}, itself intended as a compilation target language

[2] This should not be confused with the phase distinction between compile-time and run-time explicated by Harper et al [16]. The phase distinction between link-time and run-time does not exist in the latter calculus, because it translates module-level linking (functor application) to core language operations (function application and generic instantiation).

for a more high-level module language λ^{mod}, described in [12]. The correctness properties of λ^{link} carry over to TMAL. There may be some interest in verifying a translation from λ^{link} to TMAL.

2 Modular Typed Assembly Language

In this section, we review Typed Assembly Language (TAL) and Modular Typed Assembly Language (MTAL). This review is largely based on descriptions in the literature [28,10,14]. The syntax of MTAL is given in Fig. 1. Typed Assembly Language can be explained as the result of carrying types in a high-level language through the compilation process, all the way to the final output of assembly language in the backend. Starting with a high-level language, say with procedures

$$
\begin{array}{rcl}
K \in \text{Kind} & ::= & ty \mid (K_1 \rightarrow K_2) \\
A, B \in \text{Type Cons} & ::= & t \mid int \mid \forall[t_1, \ldots, t_m]\Gamma \mid \\
 & & \langle A_1^{j_1}, \ldots, A_k^{j_k} \rangle \\
j \in \text{Initialization Flag} & ::= & 0 \mid 1 \\
\Phi \in \text{Type Heap Interface} & ::= & \{t_1 : K_1, \ldots, t_k : K_k\} \\
\Psi \in \text{Value Heap Interface} & ::= & \{x_1 : A_1, \ldots, x_k : A_k\} \\
\Gamma \in \text{Register File Type} & ::= & \{r_1 : A_1, \ldots, r_k : A_k\} \\
\Delta \in \text{Type Var Context} & ::= & \{t_1 : K_1, \ldots, t_k : K_k\} \\
 & & \\
h \in \text{Heap Value} & ::= & \mathtt{code}[t_1, \ldots, t_m]\Gamma.I \mid \langle w_1, \ldots, w_k \rangle \\
r \in \text{Register Name} & ::= & \mathtt{r0}, \mathtt{r1}, \ldots \\
w \in \text{Word Value} & ::= & n \mid x \mid w[A_1, \ldots, A_k] \mid \ldots \\
v \in \text{Small Value} & ::= & w \mid r \\
TH \in \text{Type Heap} & ::= & \{t_1 \mapsto A_1, \ldots, t_k \mapsto A_k\} \\
VH \in \text{Value Heap} & ::= & \{x_1 \mapsto h_1, \ldots, x_k \mapsto h_k\} \\
R \in \text{Register File} & ::= & \{r_1 \mapsto w_1, \ldots, r_k \mapsto w_k\} \\
I \in \text{Instruction Sequence} & ::= & i_1; \ldots; i_k \\
i \in \text{Instruction} & ::= & \mathtt{add}\ r_1, r_2, v \mid \mathtt{malloc}\ r[\overline{A}] \mid \mathtt{jmp}\ v \mid \ldots \\
 & & \\
Int \in \text{Interface} & ::= & (\Phi, \Psi) \\
O \in \text{Object File} & ::= & [Int_I \Rightarrow (TH, VH) : Int_E] \\
E \in \text{Executable} & ::= & (TH, VH, x) \\
P \in \text{Program State} & ::= & (TH, VH, R, I)
\end{array}
$$

Fig. 1. Syntax of MTAL

and records, programs are translated to an assembly language where procedures have been translated to code segments (with code for environment-handling) and records have been translated to heap blocks. Thus for example the procedure definition:

```
int fact (int x) {
   int y = 1;
   while (x != 0) y = (x--) * y;
   return y;
}
```

is translated to the code segment:

```
fact: code[]{a0:int,ra:∀[]{v0:int}}.
      mov   v0,1
      jmp   loop
loop: code[]{a0:int,v0:int,ra:∀[]{v0:int}}.
      bz    a0,ra
      mul   v0,a0,v0
      sub   a0,a0,1
      jmp   loop
```

The register `ra` is the continuation or return address register, pointing to the code to be executed upon return. The `fact` procedure expects an integer in the argument register `a0`, and returns to its caller with an integer in the value return register `v0`. We use MIPS gcc calling conventions to name the registers in examples.

In general heap values h have the form:

1. A code segment $\texttt{code}[t_1,\ldots,t_m]\Gamma.I$, with register file type $\Gamma = \{r_1 : A_1,\ldots,r_n : A_n\}$. This is a code segment parameterized over m type variables $t_1,\ldots,t_m$ and expecting its n arguments in the argument registers $r_1,\ldots,r_n$. The types of the values in the argument registers are specified in the register file type. I is the sequence of assembly instructions for the code sequence. This segment has the code type $\forall[t_1,\ldots,t_m]\Gamma$.
2. A heap block $\langle w_1,\ldots,w_k\rangle$ where the k values $w_1,\ldots,w_k$ are word values. Such a heap block has a heap block type $\langle A_1^{j_1},\ldots,A_k^{j_k}\rangle$, where each $j_h \in \{0,1\}$ indicates if the hth slot has been initialized. Note that the tuple type $\langle A_1^{j_1},\ldots,A_k^{j_k}\rangle$ should not be confused with tuples of types; we do not therefore have tuple kinds, although they could be added straightforwardly.

Parametric polymorphism is used in an essential way to abstract over the call stack in typing a procedure definition. For example the most general definition of `fact` is:

```
fact: code[EnvT]{a0:int,sp:EnvT,ra:∀[]{v0:int,sp:EnvT}}. ...
```

where the `sp` register points to the environment of the calling procedure. The type parameter `EnvT` ensures that the continuation is passed the calling procedure's environment upon return.

An operational semantics is specified using program states of the form (VH, R, I), where

1. $VH = \{\overline{x \mapsto h}\}$ is a value heap, a mapping from labels to heap values h;
2. $R = \{\overline{r \mapsto h}\}$ is a register file, a mapping from register names to values; and
3. I is a sequence of typed assembly instructions.

Program states are typed using register file types $\Gamma = \{\overline{r : A}\}$ and heap types $\Psi = \{\overline{x : A}\}$, where the latter maps from labels to types. The heap contents are unordered and may contain circular references.

Modular TAL (MTAL) extends these concepts to object files for independent compilation and type-safe linking. An untyped object file imports some values and exports some values, identified by labels pointing into the object file heap. A MTAL object file places types on the imported and exported labels. Furthermore, to support the exportation of abstract data types, an MTAL object file imports and exports types and type operators, identified by labels pointing into a type heap in the object file. An object file O in MTAL has the form

$$[(\Phi_I, \Psi_I) \Rightarrow (TH, VH) : (\Phi_E, \Psi_E)]$$

where Φ_I and Φ_E are type interfaces mapping labels to kinds, Ψ_I and Ψ_E are value interfaces mapping labels to types, $TH = \{\overline{t \mapsto A}\}$ is a type heap mapping labels to type and type operator definitions and $VH = \{\overline{x \mapsto h}\}$ is a value heap mapping labels to initial values. Φ_I and Ψ_I provide the interfaces for imported types and values, while Φ_E and Ψ_E provide the interfaces for exported types and values. An interface is a pair $Int = (\Phi, \Psi)$ of type and value heap interfaces.

There are three operations in the MTAL module language:

1. Linking: O_1 `link` $O_2 \rightsquigarrow O$ combines the object files O_1 and O_2 into the single object file O. Imports in O_1 and O_2 may be resolved during linking. Interface checking ensures that resolved imports have the correct type.
2. Executable formation: $(O, x) \overset{\text{prg}}{\rightsquigarrow} E$ identifies the label for executing the code of the object file. Type-checking ensures that this label is bound in the value heap, and that all imports have been resolved.
3. Execution of an executable: $E \overset{\text{exec}}{\rightsquigarrow} P$ produces a program state of the operational semantics from an executable. Program states are extended to include a type heap, and have the form (TH, VH, R, I).

3 Type Heap Reconsidered

Before giving a description of TMAL, it is useful to explain how our treatment of the type heap and type identity differs from that of MTAL. In MTAL there are two views of a type:

1. Within an object file, a type exported by that object file is completely transparent. The definition of a type label is given by its binding in the type heap, TH. Because the type heap may contain circular bindings, there are word

value operations $\texttt{unroll}(w)$ and $\texttt{roll}^t(w)$ that unfold and fold the definition of a type label in the type of w, respectively. For example if a file system module defines a file abstract type t as $\langle \texttt{int}^1, \texttt{int}^1 \rangle$, and w is a word value with this type, then $\texttt{roll}^t(w)$ gives a word value with type t, that is with the concrete type folded to the defined type. This means that all types defined in object files are datatypes. In other words, there is no equality theory for implicitly ununfolding the definitions of type identifiers exported by object files, so type equivalence for such type identifiers is based on name equivalence rather than structural equivalence.

2. Outside of an object file, a type exported by that object file may be transparent or opaque. The interface only provides the kind, and the type heap is only visible within the module. Hicks et al [9] use a module system similar to MTAL, except that they also allow an object file to export some of its type definitions, so types may be made transparent to clients.

The advantage of requiring all defined types to be datatypes is that recursive types are assured to be iso-recursive types[3], thus greatly simplifying the problem of type-checking. The problem with this approach is that it does not adequately handle type sharing for shared libraries. This is explained in more detail in [12]. Consider for example the following Objective ML code [31]:

```
module type S = sig type t; val x:t end
module S1 : S = struct type t = C; val x = C end
module S2 : (S where type t = S1.t) = S1
if true then S1.x else S2.x
```

The module `S1` defines a datatype `t` with single constructor `C`, and binds the field `x` to this constructor. The last conditional type-checks because `S2.x` has type `S2.t`, and the type of `S2` includes the constraint `t=S1.t`, which is also the type of `S1.x`. The structure `S1` is an example of a *shared library*, in the sense that the identity of its (abstract) type component `S1.t` is shared with `S2.t`. The datatype restriction, on the other hand, requires the insertion of marshalling and unmarshalling code at the interface of a shared library, severely curtailing its usability. An example is provided in [12].

It is informally mentioned in the description of MTAL that the implementation includes singleton kinds to expose type definitions to clients of object files. However this is not formalized in the type system and therefore several important issues are left unresolved. For example it is not hard, using singleton kinds, to define two mutually recursive types in separate object files, and linking those files then results in equ-recursive types. This problem can be avoided by only allowing singleton kinds to contain type labels, where the definitions remain encapsulated in the type heap in the object file. In terms of the type

[3] Harper, Crary and Puri [8] make the distinction between *iso-recursive* and *equ-recursive* types. The latter require an equality theory for types that includes a rule for implicitly unrolling a recursive type. The former do not require this equality, and instead rely on operations in the language for explicitly folding and unfolding recursive types.

system presented here, this amounts to only allowing type sharing constraints in the interface, and not allowing type definitions to be exposed.

In our type system we allow both exposure of type definitions, and type sharing, to be expressed in module interfaces. This is done without allowing equ-recursive types in the type system. This is done by separating these two uses of type information in the interface:

1. Exposure of type definitions is expressed using *box kinds*. Box kinds differ from singleton kinds in the following way: whereas singleton kinds allow implicit equality of a type identifier with the type in its singleton kind, box kinds require explicit coercions in the term language between a type identifier and the type in its box kind.
2. Type sharing is expressed using *type sharing constraints*. The type system includes an equality theory that is merely the congruence closure of an equality between type identifiers defined by a context of type sharing constraints. Since equality is only between identifiers, there is no problem with analysing recursive constraints. This is particularly important when we consider dynamic type-checking of DLLs.

TMAL replaces the $\mathtt{roll}^t$ and `unroll` operations of MTAL, with operations for constructing and deconstructing values of types with box kind:

	Introduction	Elimination
MTAL Expression	$\mathtt{roll}^t(w)$	$\mathtt{unroll}(w)$
MTAL Side-Condition	$w : A,\ TH(t) = A$	$w : t,\ TH(t) = A$
TMAL Expression	$\mathtt{fold}_t(w)$	$\mathtt{unfold}_t(w)$
TMAL Side-Condition	$t : \boxtimes A,\ w : A$	$t : \boxtimes A,\ w : t$

Because the TMAL operations are typed independently of the type heap, box kinds can be used to expose type definitions in the interface of an object file. In contrast with singleton kinds, because explicit coercions are required between a type with box kind and the type in its kind, recursive types are guaranteed to be iso-recursive types.

4 Typed Module Assembly Language

Fig. 2 provides the syntax of Typed Module Assembly Language. In comparison with MTAL, the major changes in module interfaces are:

1. We enrich kinds with box kinds $\boxtimes A$. For simplicity we only consider simple types in this account. Box kinds generalize to type operators with some care [12].
2. We enrich import and export interfaces *Int* with a type sharing context Ξ. This is a set of equality constraints between type identifiers.

$$
\begin{array}{rcl}
K \in \text{Kind} & ::= & ty \mid \boxtimes A \\
A, B \in \text{Type Cons} & ::= & t \mid int \mid \forall[t_1 : K_1, \ldots, t_m : K_m]\Gamma \\
& \mid & \langle A_1^{j_1}, \ldots, A_k^{j_k} \rangle \mid \langle\langle\,\rangle\rangle \mid OT \mid Int \\
j \in \text{Initialization Tag} & ::= & 0 \mid 1 \\
\Phi \in \text{Type Heap Interface} & ::= & \{t_1 :: \mathbf{t_1} : K_1, \ldots, t_k :: \mathbf{t_k} : K_k\} \\
\Psi \in \text{Value Heap Interface} & ::= & \{x :: \mathbf{x}_1 : A_1, \ldots, x :: \mathbf{x}_k : A_k\} \\
\Xi \in \text{Type Sharing Cons} & ::= & \{t_1 \cong t_1' \in K_1, \ldots, t_k \cong t_k' \in K_k\} \\
\Gamma \in \text{Register File Type} & ::= & \{r_1 : A_1, \ldots, r_k : A_k\} \\
\Delta \in \text{Type Var Context} & ::= & \{t_1 : K_1, \ldots, t_k : K_k\} \\
\\
h \in \text{Heap Value} & ::= & \texttt{code}[t_1 : K_1, \ldots, t_m : K_m]\Gamma.I \\
& \mid & \langle w_1, \ldots, w_k \rangle \mid \langle\langle w, OT \rangle\rangle \mid O \mid ST \\
r, r^m, r^s \in \text{Register Name} & ::= & \mathtt{r0}, \mathtt{r1}, \ldots \\
w \in \text{Word Value} & ::= & n \mid x \mid w[A_1, \ldots, A_k] \mid \ldots \\
v \in \text{Small Value} & ::= & w \mid r \\
TH \in \text{Type Heap} & ::= & \{t_1 :: \mathbf{t_1} : K_1\mathcal{B}_1^A, \ldots, t_k :: \mathbf{t_k} : K_k\mathcal{B}_k^A\} \\
\mathcal{B}^A \in \text{Type Binding} & ::= & \triangleq A \quad \text{(Type Definition)} \\
& \mid & \cong t \quad \text{(Shared Type Binding)} \\
VH \in \text{Value Heap} & ::= & \{x_1 :: \mathbf{x_1} : A_1\mathcal{B}_1^e, \ldots, x_k :: \mathbf{x_k} : A_k\mathcal{B}_k^e\} \\
\mathcal{B}^e \in \text{Value Binding} & ::= & \triangleq h \quad \text{(Value Definition)} \\
& \mid & \cong x \quad \text{(Shared Value Binding)} \\
R \in \text{Register File} & ::= & \{r_1 \mapsto w_1, \ldots, r_k \mapsto w_k\} \\
\rho \in \text{Renaming Substitution} & ::= & \{\mathbf{n}_1 \mapsto \mathbf{n}_1', \ldots, \mathbf{n}_k \mapsto \mathbf{n}_k'\} \\
I \in \text{Instruction Sequence} & ::= & i_1; \ldots; i_k \\
i \in \text{Instruction} & ::= & \texttt{add}\ r_1, r_2, v \mid \texttt{malloc}\ r[\overline{A}] \mid \texttt{jmp}\ v \mid \ldots \\
\\
Int \in \text{Interface} & ::= & (\Phi, \Psi, \Xi) \\
OT \in \text{Object File Type} & ::= & [Int_I \Rightarrow Int_E] \\
O \in \text{Object File} & ::= & [Int_I \Rightarrow (TH, VH) : Int_E] \\
ST \in \text{Symbol Table} & ::= & \{\overline{\mathbf{t}} \mapsto \overline{t},\ \overline{\mathbf{x}} \mapsto \overline{y}\} \\
P \in \text{Program State} & ::= & (TH, VH, R, I)
\end{array}
$$

Fig. 2. Syntax of TMAL

Purpose	Instruction	Semantics
Linking,	`dllink` r_1^m, r_2^m, r_3^m	Link modules
interface	`dlcoerce` r_1^m, r_2^m, OT	Coerce to interface
matching	`dlrename` r_1^m, r_2^m, ρ	Rename external labels
Dynamic	`dlopen` r^s, r^m	Initialize module
imports	`dlsym_t` $[t : K]r_1^s, r_2^s, \mathbf{t}$	Import type
	`dlsym_v` $r, r^s, \mathbf{x}$	Import value
Shared	`dlsetsym_t` $r_1^m, r_2^m, t, \mathbf{t}$	Set shared type
definitions	`dlsetsym_v` $r_1^m, r_2^m, v, \mathbf{x}$	Set shared value
Dynamic	`dldynamic` r, v, OT	Construct DLL
linking	`dlload` r^m, r_1, r_2, OT	Extract module

Fig. 3. Summary of TMAL instructions

3. To support coercive interface matching, we add external labels to type and value heap interfaces. As explained in the next section, this allows some of the fields in a module to be safely made private, whereas allowing private fields in MTAL leads to the possibility of run-time name clashes.

There are two forms of module values in TMAL:

1. Modules or object files $O \equiv [Int_I \Rightarrow (TH, VH) : Int_E]$. This defines a type heap TH and a value heap VH, that may be linked with other such heaps using the TMAL operations. $Int_I \equiv (\Phi_I, \Psi_I, \Xi_I)$ is the interface of symbols imported by the module, while $Int_E \equiv (\Phi_E, \Psi_E, \Xi_E)$ is the interface of symbols exported to clients of the module.
2. Symbol tables $ST \equiv \{\overline{\mathbf{t}} \mapsto \overline{t}, \overline{\mathbf{x}} \mapsto \overline{x}\}$. A symbol table arises from the initialization of a module. Initializing a module adds its type and value definitions to the type and value heaps, respectively, of the running program. The symbol table provides mappings from the external labels of the module to the heap addresses of its definitions. TMAL provides operations for dynamically importing these addresses into a running program, using a symbol table to perform a run-time lookup based on external labels.

A type heap definition $t :: \mathbf{t} : K\mathcal{B}^A$ has one of two forms:

1. A definition of the form $t :: \mathbf{t} : K \triangleq A$ defines a branded type t with external name $\mathbf{t}$ and definition A. External names are explained in the next section. The most general kind for such a type is $\boxtimes A$, revealing the structure of the type definition. This is a subkind of ty, the kind of simple types that makes type definitions opaque.

2. A definition of the form $t :: \mathbf{t} : K \cong t'$ defines a shared type t that is equated to the type t'. Such a type sharing definition can be exposed in an interface by a type sharing constraint $t \cong t' \in K$.

Similarly a value heap definition $x :: \mathbf{x} : A\mathcal{B}^e$ has one of the two forms $x :: \mathbf{x} : A \triangleq h$ (analogous to a value heap definition $x \mapsto h$ in MTAL) or $x :: \mathbf{x} : A \cong y$ (a value sharing definition). Module initialization transforms a value sharing definition to a value heap definition $x :: \mathbf{x} : A \triangleq h$ by looking up the definition of y in the heap. Initialization may detect circular value sharing definitions, which correspond to values with no clearly defined initial values.

Are first-class modules necessary for dynamic linking? In TMAL, modules are manipulated (loaded, coerced and linked) at run-time. This in itself does not necessarily require modules as first-class values, and indeed TMAL is based on a module language where there is a strict separation between module values and simple values [12]. Nevertheless a critical part of the transition from a high-level language to TAL is closure conversion, where environment slots are allocated for local variables in a procedure, and the contents of the register file are saved to the environment on a procedure call. Since some local variables may be bound to module values, it is therefore necessary in TMAL to make modules into first-class values. For example, the kernel language described in [12] includes a `letmod` construct for binding a local module identifier to a module:

$$\texttt{letmod}\ s = \mathit{Mod}\ \texttt{in}\ \mathit{Expr}$$

where *Mod* is a module language expression and *Expr* a core language expression. Closure conversion then requires that an environment slot be allocated for the free module identifier s, leading to the need for first-class modules.

This potentially has some unpleasant consequences. For example Lillibridge [22] has demonstrated that type-checking is undecidable for a type system with first-class modules. The source of this undecidability is a subtype relation between modules that allows fields to be made private, and allows type definitions to be made opaque. There is no such subtype relation in the core language of TMAL, and therefore no such subtyping for modules. This makes "first-class" modules in TMAL strictly less powerful than general first-class modules. For example with general first-class modules, it is possible for the two arms of a conditional to return modules with different interfaces, by having the result interface contain the intersection of the fields of the two modules. However the weak type system for modules in TMAL is sufficient for the purposes of closure conversion, and avoids the undecidability problems with more general type systems.

Rather than allowing type subsumption for modules, TMAL has a `dlcoerce` instruction for explicitly coercing a module to a required type. This coercion operation requires that the module's type be a subtype of the required type:

$$\begin{array}{rcl} OT \preceq OT' & \iff & OT \equiv [\mathit{Int}_I \Rightarrow \mathit{Int}_E],\ OT' \equiv [\mathit{Int}'_I \Rightarrow \mathit{Int}'_E], \\ & & \mathit{Int}'_I \preceq \mathit{Int}_I \text{ and } \mathit{Int}_E \preceq \mathit{Int}'_E \\ \mathit{Int} \preceq \mathit{Int}' & \iff & \mathit{Int} \equiv (\Phi, \Psi, \Xi),\ \mathit{Int}' \equiv (\Phi', \Psi', \Xi'), \end{array}$$

$$\Phi \leq \Phi',\ \Psi \leq \Psi',\ \text{and}\ \Xi\ \text{entails}\ \Xi'$$

$$\Phi \leq \Phi' \iff \Phi \equiv \{\overline{t_k :: \mathbf{t_k} : K_k}\},\ \Phi' \equiv \{\overline{t_m :: \mathbf{t_m} : K_m}\},\ k \geq m,\ \overline{K_m} \leq \overline{K'_m}$$

$$\Psi \leq \Psi' \iff \Psi \equiv \{\overline{x_k :: \mathbf{x_k} : A_k}\},\ \Psi' \equiv \{\overline{x_m :: \mathbf{x_m} : A_m}\},\ k \geq m,\ \overline{A_m} = \overline{A'_m}$$

So interface containment reduces to kind containment (where the only containments are of the form $\boxtimes A \leq ty$) and equality between types. The latter equality relation includes entailment based on sharing constraints in the context. The latter constraints can only relate type identifiers, so the equality relation includes rules for forming the congruence closure of these equalities. Because sharing constraints can only relate type identifiers, it is straightforward to extend the language of types with type operators (λ-abstraction) and β-conversion of types.

The type formation rules for modules (object files) and symbol tables are provided in App. A. These operations are discussed in Sect. 5–8, and formally specified in App. B.

5 Coercive Interface Matching

MTAL assumes that all field names are globally defined, and interface matching is based on these global field names. Any "implicit" renaming of an identifier requires it to be rewritten globally. There is no notion (as in our approach) of differentiating between external and internal names, with internal names locally bound, and therefore allowing local renaming of these internal names to avoid name clashes during linking. In the MTAL approach, if two modules have fields with the same name, these names are references to the same global symbol, and any renaming of the symbol must be performed in both modules. As a consequence, if fields of an object file are made private in MTAL, there is no way to rename the private fields in order to avoid name clashes when this object file is linked with other object files.

We want to support run-time linking where a library is loaded from disk into the program address space and linked with other libraries. Type safety requires a run-time type check at some point in this scenario. This type check requires that the labels do not admit implicit renaming (such as alpha-conversion in the lambda-calculus). We do not expect that all labels of the loaded library are known, only those labels specified in the expected interface in the run-time type check. Following the MTAL approach, there is the potential for confusion of labels because some of the "hidden" labels in the loaded library may be the same as labels in the libraries it is linked with.

This is the motivation for generalizing labels in type and value heap interfaces to include external names $\mathbf{t}$ and $\mathbf{x}$. Type and value heap interfaces have the form

$$\Phi = \{\overline{t :: \mathbf{t} : K}\}\ \text{and}\ \Psi = \{\overline{x :: \mathbf{x} : A}\}$$

The internal names t and x represent local (type and value) heap addresses. These names admit implicit renaming or alpha-conversion, corresponding to relocating symbols in a heap. The external names $\mathbf{t}$ and $\mathbf{x}$ represent external labels that allow reference to the internal contents of a heap component of a module from outside. To allow fields of a module to be made private, external type and value names in type and value heaps include the special symbol $\star$, the name of a private field. Fields in a module are made private using the `dlcoerce` instruction, that changes the external names of fields made private to $\star$. The private external name $\star$ should never appear in a type or value heap type.

Before the contents of a module can be used by a running program, its heaps must be combined with the program heaps. This combination ensures that the internal labels of the module heaps are distinct from the internal labels in the program heaps.

Following [12], we provide three operations for combining and adapting modules. The choice of these operations is informed by an analogy between module combination and process composition in process algebras such as CCS [25]:

Operation	TMAL	CCS
Linking	`dllink` r_1^m, r_2^m, r_3^m	$(P \mid Q)$
Coercion	`dlcoerce` r_1^m, r_2^m, OT	$(P \setminus x)$
Renaming	`dlrename` r_1^m, r_2^m, ρ	$P[\rho]$

The `dllink` instruction links together two modules, combining the type and value heaps. The modules being linked together are in the source registers r_2^m and r_3^m, and the result of linking is left in the destination register r_1^m. The exports of the resulting module are the union of the exports of the two modules, while the imports are the union of the imports of the linked modules minus any imports that are resolved by linking. To obtain a coherent result, the type rules require that the external labels of the exports of the two linked modules are distinct. To maintain this restriction, the external labels of a module must always be visible in the type of the module. The linking operation also requires that the internal labels of the exports of the modules be distinct. Since internal names are bound within a module, they can be renamed to avoid name clashes when merging the fields of the modules being linked. In a concrete implementation, this renaming is handled straightforwardly by relocating the internal addresses of two object files that are linked together.

The `dlcoerce` instruction is necessary because of the absence of a subsumption rule based on interface containment for modules. This latter subsumption rule is not allowable because of the requirement that the external labels of a module must always be visible in its type. The coercion operation performs a run-time adaptation of a module, removing some of its external labels. The corresponding definitions are no longer visible to external clients of the module, but are still accessible via their internal labels to other definitions within the module. The source module is in register r_2^m, while the result of coercion is left in the destination register r_1^m. The type to which the module is coerced is specified by the object file type OT. This type annotation is mostly only for type-checking, and can be removed before execution. The part of the annotation that must be preserved during execution is the association between external names and internal names; TMAL includes instructions for looking up a field in an initialized module based on its external name.

The **dlrename** instruction is a second operation for coercive interface matching, and renames some of the external labels in a label. A renaming substitution ρ is an injective mapping from external labels to external labels. Since external names are used at run-time, this renaming substitution must be applied at run-time.

6 Dynamic Imports

The instructions given in the previous section operate on values at the module language level. At the heart of the TMAL approach are the instructions that connect the module language level to the core language level. In the λ^{mod} module language described in [12], this connection is provided by an `init` operation that initializes a module and introduces its definitions into a local scope in a core language program. In TMAL the `init` operation is realized by three instructions, for initializing a module and for importing its definitions into the scope of a running thread:

Operation	TMAL
Initialize module	`dlopen` r^s, r^m
Import type	`dlsym_t` $[t : K] r^s_1, r^s_2, \mathtt{t}$
Import value	`dlsym_v` $r, r^s, \mathbf{x}$

These operations allow a program to import some of the symbols from a DLL, using the external labels of a DLL to access its definitions.

The **dlopen** instruction expects a pointer to a module in register r^m. The instruction initializes the module, addings its type and heap bindings to the program heaps, and building a symbol table with mappings from the module fields to their bindings in the program heaps. A pointer to this symbol table is left in register r^s.

The **dlsym_t** instruction imports a type definition into the local context of the current thread, while the **dlsym_v** instruction imports a value definition. The **dlsym_t** operation imports a type symbol from a DLL into a register, using the external label of the type symbol and the symbol table of the DLL to map to the internal label. Note that the internal label cannot be known statically; the internal label is chosen at the point where the DLL is initialized and its value definitions are added to the program's value heap. This is in contrast with MTAL, where heap locations are referenced by globally bound internal names, and where renaming to avoid name clashes is not possible. In TMAL, the internal label is chosen so that there is no clash with the labels already given to program heap contents. Since the complete contents of the program heap are not known until run-time, there is no way to know the internal label during type-checking.

The dlsym_t instruction expects a pointer to a pointer to a symbol table in register r_2^s, and specifies the external name **t** of the type symbol to be imported in the local thread address space. The instruction binds the type parameter t in subsequent instructions to the type heap address corresponding to this external name. The symbol table type must be modified so that references to the global heap address are rebound to this local type parameter, for type-checking subsequent importations of definitions that rely on this type symbol. Register r_1^s is left with a pointer to a symbol table of this modified type.

The dlsym_v operation imports (the heap address of) a value definition from a DLL into a register, using the external label of the value definition and the symbol table of the DLL to map to the internal label. The external name **x** of the definition is specified in the instruction, and the instruction leaves the value heap address of the definition in the value register r.

```
// Assume s1 points to loaded file system module
dlopen    s2,s1               // Initialize module
dlsym_t   [FileT:ty] s3,s2,File // Import file type
dlsym_v   s4,s3,open          // Import file open operation
mov       a0,file_name        // Load file name
mov       ra,retpt[FileT]     // Load continuation
jmp       s4[EnvT]            // Jump to file open operation

retpt:      code[FileT]{v0:FileT,sp:EnvT} ...
file_name: "/etc/passwd"
```

Fig. 4. Example of dynamic imports

Fig. 4 gives an example of the use of these operations. Assuming the s1 register points to a module, the dlopen instruction initializes that module, addings its type and value heap definitions to those of the running program. The result of initialization is a pointer, in the s2 register, to a symbol table mapping from the external labels of the module to the addresses of its definitions in the program heaps.

The important proviso in the dlsym_v operation is that none of the free type variables in the type of a value definition are bound by the type heap definitions addressed by the symbol table. For example, recalling the example in Fig. 4, assume that the symbol table resulting from initializing the file system module has type:

```
type File::File : ty
val open::open :
    ∀[EnvT:ty]{a0:String,sp:EnvT,ra:∀[]{v0:File,sp:EnvT}
```

The abstract file type `File` occurs free in the type of the `open` operation. Therefore the `dlsym_v` instruction cannot import this definition immediately. The reason is that the register file type resulting from this importation would have no binding for the type identifier `File` in the type of the `v0` register.

In order to import the `open` operation, the type identifier `File` that occurs free in its type must first be imported from the DLL. This is done using the `dlsym_t` operation. In the example in Fig. 4, the `dlsym_t` instruction binds a local type identifier `FileT` to the abstract type `File` defined by the DLL. The `s3` register is bound to a new symbol table with type:

```
val open::open :
    ∀[EnvT:ty]{a0:String,sp:EnvT,ra:∀[]{v0:[FileT],sp:EnvT}
```

The abstract file type in the type of the `open` operation has been relocated to a type bound in the local context of the current thread, therefore it is now possible to import the `open` definition from the DLL.

7 Shared Libraries

Heaps in modules may contain shared type bindings $t :: \mathbf{t} : K \cong t'$ and shared value bindings $x :: \mathbf{x} : A \cong y$. If all linking is performed before a program runs, then shared bindings are unnecessary. However shared bindings become crucial in an environment where modules are initialized at run-time.

For example, consider a module implementing a network protocol. This implementation requires some operations and types that are only provided by the operating system. Module linking can be used to combine these modules into a single module implementing the operating system with that protocol:

```
// Assume s1 points to loaded OS module
// Assume s2 points to loaded protocol module
dllink   s3,s1,s2             // Link OS, protocol modules
dlopen   s4,s3                // Initialize module
dlsym_t  [Conn:ty] s5,s4,Conn // Import connection type
dlsym_v  s6,s5,open           // Import conn open operation
```

However there is a difficulty with this approach: the operating system will have already been initialized when the program runs. In fact the operating system is really the first module to be initialized, and a running program is just another module that has been loaded and initialized by code defined in the operating system module.

Similar remarks apply to access to OS operations from a process. The process must somehow have access to labels into the OS type and value heaps[4], but it is unrealistic to expect a program to be linked with its own copy of the OS module

[4] As mentioned in Sect. 1, approaches such as typed assembly language should be regarded as an alternative to current heavyweight protection mechanisms such as hardware-based memory protection and the use of library stubs to trap to the OS.

before execution can begin. The OS is one example of a shared library, a library that is loaded and initialized once, and that is subsequently available to other libraries as they are loaded.

The following instructions allow a program to construct a shared library:

Operation	TMAL
Set shared type	dlsetsym_t $r_1^m, r_2^m, t,$ **t**
Set shared value	dlsetsym_v $r_1^m, r_2^m, r,$ **x**

The dlsetsym_t instruction allows a reference to a type to be added to the export list of a module, while dlsetsym_v instruction allows a reference to a value to be added. These are not the only way that shared value and heap definitions can be constructed. For example, the initial value heap in a module may contain the definition of another module (manipulated by the parent module at run-time) that has aliases for value and type bindings, where the child module definitions that are shared are bound in the parent module heaps, or are imported or exported by the child module. However the aforesaid instructions are the only way to introduce aliases into a module, for shared bindings that are not available until run-time. For example, they are the only way to add bindings for OS types and operations into a module that requires those OS definitions. Once such a shared library has been constructed, the dllink instruction allows it to be linked with other modules.

The dlsetsym_t instruction expects a pointer to a module in register r_2^m, and a pointer into the type heap in type "register" t. The module should import a type definition with external label **t** and with a kind compatible with t. The instruction moves the type field with label **t** from the import list of the module to the export list, binding to the field to the type heap pointer given by t, and the resulting module is given in register r_1^m.

The dlsetsym_v instruction expects a pointer to a module in register r_2^m, and a heap address in register r. The field labelled with **x** in the module is moved from the import list to the export list, bound to the value heap pointer in r, and a pointer to the resulting module is left in register r_1^m.

Returning to the example above of a protocol module, suppose that this module requires a type ProtId of protocol identifiers and an operation deliver from the OS. The latter operation is used by this protocol module to deliver a protocol data unit to the next protocol above it in the protocol stack.

```
// Assume s1 points to initialized OS module
// Assume s2 points to loaded protocol module (PM)
dlsym_t     [ProtId:ty] s1,s1,ProtId  // Import prot id type
dlsym_v     s3,s1,deliver          // Import deliver operation
dlsetsym_t  s2,s2,ProtId,ProtId // Export protocol id to PM
dlsetsym_v  s2,s2,s3,deliver       // Export deliver to PM
dlopen      s4,s2                  // Initialize PM
```

Alternatively, if the code for initializing the protocol module is in the OS itself, then this code can be defined as:

```
// Assume s2 points to loaded protocol module (PM)
dlsetsym_t  s2,s2,ProtId,ProtId   // Export protocol id to PM
dlsetsym_v  s2,s2,deliver,deliver // Export deliver to PM
dlopen      s4,s2                 // Initialize PM
```

where `ProtId` and `deliver` are direct references into the type and value heaps, respectively, in the module implementing the OS.

For example, considering the example above of assigning the `ProtId` and `deliver` fields of a protocol module, assume that the protocol module has type:

```
import type ProtId::ProtId
import val deliver::deliver : ∀[EnvT]{a0:ProtId,...}
export type Conn::Conn
export val open::open : ∀[EnvT]{a0:String,...}
```

Then setting the `ProtId` field with the `ProtId` type defined in the OS module results in a module with type:

```
export type ProtId1::ProtId
import val deliver::deliver : ∀[EnvT]{a0:ProtId1,...}
export type Conn::Conn
export val open::open : ∀[EnvT]{a0:String,...}
sharing type ProtId1 ≅ ProtId
```

In this case the internal type name `ProtId1` is a renaming of the internal name for the type of protocol identifiers, so as to avoid a name clash with the internal type name `ProdId` in the OS module. If the OS module has a value heap label `deliver` with type

$$\forall\texttt{[EnvT]}\{\texttt{a0:ProtId,...}\}$$

then the type sharing constraint allows this type to be equated with the type of the `deliver` heap label in the protocol module. This allows the `dlsetsym_v` instruction to be used to assign this value field.

8 Dynamic Loading

The final set of instructions are used to attach run-time type information to a DLL. This type information is used in a run-time type check, to ensure that a DLL that is loaded from disk or from the network has the required module type. There is an instruction `dldynamic` for bundling a value with a type description, and another instruction `dlload` for checking that a DLL has a specified type.

Operation	TMAL
Construct DLL	`dldynamic` r, v, OT
Extract module	`dlload` r^m, r_1, r_2, OT

The type expression $\langle\langle\ \rangle\rangle$ denotes the type of a DLL. The `dldynamic` instruction associates a type descriptor OT with the heap address of a module in a DLL value $\langle\langle w, OT\rangle\rangle$, of DLL type. To be completely accurate, object files should be stripped of unnecessary type information before run-time. Then the only places where type information is required are (a) the external labels of import and export lists (since these labels are used by various instructions to look up fields in modules and symbol tables, and (b) in the `dldynamic` and `dlload` instructions above, and DLL values. We forgoe specifying this type-erasure semantics for lack of space.

The `dlload` instruction extracts a module from a DLL. This instruction also requires the value representation of a module type, the type that is expected of the module in the DLL. The instruction performs a run-time interface containment check, and if this succeeds it coerces the module in the DLL to the required type. If the interface check fails, control transfers to the failure continuation in register r_2.

The interface check includes a check for entailment of type sharing constraints. The simple form of type sharing constraints, only relating type identifiers, and the fact that the bindings in the type heap are opaque, facilitate this entailment check. The fact that type heap bindings are opaque also has the benefit that the dynamic type check cannot violate encapsulation of abstract types; this is explained in more detail in [12].

9 Related Work

There has been a great deal of work on the semantics of module interconnection languages, particularly in the context of the ML module system [16,15,18,19, 33]. The notion of separating external and internal field names, with the latter allowing renaming to avoid name clashes, originated with Harper and Lillibridge [15]. A related idea is used by Riecke and Stone to allow fields of an object to be made private, and the object then extended with a field with the same external name. Similar notions of internal and external names appear in the module calculi of Ancona and Zucca [4] and Wells and Vestergaard [38].

Cardelli [7] gives a semantics for Unix-style linking in terms of a simple λ-calculus, ensuring that all symbols in a program are resolved before it is executed. Flatt and Felleisen [13] and Glew and Morrisett [14] extend this work to consider typed module contents and circular import dependencies. It is not clear what the type of a module is in these approaches (linking simply resolves imports against exports in a type-safe way). Glew and Morrisett do not support shared libraries (type sharing) or dynamic linking. Flatt and Felleisen allow dynamic linking of units. However the *invoke* operation for initializing a unit returns a single core language value; there is no other way for a program to access the contents of a unit. The *invoke* operation takes as arguments types and values from the running program that can be provided as imports to a library before initialization. So there are really two linking operations with units: the linking operation for merging units and the more limited linking that is implicitly part of the semantics of initialization. Our approach provides a single linking operation, and addresses the problem of sharing type (and value) identity that is not considered by these other approaches. In our system, the *invoke* operation of units would translate into a sequence of `dlsetsym_t` and `dlsetsym_v` instructions, to build the imports for the unit, followed by a `dlopen` instruction to initialize the unit, followed by a `dlsym_v` instruction to retrieve the single value returned by unit initialization.

Crary et al [8] give an explanation of recursive modules in terms of the structure calculus [16]. Their work is predicated on the assumption that module linking is based on functor instantiation, and phase-splitting allows this to be transformed to core-language function application. As discussed in [12], it is difficult to generalize this model of linking to the kinds of module operations we consider.

Work on dynamic linking in ML has focused on dynamic types [2,20,1,34,11]. With these approaches a dynamic value tags a value with a runtime type tag, of type *Dynamic*. This is similar to our approach to dynamic linking, but extended to modules rather than simple values, as a way of reifying modules into the core language.

A perennial problem with dynamics is that they violate encapsulation, in the sense that the underlying representation type of a value with abstract type can be exposed, by first bundling the value as a dynamic and then using runtime type checks to examine the representation type. This is an artifact of the fact that types are bound at runtime using beta-reduction. As mentioned in Sect. 8, our approach to DLLs avoids this problem, because the bindings in the type heap remain opaque during program execution. A similar approach is possible in the system of Hicks et al [9,17]

Russo [32] considers an approach to adding first-class modules to ML, based on converting module values to core language values and back again. Explicit type annotations for modules ensure there are no unpleasant interactions with type inference. Russo avoids the undecidability of type-checking with first-class modules by omitting type subsumption for modules converted to core language values. This is similar to our approach to ensuring decidability with first-class modules. Our reflective treatment of DLLs is different from Russo's treatment of first-class modules. A module reified into the core language in Russo's approach retains its type, though reified to a core language type. In contrast, our reification operation (for building a DLL) masks the type entirely, and there must then be a reflection operation (with a dynamic type check) that extracts a module from a DLL. Dynamic typing is not necessary with Russo's approach, since his purpose is not to provide DLLs.

Ancona and Zucca [4], building on earlier work in mixin modules [3], provide a primitive calculus of modules that supports circular dependencies. Types are restricted to branded types, that is, types where equivalence is based on name equivalence rather than structural equivalence. They do not consider dynamic linking or shared libraries (and the resulting issues with recursive type constraints).

Wells and Vestergaard [38] present a calculus for equational reasoning about first-class modules. They do not place any restrictions on circular import dependencies (including dependencies between value components), allowing circular definitions that lazily unwind. They verify strong normalization and confluence for their calculus, relying on a lazy reduction semantics. They do not consider typing aspects of their calculus. So for example they do not consider the problem of equ-recursive versus iso-recursive types, and they provide no support for shared libraries. Finally as with Russo's work there is no consideration of narrowing a DLL to a specific interface, an important practical facility for dynamic linking.

Crary, Hicks and Weirich [9,17] extend TAL with primitive operations for building type-safe DLLs, on top of which more expressive dynamic linking mechanisms can be constructed. For example they are able to provide a type-safe implementation of the Unix dynamic linking API, as well as an implementation of units. Their approach amounts to extending the TAL kernel with type-safe checked casting [37]. Although their approach is type-safe, it is also more low-level than the approach described here, and so some errors that are caught statically in our type system are only caught dynamically by checked casting in their approach. The single type failure point in our calculus is the `dlload` operation, that reflects a DLL from the core language into the module language. The difference is really one of level; their approach could for example be the basis for an implementation of TMAL.

The module type system underlying that of Crary et al is MTAL, and therefore it shares the limitations of MTAL: the absence of coercive interface matching, and the absence of sharing. There are no operations for linking modules together at run-time, rather modules are loaded into a running program and their imports resolved against bindings in the global program heaps. Crary et al allow a module's contents to be accessed before all of its imports have been resolved, allowing "lazy" resolution. In our approach a continuation can specify (as a module) the definitions it requires, and the continuation argument can be linked with other modules. To ensure that a module is initialized (opened) no more than once, a module cache can be implemented: the first time a module is initialized, a shared library is constructed (using `dlsetsym_t` and `dlsetsym_v`) with the same interface, and this shared library saved in the cache with the same module name used to load the original module. Subsequent searches for this library will find the cached version, and it can be used for example to resolve the imports of subsequent DLLs. In this way a form of "lazy loading" as found in Java class loaders can be implemented on top of our module system.

10 Conclusions

We have described Typed Module Assembly Language (TMAL), an extension of typed assembly language with instructions for manipulating modules at run-time. These instructions include support for coercive interface matching, dynamically importing definitions from a library, constructing shared libraries, and using DLLs in a type-safe manner. A possible application of these mechanisms is in component-based programming environments, as demonstrated by commercial platforms based on COM or Java. The mechanisms described here can be used to enrich such environments with flexible but type-safe operations for interconnecting modules under program control.

It is plausible that this is not the final word on the choice of instruction set for TMAL. Although the instructions for dynamic imports and shared libraries are fairly RISC-y, this is not true of the `dllink`, `dlcoerce` and `dlrename` instructions, nor is it true of the `dlload` and `dldynamic` instructions. We are considering how these instructions could be decomposed into simpler instructions, to weaken the atomicity requirements of the current instruction set.

Acknowledgements. Thanks to Michael Hicks and J. Gregory Morrisett for helpful discussions. Thanks to the anonymous reviewers for their excellent feedback, comments and suggestions for improvement.

References

1. Martin Abadi, Luca Cardeli, Benjamin Pierce, and Didier Remy. Dynamic typing in polymorphic languages. In Peter Lee, editor, *Proceedings of the ACM SIGPLAN Workshop on ML and its Applications*, San Francisco, California, June 1992. Carnegie-Mellon University Technical Report CMU-CS-93-105.
2. Martin Abadi, Luca Cardelli, Benjamin Pierce, and Gordon Plotkin. Dynamic typing in a statically typed language. *ACM Transactions on Programming Languages and Systems*, 13(2):237–268, 1991.
3. David Ancona and Elena Zucca. A theory of mixin modules: Basic and derived operators. *Mathematical Structures in Computer Science*, 8(4):401–446, 1998.
4. David Ancona and Elena Zucca. A primitive calculus for module systems. In *Proceedings of the International Conference on Principles and Practice of Declarative Programming*, Paris, France, September 1999. Springer-Verlag.
5. B. N. Bershad, S. Savage, P. Pardyak, E. G. Sirer, M. E.Fiuczynski, D. Becker, C. Chambers, and S. Egger. Extensibility, safety and performance in the SPIN operating system. In *Symposium on Operating Systems Principles*, pages 267–283, Copper Mountain, CO, 1995. ACM Press.
6. Edoardo Biagioni, Robert Harper, Peter Lee, and Brian G. Milnes. Signatures for a network protocol stack: A systems application of standard ML. In *Proceedings of ACM Symposium on Lisp and Functional Programming*, pages 55–64, Orlando, Florida, January 1994. ACM Press.
7. Luca Cardelli. Program fragments, linking and modularization. In *Proceedings of ACM Symposium on Principles of Programming Languages*, pages 266–277. ACM Press, January 1997.
8. Karl Crary, Robert Harper, and S. Puri. What is a recursive module? In *Proceedings of ACM SIGPLAN Conference on Programming Language Design and Implementation*, Atlanta, GA, 1999. ACM Press.
9. Karl Crary, Michael Hicks, and Stephanie Weirich. Safe and flexible dynamic linking of native code. In *Workshop on Types in Compilation*, Lecture Notes in Computer Science, Montreal, Quebec, Canada, September 2000. Springer-Verlag.

10. Karl Crary and Greg Morrisett. Type structure for low-level programming languages. In *Proceedings of the International Conference on Automata, Languages and Programming*, Lecture Notes in Computer Science. Springer-Verlag, 1999.
11. Dominic Duggan. Dynamic typing for distributed programming in polymorphic languages. *ACM Transactions on Programming Languages and Systems*, 21(1):11–45, January 1999.
12. Dominic Duggan. Type-safe dynamic linking with recursive DLLs and shared libraries. Technical report, Stevens Institute of Technology, 2000.
13. M. Flatt and M. Felleisen. Units: Cool modules for HOT languages. In *Proceedings of ACM SIGPLAN Conference on Programming Language Design and Implementation*, 1998.
14. Neal Glew and Greg Morrisett. Type-safe linking and modular assembly languages. In *Proceedings of ACM Symposium on Principles of Programming Languages*, San Antonio, Texas, January 1999. ACM Press.
15. Robert Harper and Mark Lillibridge. A type-theoretic approach to higher-order modules with sharing. In *Proceedings of ACM Symposium on Principles of Programming Languages*, pages 123–137, Portland, Oregon, January 1994. ACM Press.
16. Robert Harper, John Mitchell, and Eugenio Moggi. Higher-order modules and the phase distinction. In *Proceedings of ACM Symposium on Principles of Programming Languages*, pages 341–354. Association for Computing Machinery, 1990.
17. Michael Hicks and Stephanie Weirich. A calculus for dynamic loading. Technical Report MS-CIS-00-07, University of Pennsylvania, 2000.
18. Xavier Leroy. Manifest types, modules, and separate compilation. In *Proceedings of ACM Symposium on Principles of Programming Languages*, pages 109–122, Portland, Oregon, January 1994. acmp.
19. Xavier Leroy. Applicative functors and fully transparent higher-order modules. In *Proceedings of ACM Symposium on Principles of Programming Languages*, pages 154–163, San Francisco, California, January 1995. ACM Press.
20. Xavier Leroy and Michel Mauny. Dynamics in ML. *Journal of Functional Programming*, 3(4):431–463, 1993.
21. Sheng Liang and Gilad Bracha. Dynamic class loading in the Java virtual machine. In *Proceedings of ACM Symposium on Object-Oriented Programming: Systems, Languages and Applications*. ACM Press, October 1998.
22. Mark Lillibridge. *Translucent Sums: A Foundation for Higher-Order Module Systems*. PhD thesis, Carnegie-Mellon University, Pittsburgh, PA, May 1997. Technical Report CMU-CS-97-122.
23. David MacQueen. Using dependent types to express modular structure. In *Proceedings of ACM Symposium on Principles of Programming Languages*, pages 277–286. ACM Press, 1986.
24. David MacQueen and Mads Tofte. A semantics for higher-order functors. In *European Symposium on Programming*, volume 788 of *Lecture Notes in Computer Science*, pages 409–423. Springer-Verlag, 1994.
25. Robin Milner. *Communication and Concurrency*. Prentice-Hall, 1989.
26. Robin Milner, Mads Tofte, Robert Harper, and David MacQueen. *The Revised Definition of Standard ML*. The MIT Press, 1997.
27. Greg Morrisett, Karl Crary, Neal Glew, Dan Grossman, Richard Samuels, Frederick Smith, David Walker, Stephanie Weirich, and Steve Zdancewic. TALx86: A realistic typed assembly language. In *Workshop on Compiler Support for Software Systems (WCSSS)*, Atlanta, GA, May 1999.

28. Greg Morrisett, David Walker, Karl Crary, and Neal Glew. From System F to typed assembly language. In *Proceedings of ACM Symposium on Principles of Programming Languages*, 1998.
29. George Necula. Proof-carrying code. In *Proceedings of ACM Symposium on Principles of Programming Languages*, 1997.
30. George Necula and Peter Lee. Safe kernel extensions without run-time checking. In *Operating Systems Design and Implementation*, 1996.
31. Didier Rémy and Jérôme Vouillon. Objective ML: An effective object-oriented extension to ml. *Theory and Practice of Object Systems*, 4(1):27–50, 1998.
32. Claudio Russo. Adding first-class modules to Standard ML. In *European Symposium on Programming*, Berlin, Germany, April 2000. Springer-Verlag.
33. Zhong Shao. Transparent modules with fully syntactic signatures. In *Proceedings of ACM International Conference on Functional Programming*, Paris, France, September 1999.
34. Mark Shields, Tim Sheard, and Simon Peyton-Jones. Dynamic typing as staged type inference. In *Proceedings of ACM Symposium on Principles of Programming Languages*, pages 289–302, San Diego, California, January 1998. ACM Press.
35. Robert Wahbe, Steven Lucco, Thomas E.Anderson, and Susan L.Graham. Efficient software-based fault isolation. In *Symposium on Operating Systems Principles*, pages 203–216. ACM Press, 1993.
36. Dan S. Wallach, Dirk Balfanz, Drew Dean, and Edward W. Felten. Extensible security architectures for Java. In *Symposium on Operating Systems Principles.* ACM Press, 1997.
37. Stephanie Weirich. Type-safe cast (functional pearl). In *Proceedings of ACM International Conference on Functional Programming*, Montreal, Canada, September 2000. ACM Press.
38. Joseph B. Wells and René Vestergaard. Equational reasoning for linking with first-class primitive modules. In *European Symposium on Programming*, Berlin, Germany, April 2000. Springer-Verlag.

A Type Rules for Modules and Symbol Tables

This appendix summarizes the type rules for modules and symbol tables. The type rules for values and heaps are specified using judgements of the form given in Fig. 5. The contexts of type and value heap bindings are defined by:

$$\widetilde{\Phi} = \{(t : K) \mid (t :: \mathbf{t} : K) \in \Phi\}$$
$$\widetilde{\Psi} = \{(x : A) \mid (x :: \mathbf{x} : A) \in \Psi\}$$

The type rules for modules (object files) require that the type heap satisfies the exported type heap interface, that the value heap satisfies the exported value heap interface, and that the exported type sharing constraints are entailed by the type sharing implied by the type heap, the type sharing context, and the type sharing constraints imposed on the imports.

$\widetilde{\Phi}; \Delta \vdash \diamond$	Type context formation
$\widetilde{\Phi}; \Delta \vdash \Phi'$	Type heap interface
$\widetilde{\Phi}; \Delta; \Xi \vdash \Phi' = \Phi''$	Type heap interface equality
$\widetilde{\Phi}; \Delta; \Xi \vdash \Phi' \leq \Phi''$	Type heap interface containment
$\widetilde{\Phi}; \Delta; \Xi \vdash TH : \Phi'$	Type heap
$\widetilde{\Phi}; \Delta \vdash \Xi$	Sharing heap interface
$\widetilde{\Phi}; \Delta; \Xi \vdash \Xi'$	Entailment of type sharing constraints
$\widetilde{\Phi}; \Delta \vdash \Psi$	Value heap interface
$\widetilde{\Phi}; \Delta; \Xi \vdash \Psi' = \Psi''$	Value heap interface equality
$\widetilde{\Phi}; \Delta; \Xi \vdash \Psi' \leq \Psi''$	Value heap interface containment
$\widetilde{\Phi}; \Delta; \Xi; \widetilde{\Psi} \vdash VH : \Psi'$	Value heap
$\widetilde{\Phi}; \Delta \vdash K$	Kind formation
$\widetilde{\Phi}; \Delta; \Xi \vdash K = K'$	Kind equality
$\widetilde{\Phi}; \Delta; \Xi \vdash K \leq K'$	Kind containment
$\widetilde{\Phi}; \Delta \vdash A : K$	Type formation
$\widetilde{\Phi}; \Delta; \Xi \vdash A = B \in K$	Type equality
$\widetilde{\Phi}; \Delta; \Xi \vdash [Int_I \Rightarrow Int_E] \preceq [Int'_I \Rightarrow Int'_E]$	Module type containment
$\widetilde{\Phi}; \Delta; \Xi; \widetilde{\Psi} \vdash h : A$	Type of heap value
$\widetilde{\Phi}; \Delta; \Xi; \widetilde{\Psi} \vdash w : A$	Type of word value
$\widetilde{\Phi}; \Delta \vdash \Gamma$	Register file type
$\widetilde{\Phi}; \Delta; \Xi; \widetilde{\Psi} \vdash R : \Gamma$	Register file
$\widetilde{\Phi}; \widetilde{\Psi}; \Xi \vdash \{\Delta; \Gamma\}\ I\ \{\Delta'; \Gamma'\}$	Instruction formation

Fig. 5. Judgement Forms of TMAL

$$\frac{\begin{array}{c}\widetilde{\Phi}; \{\}; \Xi \vdash [Int_I \Rightarrow Int_E] : ty \quad Int_I = (\Phi_I, \Psi_I, \Xi_I) \quad Int_E = (\Phi_E, \Psi_E, \Xi_E) \\ \widetilde{\Phi'} = \widetilde{\Phi} \cup \widetilde{\Phi_I} \cup TENV(TH) \quad \Xi' = \Xi \cup \Xi_I \cup SHARE(TH) \\ \widetilde{\Phi'}; \Xi' \vdash TH : \Xi_E \quad \widetilde{\Phi'}; \Xi' \vdash TH : \Phi_E \\ \Phi; \widetilde{\Phi'}; \Delta; \Xi'; \widetilde{\Psi} \cup \widetilde{\Psi_I} \cup VENV(VH); \Delta \vdash_{\text{val}} VH : \Psi_E\end{array}}{\Phi; \widetilde{\Phi}; \Delta; \Xi; \widetilde{\Psi}; \Delta \vdash_{\text{val}} [Int_I \Rightarrow (TH, VH) : Int_E] : [Int_I \Rightarrow Int_E]} \quad \text{(Val Object File)}$$

$$\frac{\Phi; \widetilde{\Phi}; \Delta; \Xi; \widetilde{\Psi}; \Delta \vdash_{\text{val}} e : A \quad \mathbf{x} \neq \star}{\Phi; \widetilde{\Phi}; \Delta; \Xi; \widetilde{\Psi}; \Delta \vdash_{\text{val}} \{x :: \mathbf{x} : A \triangleq e\} : \{x :: \mathbf{x} : A\}} \quad \text{(Heap Val Def)}$$

$$\frac{(y : A') \in \widetilde{\Psi} \quad \widetilde{\Phi}; \Delta; \Xi \vdash A = A' : ty \quad \mathbf{x} \neq \star}{\Phi; \widetilde{\Phi}; \Delta; \Xi; \widetilde{\Psi}; \Delta \vdash_{\text{val}} \{x :: \mathbf{x} : A \cong y\} : \{x :: \mathbf{x} : A\}} \quad \text{(Heap Val Share)}$$

$$\frac{\widetilde{\Phi}; \{\}; \Xi \vdash A : K \quad \mathbf{t} \neq \star}{\widetilde{\Phi}; \Xi \vdash \{type\ t :: \mathbf{t} :: K \triangleq A\} : \{t :: \mathbf{t} : K\}} \quad \text{(Heap Type Def)}$$

$$\frac{t' \in Names(\widetilde{\Phi}) \quad \widetilde{\Phi}; \{\}; \Xi \vdash t' : K \quad \mathbf{t} \neq \star}{\widetilde{\Phi}; \Xi \vdash \{type\ t :: \mathbf{t} :: K \cong t'\} : \{t :: \mathbf{t} : K\}} \quad \text{(Heap Type Share)}$$

$$\frac{\widetilde{\Phi}; \{\}; \Xi \vdash A : K}{\widetilde{\Phi}; \Xi \vdash \{t :: \mathbf{t} : K \triangleq A\} : \{\}} \quad \text{(Heap Share Def)}$$

$$\frac{t' \in Names(\widetilde{\Phi})}{\widetilde{\Phi}; \Xi \vdash \{t :: \ell : K \cong t'\} : \{t \cong t' \in ty\}} \quad \text{(Heap Share Share)}$$

There are also rules for typing "private" type and value fields of a modules (private fields have the special external name $\star$).

The type rule for symbol tables is relatively straightforward. A symbol table is a mapping from type and value external names to type and value labels, respectively, in the global type and value heaps. The side-conditions that $\widetilde{\Phi'} \subseteq \widetilde{\Phi}$ means that, in checking the well-formedness of types and kinds, global type heap labels are chosen to be consistent with the internal type names used in the interface of the symbol table.

$$\frac{\begin{array}{c} Int_E = (\Phi', \Psi', \Xi') \quad ST = \{\overline{\mathbf{t}} \mapsto \overline{t},\ \overline{\mathbf{x}} \mapsto \overline{x}\} \\ \widetilde{\Phi}; \Delta \vdash \Phi' \quad \widetilde{\Phi}; \Delta \vdash \Psi' \quad \widetilde{\Phi}; \Delta; \Xi \vdash \Xi' \\ \Phi' = \{\overline{t :: \mathbf{t} : K}\} \quad \widetilde{\Phi'} \subseteq \widetilde{\Phi} \quad \Psi' = \{\overline{x :: \mathbf{x} : A}\} \end{array}}{\widetilde{\Phi}; \Delta; \Xi; \widetilde{\Psi} \vdash ST : Int_E} \quad \text{(Val Symbol Table)}$$

The *VENV*, *TENV* and *SHARE* metafunctions are defined as follows:

$$\begin{aligned} VENV(VH) &= \{(x : A) \mid (x :: \ell : A\ \mathcal{B}^e) \in VH\} \\ TENV(TH) &= \{(t : K) \mid (t :: \mathbf{t} : K\mathcal{B}^A) \in TH\} \\ SHARE(TH) &= \{(t_1 \cong t_2 \in ty) \mid (t_1 :: \mathbf{t_1} : K \cong t_2) \in TH\} \end{aligned}$$

B Semantics of Module Linking Instructions

In this appendix we provide more details of the static and dynamic semantics of the instructions of TMAL. The reduction rules use program states of the form

$$(\widetilde{TH}, \widetilde{VH}, R, I)$$

where R is a register file and I an instruction stream, and

$$\begin{aligned} \widetilde{TH} &= \{(t\mathcal{B}^A) \mid (t :: \mathbf{t} : K\mathcal{B}^A) \in TH\} \\ \widetilde{VH} &= \{(x\mathcal{B}^e) \mid (x :: \mathbf{x} : A\mathcal{B}^e) \in VH\} \end{aligned}$$

The global type and value heaps never contain shared bindings; such bindings are removed from an object file's type and value heaps, as part of initialization, before they are merged with the global heaps.

The type rules for `dllink`, `dlcoerce` and `dlrename` are similar to that for similar constructs described in [12]. We omit the rules here for lack of space. The reduction rules for these instructions are given by:

$$\frac{\begin{array}{c} R(r_i^m) = x_i \text{ and } \widetilde{VH}(x_i) = [Int_I^i \Rightarrow (TH_i, VH_i) : Int_E^i],\ i = 2,3 \\ Int_E^1 = (Int_E^2 \cup Int_E^3) \quad Int_I^1 = (Int_I^2 \sqcup Int_I^3) \setminus \{n \mid n \in idom(Int_E^1)\} \\ TH_1 = TH_2 \cup TH_3 \quad VH_1 = VH_2 \cup VH_3 \quad x_1 \notin dom(\widetilde{VH}) \\ idom(TH_1) \cap idom(TH_2) = \{\} \quad idom(VH_1) \cap idom(VH_2) = \{\} \\ \widetilde{VH}' = \widetilde{VH} \cup \{x_1 \triangleq [Int_I^1 \Rightarrow (TH_1, VH_1) : Int_E^1]\} \end{array}}{(\widetilde{TH}, \widetilde{VH}, R, (\texttt{dllink}\ r_1^m, r_2^m, r_3^m;\ I)) \longrightarrow (\widetilde{TH}, \widetilde{VH}', R[r_1^m \mapsto x_1], I)}$$

(RED DL LINK)

$$\frac{\begin{array}{c} R(r_2^m) = x_2 \text{ and } \widetilde{VH}(x_2) = [Int_I' \Rightarrow (TH', VH') : Int_E'] \\ OT = [Int_I \Rightarrow Int_E] \quad x_1 \notin dom(\widetilde{VH}) \\ \widetilde{VH}'' = \widetilde{VH} \cup \{x_1 \triangleq [Int_I \Rightarrow (COERCE(TH', Int_E'), COERCE(VH', Int_E')) : Int_E]\} \end{array}}{(\widetilde{TH}, \widetilde{VH}, R, (\texttt{dlcoerce}\ r_1^m, r_2^m, OT;\ I)) \longrightarrow (\widetilde{TH}, \widetilde{VH}'', R[r_1^m \mapsto x_1], I)}$$

(RED DL COERCE)

$$\frac{\begin{array}{c} R(r_2^m) = x_2 \text{ and } \widetilde{VH}(x_2) = [Int_I \Rightarrow (TH', VH') : Int_E] \\ x_1 \notin dom(\widetilde{VH}) \quad \widetilde{VH}'' = \widetilde{VH} \cup \{x_1 \triangleq [\rho(Int_I) \Rightarrow (\rho(TH'), \rho(VH')) : \rho(Int_E)]\} \end{array}}{(\widetilde{TH}, \widetilde{VH}, R, (\texttt{dlrename}\ r_1^m, r_2^m, \rho;\ I)) \longrightarrow (\widetilde{TH}, \widetilde{VH}'', R[r_1^m \mapsto x_1], I)}$$

(RED DL RENAME)

The RED DL LINK type rule for the `dllink` instruction computes the new import list using the join operation *sqcup*, rather than simply unioning the import lists of the two object files being merged. This is because, for an import definition that is imported by both object files, the new import list must constrain the import to one compatible with both of the preceding import lists. For example, if one of the argument object files imports a type field t with kind ty, while another imports a type field t with kind ⊠`int`, then the new object file resulting from merging imports a definition of t with kind ⊠`int`. In computing the new import list, the `dllink` instruction removes from the import list any symbols that can be resolved against the combined export list. This operation is defined in [12].

The `dlcoerce` instruction uses the *COERCE* metafunction to hide bindings in the heaps (renaming their external name to $\star$) that are made private by the new object file type and export interface. A definition of this metafunction is provided in [12].

The following type rule and reduction rule explain the semantics of the `dlopen` operation. The metafunction *dom* denotes the domain of a mapping, while $idom(TH) = dom(\widetilde{TH})$ and $idom(VH) = dom(\widetilde{VH})$. $\Gamma[r : A]$ denotes the replacement of the type of r (if any) in the register file type Γ with the new type A. $R[r \mapsto w]$ denotes the replacement of the contents of r in the register file R with the new contents w. The `dlopen` operation expects register r^m to point to a module with type $[Int_I \Rightarrow Int_E]$, where $Int_I = (\{\},\{\},\{\})$. The operation leaves in register r^s a pointer to a symbol table with interface Int_E, after adding the heaps of the module to the program heaps:

$$\frac{\widetilde{\Phi};\Delta;\widetilde{\Psi};\Xi \vdash r^m : [(\{\},\{\},\{\}) \Rightarrow Int_E] \quad \Gamma' = \Gamma[r^s : Int_E]}{\widetilde{\Phi};\widetilde{\Psi};\Xi \vdash \{\Delta;\Gamma\}\ (\mathtt{dlopen}\ r^s, r^m)\ \{\Delta;\Gamma'\}} \quad (\text{INSTR DL OPEN})$$

$$\frac{\begin{array}{c} R(r^m) = x \text{ and } \widetilde{VH}(x) = [(\{\},\{\},\{\}) \Rightarrow (TH', VH') : Int_E] \\ ST = \{(\mathbf{t} \mapsto t) \mid (t :: \mathbf{t} : K) \in Int_E\} \cup \{(\mathbf{x} \mapsto x) \mid (x :: \mathbf{x} : A) \in Int_E\} \\ x' \notin idom(VH) \cup idom(VH') \quad idom(\widetilde{TH}) \cap idom(TH') = \{\} \quad \widetilde{TH''} = \widetilde{TH} \cup \widetilde{TH'} \\ idom(VH) \cap idom(VH') = \{\} \quad \widetilde{VH''} = CLOS(\widetilde{VH} \cup \widetilde{VH'} \cup \{x' \triangleq ST\}) \end{array}}{(\widetilde{TH}, \widetilde{VH}, R, (\mathtt{dlopen}\ r^s, r^m;\ I)) \longrightarrow (\widetilde{TH''}, \widetilde{VH''}, R[r^s \mapsto x'], I)}$$

(RED DL OPEN)

The $CLOS(VH)$ operation removes shared value bindings of the form $x : A \cong y$ from the value heap, by dereferencing y to its heap value definition:

$$CLOS(\widetilde{VH}) = \{(x \triangleq h) \mid x \in dom(\widetilde{VH}),\ h = DEREF_{\widetilde{VH}}(x)\}$$

$$DEREF_{\widetilde{VH}}(x) = \begin{cases} h \text{ if } (x \triangleq h) \in \widetilde{VH} \\ h \text{ if } (x \cong y) \in \widetilde{VH},\ h = DEREF_{\widetilde{VH}}(y) \end{cases}$$

The result of $CLOS(\widetilde{VH})$ is undefined if $\widetilde{VH}$ contains circular shared value bindings. This corresponds to an initialization failure due to cycles in the specification of initial values.

The type rule and reduction rule for the `dlsym_v` instruction are as follows:

$$\frac{\begin{array}{c} \widetilde{\Phi};\Delta;\widetilde{\Psi};\Xi \vdash r^s : (\Phi', \Psi', \Xi') \\ (x :: \mathbf{x} : A) \in \Psi' \quad FV(A) \cap idom(\Phi') = \{\} \quad \Gamma' = \Gamma[r : A] \end{array}}{\widetilde{\Phi};\widetilde{\Psi};\Xi \vdash \{\Delta;\Gamma\}\ (\mathtt{dlsym\_v}\ r, r^s, \mathbf{x})\ \{\Delta;\Gamma'\}} \quad (\text{INSTR DL SYMV})$$

$$\frac{R(r^s) = x \text{ and } \widetilde{VH}(x) = ST}{(\widetilde{TH}, \widetilde{VH}, R, (\mathtt{dlsym\_v}\ r, r^s, \mathbf{x};\ I)) \longrightarrow (\widetilde{TH}, \widetilde{VH}, R[r \mapsto ST(\mathbf{x})], I)}$$

(RED DL SYMV)

$\widehat{R}(v)$ denotes the application of the register file R to the small value (register or word value) v:

$$\widehat{R}(v) = \begin{cases} w & \text{if } v = w \\ R(r) & \text{if } v = r \end{cases}$$

The type rule and reduction rule for the dlsym_t instruction are as follows:

$$\frac{\begin{array}{c}\widetilde{\Phi}; \Delta; \widetilde{\Psi}; \Xi \vdash r_2^s : (\Phi', \Psi', \Xi') \\ (t :: \mathbf{t} : K) \in \Phi' \quad \widetilde{\Phi} \cup \widetilde{\Phi'}; \Delta; \Xi \cup \Xi' \vdash K \leq K' \quad t \notin dom(\widetilde{\Phi}) \\ \Delta' = \Delta \cup \{t : K'\} \quad \Gamma' = \Gamma[r_1^s : (\Phi_1 \cup \Phi_2, \Psi', \Xi')]\end{array}}{\widetilde{\Phi}; \widetilde{\Psi}; \Xi \vdash \{\Delta; \Gamma\}\ (\texttt{dlsym\_t}\ [t : K'] r_1^s, r_2^s, \mathbf{t})\ \{\Delta'; \Gamma'\}} \quad \text{(INSTR DL SYMT)}$$

$$\frac{R(r_2^s) = x \text{ and } \widetilde{VH}(x) = ST \quad ST = ST' \uplus \{\mathbf{t} \mapsto t\} \quad R' = R[r_1^s \mapsto ST']}{(\widetilde{TH}, \widetilde{VH}, R, (\texttt{dlsym\_t}\ [t' : K'] r_1^s, r_2^s, \mathbf{t};\ I)) \longrightarrow (\widetilde{TH}, \widetilde{VH}, R', \{t/t'\}I)} \quad \text{(RED DL SYMT)}$$

In the reduction rule, the local type identifier t' is bound to the global type heap address t of the type definition pointed to by the symbol table. This allows the remainder of the instruction stream I to access the value heap definitions, pointed to by the symbol table, that have references to this type heap address.

Type heap addresses and type identifiers serve only to support type-checking of the assembly code, and are stripped for run-time execution. The substitution $\{t/t'\}I$ is performed only in the abstract reduction semantics. Although we do not elaborate on it further here, the dlsym_t instruction can be generalized to import run-time type tags from a DLL, for languages such as Java and Modula-3 that associate type tags with some values.

For the next two instructions, we abuse notation slightly by allowing union and set difference operations to be applied to interfaces. These are to be understood as the operations distributing over the components of the interfaces, for example:

$$\begin{array}{c}(\Phi_1, \Psi_1, \Xi_1) \cup (\Phi_2, \Psi_2, \Xi_2) = (\Phi_1 \cup \Phi_2, \Psi_1 \cup \Psi_2, \Xi_1 \cup \Xi_2) \\ (\Phi, \Psi, \Xi) \cup \Phi' = (\Phi \cup \Phi', \Psi, \Xi)\end{array}$$

The type rule for the dlsetsym_v instruction is reasonably straightforward. The only complication is that the type of the value field being assigned may have free type identifiers that are bound in the module. The typing rule relies on type sharing constraints in the module type that relate these locally bound type identifiers to global identifiers bound by the program type heap:

$$\frac{\begin{array}{c}\widetilde{\Phi}; \Delta; \widetilde{\Psi}; \Xi \vdash v : A \quad \widetilde{\Phi}; \Delta; \widetilde{\Psi}; \Xi \vdash r_2^m : [Int_I \Rightarrow Int_E] \\ Int_I = (\Phi_I, \Psi_I, \Xi_I) \quad Int_E = (\Phi_E, \Psi_E, \Xi_E) \quad (x :: \mathbf{x} : B) \in \Psi_I \\ \widetilde{\Phi} \cup \widetilde{\Phi_I} \cup \widetilde{\Phi_E}; \Delta; \Xi \cup \Xi_I \cup \Xi_E \vdash A = B \in ty \\ \Gamma' = \Gamma[r_1^m \mapsto [(Int_I - \{x :: \mathbf{x} : B\}) \Rightarrow (Int_E \cup \{x :: \mathbf{x} : B\})]]\end{array}}{\widetilde{\Phi}; \widetilde{\Psi}; \Xi \vdash \{\Delta; \Gamma\}\ (\texttt{dlsetsym\_v}\ r_1^m, r_2^m, v, \mathbf{x})\ \{\Delta; \Gamma'\}} \quad \text{(INSTR DL SETSYMV)}$$

$$\frac{\begin{array}{c} R(r_2^m) = x \text{ and } \widetilde{VH}(x) = [Int_I \Rightarrow (TH', VH') : Int_E] \quad (x :: \mathbf{x} : A) \in Int_I \quad \widehat{R}(v) = y \\ Int_I' = Int_I - \{x :: \mathbf{x} : A\} \quad Int_E' = Int_E \cup \{x :: \mathbf{x} : A\} \\ z \notin dom(\widetilde{VH}) \quad \widetilde{VH''} = \widetilde{VH} \cup \{z \triangleq [Int_I' \Rightarrow (TH', VH' \cup \{x :: \mathbf{x} : A \cong y\}) : Int_E']\} \end{array}}{(\widetilde{TH}, \widetilde{VH}, R, (\texttt{dlsetsym\_v}\ r_1^m, r_2^m, v, \mathbf{x};\ I)) \longrightarrow (\widetilde{TH}, \widetilde{VH''}, R[r_1^m \mapsto z], I)}$$

(RED DL SETSYMV)

The **dlsetsym_t** instruction for assigning a type field in a module similarly relies on type sharing to equate any local type identifiers with global type identifiers in the kind of the type being assigned. Free type identifiers may appear free in the kind of a field with box kind. Once a type field has been assigned, a type sharing constraint is added to the export interface of the module, to allow subsequent value fields to be assigned:

$$\frac{\begin{array}{c} \widetilde{\Phi}; \Delta \vdash t' : K \quad \widetilde{\Phi}; \Delta; \widetilde{\Psi}; \Xi \vdash r_2^m : [Int_I \Rightarrow Int_E] \\ Int_I = (\Phi_I, \Psi_I, \Xi_I) \quad Int_E = (\Phi_E, \Psi_E, \Xi_E) \quad (t :: \mathbf{t} : K') \in \Phi_I \\ \widetilde{\Phi} \cup \widetilde{\Phi_I} \cup \widetilde{\Phi_E}; \Delta; \Xi \cup \Xi_I \cup \Xi_E \vdash K = K' \\ \Gamma' = \Gamma[r_1^m \mapsto [(Int_I - \{t :: \mathbf{t} : K'\}) \Rightarrow (Int_E \cup \{(t :: \mathbf{t} : K'), (t \cong t' \in K')\})]] \end{array}}{\widetilde{\Phi}; \widetilde{\Psi}; \Xi \vdash \{\Delta; \Gamma\}\ (\texttt{dlsetsym\_t}\ r_1^m, r_2^m, t', \mathbf{t})\ \{\Delta; \Gamma'\}}$$

(INSTR DL SETSYMT)

$$\frac{\begin{array}{c} R(r_2^m) = x \text{ and } \widetilde{VH}(x) = [Int_I \Rightarrow (TH', VH') : Int_E] \quad (t :: \mathbf{t} : K) \in Int_I \\ Int_I' = Int_I - \{t :: \mathbf{t} : K\} \quad Int_E' = Int_E \cup \{(t :: \mathbf{t} : K), (t \cong t' \in K)\} \\ z \notin dom(\widetilde{VH}) \quad \widetilde{VH''} = \widetilde{VH} \cup \{z \triangleq [Int_I' \Rightarrow (TH' \cup \{t :: \mathbf{t} : K \cong t'\}, VH') : Int_E']\} \end{array}}{(\widetilde{TH}, \widetilde{VH}, R, (\texttt{dlsetsym\_t}\ r_1^m, r_2^m, t', \mathbf{t};\ I)) \longrightarrow (\widetilde{TH}, \widetilde{VH''}, R[r_1^m \mapsto z], I)}$$

(RED DL SETSYMT)

Finally the reduction rules for the instructions for creating a DLL, and for extracting a module from a DLL, are as follows:

$$\frac{x \notin dom(VH) \quad \widetilde{VH'} = \widetilde{VH} \cup \{x \triangleq \langle\langle \widehat{R}(v), OT \rangle\rangle\}}{(\widetilde{TH}, \widetilde{VH}, R, (\texttt{dldynamic}\ r, v, OT;\ I)) \longrightarrow (\widetilde{TH}, \widetilde{VH'}, R[r \mapsto x], I)}$$

(RED DL DYNAMIC)

$$\frac{\begin{array}{c} R(r_1) = x \text{ and } \widetilde{VH}(x) = \langle\langle y, OT \rangle\rangle \\ OT = [Int_I \Rightarrow Int_E] \quad OT'' = [Int_I'' \Rightarrow Int_E''] \quad \widetilde{VH}(y) = [Int_I' \Rightarrow (TH', VH') : Int_E'] \\ TENV(\widetilde{TH}); \{\}; SHARE(\widetilde{TH}) \vdash [Int_I \Rightarrow Int_E] \preceq [Int_I'' \Rightarrow Int_E''] \\ z \notin dom(\widetilde{VH}) \quad \widetilde{VH''} = \widetilde{VH} \cup \{z \triangleq [Int_I'' \Rightarrow (TH', VH') : Int_E'']\} \end{array}}{(\widetilde{TH}, \widetilde{VH''}, R, (\texttt{dlload}\ r^m, r_1, r_2, OT'';\ I)) \longrightarrow (\widetilde{TH}, \widetilde{VH''}, R[r^m \mapsto z], I)}$$

(RED DL LOAD SUCC)

The last rule handles the case where loading a DLL (reflecting a DLL from the core language into the module language) succeeds with a runtime type check.

There is also an associated rule for when the runtime type check fails; in this case, control transfers to the address specified by the address register r_2, i.e., r_2 contains a pointer to a failure continuation that should be invoked if the runtime type check fails.

Scalable Certification for Typed Assembly Language

Dan Grossman and Greg Morrisett*

Department of Computer Science, Cornell University

Abstract. A type-based certifying compiler maps source code to machine code and target-level type annotations. The target-level annotations make it possible to prove easily that the machine code is type-safe, independent of the source code or compiler. To be useful across a range of source languages and compilers, the target-language type system should provide powerful type constructors for encoding higher-level invariants. Unfortunately, it is difficult to engineer such type systems so that annotation sizes are small and verification times are fast.

In this paper, we describe our experience writing a certifying compiler that targets Typed Assembly Language (TALx86) and discuss some general techniques we have used to keep annotation sizes small and verification times fast. We quantify the effectiveness of these techniques by measuring their effects on a sizeable application — the certifying compiler itself. Using these techniques, which include common-subexpression elimination of types, higher-order type abbreviations, and selective reverification, can dramatically change certificate size and verification time.

1 Background

A certifying compiler takes high-level source code and produces target code with a *certificate* that ensures that the target code respects a desired safety or security policy. To date, certifying compilers have primarily concentrated on producing certificates of type safety. For example, Sun's `javac` compiler maps Java source code to statically typed Java Virtual Machine Language (JVML) code. The JVML code includes type annotations that a verifier based on dataflow analysis can use to ensure that the code is type-safe.

However, both the instructions and the type system of JVML are at a relatively high level and are specifically tailored to Java. Consequently, JVML is ill-suited for compiling a variety of source-level programming languages to high-performance code. For example, JVML provides only high-level method-call and

* This material is based on work supported in part by the AFOSR grant F49620-97-1-0013, ARPA/RADC grant F30602-1-0317, and a National Science Foundation Graduate Fellowship. Any opinions, findings, and conclusions or recommendations expressed in this publication are those of the authors and do not reflect the views of these agencies.

R. Harper (Ed.): TIC 2000, LNCS 2071, pp. 117–145, 2001.

method-return operations. Also, it provides no provision for performing general tail-calls on methods. Therefore, JVML is a difficult target for compilers of functional languages such as Scheme that require tail-call elimination.

In addition, current platforms for JVML either interpret programs or compile them further to native code. Achieving acceptable performance seems to demand compilation with a good deal of optimization. To avoid security or safety holes, the translation from JVML to native code should also be done by a certifying compiler. That way, we can verify the safety of the resulting code instead of trusting the "just-in-time" compiler.

Another example of a certifying compiler is Necula and Lee's Touchstone compiler [22]. Touchstone compiles a small, type-safe subset of C to optimized DEC-Alpha assembly language. The key novelty of Touchstone is that the certificate it produces is a formal "proof" that the code is type-correct. Checking the proof for type-correctness is relatively easy, especially compared to the *ad hoc* verification process for JVML. As such, the Touchstone certificates provide a higher degree of trustworthiness.

The proofs of the Touchstone system are represented using the general-purpose logical framework LF [11]. The advantage of using LF to encode the proofs is that, from an implementation perspective, it is easy to change the type system of the target language. In particular, the proof checker is parameterized by a set of primitive axioms and inference rules that effectively define the type system. The checker itself does not need to change if these rules are changed. Consequently, the use of LF makes it easy to change type systems to adapt to different source languages or different compilation strategies. Indeed, more recent work uses a very different type system for certifying the output of Special J [5,24], a compiler for Java.

Although changing the type system is easy for the implementor, doing so obligates one to an enormous proof burden: Every change requires a proof of the soundness of the type system with respect to the underlying machine's semantics. Constructing such proofs is an extremely difficult task. In the absence of a proof, it is not clear what assurances a verifier is actually providing.

1.1 An Alternative Approach

Our goal is to make it easy for certifying compilers to produce provably type-correct code without having to change the type system of the target language. That way, it suffices to write and trust one verifier for one type system. Toward this end, we have been studying the design and implementation of general-purpose type systems suitable for assembly language [20,19]. Ultimately, we hope to discover typing constructs that support certifying compilation of many orthogonal programming-language features.

Our current work focuses on the design of an extremely expressive type system for Intel's IA32 assembly language and a verifier we call TALx86 [18]. Where possible, we have avoided including high-level language abstractions like procedures, exception handlers, or objects. In fact, the only high-level operation that is a TALx86 primitive is memory allocation. We also have not "baked in" compiler-specific abstractions such as activation records or calling conventions. Rather, the type system of TALx86 provides a number of primitive type constructors, such as parametric polymorphism, label types, existential types, products, recursive types, etc., that we can use to encode language features and compiler invariants. These type constructors have either been well studied in other contexts or modeled and proven sound by our group.

In addition, we and others have shown how to encode a number of important language and compiler features using our type constructors. For example, our encoding of procedures easily supports tail-call optimizations because the control-flow transfers are achieved through simple machine-level jumps. In other words, we do not have to change the type system of TALx86 to support these optimizations. Type soundness of TALx86 ensures that compilers targeting TALx86 produce only code with safe run-time behavior. Some specific assurances are that the program counter will always point to executable code, unallocated memory will never be dereferenced, and system routines (such as input/output) will never be called with inappropriate arguments. In these respects, TALx86 provides an attractive target for certifying compilers.

1.2 The Problem

Unfortunately, there is a particularly difficult engineering tradeoff that arises when a certifying compiler targets a general-purpose type system like TALx86: Encoding high-level language features, compiler invariants, and optimizations into primitive type constructors results in extremely large types and type annotations — *often much larger than the code itself.* Thus, there is a very real danger that our goal of using one general-purpose type system will be defeated by practical considerations of space and time.

The work presented here is a case study in writing a certifying compiler that targets the general-purpose typed assembly language TALx86. The source language for our compiler, called Popcorn, shares much of its syntax with C, but it has a number of advanced language features including first-class parametric polymorphism, non-regular algebraic datatypes with limited pattern matching, function pointers, exceptions, first-class abstract data types, modules, etc. Indeed, the language is suitably high-level that we have ported various ML libraries to Popcorn without needing to change their structure substantially. The certifying compiler for Popcorn is itself written in Popcorn.

Although the TALx86 type system is very expressive, it is far from being able to accept all safe assembly programs. However, we have found that it is expressive enough to allow a reasonable translation of Popcorn's linguistic features. Because the compiler's invariants are encoded in the primitive typing constructs of TALx86, the most difficult aspect of efficient, scalable verification is handling the potentially enormous size of the target-level types. We use our experience to suggest general techniques for controlling this overhead that we believe transcend the specifics of our system. The efficacy of these techniques is demonstrated quantitatively for the libraries and compiler itself. In particular, the size of the type annotations and the time needed to verify the code are essentially linear in the size of the object code. The constant factors are small enough to permit verification of our entire compiler in much less than one minute.

In the next section, we give a taxonomy for general approaches to reducing type-annotation overhead and further discuss other projects related to certifying compilation. Although it is an informal description of existing techniques, we have found this classification useful and we know of no other attempt to classify the approaches.

In Section 3, we summarize relevant aspects of the TALx86 type system, annotations, and verification process. We then show how these features are used to encode the provably safe compilation of the control-flow aspects of Popcorn, including procedures and exceptions. This extended example demonstrates that an expressive type system can permit reasonable compilation of a language for which it is not specifically designed. It also shows qualitatively that if handled naively, type-annotation size becomes unwieldy.

In Section 4, we use the example to analyze several approaches that we have examined for reducing type-annotation overhead. Section 5 presents the quantitative results of our investigation; we conclude that the TALx86 approach scales to verify our Popcorn compiler, the largest Popcorn application we have written. Moreover, all of the techniques contribute significantly to reducing the overhead of certifying compilation. Finally, we summarize our conclusions as a collection of guidelines for designers of low-level safety policies.

2 Approaches to Efficient Certification

Keeping annotation size small and verification time fast in the presence of optimizations and advanced source languages is an important requirement for a practical system that relies on certified code. In this section, we classify some approaches to managing the overhead of certifying compilation and discuss their relative merits. None of the approaches are mutually exclusive; any system will probably have elements of all of them.

The "Bake it in" Approach. If the type system supports only one way of compiling something, then compilers do not need to write down that they are using that way. For example, the type system could fix a calling convention and require compilers to group code blocks into procedures. JVML, Touchstone, and Special J all use this approach.

Baking in assumptions about procedures eliminates the need for any annotations describing the interactions between procedures. However, it inhibits some inter-procedural optimizations, such as inter-procedural register allocation, and makes it difficult to compile languages with other control features, such as exception handlers. In general, the "bake it in" approach reflects particular source features into the target language rather than providing low-level constructors suitable for encoding a variety of source constructs. For example, the certifier for Special J first processes a, "class descriptor whose form is very close to that of the JVM class descriptors" [24], so only programs conforming to the JVML class hierarchy and type system are certifiable by this checker.

Even general frameworks inevitably bake in more than the underlying machine requires. A TALx86 example is that labels are abstract — well-formed code cannot examine the actual address used to implement a label. This abstraction prevents some clever implementation techniques. Any verifiable safety policy must impose some conservative restrictions; choosing the restrictions is a crucial design decision that is a fundamental part of a policy.

The "Don't optimize" Approach. If a complicated analysis is necessary to prove an optimization safe, then the reasoning involved must be encoded in the annotations. For example, when compiling dynamically typed languages such as Scheme, dynamic type tests are in general necessary to ensure type safety. A simple strategy is to perform the appropriate type test before every operation. With this approach, a verifier can easily ensure safety with a minimum of annotations. This strategy is the essence of the verification approach suggested by Kozen [14]. Indeed, it results in relatively small annotations and fast verification, but at the price of performance and flexibility.

In contrast, an optimizing compiler may attempt to eliminate the dynamic checks by performing a "soft-typing" analysis [30]. However, the optimized code requires a more sophisticated type system to convince the verifier that type tests are unnecessary. To make verification tractable, such type systems require additional annotations. For example, the Touchstone type system supports static elimination of array-bounds checks, but it requires additional invariants and proof terms to support the optimization.

Another example is record initialization: An easy way to prove that memory is properly initialized is to write to the memory in the same basic block in which the memory is allocated. Proving that other instruction schedules are safe may require dataflow annotations that describe the location of uninitialized memory.

Unoptimized code also tends to be more uniform, which in turn makes the annotations more uniform. For example, if a callee-save register is always pushed onto the stack by the callee (even when the register is not used), then the annotations that describe the stack throughout the program will have more in common. Such techniques can improve the results of the "Compression" approach (discussed below) at the expense of efficiency.

The "Reconstruction" Approach. If it is easy for the verifier to infer a correct annotation, then such annotations can be elided. For example, Necula shows how simple techniques may be used for automatically reconstructing large portions of the proofs produced by the Touchstone compiler [23].

It is important that verification time not unduly suffer, however. For this reason, code producers should know the effects that annotation elision can have. Unfortunately, in expressive systems such as TALx86, many forms of type reconstruction are intractable or undecidable. The verifier could provide some simple heuristics or default guesses, but such maneuvers are weaker forms of the "bake it in" approach.

A more extreme approach to reconstruction would be to include a general-purpose theorem prover in the verification system. Unless the prover generates proofs that are independently checked, the trusted computing base would become larger and more complex. Any generated proofs would need to be concise as well. The TALx86 project has maintained the design goal that type-checking should be essentially syntax-directed; search and backtracking seem beyond the realm of efficient verification. However, recent work by Necula and Rahul [24] suggests using annotations not to provide a proof, but instead to guide the prover's non-determinism. In essence, the insight is that a compiler that knows enough about the verifier's decision procedure can guide reconstruction to avoid the overhead of search.

Certification systems invariably use reconstruction when the type of a construct is straightforward to compute from the types of its parts. For example, explicitly typed source languages never require explicit types for every term; these types are reconstructed from the explicit types of variables. Similarly, low-level systems do not explicitly describe how every single instruction changes the abstract state of the program. For most instructions, it is just as efficient to examine the instruction and recompute this information.

The "Compression" Approach. Given a collection of annotations, we could create a more concise representation that contains the same information. One technique for producing a compact wire format is to run a standard program such as `gzip` on a serialized version. If the repetition in the annotations manifests itself as repetition in the byte stream, this technique can be amazingly effective (see Section 5). However, it does not help improve the time or space required for verification if the byte stream is uncompressed prior to processing.

A slightly more domain-specific technique is to create a binary encoding that shares common subterms between annotations. This approach is effectively common-subexpression elimination on types. Because the verifier is aware of this sharing, it can exploit it to consume less space. There is an interesting tradeoff with respect to in-place modification, however. If a simplification (such as converting an annotation to a canonical form for internal use) is sound in all contexts, then it can be performed once on the shared term. However, if a transformation is context-dependent, the verifier must make a copy in the presence of sharing.

Work on reducing the size of JVML annotations has largely followed the compression approach [25,2]. For example, projects have found ways to exploit similarities across an entire archive of class files. Also, they carefully design the wire format so that downloading and verification may be pipelined. The TALx86 encoding does not currently have this property, but there is nothing essential to the language that prevents it.

Shao and associates [26] have investigated the engineering tradeoffs of sharing in the context of typed intermediate languages. They suggest a consistent use of hash-consing (essentially on-line common-subexpression elimination) and suspension-based lambda encoding [21] as a solution. Their hash-consing scheme also memoizes the results of type reductions so that identical reductions in the future require only retrieving the answer from a table. The problem of managing low-level types during compilation is quite similar to the problem of managing them during verification, but in the case of type-directed compilation, it is appropriate to specialize the task to the compiler.

Finally, we should note that comparing the size of compressed low-level types to the size of uncompressed object code is somewhat misleading because object code compresses quite well [16,7]. Domain-specific techniques include taking the instruction format into account (instead of the generic compression technique of processing entire bytes); detecting common sequences of instructions; and detecting similarity modulo a rarely repeated field, such as a branch target address. Analogous techniques may prove useful for annotations as well, but we know of no work that has tried them.

The "Abbreviation" Approach. The next step beyond simple sharing is to use *higher-order* annotations to factor out common portions. Such annotations are essentially functions at the level of types. Tarditi and others used this approach in their TIL compiler [28]. As we show in Section 4, this approach can exploit similarities that sharing cannot. Furthermore, higher-order annotations make it relatively easy for a compiler writer to express high-level abstractions within the type system of the target language. In our experience, using abbreviations places no additional burden on the compiler writer because she is already reasoning in terms of these abstractions. However, if the verifier must expand the abbreviations in order to verify the code, verification time may suffer.

Higher-order abbreviations are also an important component in the certified-code framework that Appel and Felty [1] propose. They suggest formalizing a machine's semantics and a safety policy in a higher-order logical framework. The code producer must then supply a formal proof that a program obeys the policy. Because a proof expressed directly in terms of a machine's semantics would presumably be enormous, Appel and Felty suggest that a compiler would first prove that a collection of lemmas are sound with respect to the semantics and then apply the lemmas to a program. In a sense, these lemmas are parameterized abbreviations that define a suitably concise type system.

In our system, we use *all* of these approaches to reduce annotation size and verification time. However, we have attempted to minimize the "bake it in" and "don't optimize" approaches in favor of the other techniques. Unlike `javac`, Touchstone, or Special J, TALx86 makes no commitment to calling convention or data representation. In fact, it has no built-in notion of functions; all control flow is just between blocks of code. The design challenge for TALx86, then, is to provide generally useful constructors that compilers can use in novel ways to encode the safety of their compilation strategies.

As a type system, TALx86 does "bake in" more than a primitive logical description of the machine. For example, it builds in a distinction between integers and pointers. As a result, programs cannot use the low bits of pointers to store information and then mask these bits before reading memory. Also, memory locations are statically divided into code and data (although extensions support run-time code generation [12]). In order to investigate the practicality of expressive low-level safety policies, we have relied on a rigorous, hand-written proof of type soundness and a procedural implementation of the verifier. A more formal approach would be to encode the proof in a logical framework and use a verifier produced mechanically from the proof.

Using our approach, we have been able to examine the feasibility of compiler-independent safety policies on a far larger scale than has been previously possible. To date, certifiers based on proof-carrying code technology have all had compiler-specific safety policies and no compiler has targeted the compiler-independent safety policies of Appel and Felty. Not only was TALx86 designed to be compiler-independent, but we and others have written three separate compilers that target TALx86. In this paper, we discuss our optimizing Popcorn compiler.[1] This compiler, itself a certified TALx86 program, is a several-hundred kilobyte executable compiled from over eighteen thousand lines of source code.

3 Compiling to TALx86: An Extended Example

In this section, we briefly review the structure of the TALx86 type system, its annotations, and the process of verification. In what follows, we present relevant TALx86 constructs as necessary, but for the purposes of this paper, it is sufficient to treat the types as low-level syntax for describing pre-conditions. Our purpose is not to dwell on the artifacts of TALx86 or its relative expressiveness. Rather, we want to give some intuition for the following claims, which we believe transcend TALx86:

- If the safety policy does not bake in data and control abstractions, then the annotations that the compiler uses to encode them can become large.
- In fact, the annotations describing compiler conventions consume much more space than the annotations that are specific to a particular source program.
- Although the annotations for compiler conventions are large, they are also very uniform and repetitious, though they become much less so in the presence of optimizations.

Because of this focus, we purposely do not explain some aspects of the annotations other than to mention the general things they are encoding. The reader interested in such details should consult the literature [20,19,10,18,9,27].

A TALx86 object file consists of IA32 assembly-language instructions and data. As in a conventional assembly language, the instructions and data are organized into labeled sequences. Unlike conventional assembly language, some labels are equipped with a type annotation. The type annotations on the labels of instruction sequences, called *code types*, specify a pre-condition that must be satisfied before control may be transferred to the label. The pre-condition specifies, among other things, the types of registers and stack slots. For example, if the code type annotating a label `L` is `{eax:int4, ebx:S(3), ecx: ^`

[1] The other compilers are a simple stack-based compiler for Popcorn and a compiler for a core subset of Scheme.

[int4,int4]}, then control may be transferred to the address L only when the register eax contains a 4-byte integer, the register ebx contains the integer value 3, and the register ecx contains a pointer (^) to a record ([...]) of two 4-byte integers.

Verification of code proceeds by taking each labeled instruction sequence and building a typing context that assumes registers have values with types as specified by the pre-condition. Each instruction is then type-checked, in sequence, under the current set of context assumptions, possibly producing a new context. For most instructions, the verifier automatically infers a suitable typing post-condition in a style similar to dataflow analysis or strongest post-conditions. Some instructions require additional annotations to help the verifier. For example, it is sometimes necessary to explicitly coerce values to a supertype, or to explicitly instantiate polymorphic type variables.

Not all labels require type annotations. However, code blocks without annotations may be checked multiple times under different contexts, depending on the control-flow paths of the program. To ensure termination of verification, the type-checker requires annotations on labels that are moved into a register, the stack,[2] or a data structure (such as a closure); on labels that are the targets of backwards branches (such as loop headers); and on labels that are exported from the object file (such as function entry points). These restrictions are sufficient for verification to terminate. We discuss labels without explicit types in more detail in Section 4.3.

As in a conventional compiler, our certifying compiler translates the high-level control-flow constructs of Popcorn into suitable collections of labeled instruction sequences and control transfers. For present purposes, control flow in Popcorn takes one of three forms:

- an intra-procedural jump
- a function call or return
- an invocation of the current exception handler

Currently, our compiler performs only intra-procedural optimizations, so the code types for function-entry labels are quite uniform and can be derived systematically from the source-level function's type. For simplicity, we discuss these code types first. We then discuss the code types for labels internal to functions, focusing on why they are more complicated than function entries. We emphasize that the distinction between the different flavors of code labels (function entries, internal labels, exception handlers) is a Popcorn convention encoded in the preconditions and is in no way specific to TALx86. Indeed, we have constructed other toy compilers that use radically different conventions.

3.1 Function-Entry Labels

As a running example, we consider a Popcorn function foo that takes one parameter, an int, and returns an int. The Popcorn type int is compiled to the

[2] Return addresses are an important exception; they do not need explicit types.

TALx86 type int4. Arithmetic operations are allowed on values of this type; treating them as pointers is not. Our compiler uses the standard C calling convention for the IA32 architecture. Under this convention, the parameters are passed on the stack, the return address is shallowest on the stack, the return value is passed in register eax, and the caller pops the parameters upon return. All of these specifics are encoded in TALx86 by giving foo this pre-condition:

```
foo: ∀s:Ts. {esp: { eax: int4
                    esp: int4::s}
                 ::int4
                 ::s}
```

The pre-condition for foo concerns only esp (the stack pointer) and requires that this register point to a stack that contains a return address (which itself has a pre-condition), then an int4 (*i.e.* the parameter), and then some stack, s. The return address expects an int4 in register eax and the stack to have shape int4::s. (The int4 is there because the caller pops the parameters.) The pre-condition is polymorphic over the "rest" of the stack as indicated by the universal quantification over the stack-type variable s. This technique allows a caller to abstract the current type of the stack upon entry, and it ensures that the type is preserved upon return. Types in TALx86 are classified into kinds (types of types), so that we do not confuse "standard" types such as int4 with "non-standard" types such as stack types. To maintain the distinction, we must label the bound type variable s with its kind (Ts).

Notice that our annotation already includes much more information than it would need to if the safety policy dictated a calling convention. In that case, we would presumably just give the parameter types and return type of the function. Some systems, including the certifier for Special J [5], go even further — they encode the types in the string for the label, so it appears that no annotation is necessary. Of course, the safety policy now attaches specific meaning to the characters in a label; the annotations are encoded in the assembly listing.

Our annotation does not quite describe the standard C calling convention. In particular, the standard requires registers ebx, esi, and edi to be callee-save. (It also requires ebp, traditionally the frame pointer, to be callee-save. Our compiler uses ebp for the exception handler.) We encode callee-save registers using polymorphism:[3]

```
foo: ∀s:Ts a1:T4 a2:T4 a3:T4 .
 {esp: {eax:int4 esp: int4::s ebx:a1 esi:a2 edi:a3}
       ::int4::s
  ebx:a1 esi:a2 edi:a3}
```

This pre-condition indicates that for any standard types a1, a2, a3,[4] the appropriate registers must have those types before foo is called and again when

[3] Here and below, underlining is only for emphasis.

[4] The kind T4 includes all types whose values fit in a register.

the return address is invoked. This annotation restricts the behavior of `foo` to preserve these registers because it does not know of any other values with these types. More formally, this fact follows from parametricity [6,29]. Notice that if we wish to use different conventions about which registers should be callee-save, then we need to change only the pre-condition on `foo`. In particular, we do not need to change the underlying type system of TALx86.

Much more detail is required to encode our compiler's translation of exception handling [19], so we just sketch the main ideas. We reserve register `ebp` to point into the middle of the stack where a pointer to the current exception handler resides. This handler expects an exception packet in register `eax`. Because `foo` might need to raise an exception, its pre-condition must encode this strategy. Also, it must encode that if `foo` returns normally, the exception handler is still in `ebp`. We express all these details below, where `@` is an infix operator for appending two stack types.

```
foo: ∀s1:Ts s2:Ts a1:T4 a2:T4 a3:T4 .
 {esp: {eax:int4
        esp: int4::s1@{esp:s2 eax:exn}::s2
        ebp: {esp:s2 eax:exn}::s2
        ebx:a1 esi:a2 edi:a3}
       ::int4::s1@{esp:s2 eax:exn}::s2}
  ebp: {esp:s2 eax:exn}::s2
  ebx:a1 esi:a2 edi:a3}
```

We urge the reader not to focus on the details other than to notice that none of the additions are particular to `foo`, nor would it be appropriate for a safety policy to bake in this specific treatment of exception handlers. Also, we have assumed there is a type `exn` for exception packets. TALx86 does not provide this type directly, so our compiler must encode its own representation using an extensible sum [9]. Each of the four occurrences of `exn` above should in fact be replaced by the type

```
∃c:Tm ^*[(^T^rw(c)*[int4^rw])^rw,c]
```

but in the interest of type-setting, we spare the reader the result.

For the sake of completeness, we offer a final amendment to make this pre-condition correct. Our compiler schedules function calls while some heap records may be partially initialized. This strategy is arguably better than the "don't optimize" approach of always initializing records within a basic block, but it requires that we convince the verifier that no aliases to partially initialized records escape. In particular, the pre-condition for `foo` uses two *capability variables* [27], as shown below,[5] to indicate that it does not create any aliases to partially initialized records reachable from the caller or exception handler.

[5] The constructor `&[...]` joins two capabilities to produce a harder-to-satisfy capability; we omit its definition.

```
foo: ∀s1:Ts s2:Ts e1:Tcap e2:Tcap a1:T4 a2:T4 a3:T4 .
 {esp: {eax:int4
        esp: int4::s1@{esp:s2 eax:exn cap:e2}::s2
        ebp: {esp:s2 eax:exn cap:e2}::s2
        ebx:a1 esi:a2 edi:a3
        cap: &[e1,e2]}
       ::int4::s1@{esp:s2 eax:exn cap:e2}::s2}
  ebp: {esp:s2 eax:exn cap:e2}::s2
  ebx:a1 esi:a2 edi:a3
  cap: &[e1,e2]}
```

In short, because our compiler has complicated inter-procedural invariants, the naive encoding into TALx86 is anything but concise. (The unconvinced reader is invited to encode a function that takes a function pointer as a parameter.) However, the only parts particular to our example function `foo` are the return type, which is written once, and the parameter types, which are written twice. Even these parts are the same for all functions that take and return integers.

3.2 Internal Labels

In this section, we present the pre-conditions for labels that are targets of intra-procedural jumps. For simplicity, we consider only functions that do not declare any local exception handlers. This special case is by far the most common, so it is worth considering explicitly. Because our compiler does perform intra-procedural optimizations, most relevantly register allocation, the pre-conditions for internal labels are less uniform than those for function-entry labels. Specifically, they must encode several properties about the program point that the label designates:

- A local variable may reside in a register or on the stack.
- Some stack slots may not hold live values, so along different control-flow paths to the label, a stack slot may have values of different types.
- Some callee-save values may reside on the stack while others remain in registers.
- Some heap records may be partially initialized.

First we describe the relevant aspects of our term translation: Any callee-save values that cannot remain in registers are stored on the stack in the function prologue and restored into registers in the function epilogue. The space for this storage is just shallower than the return address. Local variables that do not fit in registers are stored in "spill slots" that are shallowest on the stack. The number of spill slots remains constant in the body of a function. This strategy is fairly normal, but it is far too specific to be dictated by TALx86. Indeed, our original Popcorn compiler did not perform register allocation; it simply pushed and popped variables on the stack as needed.

The pre-condition for internal labels gives the type and location (register or spill slot) for each live local variable. If a stack slot is not live, we must still give it some "place-holder" type so that the stack type describes a stack of the correct size. Different control-flow paths may use the same stack slot for temporary variables of different types. In these cases, no previously seen type can serve as this place-holder. TALx86 provides a primitive type `top4` which is a supertype of all types ranging over word-sized values. We give this type to the dead stack slots at the control-flow join; the appropriate subtyping on control transfers is handled implicitly by the verifier.[6]

In addition to live variables, all of the invariants involving the stack, the exception handler, etc. must be preserved as control flows through labels, so this information looks much as it does for function-entry labels.

For example, suppose our function `foo` uses all of the callee-save registers and needs three spill slots. Furthermore, suppose that at an internal label, `l`, there are two live variables, both of type `int4`, one in register `esi` and one in the middle spill slot. Then a correct pre-condition for `l` is:

```
l: ∀s1:Ts s2:Ts e1:Tcap e2:Tcap a1:T4 a2:T4 a3:T4.
 {esp:
      top4::int4::top4::a3::a2::a1
      ::{eax:int4
         esp: int4::s1@{esp:s2 eax:exn cap:e2}::s2
         ebp: {esp:s2 eax:exn cap:e2}::s2
         ebx:a1 esi:a2 edi:a3
         cap: &[e1,e2]}
      ::int4::s1@{esp:s2 eax:exn cap:e2}::s2}
  ebp: {esp:s2 eax:exn cap:e2}::s2
  cap: &[e1,e2]
  esi: int4}
```

Our register allocator tries not to use callee-save registers so that functions do not have to save and restore them. For example, suppose registers `esi` and `edi` are not used in a function. Then internal labels will encode that a value of type `a1` is on the stack in the appropriate place, `esi` contains a value of type `a2`, and `edi` contains a value of type `a3`.

If one or more records were partially initialized on entry to `l`, then the pre-condition would have a more complicated capability; we omit the details. What should be clear at this point is that the type annotations for internal labels are considerably less uniform than function-entry annotations.

4 Recovering Conciseness and Efficiency

Continuing the examples from the previous section, we describe three techniques for reducing the size of annotations. We then discuss techniques, most notably hash-consing, that can reduce the space and time required during verification. The next section quantifies the effectiveness of these and other techniques.

[6] It is theoretically possible to use polymorphism instead of a supertype, but in practice we found doing so very unwieldy.

4.1 Sharing Common Subterms

Because the annotations repeat information, we can greatly reduce their total size by replacing identical terms with a pointer to a shared term. As an example, consider again the pre-condition for the function `foo`, which takes and returns an `int`:

```
type exn = ∃c:Tm ^*[(^T^rw(c)*[int4^rw])^rw,c]
foo: ∀s1:Ts s2:Ts e1:Tcap e2:Tcap a1:T4 a2:T4 a3:T4 .
 {esp: {eax:int4
        esp: int4::s1@{esp:s2 eax:exn cap:e2}::s2
        ebp: {esp:s2 eax:exn cap:e2}::s2
        ebx:a1 esi:a2 edi:a3
        cap: &[e1,e2]}
       ::int4::s1@{esp:s2 eax:exn cap:e2}::s2}
  ebp: {esp:s2 eax:exn cap:e2}::s2
  ebx:a1 esi:a2 edi:a3
  cap: &[e1,e2]}
```

Removing some common subterms by hand, we can represent the same information with the following pseudo-annotation:

```
1 = ∃c:Tm ^*[(^T^rw(c)*[int4^rw])^rw,c]
2 = &[e1,e2]
3 = {esp:s2 eax: [1] cap:e2}::s2
4 = int4::s1@ [3]
5 = {eax:int4 esp: [4] ebp: [3]
     ebx:a1 esi:a2 edi:a3 cap: [2] }::[4]

foo: ∀s1:Ts s2:Ts e1:Tcap e2:Tcap a1:T4 a2:T4 a3:T4 .
 {esp: [5] ebp: [3] ebx:a1 esi:a2 edi:a3 cap: [2] }
```

Other pre-conditions can share subterms with this one. For example, the pre-condition for `l` from the previous section can be rewritten as:

```
l: ∀s1:Ts s2:Ts e1:Tcap e2:Tcap a1:T4 a2:T4 a3:T4.
 {esp: top4::int4::top4::a3::a2::a1::[5]
  ebp: [3] cap: [2] esi:int4}
```

Despite exploiting significant sharing, this example illustrates some limitations of sharing common subterms. First, we would like to share all the occurrences of "`s1:Ts s2:Ts ... a3:T4`", but whether or not we can do so depends on the abstract syntax of the language. Second, pre-conditions for functions with different parameter types or return types cannot exploit subterms 4 or 5. Another possible shortcoming not demonstrated is that alpha-equivalent terms may not appear to be the same. In practice, compilers can re-use variable names for compiler-introduced variables, so detecting alpha-equivalence for the purpose of sharing is not so important.

4.2 Parameterized Abbreviations

TALx86 provides user-defined (*i.e.* compiler-defined) higher-order type constructors. These functions from types to types have several uses. For example, they are necessary to encode source-level type constructors, such as array, list, or object types. Here we show how to use higher-order type constructors to define parameterized abbreviations. These abbreviations can exploit sharing among different types that sharing common subterms cannot. However, our verifier is unable to exploit such abbreviations during verification for reasons we explain below.

Because every function-entry pre-condition that our compiler creates is the same except for its parameter types and return type, we can create a parameterized abbreviation that describes the generic situation. Then at each function-entry label, we apply the abbreviation to the appropriate types.

```
type F = fn params:Ts ret:T4.
 ∀s1:Ts s2:Ts e1:Tcap e2:Tcap a1:T4 a2:T4 a3:T4.
 {esp: {eax: ret
        esp: params@s1@{esp:s2 eax:exn cap:e2}::s2
        ebp: {esp:s2 eax:exn cap:e2}::s2
        ebx:a1 esi:a2 edi:a3
        cap: &[e1,e2]}
       ::params@s1@{esp:s eax:exn cap:e2}::s2}
  ebp: {esp:s2 eax:exn cap:e2}::s2
  ebx:a1 esi:a2 edi:a3
  cap: &[e1,e2]}

foo: F int4::se int4
```

The only new feature other than the abbreviation is the type `se` which describes empty stacks. We use it here to terminate a list of parameter types. The use of abbreviations greatly simplifies the structure of the compiler because it centralizes invariants such as calling conventions.

It is not clear how a compiler-independent verifier could exploit an abbreviation like `F` during verification. Suppose the first instruction in block `foo` increments the input parameter. The verifier must check that given the pre-condition `F int4::se int4`, it is safe to perform an increment of the value on top of the stack. This verification requires inspecting the result of the abbreviation application — the verifier does not know that the argument `int4::se` describes the top of the stack. As we show in Section 5, using abbreviations sometimes slows down verification because of this phenomenon.

The abbreviation `F` is widely useful because all function-entry pre-conditions are similar. To use abbreviations for internal labels, we must capture the additional properties that distinguish these pre-conditions. In addition to `F`'s parameters, we also need parameters for the spill slots, the live registers, and something to do with partial-initialization issues. We also use a primitive type constructor (&) for combining two pre-conditions. That way we can pass in the live registers as one pre-condition and merge it with a pre-condition that describes the reserved registers.

```
type L =
fn params:Ts ret:T4 spills:Ts part:Tcap regs:Tpre.
 ∀s1:Ts s2:Ts e1:Tcap e2:Tcap a1:T4 a2:T4 a3:T4.
 {esp:
      spills@a3::a2::a1
      ::{eax: ret
         esp: params@s1@{esp:s2 eax:exn cap:e2}::s2
         ebp: {esp:s2 eax:exn cap:e2}::s2
         ebx:a1 esi:a2 edi:a3
         cap: &[e1,e2]}
      ::params@s1@{esp:s2 eax:exn cap:e2}::s2}
 ebp: {esp:s2 eax:exn cap:e2}::s2
 cap: &[part,e1,e2]}
 & regs

l: L int4::se int4
     top4::int4::top4::se ce {esi:int4}
```

L is correct, but it is useful only for labels in functions where all three callee-save values are stored on the stack. With a "don't optimize" approach, we could make all functions meet this description, but we lose most of the advantages of callee-save registers as a result. A better approach is to provide $2^3 = 8$ different abbreviations, one for each combination of callee-save values being stored on the stack. In fact, we need only 4 such abbreviations because our register allocator uses the callee-save registers in a fixed order. Because the compiler provides the abbreviations, this specialization is possible and appropriate.

Rather than require the compiler-writer to write and use higher-order abbreviations, one might hope to write a tool that took a collection of TALx86 types and re-wrote them in terms of some automatically generated abbreviations. Creating an optimal result appears at least as difficult as finding the shortest simply-typed lambda calculus term equivalent to a given one. We have not investigated using heuristics to discover useful abbreviations.

4.3 Eliding Pre-conditions

Recall that the verifier checks a code block by assuming its pre-condition is true and then processing each instruction in turn, checking it for safety and computing a pre-condition for the remainder of the block. At a control transfer to another block, it suffices to ensure that the current pre-condition implies the pre-condition on the destination label.

TALx86 uses a reconstruction approach by allowing many label pre-conditions to be elided. Clearly, the result of eliding a pre-condition is a direct decrease in annotation size. To check a control transfer to a block with an elided pre-condition, the verifier simply uses the current pre-condition at the source of the transfer to check the target block. Hence, if a block with elided pre-condition has multiple control-flow predecessors, it is verified multiple times under (possibly) different pre-conditions.

To ensure that the verifier terminates, we prohibit annotation-free loops in the control-flow graph. For this reason, TALx86 allows a pre-condition to be elided only if the block is only the target of forward jumps. Even with this restriction, the number of times a block is checked is the number of *paths* through the control-flow graph to the block such that no block on the path has an explicit pre-condition. This number can be exponential in the number of code blocks, so it is unwise to elide explicit pre-conditions indiscriminantly. As the next section demonstrates, an exponential number of paths is rare, but it does occur and it can have a disastrous effect on verification time.

The approach our compiler takes is to set an *elision threshold*, T, and insist that no code block is verified more than T times. Notice $T = 1$ means all merge points have explicit pre-conditions. We interpret $T = 0$ to mean that all code labels, even those with a single predecessor, have explicit pre-conditions. For higher values of T, we expect space requirements to decrease, but verification time to increase. Given a value for T, we might like to minimize the number of labels that have explicit pre-conditions. Unfortunately, we have proven that this problem is NP-Complete for $T \geq 3$. (We do not know the tractability when $T = 2$.) Currently, the compiler does a greedy depth-first traversal of the control-flow graph, leaving off pre-conditions until the threshold demands otherwise. In pathological cases, this heuristic can do arbitrarily poorly, but it seems to do well in practice.

Using an elision threshold is actually over-constraining the problem — it is more important to minimize the total number of times that we verify blocks. That is, we would prefer to verify some block more than T times in order to verify several other blocks many fewer times. For structured programs (all intra-procedural jumps are for loops and conditionals), it appears that this relaxed problem can be solved in polynomial time ($O(n^9)$ where n is the number of blocks [13]), but the algorithm seems impractical.

4.4 Hash-Consing and Fast Type Operations

So far, we have discussed techniques for reducing the size of the annotations that the code producer writes. For the verifier, these explicit types provide guidance to check that each assembly instruction is safe. To do this checking, the verifier determines the type of the context (i.e., the registers and the stack) before the instruction, the types of the operands, and the type of the context after the instruction. The operands must be subtypes of the types that the instruction requires. In short, the verifier itself creates many type expressions and often checks that one is a subtype of another. Therefore, it is important that these operations consume as little time and space as possible.

Our primary technique for reducing space is hash-consing, which is essentially just the on-line form of sharing. As types are created, we first check a table to see if they have been created before. If so, we return a pointer to the table entry;

if not, we put the type in the table. As a result, types consume less space, but we incur the overhead of managing a table. It would be correct to return any alpha-equivalent type from the table, but in the interest of fast lookup operations, we find only a syntactically identical type.

In the most general case, to decide if τ is a subtype of τ', we should convert both types to normal form and then do a structural subtyping comparison. One common case for which it is easy to optimize is when τ and τ' are the same object, that is, they are pointer-equal. With hash-consing, syntactically equal types should always be pointer-equal. Even when the two types are not the same object (for example, one is a strict subtype of the other), many parts of the two types may be pointer-equal, so we can usually avoid a full structural comparison.

There are complications with pointer equality, however: We must consider alpha-equivalent types to be equal. To do so, we maintain a separate variable-substitution map rather than actually performing costly type substitutions. In the presence of a non-empty map, it is not necessarily correct that pointer-equal types are equal because the substitution has not been applied. Fortunately, our compiler uses the same type variables consistently, so the variable-substitution map is almost always empty.

Hash-consing has another positive effect on verification time: When we reduce τ to τ' (for example, by applying an abbreviation), we do an in-place update of τ. Hence, all pointers to a shared τ will use the result of the single reduction. However, the original τ will no longer appear to be in the hash-cons table. We could add a level of indirection to alleviate this shortcoming (keep τ in the table for the purpose of future sharing and have it point to its reduced form τ'), but our implementation does not currently do so.

Another common operation on types is substitution, that is, substituting τ' for a variable α in τ. Operations that need substitution include applying abbreviations and instantiating polymorphic types. We need to recursively substitute for α in all the constituent types within τ, but we expect that most of them do not contain α. To optimize for this common case and avoid crawling over much of τ, we memoize the free variables of each type and store this set with the type.

As discussed in Section 5.4, we might expect further benefits from using de Bruijn indices and performing type substitutions lazily. Unfortunately, this change was so pervasive that we chose not to investigate it in the experiments that we discuss in the next section.

5 Experimental Results

In this section, we present our quantitative study of certifying a real program in TALx86. We conclude that targeting compiler-independent safety policies is practical and scalable when appropriate techniques are used.

Our example is the Popcorn compiler itself. The compiler consists of 39 Popcorn source files compiled separately. The more interesting optimizations performed are Chaitin-style intra-procedural register allocation [4] (using optimistic spilling [3] and conservative coalescing [8]) and the elimination of fully redundant null-checks for object dereferences. The entire compiler is roughly 18,000 lines of source code and compiles to 816 kilobytes of object code (335 kilobytes after running `strip`).

The sizes we report include the sum across files of all annotations, not just those for code labels. They do not include the separate module-interface files that the TALx86 link-checker uses to ensure type-safe linking. All execution times were measured on a 266MHz Pentium II with 64MB of RAM running Windows NT 4.0. The verifier and assembler are written in Objective Caml [15] and compiled to native code.

We first show that naive choices in the annotation language and compiler can produce a system with unacceptable space and/or time overhead. Then we show that our actual implementation avoids these pitfalls. Next we adjust various parameters and disable various techniques to discover the usefulness of individual approaches and how they interact. Finally, we discuss how we could extend our techniques to further lower the TALx86 overhead.

5.1 Two Bad Approaches

A simple encoding of the TALx86 annotations is insufficient. First, consider a system where we do not use the abbreviations developed in Section 4, our type annotations repeat types rather than share them, and we put types on all code labels. Then the total annotation size for our program is over 4.5 megabytes, several times the size of the object code. As for verification time, if we make no attempt to share common subterms created during verification, then it takes 59 seconds to verify all of the files.

A second possibility is to remove as many pre-conditions as possible. That is, we put an explicit pre-condition on a code label only if the label is used as a call destination, a backwards-branch destination, or a first-class value. Indeed, the total size of our annotations drops to 1.85 megabytes. However, the verifier now checks some code blocks a very large number of times. Total verification time rises to 18 minutes and 30 seconds.

These two coarse experiments yield some immediate conclusions. First, the actual amount of safety information describing a compiled program is large. Second, the number of loop-free paths through our application code is, in places, much larger than the size of the code. Therefore, it is unwise to make verification time proportional to the number of loop-free paths as the second approach does.

The latter conclusion is important for certified-code frameworks that construct verification conditions at verification time via a form of weakest pre-condition computation. Essentially, such systems construct pre-conditions for loop-free code segments using a backward flow analysis. In an expressive system, the pre-condition at a backward merge-point could be the logical disjunction of two conditions. Hence, if done naively, the constructed condition can have exponential size by having a different clause for every loop-free path.

When the number of loop-free paths is large, it is clear that constructing an enormous pre-condition is wasteful. For a compiler to exploit the weakness of such a pre-condition, it would need to have optimized based on an exponential amount of path-sensitive information. We conclude that constructing weakest pre-conditions in this way is impractical. Instead, annotations should guide the construction of the verification condition; the optional code pre-conditions of TALx86 fill this role.

5.2 A Usable System

Having shown how bad matters can get, we now present the actual overhead that our system achieves. First, we identify the main techniques used and the overhead that results. Then we show that verification time is roughly proportional to file size; this fact suggests that our approach should scale to larger applications. Finally, we partition the source code into several styles, show that the overhead is reasonable for all of them, and discuss salient differences.

Unlike the "straw man" systems constructed above, the real encoding of TALx86 annotations uses several tables to share common occurrences. Specifically, uses of identifiers, types, kinds, and coercions are actually indices into tables that contain the annotations. The code producer can avoid duplicates when constructing the tables. The benefit of this approach is proportional to the amount of repetition; there is a small penalty for annotations that occur only once. We call this technique "sharing"; more specifically it is full common-subexpression elimination on types at the file level. Sharing is just off-line hash-consing; we use the latter term to refer to sharing within the verifier for types created during verification.

Sharing does not create parameterized abbreviations, so we also use the abbreviations developed in Section 3. The compiler provides the abbreviations and uses them in a text version of TALx86. An independent tool converts the text version into a binary version that has sharing. In this sense, we use abbreviations "before" sharing.

We set the elision threshold to four. At this value, many forward control-flow points will not need explicit pre-conditions, but no block is verified more than four times.

Finally, the verifier uses hash-consing to share types that are created during verification. That is, when creating a new type, the verifier consults a table to see if it has encountered the type previously. If so, it uses the type in the table. Because the entire sharing table is parsed prior to verification, any types in the table will be used rather than repeated. Reductions on higher-order type constructors are performed in a lazy manner. In particular, we use a weak-head normalization strategy with memoization to avoid both unnecessary reductions and duplicated reductions. As such, other uses of the type will not have to recompute the reduction. Shao and associates use a similar strategy [26]. Because of complications with the scope of abbreviations, the hash-consing table is emptied before verifying each file. If memory becomes scarce, we could empty the table at any point, but this measure has not been necessary in practice. Note that the use of hash-consing cannot affect the size of explicit annotations; hash-consing attempts to share types created during verification.

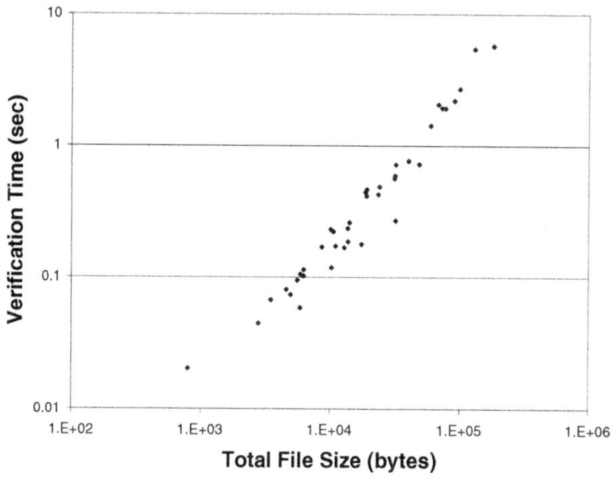

Fig. 1. Verification Time vs. File Size

With this system, total annotation size drops from 4.5 megabytes to 419 kilobytes and verification time drops from 59 to 34.5 seconds. As for compilation time, our compiler takes 40 seconds to compile the Popcorn source files into ASCII TALx86 files, which are essentially Microsoft Assembler (MASM) files augmented with annotations. A separate tool takes 23 seconds to assemble all of these files; this time includes the creation of the binary encoding of the annotations with sharing. As we add more optimizations to our compiler, we expect compilation time to increase more than verification time. The latter may actually decrease as object-code size decreases.

Performing `gzip` compression on the 419 kilobytes of annotations reduces their size to 163 kilobytes. The ratio of compression is similar to that for our object files; the unstripped files compress from 816 to 252 kilobytes and the stripped files compress from 335 to 102 kilobytes.

A desirable property is that verification time is generally proportional to file size. Without eliding pre-conditions, the time to verify TALx86 code is proportional to the size of the code plus the size of the *normalized* types used as annotations plus the time to look up types in the context. However, with higher-order abbreviations, normalizing types could, in theory, take non-elementary time [17]. We are pleased to see that such inefficiency has not occurred in practice: Figure 1 plots verification time against total size (object code plus annotations) for all of the files in the compiler. The time stays roughly proportional as file size grows by over an order of magnitude. Small files take proportionally longer to verify because of start-up costs and the overhead of using hash-consing. Such files take just a fraction of a second to verify, so we consider these costs insignificant.

So far we have presented results for the entire compiler as a whole. By analyzing the results for different styles of code, we can gain additional insight. Of course, all of the code is in the same source language, compiled by the same

Style	Object Code (kB)	Annotations (kB)	Verification Time (sec)	Size Ratio	Time Ratio
Polymorphic Libraries	36.4	19.6	1.19	.54	46.9
Monomorphic Libraries	34.8	15.1	.94	.43	53.1
Mostly Type Definitions	45.7	30.6	1.29	.67	58.9
Machine generated	148.4	82.0	6.30	.55	36.6
Compilation	550.0	271.4	22.3	.49	36.8

Fig. 2. Effect of Different Code Styles

compiler, and written by the authors. Nonetheless, we can partition the files into several broad categories:

- Polymorphic libraries: These files provide generally useful utilities such as iterators over generic container types. Examples include files for lists, dictionaries, sets, and resizing arrays.
- Monomorphic libraries: Examples include files for bit vectors and command-line arguments.
- Mostly Type Definitions: These files primarily define types used by the compiler and provide only simple code to create or destruct instances of the type. Examples include files for the abstract syntax of Popcorn, the compiler's intermediate language, an abstract syntax for TALx86, and an environment maintained while translating from the intermediate language to TALx86.
- Machine generated: These files include the scanner and the parser. Compared to other styles of code, they are characterized by a small number of large functions that contain switch statements with many cases. They also have large constant arrays.
- Compilation: These files actually do the compilation. Examples include files for type checking, register allocation, and printing the output.

Figure 2 summarizes the annotation size and verification time relative to the categorization.[7] The "Size Ratio" is annotation size divided by the object code size (smaller is better). The "Time Ratio" is the sum of the two sizes divided by the verification time (larger is better).

Most importantly, all of the size ratios are well within a factor of two and the time ratios are even closer to each other. We conclude that no particular style of code we have written dominates the overhead of producing provably safe object code. Even so, the results differ enough to make some interesting distinctions.

The files with mostly type definitions have the largest (worst) size ratio and largest (best) time ratio. The former is because type definitions are compiled into annotations that describe the corresponding TALx86 types, but there is no associated object code. The size ratio can actually be arbitrarily high as the

[7] The sum of the verification times is slightly less than the time to verify all the files together due to secondary effects.

		Annotation Size (kB)		Verification Time (sec)	
Sharing	Abbreviations	Uncompressed	Compressed	No hash-consing	Hash-consing
no	no	2041	155	50	38
no	yes	793	132	42	36
yes	no	503	205	37.5	34.5
yes	yes	419	163	40.5	34.5

Fig. 3. Effect of Abbreviations, Sharing Subterms, and Hash-Consing

amount of code in a source file goes to zero. The time ratio is also not surprising; the time-consuming part of verification is checking that each instruction is safe given its context.

The relatively high size ratio for machine-generated code is an artifact of how parsers are generated. Essentially, all of the different token types are put into a large union. The code that processes tokens is therefore filled with annotations that coerce values into and out of this union.

The size ratio for polymorphic libraries is slightly larger than we expected. A source-level function that is polymorphic over some types needs to explicitly name those types only once. Because TALx86 has no notion of function, all of the labels for such a function must enumerate their type variables.[8] Furthermore, control transfers between these labels must explicitly instantiate the additional type variables.

Finally, the time ratio is noticeably worse for the compilation code. This style of code contains a much higher proportion of function calls than libraries, which mostly contain leaf procedures. Because of the complicated type instantiations that occur at a call site, call instructions take the most time to verify.

5.3 Effectiveness of Individual Techniques

We have shown that our system achieves reasonable performance and uses a number of techniques for controlling annotation overhead, but we have not yet discussed which of the techniques are effective. In this section, we examine what happens if we selectively disable some of these techniques.

Figure 3 summarizes the total annotation size when the elision threshold is four and the other techniques are used selectively. When "Sharing" is no, we do not use tables for sharing types and coercions. Instead, we repeat the types directly in the annotations. We still share identifiers so that the lengths of strings is insignificant. If "Abbreviations" is no, then all abbreviations are fully expanded before the annotations are written. "Uncompressed" is the total size of all the annotations. "Compressed" is the sum of the result of running `gzip` on each file's annotations separately. The final two columns give total verification time with and without hash-consing enabled.

[8] Pre-conditions can still be elided, fortunately.

We first discuss the effect of sharing and abbreviations on the explicit annotation size. Both techniques appear very effective if we ignore the effect of `gzip`. Abbreviations alone reduce size by a factor of 2.57 whereas sharing alone reduces size by a factor of 4.06. Using abbreviations and sharing reduces size by another seventeen percent as compared to a system with just sharing. Hence neither technique subsumes the other, but they recover much of the same repetition.

However, if what we really care about is the size of annotations that must be sent to a code consumer, then we should consider running `gzip`. It is clear that `gzip` is extremely effective; our worst result for compressed annotations is a factor of two better than our best result for uncompressed annotations. More subtle is the fact that `gzip` achieves a smaller result when sharing is *not* used in our binary encoding. This result, which surprised us, is a product of how our tables are implemented and how `gzip` performs compression. In short, `gzip` constructs its own tables and uses a much more compact format than our encoding. Worse, our tables hide repetition from `gzip`, which looks for common strings. We conclude that if annotation size is the primary concern, then the binary encoding should remain "`gzip`-friendly".

Abbreviations are actually much more effective than the data in the figure suggests. The compiler's abbreviations are used only for code pre-conditions, so optimizing this one aspect of annotation size must eventually demonstrate Amdahl's Law.[9] We considered what the total annotation size would be if we removed *all* explicit code pre-conditions. Of course, the result of this drastic measure is unverifiable, but it provides a rough lower bound for the effectiveness of the abbreviations. The total size is still 377 kilobytes, so abbreviations reduced the size of code pre-conditions by about a factor of four $((2041-377)/(793-377))$.

We now discuss the effect of the techniques on verification time. Here `gzip` is useless because our verifier works on uncompressed annotations. Without hash-consing, sharing significantly reduces verification time. While the verifier under these conditions does not share types that it creates during verification, it does share types that originally occur in the annotations. The result suggests that these types cover many of those used during verification.[10] Without sharing, abbreviations are a great help because they recover the most common occurrences. However, with sharing, abbreviations actually *hurt* verification time. The time to expand the abbreviations during verification outweighs the time that the additional sharing gains.

With hash-consing, the different verification times are much closer to each other. Using a hash-consing table rediscovers any sharing, so without sharing initially we have to pay only the cost to achieve this rediscovery. More interestingly, the penalty for abbreviations disappears. We believe this result is due to the fact that with hash-consing, any abbreviation applied to the same argument is expanded only once and then the result is used in multiple places.

[9] Actually, there are a few other places where the abbreviations are used, such as when a polymorphic function is instantiated at a function type, but such situations are rare in our code.

[10] Parsing time is a small but noticeable fraction of the difference.

Hash-consing reduces verification time significantly, but only with a careful implementation of the hashing. For example, if we give our hash-cons table a size near a power of two (as number theory warns against), verification time takes longer than without hash-consing. The good news is that optimizing the verifier can sometimes be reduced to fundamental properties of data structures. The bad news is the difference between verification times under different parameters is more brittle than we would like.

One reason hash-consing improves verification time is that types occupy less space, so we expect better cache performance and fewer garbage collections. Another reason is that the verifier's function for determining if one type is a subtype of another returns immediately when two types are pointer-equal. This function is called about 170,000 times when verifying our compiler. Without hash-consing (but with sharing and abbreviations), 45,000 of the calls are with pointer-equal arguments. With hash-consing, the figure rises to 82,000. Even when the entire types are not pointer-equal, we can avoid much of the structural comparison when parts of them are pointer-equal. Without hash-consing, we make about 1,400,000 recursive calls. With hash-consing, the number of recursive calls drops to 730,000.

As explained in the previous section, TALx86 code blocks that are targets of only forward branches do not need annotations, but they will be reverified along every unannotated control-flow path. Given an elision threshold T, our compiler ensures that no block will be verified more than T times. Subject to this constraint, it uses a simple greedy algorithm to leave annotations off labels. Figure 4 shows the effect of changing the value of T. We use sharing and abbreviations.

The top chart in Figure 4 shows that total annotation size drops by over fifteen percent as T is 1 instead of 0. We conclude that low-level systems should not require pre-conditions on all blocks. However, the additional space savings as T takes values larger than 8 are quite small. This fact justifies the use of $T = 4$ for the other experiments.

The bottom charts in Figure 4 show the verification time for different values of T. Verification time initially drops as T gets the value 1 instead of 0. This phenomenon indicates that it takes a lot of time to process an explicit annotation and compare it to a pre-condition. As T takes values 2, 4, 8, and 16, verification time rises noticeably but only by a few seconds. We conclude that this range of values allows for reasonable time-space tradeoffs. As T takes larger values, verification time rises sharply. Although very few additional blocks have their pre-conditions elided, these blocks are then checked a very large number of times. In fact, for large T, the time spent verifying different files varies drastically because most files do not have any such blocks. (A value of infinity for T means we put explicit annotations only where the verifier requires them.)

5.4 Useful Extensions

We have presented a system where uncompressed safety annotations consume roughly half the space of the object code they describe, and we have given

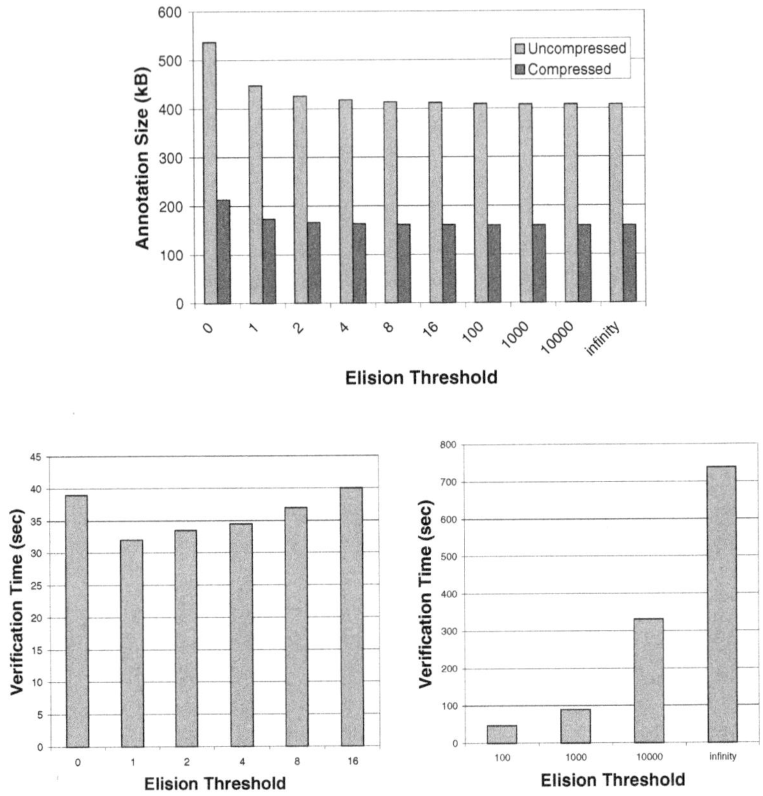

Fig. 4. Effect of Elision Threshold

techniques (sharing, abbreviations, and elision) that help in this regard. Now we investigate whether the current system is the best we can hope to achieve or if the techniques could contribute more to reducing the TALx86 overhead. By moving beyond what the current system supports, we demonstrate the latter.

First, notice that sharing common subterms is so effective because we share annotations across an entire file. The file level is currently the best we can do because we compile files separately. In a scenario where all of the object files are packaged together, we could share annotations in a single table for the entire package. Although our current tools cannot process such a package, we are able to generate it and measure its size. The total size drops from 419 kilobytes to 338 kilobytes. We conclude that different files in our project have many similar annotations; we should be able to exploit this property to further reduce overhead.

This improvement does not rely on understanding the compiler's conventions, so a generic TALx86 tool could put separately compiled object files into a package.

Second, the annotations that describe what coercions apply at each instruction are not currently shared. Although there are many common occurrences, some of them take only one byte to represent, so sharing these annotations must carefully avoid increasing space requirements.

Third, verification time suffers significantly from memory allocation and garbage collection. Although we have implemented hash-consing to address this bottleneck, Shao and associates [26] use their experience building type-directed compilers to suggest that suspension-based lambda encoding [21] (essentially de Bruijn indices and lazy substitution) can further improve performance. We relegate to future work modifying the verifier to experiment with these techniques.

Fourth, some well-chosen uses of type reconstruction could eliminate many of the explicit annotations. For example, if the verifier performed unification of (first-order) type variables, then the compiler could eliminate all of the type applications at control transfer points. This elision would improve our annotation size to 330 kilobytes. (To compute this figure, we elided the instantiations even though the verifier cannot process the result.) Reconstruction approaches improve the size even in the presence of `gzip`; the compressed annotations drop from 163 kilobytes to 141 kilobytes in this case.

In summary, the TALx86 system shows that techniques such as sharing and elision make certified code scalable and practical, but even TALx86 could use these techniques more aggressively to achieve lower overhead.

6 Conclusions

Our Popcorn compiler encodes the safety of its output in TALx86. As a Popcorn application itself, it also serves as the largest application we know of that has been compiled to a safe machine language. Because we believe safety policies should not be tailored to a particular compiler, we encode the aspects of Popcorn compilation relevant to safety in the more primitive constructs of TALx86. We have found that the most important factor in the scalability of certifying compilation is the size of code pre-conditions.

Based on our experience, we present the following conclusions for compiler-independent certification systems.

- Common-subexpression elimination of explicit annotations is a practical necessity. Sharing terms created during verification is also helpful, but it is important to carefully manage the overhead inherent in doing so.
- Compilers can effectively exploit parameterized abbreviations to encode their invariants. Although abbreviations improve the size of explicit annotations, it is more difficult to exploit abbreviations during verification.
- Serial compression utilities, such as `gzip`, are very helpful, but they are not a complete substitute for other techniques. Moreover, if good compression is a system requirement, one should understand the compression algorithm when designing the uncompressed format.

– Overhead should never be proportional to the number of loop-free control-flow paths in a program.

We believe these suggestions will help other projects avoid common pitfalls and focus on the important factors for achieving expressiveness and scalability.

Acknowledgments. The TALx86 infrastructure is a product of the TAL research group. Fred Smith contributed greatly to the prototype Popcorn compiler used for bootstrapping. We proved that optimal annotation elision is NP-complete for an elision threshold greater than five; David Kempe proved the other complexity results. The anonymous reviewers provided many helpful comments. David Walker generously encouraged us to write this report.

References

1. Andrew W. Appel and Amy P. Felty. A semantic model of types and machine instructions for proof-carrying code. In *Twenty-Seventh ACM Symposium on Principles of Programming Languages*, pages 243–253, Boston, MA, January 2000.
2. Quetzalcoatl Bradley, R. Nigel Horspool, and Jan Vitek. Jazz: An efficient compressed format for Java archive files. In *CASCON'98*, November 1998.
3. Preston Briggs, Keith Cooper, and Linda Torczon. Improvements to graph coloring register allocation. *ACM Transactions on Progamming Languages and Systems*, 16(3):428–455, May 1994.
4. G. Chaitin, M. Auslander, A. Chandra, J. Cocke, M. Hopkins, and P. Markstein. Register allocation via coloring. *Computer Languages*, 6:47–57, 1981.
5. Christopher Colby, Peter Lee, George Necula, and Fred Blau. A certifying compiler for Java. In *ACM Conference on Programming Language Design and Implementation*, pages 95–107, Vancouver, Canada, 2000.
6. Karl Crary. A simple proof technique for certain parametricity results. In *Fourth ACM International Conference on Functional Programming*, pages 82–89, Paris, France, September 1999.
7. Jens Ernst, William Evans, Christopher W. Fraser, Todd A. Proebsting, and Steven Lucco. Code compression. In *ACM Conference on Programming Language Design and Implementation*, pages 358–365, Las Vegas, NV, June 1997.
8. Lal George and Andrew W. Appel. Iterated register coalescing. *ACM Transactions on Progamming Languages and Systems*, 18(3):300–324, May 1996.
9. Neal Glew. Type dispatch for named hierarchical types. In *Fourth ACM International Conference on Functional Programming*, pages 172–182, Paris, France, September 1999.
10. Neal Glew and Greg Morrisett. Type safe linking and modular assembly language. In *Twenty-Sixth ACM Symposium on Principles of Programming Languages*, pages 250–261, San Antonio, TX, January 1999.
11. R. Harper, F. Honsell, and G. Plotkin. A framework for defining logics. *Journal of the ACM*, 40(1):143–184, 1993.
12. Luke Hornof and Trevor Jim. Certifying compilation and run-time code generation. In *ACM Workshop on Partial Evaluation and Semantics-Based Program Manipulation*, pages 60–74, San Antonio, TX, January 1999.
13. David Kempe. Personal communication.

14. Dexter Kozen. Efficient code certification. Technical Report 98-1661, Department of Computer Science, Cornell University, Ithaca, NY, January 1998.
15. Xavier Leroy. *The Objective Caml system, documentation, and user's guide*, 1998.
16. Steven Lucco. Split-stream dictionary program compression. In *ACM Conference on Programming Language Design and Implementation*, pages 27–34, Vancouver, Canada, June 2000.
17. Harry Mairson. A simple proof of a theorem of Statman. *Theoretical Computer Science*, 103(2):387–394, September 1992.
18. Greg Morrisett, Karl Crary, Neal Glew, Dan Grossman, Richard Samuels, Frederick Smith, David Walker, Stephanie Weirich, and Steve Zdancewic. TALx86: A realistic typed assembly language. In *Second ACM SIGPLAN Workshop on Compiler Support for System Software*, pages 25–35, Atlanta, GA, 1999. Published as INRIA Technical Report 0288, March, 1999.
19. Greg Morrisett, Karl Crary, Neal Glew, and David Walker. Stack-based typed assembly language. In *Workshop on Types in Compilation*, volume 1473 of *Lecture Notes in Computer Science*, pages 28–52, Kyoto, Japan, March 1998. Springer-Verlag.
20. Greg Morrisett, David Walker, Karl Crary, and Neal Glew. From System F to typed assembly language. *ACM Transactions on Progamming Languages and Systems*, 21(3):528–569, May 1999.
21. Gapolan Nadathur. A notation for lambda terms II: Refinements and applications. Technical Report CS-1994-01, Duke University, Durham, NC, January 1994.
22. George Necula and Peter Lee. The design and implementation of a certifying compiler. In *ACM Conference on Programming Language Design and Implementation*, pages 333–344, Montreal, Canada, June 1998.
23. George Necula and Peter Lee. Efficient representation and validation of proofs. In *Thirteenth Symposium on Logic in Computer Science*, pages 93–104, Indianapolis, IN, June 1998.
24. George Necula and S. P. Rahul. Oracle-based checking of untrusted software. In *Twenty-Eigth ACM Symposium on Principles of Programming Languages*, pages 142–154, London, United Kingdom, January 2001.
25. William Pugh. Compressing Java class files. In *ACM Conference on Programming Language Design and Implementation*, pages 247–258, Atlanta, GA, May 1999.
26. Zhong Shao, Christopher League, and Stefan Monnier. Implementing typed intermediate languages. In *Third ACM International Conference on Functional Programming*, pages 313–323, Baltimore, MD, September 1998.
27. Fred Smith, David Walker, and Greg Morrisett. Alias types. In *Ninth European Symposium on Programming*, volume 1782 of *Lecture Notes in Computer Science*, pages 366–381, Berlin, Germany, March 2000. Springer-Verlag.
28. D. Tarditi, G. Morrisett, P. Cheng, C. Stone, R. Harper, and P. Lee. TIL: a type-directed optimizing compiler for ML. In *ACM Conference on Programming Language Design and Implementation*, pages 181–192, Philadelphia, PA, May 1996.
29. Philip Wadler. Theorems for free! In *Fourth International Conference on Functional Programming Languages and Computer Architecture*, pages 347–359, London, United Kingdom, September 1989.
30. Andrew K. Wright and Robert Cartwright. A practical soft type system for Scheme. *ACM Transactions on Progamming Languages and Systems*, 19(1):87–152, January 1997.

Safe and Flexible Dynamic Linking of Native Code

Michael Hicks[1], Stephanie Weirich[2], and Karl Crary[3]

[1] University of Pennsylvania, Philadelphia PA 19104, USA,
mwh@dsl.cis.upenn.edu,
http://www.cis.upenn.edu/~mwh
[2] Cornell University, Ithaca NY 14853, USA,
sweirich@cs.cornell.edu,
http://www.cs.cornell.edu/sweirich
[3] Carnegie Mellon University, Pittsburgh PA 15213, USA
crary@cs.cmu.edu,
http://www.cs.cmu.edu/~crary

Abstract. We present the design and implementation of the first complete framework for flexible and safe dynamic linking of native code. Our approach extends Typed Assembly Language with a primitive for loading and typechecking code, which is flexible enough to support a variety of linking strategies, but simple enough that it does not significantly expand the trusted computing base. Using this primitive, along with the ability to compute with types, we show that we can *program* many existing dynamic linking approaches. As a concrete demonstration, we have used our framework to implement dynamic linking for a type-safe dialect of C, closely modeled after the standard linking facility for Unix C programs. Aside from the unavoidable cost of verification, our implementation performs comparably with the standard, untyped approach.

1 Introduction

A principle requirement in many modern software systems is dynamic extensibility—the ability to augment a running system with new code without shutting the system down. Equally important, especially when extensions may be untrusted, is the condition that extension code be *safe*: an extension should not be able to compromise the integrity of the running system. Two examples of systems allowing untrusted extensions are extensible operating systems [4], [11] and applet-based web browsers [22]. Extensible systems that lack safety typically suffer from a lack of robustness; for example, if the interface of a newer version of a dynamically linked library (DLL) changes from what is expected by the loading program, its functions will be called incorrectly, very possibly leading to a crash. These sorts of crashes are accidental, so in the arena of untrusted extensions the problem is greatly magnified, since malicious extensions may intentionally violate safety.

R. Harper (Ed.): TIC 2000, LNCS 2071, pp. 147–176, 2001.

The advent of Java [3] and its virtual machine [29] (the JVM) has popularized the use of language-based technology to ensure the safety of dynamic extensions. The JVM bytecode format for extension code is such that the system may *verify* that extensions satisfy certain safety constraints before it runs them. To boost performance, most recent JVM implementations use just-in-time (JIT) compilers. However, because JIT compilers are large pieces of software (typically tens of thousands of lines of code), they unduly expand the *trusted computing base* (TCB), the system software that is required to work properly if safety is to be assured. To minimize the likelihood of a security hole, a primary goal of all such systems is to have a small TCB.

An alternative approach to verifiable bytecode is verifiable native code, first proposed by Necula and Lee [35] with Proof-Carrying Code (PCC). In PCC, code may be heavily optimized, and yet still verified for safety, yielding good performance. Furthermore, the TCB is substantially smaller than in the JVM: only the verifier and the security policy are trusted, not the compiler. A variety of similar architectures have been proposed [2], [25], [33].

While verifiable native code systems are fairly mature, all lack a well-designed methodology for dynamic linking, the mechanism used to achieve extensibility. In the PCC Touchstone system, for example, dynamic linking has only been performed in an ad-hoc manner, entirely within the TCB [35], and the current Java to PCC compiler, Special J, does not support dynamic linking [6]. Most general-purpose languages support dynamic linking [3], [9], [13], [27], [36], [37], so if we are to compile such languages to PCC, then it must provide some support for implementing dynamic linking. We believe this support should meet three important criteria:

1. **Security**. It should only minimally expand the TCB, improving confidence in the system's security. Furthermore, soundness should be proved within a formal model.
2. **Flexibility**. We should be able to compile typical source language linking entities, *e.g.*, Java classes, ML modules, or C object files; and their loading and linking operations.
3. **Efficiency**. This compilation should result in efficient code, in terms of both space and time.

In this paper, we present the design and implementation of the first complete framework for dynamic linking of verifiable native code. We have developed this framework in the context of Typed Assembly Language [33] (TAL), a system of typing annotations for machine code, similar to PCC, that may be used to verify a wide class of safety properties. Our framework consists of several small additions to TAL that enable us to *program* dynamic linking facilities in a type-safe manner, rather than including them as a monolithic addition to the TCB. Our additions are simple enough that a formal proof of soundness is straightforward. The interested reader is referred to the companion technical report [20] for the full formal framework and soundness proof.

To demonstrate the flexibility and efficiency of our framework, we have used it to program a type-safe implementation of DLopen [9], a UNIX library that provides dynamic linking services to C programs. Our version of DLopen has performance comparable to the standard ELF implementation [40], and has the added benefit of safety. Furthermore, we can program many other dynamic linking approaches within our framework, including Java classloaders [23], Windows DLLs and COM [7], Objective Caml's Dynlink [27], [37], Flatt and Felleisen's Units [13], and SPIN's domains [38], among others.

The remainder of this paper is organized as follows. In the next section we motivate and present our framework, which we call TAL/Load. In Section 3 we describe a type-safe version of DLopen programmed using TAL/Load. In Section 4 we compare the performance of our type-safe version to the standard version of DLopen. We discuss how we can program other linking approaches using TAL/Load in Section 5, and discuss other related work. We conclude in Section 6.

2 Our Approach

We begin our discussion by considering a straightforward but flawed means of adding dynamic linking in TAL, to motivate our actual approach, described later. Consider defining a primitive, load_0, that dynamically instantiates, verifies, and links TAL modules into the running program. Informally, load_0 might have the type:

$$\mathsf{load}_0 : \quad \forall\alpha : \mathsf{sig}.\, \mathtt{bytearray} \rightarrow \alpha\ \mathtt{option}$$

To dynamically load a module, the application first obtains the binary representation of the module as a **`bytearray`**, and provides it to load_0 preceded by the module's expected signature type α. Then load_0 parses the bytearray, checks it for well-formedness, and links any unresolved references in the file to their definitions in the running program. Next, it compares the module's signature with the expected one; if the signatures match, it returns the module to the caller. If any part of this process fails, load_0 returns `NONE` to signal an error. As an example, suppose the file "**`extension`**" contains code believed to implement a module containing a single function f of type `int` $\rightarrow$ `int`. In informal notation, that file is dynamically linked as follows:

```
case load0 [sig f : int -> int end]
      (read_file "extension") of
   NONE => ... handle error ...
 | SOME m => m.f(12)
```

There are many problems with this approach. First, it requires first-class modules; in the context of a rich type system, first-class modules require a complicated formalization (*e.g.*, Lillibridge [28]) with restrictions on expressiveness; as a result, in most ML variants (and TAL as well) modules are second-class [17], [26], [30]. Second, it requires a type-passing semantics as the type passed to load_0 must be checked against the actual type of the module at run-time. This kind of semantics provides implicit type information to polymorphic functions, contrary to the efforts of TAL to make all computation explicit. Third, all linking operations, including tracking and managing the exported definitions of the running program, and rewriting the unresolved references in the loaded file, occur within load_0, and thus within the TCB. Finally, we are constrained to using the particular linking approach defined within the TCB, diminishing flexibility. As we show in Sections 3 and 5, linking is the aspect of extensibility that differs most among source languages. For example, Java links unresolved references incrementally, just before they are accessed, while in C all linking generally occurs at load-time. Furthermore, extensible systems typically require more fine-grained control over linking. For example, in SPIN [4], only trusted extensions may link against certain secure interfaces, and in MMM [37], the runtime interface used during dynamic linking is a safe subset of the one used during static linking, a practice called module thinning.

Rather than place all dynamic linking functionality within the TCB, as we have outlined above with load_0, we prefer to place smaller components therein, forming a dynamic linking framework. Furthermore, these components are themselves largely composed of pre-existing TAL functionality. Therefore, this framework does not implement source-level dynamic linking approaches directly, but may be used to *program* them.

Our framework defines a primitive load similar to load_0 above, but with the following simplifications:

1. Loaded modules are required to be *closed* with respect to terms. That is, they are not allowed to reference any values defined outside of the module itself. We can compile source-language modules that allow externally-defined references to be loadable by using a "poor man's functorization," which we describe below. Modules may refer to externally-defined (*i.e.*, imported) type definitions.
2. Rather than return a first-class module, load returns a tuple containing the module's exported term definitions (and thus the type variable α now is expected to be a tuple-type, rather than a signature). Any exported type definitions are added to the global *program type interface*, a list of types and their definitions used by the current program, used to resolve the imported type definitions of modules loaded later.
3. Rather than require a type-passing semantics for the type argument to load, we make use of term-level representations of types, in the style of Crary *et al.* [8].

These simplifications serve three purposes. First, by eliminating possible type components from the value returned by load, we avoid a complicated modular theory, at a small cost to the flexibility of the system. Second, the majority of the functionality of load—parsing binary representations and typechecking—is *already* a part of the TCB. By avoiding term-level linking (since loaded modules must be closed) we can avoid adding binary rewriting and symbol management to the TCB (we do have to manage type definitions, however, as we explain in the next subsection). Finally, by adding term-level type representations, we preserve TAL's type-erasure semantics. These representations also allow the implementation of a dynamic type, making it possible to program linking facilities outside of the TCB. We call our framework TAL/Load.

While TAL/Load only permits loading closed *TAL* modules, in practice we wish to dynamically load non-closed *source* modules by resolving their external references with definitions in the running program. One way to implement this linking strategy is by translating source-level external references into "holes" (i.e. uninitialized reference cells), in a manner similar to closure-converting a function. After the module is loaded via load, these cells are linked appropriately using a library added to the program. To track the running program's symbols, we can use term-level type representations, existential types [31] and a special checked_cast operator to implement type dynamics [1], amenable to programming a type-safe symbol table.

We defer a complete discussion of how to effectively use TAL/Load until Section 3, where we describe our implementation of a full-featured dynamic linking approach for C programs. For the remainder of this section, we focus on two things. First, we look more closely at the process of closing a module with respect to its externally defined types and terms. We explain the difficulty with closing a module with respect to named types, thus motivating our solution of using the program type interface. We then describe the implementation of TAL/Load in the TALx86 [32] implementation of TAL.

2.1 Comparing Types by Name

The complications with first-class structures arise because of their type components; if M and N are arbitrary expressions of module type having a type component t, it is difficult at compile-time to determine if $M.t$ is equal to (is the same type as) $N.t$. The problem arises because we do not know the identities of types $M.t$ and $N.t$, and therefore must use their names (including the paths) to compare them.

In the absence of these named types[1], closing a module with respect to its externally-defined terms is fairly simple. For example, consider the following SML module, perhaps forming part of an I/O library, that supports the opening and reading of text files.

```
structure TextIO =
struct
  type instream = int
  val openIn : string -> instream = ...
  val inputLine : instream -> string = ...
  ...
end
```

[1] Named types are also called branded types, and can be used to implement abstract types (as in first-class modules) and generative types (such as structs in C or datatypes in ML).

A client of this module might be something like:

```
fun doit =
  let val h = TextIO.openIn "myfile.txt" in
    TextIO.inputLine h
  end
```

If we want to close this client code to make it amenable for dynamic loading, we need to remove the references to the `TextIO` module. For example, we could do:

```
val TextIO_openIn :
  (string -> int) option ref = ref NONE
val TextIO_inputLine :
  (int -> string) option ref = ref NONE
fun doit () =
  let val h = getOpt (!TextIO_openIn)
                "myfile.txt" in
    getOpt (!TextIO_inputLine) h
  end
```

We have converted the externally referenced function into a locally defined reference to a function. When the file is dynamically loaded, the reference can get filled in. This strategy is essentially a "poor man's" functorization. This process closes the file with respect to values. However, we run into difficulty when we have externally defined values of named type. Consider if `TextIO` wished to hold the type `instream` abstract. If we attempt to close the client code as before, we get:

```
val TextIO_openIn :
      (string -> TextIO.instream) option ref = ...
val TextIO_inputLine :
      (TextIO.instream -> string) option ref = ...
```

We still have the external references to the type `TextIO.instream` itself. We must have a way to load a module referring to externally defined, named types. Because types form an integral part of typechecking, a trusted operation, our solution is to support name-based type equality within the TCB. As we do not want to overly complicate the TCB, we base the support for named types on that of TAL's framework for static link verification [15]. There, paths are disregarded altogether in comparing types; only one module may export a type with a given name. A related project, TMAL [10], approaches this problem differently, as we describe in Section 5.6.

Therefore, loaded code is not closed with respect to externally defined types, but instead declares a type interface (X_I, X_E), which is a pair of maps from type names to implementations. X_I mentions the named types provided by other modules, and X_E mentions named types defined by this one. By not including the implementation of the type inside a map X (just mentioning its name), we can use this mechanism to implement abstraction. As an example, the type interface of the client code above would be something like:

$$(\{instream\}, \{\})$$

and the interface for `TextIO` would be the reverse:

$$(\{\}, \{instream\})$$

Part of the implementation of load maintains a list of the imported and exported types of all the modules in the program, called the *program type interface*. When a new module is loaded, load checks that the named type imports of the new module are consistent with the program type interface, and that the exports of the new module do not redefine, or define differently, any types in the program type interface imports. We do not require that all of a module's type imports be defined by the program interface when it is loaded. This relaxation requires a uniform representation of named types; in our case, all named types are pointer-types. Not requiring defined imports facilitates loading a file that has mutually-recursive type definitions. In particular, the loaded file indicates the type it expects from another file to be loaded. When the other file is loaded, its export is confirmed to match the previously loaded import.

We have developed a formal calculus for our framework and have proven it sound. While this formalization is interesting, our real contribution lies in the way we can program type-safe dynamic linking within our framework. We refer the interested reader to the companion technical report [20] for the full theoretical treatment.

2.2 Implementation

We have implemented TAL/Load in the TALx86 [32] implementation of TAL. The key component of TAL/Load is the load primitive:

$$\mathsf{load} : \forall\alpha.\,(R(\alpha) \times \texttt{bytearray}) \to \alpha\ \texttt{option}$$

In addition to the `bytearray` containing the module data, load takes a term representation of its type argument, following the approach of Crary *et al.'s* λ_R [8]. Informally, λ_R defines term representations for types, called R-terms, and types to classify these terms, called R-types. For example, the term to represent the type `int` would be $R_{\texttt{int}}$, and the type of this term would be $R(\texttt{int})$. The type $R(\tau)$ is a singleton type; for each τ there is only one value that inhabits it—the representation of τ. Therefore the typechecker guarantees the correspondence between a type variable checked statically and the representation of that type used at runtime.

The actions of load are illustrated in Figure 1. In the figure, the square boxes indicate unconditional actions, and the diamond boxes indicate actions that may succeed or fail. Each square and diamond box has data inputs and outputs, indicated as wavy boxes; the arrows illustrate both data- and control-flow. Using components of the TALx86 system, load performs two functions:

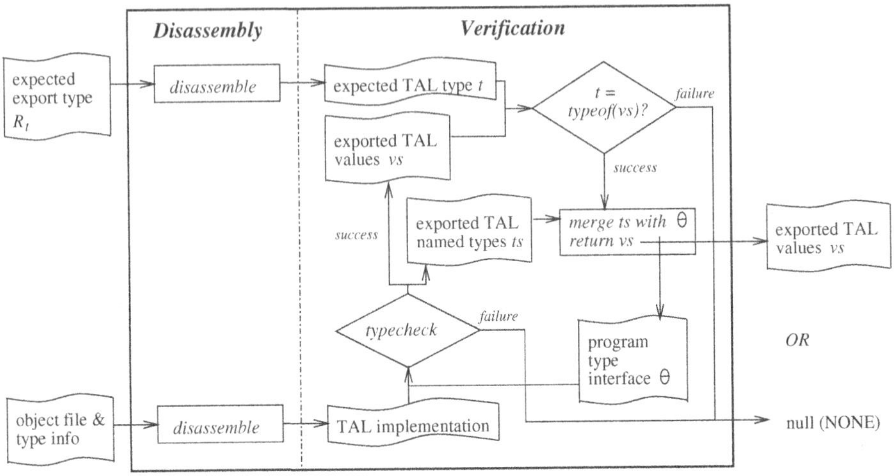

Fig. 1. The implementation of load

1. **Disassembly.** The first argument R_t indicates the expected type t of the exports, and must be disassembled into the internal representation of TAL types. Type t should always be of tuple type, where each element type represents the type of one of the object file's exported values. The second argument to load is a byte array representing the object file and the typing annotations on it; while conceptually a single argument, in practice TALx86 separates the annotations from the object code, resulting in an *object file* and a *types file*. The contents of these two files, stored in buffers, are disassembled and combined to produce the appropriate internal representation: a *TAL implementation.*
2. **Verification.** The TAL implementation is then typechecked in the context of the program's current type interface Θ, following the procedure described in the previous subsection. If typechecking succeeds, the result is a list of exported values and exported types. The values are gathered into a tuple, the type of which is compared to the expected type. If the types match, the tuple is returned (within an option type) to the caller, and the exported types are combined with Θ to form the new program type interface. On failure, *null* (*i.e.*, `NONE`) is returned.

The majority of the functionality described above results in no addition to the TAL trusted computing base. In particular, the TAL link verifier, typechecker, and disassembler are already an integral part of the the TCB; TAL/Load only makes these facilities available to programs through load. Three pieces of trusted functionality are needed, however, beyond that already provided by TAL: loading the object code into the address space of the running program, representing types as runtime values, and maintaining the program type interface Θ at runtime. We explain how these elements impact the TCB below.

Loading. Following the verification process, before returning to the caller, some C code is invoked to load the object code into the address space. This loading code is based on that used by the Linux kernel to dynamically load modules. We describe the code for ELF object files, used in TALx86 Linux implementation; COFF files, used in the Windows implementation, are similar.

First, the file is parsed, performing well-formedness checks and extracting the ELF file's section headers, which describe the file's format. The file must be a relocatable object file, as is normally produced by a compiler for separate compilation, *e.g.* by `cc -c`. The sections of interest are the code and data sections, the relocations section, and the symbol tables. Second, the code and data are logically arranged in the order and alignment specified by the file and the ELF standard, and the total required size is computed. Third, any externally-defined symbols are resolved—more on this below. Finally, an appropriately-sized buffer is allocated and the code and data are copied to that buffer (TAL uses garbage collection, so the buffer is allocated using the GC allocator).[2] This code is then relocated to work relative to the allocated buffer's address. Finally, the address of the buffer is returned to the caller (which is the result of load).

It is troublesome that we resolve (*i.e.* link) external symbols during the loading process. Much of the motivation of our approach is to perform linking outside the TCB, in part to avoid the additional complexity. In fact, the overwhelming majority of symbols *are* linked by mechanisms outside the TCB, as we show in the next section. However, there are some *trusted* symbols that cannot easily be linked in this way. These symbols are part of the *macro* instructions of TALx86. Macro instructions do not map directly to a machine instruction, but instead to a machine instruction sequence; this sequence may include references to external symbols. For example, the macro for the TALx86 `malloc` instruction consists of six machine instructions, of which two are calls to external functions, one to `GC_malloc` (to actually allocate the memory), and the other to `out_of_memory` (in case the GC allocator returns *null*). The file cannot be closed with respect to these calls, because they are primitive.

As a result, when a file containing a `malloc` instruction is dynamically loaded, the external calls to must be resolved by the loader. We do this by rewriting the code directly, using the relocations provided in the object file. Patching symbols in this manner has the unfortunate consequence that loaded code cannot be shared between (OS-level) processes because the patched symbols, like `GC_malloc`, may be at different addresses in each process.

Given that we must link some symbols implicitly—that the module does not truly have to be 'closed'—it is reasonable to ask "why not link all symbols in this way?" The answer is that it would greatly reduce our flexibility and our security.

[2] Note that this allocation is necessary; we cannot reuse the buffer containing the object file data to avoid the copy. The reason is that load effectively changes the type of the buffer argument from `bytearray` to some type α. Placing the object file contents in a fresh buffer prevents surreptitiously modifying the given buffer via an alias still having `bytearray` type. We could avoid this copy by proving that no aliases exist, *e.g.* by using alias types [41].

As motivated in §2, by moving symbol management outside of the TCB, we can better control how symbols are stored (*i.e.* what datastructure), how they are apportioned among users of various privilege levels, how they are interfaced, *etc.*, without changing to trusted computing base; instead we can rely on the system to verify that this 'untrusted' code is safe.

While implicit linking seems to be necessary for TALx86 macro instructions, it may be that our approach could be improved. In particular, if the symbols referred to by macro sequences (*e.g.* `GC_malloc`) were always loaded at the same address, then we could share the code between processes. Given that most modern operating systems support separate, per-process address spaces, and that both ELF and COFF files allow the loaded address for a program component to be specified, this should be possible. It would furthermore allow the relocation process to take place outside of the TCB, preceding the call to load. The disassembler would then check for the particular, fixed address when checking the well-formedness of macro instruction sequences, rather than looking for an external symbol reference.

Passing Types at Runtime. Term representations for types are used, among other things, to preserve TAL's type-erasure semantics. So that this addition to the TAL trusted computing base can be kept small, we do two things. First, we represent R-terms using the binary format for types already used by the TAL disassembler. Note that the binary representation of a named type is a string containing the name. Second, we do not provide any way within TAL to dynamically introduce or deconstruct R-terms, such as via appropriate syntax and `typecase` [8]. Doing so would require that we reflect the entire binary format of types into the type system of TAL. Instead, we only allow the introduction of R-terms in the static data segment by a built-in directive. Consequently, only closed types may be represented.

Aside from providing type information to load, R-types are also useful for implementing dynamic types. Dynamic types may be used to implement type-safe symbol management, as we describe in the next section. Therefore we allow limited examination of R-terms with a simple primitive called checked_cast:

$$\mathsf{checked\_cast} : \forall\alpha.\forall\beta.\,(R(\alpha) \times R(\beta) \times \beta) \rightarrow \alpha\ \texttt{option}$$

Informally, checked_cast takes a value of type β and casts it to one of type α if the types α and β are equal. This operation is trivial to add as comparing types is part of the TAL typechecker. Therefore it does not add to the TCB. With a full implementation of λ_R including `typecase`, checked_cast does not need to be primitive [42].

Maintaining the Program Type Interface. As explained in the previous subsection, the need to maintain the program's type interface at runtime derives directly from the presence of named types in TAL. We may use elements already within the TCB to implement the program type interface. Representations of type interfaces (X_I, X_E) already exist as a part of object files; they are used in verifying static link consistency. The initial Θ is initialized in a small bit of code generated by the TAL static linker after it has determined the program's type interface. Computing the new type interface at run time is done using this same trusted code for static link verification, so maintaining this information at run time does not significantly expand the TCB.

3 Programming Dynamic Linking

Having defined our dynamic linking framework TAL/Load, we now describe how to use TAL/Load to program dynamic linking services as typically defined in source languages like C and Java. As a concrete demonstration, we present a type-safe version of DLopen [9], a standard dynamic-linking methodology for C, that we have written using TAL/Load. Our version, called DLpop, provides the same functionality for Popcorn [32], a type-safe dialect of C. We chose to implement DLopen over several other dynamic linking approaches because it is the most general; we describe informal encodings of other approaches, including Java classloaders [23], in Section 5. We begin by describing DLpop and the ways in which it differs from DLopen, and then follow with a description of our implementation written in TAL/Load.

3.1 DLpop: A Type-Safe DLopen

Most Unix systems provide some compiler support and a library of utilities (interfaced in the C header file `dlfcn.h`) for dynamically linking object files. We call this methodology DLopen, after the principal function it provides. We have implemented a version of DLopen for our type-safe C-like language, Popcorn [32], which we call DLpop. The library interface is essentially identical to DLopen except that it is type-safe; it is depicted in Figure 2. We describe this interface in detail below, noting differences with DLopen; a thorough description of DLopen may be found in Unix documentation [9]. DLpop and DLopen both provide three core functions:

```
extern handle;
extern handle dlopen(string fname);
extern a dlsym<a>(handle h, string sym, <a>rep typ);
extern void dlclose(handle h);

extern exception WrongType(string);
extern exception FailsTypeCheck;
extern exception SymbolNotFound(string);
```

Fig. 2. DLpop library interface

handle dlopen(string fname)

Given the name of an object file, dlopen dynamically loads the file and returns a handle to it for future operations. Imports in the file (*i.e.*, symbols declared extern therein) are resolved with the exports (*i.e.*, symbols not declared static) of the running program and any previously loaded object files. Before it returns, dlopen will call the function _init if that function is defined in the loaded file. In DLpop (but not DLopen), dlopen typechecks the object file, throwing the exception FailsTypeCheck on failure. In addition, the exception SymbolNotFound will be raised if the loaded file imports a symbol not present in the running program, or WrongType if a symbol in the running program does not match the type expected by the import in the loaded file. DLopen functions, in general report errors with an errno-like facility.

a dlsym<a>(handle h, string sym, <a>rep typ)

In DLpop, dlsym takes a handle for a loaded object file h, a string naming the symbol s, and the representation of the symbol's type typ, dlsym returns a pointer to the symbol's value. The syntax <a> refers to the type argument a (not its representation) to dlsym. In lambda-calculus notation, dlsym therefore has the type

$$\texttt{dlsym} : \forall a.\ \texttt{handle} \times \texttt{string} \times R(a) \to a$$

In DLopen, dlsym does not receive a type argument, and the function returns an untyped pointer (*null* on failure), of C-type void *, which requires the programmer to perform an unchecked cast to the expected type. The fact that our version takes a type representation argument typ to indicate the expected type means that this type can be (and is) checked against the actual type at runtime. In practice, this type always has the form of a pointer type since the value returned is a reference to the requested symbol. As in TAL, we have extended Popcorn with representation types (<a>rep), implementing them with TAL R-types. The term representing type t in Popcorn is denoted repterm@<t>. Because we cannot create the representation of a type with free type variables in TAL, the type argument a to dlsym must also be a closed type. If the requested symbol is not present in the object file, the exception SymbolNotFound is thrown; if the passed type does not match the type of the symbol, the exception WrongType is thrown.

void dlclose(handle h)

In DLopen, dlclose *unloads* the file associated with the given handle. In particular, the file's symbols are no longer used in linking, and the memory for the file is freed; the programmer must make sure there are no dangling pointers to symbols in the file. In DLpop, dlclose only removes symbols from future linkages; if the user program does not reference the object file, then it can be garbage collected.

The current version of DLpop does not implement all of the features of DLopen, most notably: DLopen automatically loads object files upon which a dynami-

Dynamically linked code: `loadable.pop`

```
extern int foo(int);

int bar(int i) {
  return foo(i);
}
```

Static code: `main.pop`

```
int foo(int i) {
  return i+1;
}

void pop_main(){
  handle h = dlopen("loadable");
  int bar(int) = dlsym(h,"bar", repterm@<int(int)>);
  bar(3);
  dlclose(h);
}
```

Fig. 3. DLpop dynamic loading example

cally loaded file depends, allowing for recursive references; DLopen supports the ability to optionally resolve function references *on-demand*, rather than all at load-time, assuming the underlying mechanisms (*e.g.* an ELF procedure linkage table [40]) are present in the object file; and DLopen provides a sort of finalization by calling the user-defined function `_fini` when unloading object files. We foresee no technical difficulties in adding these features should the need arise. In a later version of DLpop, we implemented a variant of `dlopen` that allows the caller to specify a list of object files to load, and these files may have mutually-recursive (value) references. On-demand function symbol resolution is also feasible; a possible compilation strategy to support it is described below, and another approach is described in Section 5.1. Finally, finalization is implemented in most garbage collectors, in particular the Boehm-Demers-Weiser collector [5] used in the current TAL implementation.

Figure 3 depicts a simple use of DLpop. The user statically links the file `main.pop`, which, during execution, dynamically loads the object file `loadable.o` (the result of compiling `loadable.pop`), looks up the function `bar`, and then executes it; the type argument to `dlsym` is inferred by the Popcorn compiler. The dynamically linked file also makes an external reference to the function `foo`, which is resolved at load time from the exports of `main.pop`.

the type of the global offset table

the global offset table itself

```
struct got_t {
  int (int) foo;
}
struct got_t GOT = { dummy };
```

to avoid null checks, all fields have dummy values

```
static int dummy(int i) {
  raise (Failure);
}
```

the function recompiled to reference the global offset table

```
static int bar(int i) {
  return GOT.foo(i);
}
```

initialization function called by dlopen

resolve file's imports

add the exported function to the symbol table

```
void dyninit(a lookup<a>(string, <a>rep),
             void update<a>(string,a,<a>rep)) {

  int (int) foo = lookup("foo",repterm@<int (int)>);
  GOT.foo = foo;

  update("bar",bar,repterm@<int (int)>);
}
```

Fig. 4. Compilation of dynamically loadable code

3.2 Implementing DLpop in TAL/Load

Our implementation of DLpop is similar to implementations of DLopen that follow the ELF standard [40] for dynamic linking, which requires both library and compiler support. In ELF, dynamically loadable files are compiled so that all references to data are indirected through a *global offset table* (GOT) present in the object file. Each slot in the table is labeled with the name of the symbol to be resolved. When the file is loaded dynamically, the dynamic linker fills each slot with the address of the actual exported function or value in the running program; these exported symbols are collected in a *dynamic symbol table*, used by the dynamic linker. This table consists of a list of hashtables, one per object file, each constructed at compile-time and stored as a special section in the object file. As files are loaded and unloaded, the hashtables are linked and unlinked from the list, respectively.

We describe our DLpop implementation below, pointing out differences with the ELF approach. We first describe the changes we made to the Popcorn compiler, and then describe how we implemented the DLpop library.

Compilation. As in the ELF approach, dynamically loadable files must be specially compiled, an operation that we perform in three stages. First, the compiler must define a GOT for the file, and translate references to externally defined functions and data to refer to slots in the GOT. In ELF, the GOT is

```
int foo(int i) {                    foo is still exported (not static) so
  return i+1;                       statically linked files may refer to it
}

void pop_main() {
  handle h = dlopen("loadable");
  int bar(int) = dlsym(h,"bar",repterm@<int (int)>);
  bar(3);
  dlclose(h);
}
                                    initialization function called at startup
void dyninit(a lookup<a>(string, <a>rep),
             void update<a>(string,a,<a>rep)) {

  update("foo",foo,repterm@<int (int)>);     add the exported function
}                                            to the symbol table
```

Fig. 5. Compilation of statically linked code

a trusted part of the object file, while in DLpop the GOT is implemented in the verifiable language, TAL. As a consequence, the table is well-typed with the compiler initializing each slot to a dummy value of the correct type, where possible. For slots of abstract type, we cannot create this dummy value, so we initialize the slot to null and insert null checks for each table access in order to satisfy the typechecker.

Second, the compiler adds a special `dyninit` function that will be called at load-time to fill in the slots in the GOT with the proper symbols. This approach differs from ELF, in which the GOT is filled by a dynamic linker contained in the running program. From the loading program's point of view, the `dyninit` function abstracts the linking process. The `dyninit` function takes as arguments two other functions, `lookup` and `update`, that provide access to the dynamic symbol table. For each symbol address to be stored in the GOT, `dyninit` will look up that address by name and type using the `lookup` function, and fill in the appropriate GOT slot with the result. Similarly, `dyninit` will call `update` with the name, type, and address of each symbol that it wishes to export. Because the `dyninit` function consists only of TAL code, all linking operations are verifiably type-safe. This verification prevents, for example, `lookup` from requesting a symbol by name, then receiving a symbol of an unexpected type. In an untypechecked setting, as in DLopen, this operation could result in a crash.

Finally, because the exports of dynamically linked files are designated by `dyninit`, the object file should only export `dyninit` itself; therefore the compiler makes all global symbols `static`. Figure 4 shows the entire translation for the dynamic code in Figure 3.

Statically linked files are only changed by adding a `dyninit` to export symbols to dynamically linked files. At startup, the program calls the `dyninit` functions

```
struct got_t {
  int (int) foo;
}
struct got_t GOT = { dummy };

static int dummy(int i) {
  int (int) foo = dynlookup("foo",repterm@<int (int)>);   look up foo

  GOT.foo = foo;                                 replace dummy in the GOT

  return GOT.foo(i);                                              call it
}

static int bar(int i) {
  return GOT.foo(i);
}
                            saved lookup function as passed to dyninit
static a dynlookup<a>(string, <a>rep) = ...;

void dyninit(a lookup<a>(string, <a>rep),
             void update<a>(string,a,<a>rep)) {

  dynlookup = lookup;                           note the lookup function

  update("bar",bar,repterm@<int (int)>);
}
```

Fig. 6. Compilation of dynamically loadable code to resolve functions on-demand. Only the parts that differ from Figure 4 are commented.

of each of its statically linked files. Figure 5 shows the static code of Figure 3 compiled in this manner.

Rather than add the `dyninit` function to fill in the GOT's of loaded files and note their exported symbols, we could have easily followed the ELF approach of writing a monolithic dynamic linker, called at startup and from `dlopen`. However, we have found that abstracting the process of linking to calling a function in the loaded file has a number of benefits. First, it allows the means by which an object file resolves its imported symbols to change without affecting the DLpop library. For example, in order to save space, we could allow GOT entries to be null by changing them to `option` type, or we could eliminate the GOT altogether by using runtime code generation, as described in Section 5. If we knew that many symbols may not be used by the loading program (as is likely with a large shared library), we could resolve them on-demand by making the dummy functions perform the symbol resolution, rather than doing so in the `dyninit` function; this approach is shown in Figure 6.

Second, `dyninit` simplifies the implementation of policy decisions made by the loading code with regard to symbol management. For example, the loading code may wish to restrict access to some of its symbols based on security criteria [38]; in this case, it could customize the `lookup` function provided to `dyninit` to throw an exception if a restricted symbol is requested.

Finally, using `dyninit` allows the loaded file to customize operations performed at link-time. For example, by adding a flag to prevent calls to `update` from occurring on subsequent calls to `dyninit` (and thus only the `lookup` calls are performed), we can enable code *relinking*. This allows us to *dynamically update* the module in a running program: we load a new version of a module, link it as usual, and then relink the other modules in the program to use the new module by calling their `dyninit` functions. Any needed state translation can be performed by the new module's `_init` function. Though not described here, we have fully explored this idea with an alternative version of DLpop [19], [18], and used it to build a dynamically updateable webserver, *FlashEd* [12].

The DLpop Library. The DLpop interface in Figure 2 is implemented as a Popcorn library. The central element of the library is a type-safe implementation of the dynamic symbol table for managing the symbols exported by the running program. We first describe this symbol table, and then describe how the DLpop functions are used in conjunction with it.

DLpop encodes the dynamic symbol table as in ELF, as a list of hashtables mapping symbol names to their addresses, one hashtable per linked object file. Each time a new object file is loaded, a new hashtable is added. The dynamic symbol table is constructed at start-up time by calling the `dyninit` functions for all of the statically linked object files.

Each entry of the hashtable contains the name, value, and type representation of a symbol in the running program, with the name as the key. So that entries have uniform type, we use existential types [31] to hide the actual type of the value:[3]

`objfile_ht : <string,` $\exists\alpha.\ (\alpha \times R(\alpha))$`> hashtable`

To update the table with a new symbol (the result of calling `update` from `dyninit`), we pack the value (say of type β) and type representation (of type $R(\beta)$) together in an existential package, hiding the value's type, and insert that package into the table under the symbol's key. When looking up a symbol expected to have type α, and given a term representation `r` of type $R(\alpha)$, we do the following. First, the symbol's name is used to index the symbol hashtable, returning a package having type $\exists\beta.\beta \times R(\beta)$. During unpacking, the tuple is destructed, binding a type variable β, and two term variables, `table_value` and `table_rep`, of type β and $R(\beta)$, respectively. We then call

`checked_cast[`α`][`β`](r, table_rep, table_value)`

which compares `r` and `table_rep`, and coerces `table_value` from type β to type α if they match. This value is then returned to the caller. Otherwise, the exception `WrongType` is raised.

The DLpop library essentially consists of wrapper functions for `load` and the dynamic symbol table manipulation routines:

[3] The type `<`τ_1, τ_2`> hashtable` contains mappings from τ_1 to τ_2.

`dlopen`
: Recall that `dlopen` takes as its argument the name of an object file to load. First it opens and reads this object file into a `bytearray`. Because of the compilation strategy we have chosen, all loadable files should export a single symbol, the `dyninit` function. Therefore, we call load with the `dyninit` function's type and the `bytearray`, and should receive back the `dyninit` function itself as a result. If load returns `NONE`, indicating an error, `dlopen` raises the exception `FailsTypeCheck`. Otherwise, a new hashtable is created, and a custom `update` function is crafted that adds symbols to it. The returned `dyninit` function is called with this custom `update` function, as well as with a `lookup` function that works on the entire dynamic symbol table. After `dyninit` completes, the new hashtable is added to the dynamic symbol table, and then returned to the caller with abstract type `handle`.

`dlsym`
: This function receives a type argument (call it α) and three term arguments: a `handle`, `h`; a string representing the symbol name, `s`; and the representation of the type α, `r`. Because the `handle` object returned by `dlopen` is in actuality the hashtable for the object file, `dlsym` simply attempts to look up the given symbol in that hashtable, following the procedure outlined above, raising the exception `SymbolNotFound` if the symbol is not present, or `WrongType` if the types do not match.

`dlclose`
: The `dlclose` operation simply removes the hashtable associated with the `handle` from the dynamic symbol table. Future attempts to look up symbols using this handle will be unsuccessful. Once the rest of the program no longer references the handle's object file, it will be safely garbage-collected.

As a closing remark, we emphasize the value of implementing DLpop. We have not intended DLpop to be a significant contribution in itself; rather, the contribution lies in the *way* in which DLpop is implemented. By using TAL/Load, much of DLpop was implemented within the verifiable language, and was therefore provably safe. Only load and λ_R constitute trusted elements in its implementation, and these elements are themselves small. If some flaw exists in DLpop, the result will be object files that fail to verify, not a security hole.

We should point out that the implementation described here (and measured in the next section) is the first of two DLpop implementations. Our most recent implementation, described fully in [18], differs in two key ways from the one described here. First, rather than perform the dynamic transformation for files within the compiler, we do it source-to-source, preceding compilation. Decoupling the transformation from the compiler results in a more modular and flexible implementation, but required the addition of some features to Popcorn. Second, the newer implementation is more full-featured. It supports loading modules with mutually-recursive references, and allows for dynamically updating a module, as described above. The principles behind the two implementations are essentially the same.

4 Measurements

Much of the motivation behind TAL and PCC is to provide safe execution of untrusted code without paying the price of byte-code interpretation (as in the JVM) or sandboxing (as in the Exokernel [11]). Therefore, while the chief goal of our work is to provide flexible and safe dynamic linking for verifiable native code, another goal is to do so efficiently.

In this section we examine the time and space costs imposed by load and DLpop. We compare these overheads with those of DLopen (using the ELF implementation) and show that our overheads are competitive. In particular, our run-time overhead is exactly the same, and our space overhead is comparable. The verification operation constitutes an additional load-time cost, but we believe that the cost is commensurate with the benefit of safety, and does not significantly reduce the applicability of dynamic linking in most programs. All measurements presented in this section were taken on a 400 MHz Pentium II with 128 MB of RAM, running Linux kernel version 2.2.5. DLopen/ELF measurements were generated using `gcc` version egcs-2.91.66.

4.1 Time Overhead

The execution time overhead imposed by dynamic linking, relative to Popcorn programs that use static linking only, occurs on three time scales: run-time, load-time, and start-time. At run-time, each reference to an externally defined symbol must be indirected through the GOT. At load-time, the running program must verify and copy the loaded code with load, and then link it by executing its `dyninit` function. At startup, statically linked code must construct the initial dynamic symbol table. DLopen/ELF has similar overheads, but lacks verification and its associated benefit of safety.

Run-time Overhead. In most cases, the only run-time overhead of dynamic code is the need to access imported symbols through the GOT; this overhead is exactly the same as that imposed by the ELF approach. Each access requires one additional instruction, which we have measured in practice to cost one extra cycle. A null function call in our system costs about 7 cycles, so the dynamic overhead of an additional cycle is about 14%.

For imported values of abstract type, there is also the cost of the null check before accessing each GOT element. However, we have yet to see this overhead occur in practice. Most files do not export abstract values, but instead "constructor" functions that produce abstract values; an exception in our current code base is the Popcorn `Core` library, which defines `stdin`, `stdout`, and `stderr` to have abstract type `FILE`. These cases typically define the abstract type to allow a null value (a sort of abstract `option` type), meaning that a null-check would have occurred anyway.

Load-time Overhead. The largest load-time cost in DLpop is verification. Verification in load consists of two conceptual steps, disassembly and verification, as pictured in Figure 1, and described in Section 2.2. Verification itself is performed in two phases: consistency checking (labeled *typecheck* in the figure) and interface checking (labeled $t = typeof(vs)$? in the figure). For the `loadable.pop` file, presented in Figure 3, the total time of these operations is 47 ms, where 2% is disassembly, 96% is consistency checking, and the remaining 2% is interface checking. Detailed measurements concerning the cost of TAL verification may be found in [16], which notes that in general, verification costs are linear in the size of the file being verified.

The remaining cost is to copy the verified code and to execute the file's `dyninit` function. For `loadable.pop`, the total cost of these two operations is negligible: about 0.73 ms. This time is roughly twice the time of 0.35 ms for DLopen/ELF. The main difference here is simply that the ELF loader is more optimized. Because of its small weight relative to verification, there is little reason to optimize linking in DLpop.

Verification is by far the most expensive load-time operation, but its cost could be reduced, in three ways. First, the verification code could be more optimized for speed. In particular, proof-carrying code's Touchstone compiler [34] has demonstrated small verification times, albeit with a different type system, and even TAL's implementors recognize that further gains could be made [16]. Furthermore, disassembly has not been optimized. Second, verification could be performed in parallel with normal service. After verification completes, only linking remains, which has negligible overhead. Finally, in the case of a trusted system, we could turn off the consistency-checking phase during verification, since it can be run for each loaded file on some other machine. Leaving on link-checking and interface-checking still ensures that the loaded code meshes with the running program at the module level, but trusts that the contents of the loaded module are well-formed. Since consistency-checking is the most time-consuming operation, we greatly reduce our total update times as a result. Breaking up the verification operation onto server and client machines has been explored for Java in [39].

Even with current overheads, verification occurs but once per extension, and so should not pose a problem for most applications. Applications that load code at larger time scales, and/or for which loaded code is long-lived, will amortize the cost of verification over the entire computation. Long running systems that load extensions or updates, such as operating systems and network servers, and productivity applications that use dynamically loaded libraries fall into this category. Even those applications for which loaded code is short-lived, *e.g.*, agent systems, could be accommodated, because while verification time may be large, execution time (thanks to native code) will be small, balancing out the total cost.

Start-time Overhead. At start-time, before execution begins, each statically linked file's `dyninit` function is executed to create the initial dynamic symbol table for the program. In addition, the program type interface, generated by the linker, is properly instantiated for use by load. The costs of these operations depend on the number of symbols and type definitions exported by each file, and which libraries are used. A typical delay is on the order of tens of milliseconds, which is meaningless over the life programs that will perform dynamic linking.

In contrast, ELF imposes no start-time cost, because no type interface is used, and because the static linker generates the hashtables that make up the dynamic symbol table, storing them in the object file. This implementation trades space for time.

4.2 Space Overhead

Both DLpop and DLopen/ELF increase the size of object files relative to their compilation without dynamic linking support. Based on some simple measurements, they appear to be fairly comparable in practice. For the most part the per-symbol costs for DLpop are higher than that of DLopen/ELF, but there is a significantly smaller fixed cost. For the remainder of this section we break the down the space costs of DLpop, and compare them to those of DLopen/ELF.

For both imported and exported symbols, DLpop imposes three space costs: the string representation of the symbol name,[4] its type representation, and the instructions in the `dyninit` function that perform its linking. For imported symbols, there is the additional cost of the symbol's GOT slot and its default value. These costs are summarized in Table 1, and compared to the overheads DLopen/ELF. DLopen/ELF overheads were determined from [40] and from examining object files on our platform. The fixed cost was estimated by subtracting the per-symbol costs from the total calculated overhead shown in Figure 7.

The per-symbol cost of DLpop is about one and a half times as much as DLopen/ELF when not including type representations t. Type representations tend to be large, between 128 and 200 bytes for functions, increasing total overhead when they are considered. We mitigate this cost somewhat by sharing type representations among elements of the same type. One factor that adds to function type representation size is that the representation encodes not only the types of the function arguments and returned values, but also the calling convention. This fact suggests that sharing type components among representations would net a larger savings, since the calling convention is the same for all Popcorn functions. We could also reduce per-symbol overhead by eliminating `dyninit` and moving the linking code into the DLpop library. However, `dyninit` is a convenient, flexible way to perform linking, justifying the extra space cost.

DLopen/ELF has a much higher fixed space cost than DLpop. This comes from a number of sources, including load-time and unload-time code sequences, and datastructures that aid in linking. In ELF, each of the hashtables of the dynamic symbol table is constructed at *compile-time* and stored in the object file. Some of the hashtable overhead is per-symbol, but there is also a large fixed

[4] Popcorn strings have a length field and an extra pointer (for easier translation to/from C-style strings), adding 2 words to a C-style representation.

Table 1. Object file overheads, in bytes, for both DLpop and ELF. DLpop overheads are broken down into component costs; l is the length of a symbol's name and t is the size of its TAL type representation.

	DLpop						DLopen (ELF)
	symbol name	`dyninit` function	type rep	GOT slot	default value	total	
import function	$8+l$	24	t	8	8	$48+l+t$	$58+l$
data	$8+l$	24	t	8	8*	$48+l+t$	$32+l$
export	$8+l$	24	t	-	-	$32+l+t$	$24+l$
fixed						4	~2500

cost for the empty buckets in order to improve the hash function accuracy. In DLpop, these tables are constructed at start-time, creating a start-up penalty but avoiding the extra space cost per object file.

Figure 7 compares DLpop to DLopen/ELF for some benchmark files. Each of the four clusters of bars in the graph represents a different source file, with varying numbers of imported and exported functions, notated x**i** y**e** at the bottom of the cluster, where x and y are the number of imports and exports, respectively. When there is one exported function, its code consists of calling all of the imported functions; when there are fifteen functions, each one calls a single imported function. All functions are `void (void)` functions.[5] Each bar in the cluster represents a different compilation approach. The leftmost is the standard DLpop approach, and the rightmost is DLopen/ELF. The center bar is DLpop without the sharing of type representations, to show worst case behavior (when sharing, only one type representation for `void (void)` is needed). Each bar shows the size of object files when compiled statically, compiled to export symbols to dynamic code, and compiled to be dynamically loadable (thus importing and exporting symbols). The export-only case is not shown for ELF, as this support is added at static link time, rather than compile-time.

The figure shows that DLpop is competitive with DLopen/ELF. The figure also illustrates the benefit of type representation sharing; the overhead for the 15**i** 15**e** when not sharing is almost twice that when sharing is enabled. As the number of symbols in the file increases, the ELF approach will begin to outperform DLpop, but not by a wide margin for typical files (exporting tens of symbols). In general, we do not feel that space overheads are a problem (nor did the designers of ELF dynamic linking, it seems). We could structure our object files so that the `dyninit` function, which is used once, and type representations, which are used infrequently, will not affect the cache, and may be easily paged out. Type representations are highly compressible (up to 90% using `gzip`), and therefore need not contribute to excessive network transmission time for extensions.

[5] This is the Popcorn (C-like) notation for the type `unit` → `unit`.

* For one-word values, this is the cost of the value plus a pointer; structured values are larger.

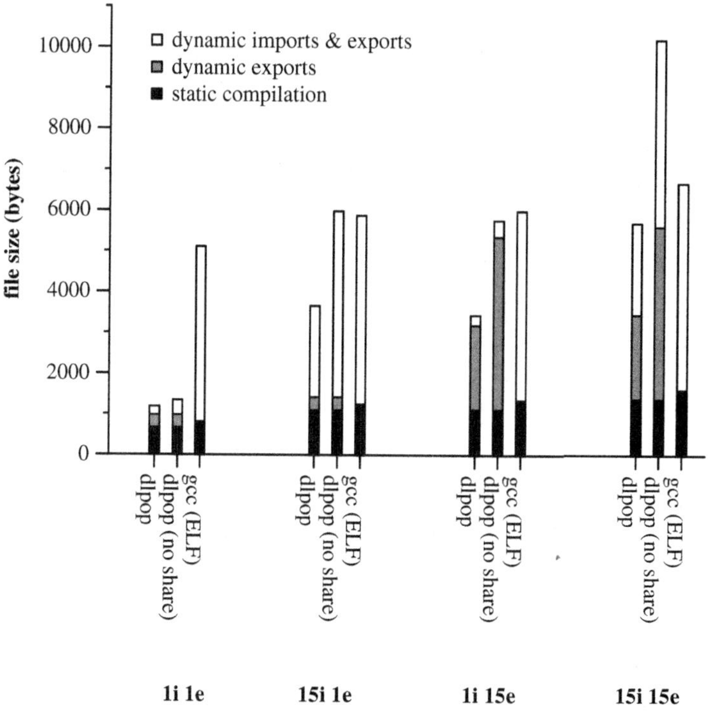

Fig. 7. Comparing the space overhead of DLpop, DLpop without type representation sharing, and DLopen/ELF for some microbenchmarks.

5 Programming Other Linking Strategies (Related Work)

Using our framework TAL/Load, we can implement safe, flexible, and efficient dynamic linking for native code, which we have illustrated by programming a safe DLopen library for Popcorn. Many other dynamic linking approaches have been proposed, for both high and low level languages. In this section we do two things. First, we describe the dynamic linking interfaces of some high level languages, describe their typical implementations, and finally explain how to program them in TAL/Load, resulting in better security due to type safety and/or reduced TCB size. Second, we look at some low-level mechanisms used to implement dynamic linking, and explain how we can program them in our framework. Overall, we demonstrate that TAL/Load is flexible enough to encode typical dynamic linking interfaces and mechanisms, but with a higher level of safety and security.

5.1 Java

In Java, user-defined classloaders [23] may be invoked to retrieve and instantiate the bytes for a class, ultimately returning a `Class` object to the caller. A classloader may use any means to locate the bytes of a class, but then relies on the trusted functions `Classloader.defineClass` and `Classloader.resolveClass` to instantiate and verify the class, respectively. When invoked directly, a classloader is analogous to `dlopen`. Returned classes may be accessed directly, as with `dlsym`, if they can be cast to some entity that is known statically, such as an interface or superclass. In the standard JVM implementation, linking occurs incrementally as the program executes: when an unresolved class variable is accessed, the classloader is called to obtain and instantiate the referenced class. In the standard JVM implementation, all linking operations occur within the TCB: checks for unresolved class variables occur as part of JVM execution, and symbol management occurs within `resolveClass`.

We can implement classloaders in TAL/Load by following our approach for DLpop: we compile classes to have a GOT and an `dyninit` function to resolve and register symbols. A classloader may locate the class bytes exactly as in Java (*i.e.*, through any means programmable in TAL), and `defineClass` simply becomes a wrapper for a function similar to `dlopen`, which calls load and then invokes the `dyninit` function of the class with the dynamic symbol table.

To support incremental linking, we can alter the compilation of Java to TAL (hypothetically speaking) in two ways. We first compile the GOT, which holds references to externally defined classes, to allow null values (in contrast to DLpop where we had default values). Each time a class is referenced through the GOT, a null check is performed; if the reference is null then we call the classloader to load the class, filling in the result in the GOT. Otherwise, we simply follow the pointer that is present. As in the strategy depicted in Figure 6, the `dyninit` function no longer fills in the GOT at load-time; it simply registers its symbols in the dynamic symbol table. This approach moves both symbol management and the check for unresolved references into the verifiable language, reducing the size of the TCB.

5.2 Windows DLLs and COM

Windows allows applications to load Dynamically Linked Libraries (DLLs) into running applications, following an interface and implementation quite similar to DLopen and ELF, respectively, with some minor differences (see Levine [24, pps 217–222]). Like DLopen and ELF, DLLs are not type-safe and would therefore benefit in this regard from an implementation in TAL/Load.

DLLs are often used as vehicle to load and manipulate Common Object Model [7] (COM) objects. COM objects are treated abstractly by their clients, providing access through one or more interfaces, each consisting of one or more function pointers. All COM objects must implement the interface **IUnknown**, which provides the function `QueryInterface`, to be called at runtime to determine if the object implements a particular interface. `QueryInterface` is called with the globally unique identifier (GUID) that names the desired interface. GUIDs are not incorporated into the type-system (at least not for source languages like C and C++), and thus, as with `dlsym`, the user is forced to cast the object's returned interface to the type expected, with a mistake likely resulting in a crash.

Implementing COM in TAL/Load would be straightforward, with the added benefit of proven type-safety for interfaces. `QueryInterface` could be changed to take type parameter $R(t)$ in addition to the GUID of the expected interface, ensuring the proper type of the returned interface.

5.3 OCaml Modules

Objective Caml [27] (OCaml) provides dynamic linking for its bytecode-based runtime system with a special *Dynlink* module; these facilities have been used to implement an OCaml applet system, MMM [37]. Dynlink essentially implements `dlopen`, but not `dlsym` and `dlclose`, and would thus be easy to encode in TAL/Load. In contrast to the JVM, OCaml does not verify that its extensions are well-formed, and instead relies on a trusted compiler. OCaml dynamic linking is similar to that of other type-safe, functional languages, *e.g.* Haskell [36].

A TAL/Load implementation of the OCaml interface would improve on its current implementation [27] in two ways. First, all linking operations would occur outside of the TCB. Second, extension well-formedness would be verified rather than assumed.

5.4 Units

Units [13] are software construction components, quite similar to modules. A unit may be dynamically linked into a static program with the **invoke** primitive, which takes as arguments the unit itself (perhaps in some binary format) and a list of symbols needed to resolve its imports. Linking consists of resolving the imports and executing the unit's initialization function. **Invoke** is similar to `dlopen`, but the symbols to link are provided explicitly, rather than maintained in a global table.

Units could be implemented following DLpop, but without a dynamic symbol table. Rather than compiling the `dyninit` function to take two functions, `lookup` and `update`, it would take as arguments the list of symbols needed to fill the imports. The function would then fill in the GOT entries with these symbols, and then call the user-defined `_init` function for the unit. The implementation for **invoke** would call load, and then call the `dyninit` function with the arguments supplied to **invoke**.

The current Units implementation [13] is similar to the one we have described above, but is written in Scheme (rather than TAL), a dynamically typed language. Therefore, while linking errors within `dyninit` may be handled gracefully in our system (since they will result in thrown exceptions), in Scheme they will result in run-time type errors, halting system service. Alternatively, run-time type checks would have to be provided for each access of the GOT.

5.5 SPIN

The extensible operating systems community has explored a number of approaches to dynamic linking. For example, the SPIN [4] kernel may load untrusted extensions written in the type-safe language Modula-3. In SPIN, dynamic linking operates on objects called domains [38], which are collections of code, data, and exported symbols. Domains are quite similar to Units, with the functionality of **invoke** spread among separate functions for creation, linking, and initialization, along with other useful operations, including unlinking and combining. All of these operations are provided by the trusted `Domain` module. Furthermore, all operations are subject to security checks based on runtime criteria. For example, when one domain is linked against the interface of another, the interface seen may depend on the caller's privilege.

We can implement domains using techniques described above, with the addition of filters to take security information into account. TAL/Load would improve on the security of the current SPIN implementation in the same ways as OCaml: less of the domain implementation must be trusted, and integrity of extensions can be verified, rather than relegated to a trusted compiler.

5.6 TMAL

The TAL module system implemented for TALx86, MTAL (Modular Typed Assembly Language [15]), provides a typed version of standard static linking facilities. Typed Module Assembly Language (TMAL) [10] is an alternative module system for TAL that provides a different model of linking, including dynamic linking. Our work in TAL/Load is an extension to TAL to allow dynamically linking MTAL modules. Therefore, TMAL and TAL/Load can be seen as two ways to solve similar problems. TMAL has not been implemented.

TMAL adds a simple notion of first-class modules to TAL; by using explicit coercions accompanied by runtime checks, the type system remains decidable. The operations provided for TMAL module values are much like those for SPIN domains, described above. Two modules can be linked together to form a third module, and the circumstances of linking can be customized. In particular, coercions are provided to remove exported names from a module, and to rename its types and/or values. In addition, modules can be linked with symbols from the program (rather than other modules).

TMAL also provides primitives for reflection. In particular, TMAL's `dlsym_v` is essentially the same as DLpop's `dlsym`. MTAL, and thus TAL/Load, makes the simplification that all named types are global, as we explained in §2.1. As a module is loaded, its type components are added into the global namespace. However, in TMAL, first-class modules can contain type components, which introduces a level of hierarchy. As a result, TMAL provides a `dlsym_t` operation for looking up a type component of a module, to be used prior to retrieving a value that has that type.

Finally, TMAL provides primitives for creating and loading dynamically-linked libraries, respectively; the latter operation is similar to load, and the former is something that we do at compile-time.

The major difference between TAL/Load and TMAL is that TAL/Load is intended for *programming* the sorts of operations that TMAL provides as primitive; the result is a smaller TCB. On the other hand, the goal of TMAL is to preserve and statically verify the constraints expressed by the source module language at the assembly language level. We could easily implement the majority of TMAL using TAL/Load, where the notion of `handle` as implemented in DLpop is analogous to a first-class module TMAL. Breaking the linking functionality out of DLpop's `dlopen` into the various TMAL linking primitives would be straightforward for values, but tricky for types, though still possible; *e.g.* our technical report [20] describes a way to implement load to hide global types from loaded modules, and we could use existential types to implement something like `dlsym_t`. However, in such an implementation, some properties that could be statically verified by TMAL, would have to be dynamically checked by load.

On the other hand, programming provides flexibility. In the case of values, we could even program additional module coercions, since they essentially control a module's symbol table. For example, we could add security information to the table to be used during linking, as is done in SPIN.

5.7 Low-Level Dynamic Linking Mechanisms

A useful reference of low-level, dynamic linking mechanisms may be found in Franz [14]. One technique that he presents, which has been used to implement some versions of DLopen (as opposed to the ELF methodology [40]), is called load-time rewriting. Rather than pay the indirection penalty of using a GOT, the dynamic linker rewrites each of the call-sites for an external reference with the correct address.

This technique is a simple form of run-time code generation. Popcorn and the TAL implementation provide facilities for type-safe run-time code generation, called Cyclone [21], that we can use to implement load-time rewriting. Rather than compile functions to indirect external references through a GOT, we instead create template functions that abstract their external references. When `dyninit` is called, each template function is invoked with the appropriate symbols (found by calling `lookup`), returning a custom version of the original function, closed with respect to the provided symbols. This function is then registered with the dynamic symbol table using `update`. The advantage of this approach is that the process of rewriting can be proven completely safe.

There are two notable disadvantages. First, mutually recursive functions are problematic because their template functions must be called in a particular order. One possible solution is to use one level of indirection for recursive calls, backpatching the correct values. Another disadvantage is that template functions make copies of the functions they abstract, rather than filling in the holes in place; Cyclone's approach is more general, but not necessary in our context. However, the overall cost of doing this should be low (especially relative to verification). We plan to experiment with this approach in future work.

6 Conclusions

We have designed, implemented, and demonstrated TAL/Load, the first complete type-safe dynamic linking framework for native code. Our approach has many advantages:

- It supports linking of native code so dynamic extensions may be written in many source languages.
- It is composed largely of components already present in the TAL trusted computing base, therefore its addition does not overly complicate the code verification system.
- It is expressive enough to support a variety of dynamic linking strategies in an efficient manner.

Furthermore, there is nothing specific to TAL in this strategy—we believe that in principle it would also be applicable to Proof Carrying Code (with some changes to verification condition generation). We see this work as the first step in a larger study of type-safe extensible systems.

References

1. M. Abadi, L. Cardelli, B. Pierce, and G. Plotkin. Dynamic typing in a statically-typed language. *ACM Transactions on Programming Languages and Systems*, 13(2):237–268, April 1991.
2. A. W. Appel and A. P. Felty. A semantic model of types and machine instructions for proof-carrying code. In *Twenty-Seventh ACM Symposium on Principles of Programming Languages*, pages 243–253, Boston, Jan. 2000.
3. K. Arnold and J. Gosling. *The Java Programming Language*. Addison-Wesley, 1996.
4. B. Bershad, S. Savage, P. Pardyak, E. G. Sirer, D. Becker, M. Fiuczynski, C. Chambers, and S. Eggers. Extensibility, safety, and performance in the SPIN operating system. In *Proceedings of the 15th ACM Symposium on Operating System Principles*, pages 267–284, Copper Mountain Resort, Colorado, 1995.
5. H. Boehm and M. Weiser. Garbage collection in an uncooperative environment. *Software—Practice and Experience*, 18(9):807–820, September 1988.
6. C. Colby, P. Lee, G. C. Necula, F. Blau, K. Cline, and M. Plesko. A certifying compiler for Java. In *Proceedings of the 2000 ACM SIGPLAN Conference on Programming Language Design and Implementation (PLDI00)*, June 2000.
7. Microsoft COM technologies. `http://www.microsoft.com/com/default.asp`.
8. K. Crary, S. Weirich, and G. Morrisett. Intensional polymorphism in type-erasure semantics. In *1998 ACM International Conference on Functional Programming*, pages 301–312, Baltimore, Sept. 1998. Extended version published as Cornell University technical report TR98-1721.
9. DLOPEN(3). Linux Programmer's Manual, December 1995.
10. D. Duggan. Sharing in Typed Module Assembly Language. In *Proceedings of the Third ACM SIGPLAN Workshop on Types in Compilation*, September 2000.
11. D. R. Engler, M. F. Kaashoek, and J. O'Toole Jr. Exokernel: an operating system architecture for application-level resource management. In *Proceedings of the 15th ACM Symposium on Operating Systems Principles*, pages 251–266, Copper Mountain Resort, Colorado, December 1995.

12. Flashed webserver. `http://flashed.cis.upenn.edu`.
13. M. Flatt and M. Felleisen. Units: Cool modules for HOT languages. In *Proceedings of SIGPLAN International Conference on Programming Language Design and Implementation*, pages 236–248. ACM, June 1998.
14. M. Franz. Dynamic linking of software components. *IEEE Computer*, 30(3):74–81, March 1997.
15. N. Glew and G. Morrisett. Type-safe linking and modular assembly language. In *Twenty-Sixth ACM Symposium on Principles of Programming Languages*, 1999.
16. D. Grossman and G. Morrisett. Scalable certification for Typed Assembly Language. In *Proceedings of the Third ACM SIGPLAN Workshop on Types in Compilation*, September 2000.
17. R. Harper, J. C. Mitchell, and E. Moggi. Higher-order modules and the phase distinction. In *Seventeenth ACM Symposium on Principles of Programming Languages*, pages 341–354, San Francisco, Jan. 1990.
18. M. Hicks. *Dynamic Software Updating*. PhD thesis, Department of Computer and Information Science, University of Pennsylvania, 2001.
19. M. Hicks, J. T. Moore, and S. Nettles. Dynamic software updating. In *Proceedings of the ACM SIGPLAN Conference on Programming Language Design and Implementation*. ACM, June 2001. To appear.
20. M. Hicks and S. Weirich. A calculus for dynamic loading. Technical Report MS-CIS-00-07, University of Pennsylvania, 2000.
21. L. Hornof and T. Jim. Certifying compilation and run-time code generation. *Journal of Higher-Order and Symbolic Computation*, 12(4), 1999. An earlier version appeared in Partial Evaluation and Semantics-Based Program Manipulation, January 22-23, 1999.
22. Hotjava browser. `http://java.sun.com/products/hotjava/index.html`.
23. Basics of java class loaders, 1996.
`http://www.javaworld.com/javaworld/jw-10-1996/jw-10-indepth.html`.
24. John R. Levine. *Linkers and Loaders*. Morgan-Kaufman, 2000.
25. D. Kozen. Efficient code certification. Technical Report 98-1661, Department of Computer Science, Cornell University, Ithaca, NY 12853-7501, January 1998.
26. X. Leroy. Manifest types, modules and separate compilation. In *Twenty-First ACM Symposium on Principles of Programming Languages*, pages 109–122, Portland, Oregon, Jan. 1994.
27. X. Leroy. *The Objective Caml System, Release 3.00*. Institut National de Recherche en Informatique et Automatique (INRIA), 2000. Available at
`http://caml.inria.fr`.
28. M. Lillibridge. *Translucent Sums: A Foundation for Higher-Order Module Systems*. PhD thesis, Carnegie Mellon University, School of Computer Science, Pittsburgh, Pennsylvania, May 1997.
29. T. Lindholm and F. Yellin. *The Java Virtual Machine Specification*. Addison-Wesley, 1996.
30. R. Milner, M. Tofte, R. Harper, and D. MacQueen. *The Definition of Standard ML (Revised)*. The MIT Press, Cambridge, Massachusetts, 1997.
31. J. C. Mitchell and G. D. Plotkin. Abstract types have existential type. *ACM Transactions on Programming Languages and Systems*, 10(3):470–502, July 1988.
32. G. Morrisett, K. Crary, N. Glew, D. Grossman, R. Samuels, F. Smith, D. Walker, S. Weirich, and S. Zdancewic. TALx86: A realistic typed assembly language. In *Second Workshop on Compiler Support for System Software*, Atlanta, May 1999.

33. G. Morrisett, D. Walker, K. Crary, and N. Glew. From System F to typed assembly language. *ACM Transactions on Programming Languages and Systems*, 21(3):527–568, May 1999. An earlier version appeared in the 1998 Symposium on Principles of Programming Languages.
34. G. Necula. Proof-carrying code. In *Twenty-Fourth ACM Symposium on Principles of Programming Languages*, pages 106–119, Paris, Jan. 1997.
35. G. Necula and P. Lee. Safe kernel extensions without run-time checking. In *Second Symposium on Operating Systems Design and Implementation*, pages 229–243, Seattle, Oct. 1996.
36. J. Peterson, P. Hudak, and G. S. Ling. Principled dynamic•code improvement. Technical Report YALEU/DCS/RR-1135, Department of Computer Science, Yale University, July 1997.
37. F. Rouaix. A Web navigator with applets in Caml. In *Proceedings of the 5th International World Wide Web Conference, in Computer Networks and Telecommunications Networking*, volume 28, pages 1365–1371. Elsevier, May 1996.
38. E. G. Sirer, M. E. Fiuczynski, P. Pardyak, and B. N. Bershad. Safe dynamic linking in an extensible operating system. In *First Workshop on Compiler Support for System Software*, Tucson, February 1996.
39. E. G. Sirer, R. Grimm, A. J. Gregory, and B. N. Bershad. Design and implementation of a distributed virtual machine for networked computers. In *Proceedings of the Seventeenth Symposium on Operating Systems Principles*, December 1999.
40. Tool Interface Standards Committee. Executable and Linking Format (ELF) specification. `http://x86.ddj.com/ftp/manuals/tools/elf.pdf`, May 1995.
41. D. Walker and G. Morrisett. Alias types for recursive data structures. In *Proceedings of the Third ACM SIGPLAN Workshop on Types in Compilation*, September 2000.
42. S. Weirich. Type-safe cast. In *Proceedings of the Fifth ACM SIGPLAN International Conference on Functional Programming Languages*, pages 58–67, September 2000.

Alias Types for Recursive Data Structures*

David Walker[1] and Greg Morrisett[2]

[1] Carnegie Mellon University
[2] Cornell University

Abstract. Linear type systems permit programmers to deallocate or explicitly recycle memory, but are severely restricted by the fact that they admit no aliasing. This paper describes a pseudo-linear type system that allows a degree of aliasing and memory reuse as well as the ability to define complex recursive data structures. Our type system can encode conventional linear data structures such as linear lists and trees as well as more sophisticated data structures including cyclic and doubly-linked lists and trees. In the latter cases, our type system is expressive enough to represent pointer aliasing and yet safely permit destructive operations such as object deallocation. We demonstrate the flexibility of our type system by encoding two common space-conscious algorithms: destination-passing style and Deutsch-Schorr-Waite or "link-reversal" traversal algorithms.

1 Introduction

Type-safe programming languages, such as Haskell, Java, and ML, do not give programmers control over memory management. In particular, these languages do not allow programmers to separate allocation and initialization of memory objects, nor do they allow explicit re-use of memory objects. Rather, allocation and initialization of objects are presented to the programmer as an atomic operation, and re-use of memory is achieved "under the covers" through garbage collection. In other words, memory management is achieved by meta-linguistic mechanisms that are largely outside the control of the programmer.

In type-unsafe languages such as C or C++, programmers have control over memory management so they can tailor routines for application-specific constraints, where the time and/or space overheads of general-purpose memory management mechanisms do not suffice. However, such languages have a far more complicated and error-prone programming model. In particular, neither the static type systems, the compilers, nor the run-time systems of these languages

* This material is based on work supported in part by the AFOSR grant F49620-97-1-0013, the National Science Foundation under Grant No. EIA 97-03470, and the Advanced Research Projects Agency CSTO under the title "The Fox Project: Advanced Languages for Systems Software", ARPA Order No.C533, issued by ESC/ENS under Contract No. F19628-95-C-0050. Any opinions, findings, and conclusions or recommendations expressed in this publication are those of the authors and do not reflect the views of these agencies.

R. Harper (Ed.): TIC 2000, LNCS 2071, pp. 177–206, 2001.

prevent the accidental use of uninitialized objects, or the accidental re-use of memory at an incompatible type. Such errors are extremely costly to diagnose and correct.

Our ultimate goal is to provide support for programmer-controlled memory management, without sacrificing type-safety, and without incurring significant overhead. In addition, we hope to discover general typing mechanisms and principles that allow greater lattitude in the design of low-level languages intended for systems applications or as the target of certifying compilers [28,30]. In this paper, we take a step further towards these goals by developing a type system that gives fine-grained control over memory management, for a rich class of recursively defined datatypes. We demonstrate the power of the type system by showing how we can safely encode two important classes of optimization, destination-passing style and link-reversal traversals of data structures.

1.1 Background

One well-known principle for proving type safety is based upon *type-invariance of memory locations*. Simply put, this property says that, when allocated, a memory object should (conceptually) be stamped with its type, and that the type of the object should not change during evaluation. When this property is maintained, it is straightforward to prove a subject-reduction or type-preservation property (see for example [44,16]), which is in turn crucial to establishing type-soundness. There are many examples from language design where this principle has been violated and resulted in an unsoundness. For instance, the naive treatment of polymorphic references in an ML-like language, or the covariant treatment of arrays in a Java-like language, both violate this basic principle.

From the type-invariance principle, it becomes clear why most type-safe languages do not support user-level initialization or memory recycling: the type τ of the memory object cannot change, so (1) it must initially have type τ and (2) must continue to have type τ after an evaluation step. Atomic allocation and initialization ensures the first invariant, and the lack of explicit recycling ensures the second. Thus, it appears that some meta-linguistic mechanism is necessary to achieve memory management when the type-invariance principle is employed.

Linear type systems [42,40] employ a different principle to achieve subject-reduction. In a linear setting, the crucial invariant is that memory objects must have exactly one reference — that is, no object can be aliased. Unlike the traditional approach, the type of a memory object can change over time and thus, explicit initialization and recycling can be performed in the language. Unfortunately, the inability to share objects through aliasing can have a steep cost: Many common and efficient data structures that use sharing or involve cycles cannot be implemented.

In recent previous work, we considered a generalization of linear types that supported a very limited degree of aliasing [36]. Like linear type systems, our alias types supported separation of allocation and initialization, and explicit re-use of memory, but unlike linear approaches, some objects could have more than one reference. To achieve subject reduction, we tracked aliasing in the type system by giving memory objects unique names, and maintained the invariant that the names were unique. We found that alias types unified a number of ad-hoc features in our Typed Assembly Language, including the treatment of initialization and control stacks. Furthermore, the alias type constructors were easy to add to our type checker for TALx86 [38].

Unfortunately, the named objects in our alias-type system were restricted to a "second-class" status; though named objects could be passed to and from functions, the type system prevented a programmer from placing these objects in a recursive datatype such as a list or tree. The problem is that our type system did not track aliasing beyond a certain compile-time "frontier", and in this respect, was similar to the k-limiting approaches used in alias analysis [18]. As a result, we could not embed linear datatypes into our language, and the opportunities for user-level memory management were greatly reduced.

In this paper, we extend alias types to cover recursive datatypes in full generality. Our type system is powerful enough to encode linear variants of lists and trees, as well as richer data structures with complex shapes and aliasing relationships, such as cyclic or doubly-linked lists and trees. The critical addition to the type system is a mechanism for combining recursive type operators with first-class store abstractions that represent repeated patterns of aliasing. In this respect, our work is inspired by the more complex approaches to alias and shape analysis that have recently appeared in the literature [11,12,33].

The generalization to recursive datatypes opens the door for users or certifying compilers to have far more control over the memory management of complex data structures. To demonstrate this fact, we show how two classes of space optimization can be encoded in a language based on recursive alias types. The first optimization, called *destination-passing style* [41,22,7,24] transforms algorithms that are "tail-recursive modulo allocation" into properly tail-recursive algorithms, thereby avoiding the space overheads of a control stack. The second optimization shows how we can safely encode Deutsch-Schorr-Waite algorithms [35] for traversing a tree using minimal additional space, based on link reversal.

In the following section, we motivate the type structure of the language by introducing a series of type-theoretic abstraction mechanisms that enable suitable approximations of the store. We then show how these constructors may be used to encode a number of common data structures, without losing the ability to explicitly manage memory. Section 3 formalizes these ideas by presenting the syntax and static semantics of a programming language that includes instructions for allocating, deallocating, and overwriting memory objects. Section 4 shows how the destination-passing style and link-reversal optimizations can be safely encoded in the language. Section 5 presents an operational semantics for the language and states a type soundness theorem. We close in Section 6 by discussing some of the limitations of this work and how they might be addressed as well as giving more detail on related research.

2 Types for Describing Store Shapes

The linear pair $\tau_1 \otimes \tau_2$ captures an extremely valuable memory management invariant: There is only one access path to any value with this type. Consequently, if x has type $\tau_1 \otimes \tau_2$ then once both its components have been extracted, it is safe to reuse x to store new values with incompatible types. Since the only way to access x's data is through x itself, there is no chance that this reuse can introduce inconsistent views of the store and unsoundness into the system.

Unfortunately, the restriction to a single access path makes it impossible to construct a number of important data structures. Our goal is to lift this restriction and yet retain the capacity to reuse or deallocate memory when there is a pointer to it. Our approach is based on the intuition that a linear data structure may be decomposed into two parts, a piece of state and a pointer to that state. Destructive operations such as memory reuse alter only the state component and leave the pointer part unchanged. Consequently, if the goal is to ensure no inconsistencies arise, only the state component need be treated linearly. The pointer may be freely copied, making it possible to construct complex data structures with shared parts. Of course, in order to actually *use* a pointer, there must be some way to relate it to the state it points to. We make this relationship explicit in the type system by introducing locations, ℓ, that contain the state component, and by specializing the type of a pointer to indicate the location it points to. Consider again the linear pair $\tau_1 \otimes \tau_2$. We factor it into two parts:

- A type for the state, called an *aliasing constraint* or *store description*, that takes the form $\{\ell \mapsto \langle \tau_1, \tau_2 \rangle\}$. This type states that at location ℓ there exists a memory block containing objects with types τ_1 and τ_2.
- A type for a pointer to the location: $ptr(\ell)$. This type is a *singleton type*—any pointer described by this type is a pointer to the one location ℓ and to no other location.

This simple trick provides a tremendous flexibility advantage over conventional linear type systems because even though constraints may not alias one another, there is no explicit restriction on the way pointer types may be manipulated.

We build complicated data structures by joining a number of aliasing constraints together using the $\otimes$ constructor. For example, the following DAG may be specified by the constraints below.

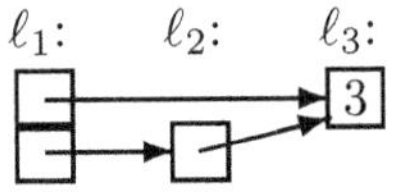

$$\{\ell_1 \mapsto \langle ptr(\ell_3), ptr(\ell_2) \rangle\} \otimes$$
$$\{\ell_2 \mapsto \langle ptr(\ell_3) \rangle\} \otimes$$
$$\{\ell_3 \mapsto \langle int \rangle\}$$

The most important property of $\otimes$ is that it joins descriptions for *separate portions* of the store. In this respect, it is identical to the "spatial conjunction" studied by Reynolds [32] and Ishtiaq and O'Hearn [17]. This separation property makes it possible to reason about potential aliasing relationships. For example, if a store is described by constraints $\{\ell_1 \mapsto \tau_1\} \otimes \cdots \otimes \{\ell_n \mapsto \tau_n\}$ then each location ℓ_i on the left-hand side of one of the constraints must be different from all other locations on the left-hand side. This invariant resembles invariants for the typing context of a standard linear type system. For example, the linear context $x_1{:}\tau_1, \ldots, x_n{:}\tau_n$ implies that the x_i are distinct values with linear types τ_i. However, the analogy is not exact because a linear type system prevents any of the x_i from being used more than once whereas our calculus allows pointers to the locations ℓ_i to be used over and over again on the right-hand sides of constraints. This flexibility makes it possible to represent aliasing. For instance, in the example above, there are two paths from location ℓ_1 to location ℓ_3, one direct, and one indirect through location ℓ_2.

One other important invariant is that the ordering of the constraints joined by $\otimes$ is not important: $\{\ell_1 \mapsto \tau_1\} \otimes \{\ell_2 \mapsto \tau_2\}$ is equivalent to $\{\ell_2 \mapsto \tau_2\} \otimes \{\ell_1 \mapsto \tau_1\}$. For the sake of brevity, we often abbreviate $\{\ell_1 \mapsto \tau_1\} \otimes \cdots \otimes \{\ell_n \mapsto \tau_n\}$ with $\{\ell_1 \mapsto \tau_1, \ldots, \ell_n \mapsto \tau_n\}$.

2.1 Abstraction Mechanisms

Any particular store can be represented exactly using these techniques[1], even stores containing cyclic data structures. For example, a node containing a pointer to itself may be represented with the type $\{\ell \mapsto \langle ptr(\ell)\rangle\}$. However, the principal difficulty in describing aliasing relationships is not specifying one particular store but being able to specify a class of stores using a single compact representation. We use the following type-theoretic abstraction mechanisms to describe a wide class of pointer-rich data structures.

Location Polymorphism. In general, the particular location ℓ that contains an object is inconsequential to the algorithm being executed. The relevant information is the connection between the location ℓ, the contents of the memory residing there, and the pointers $ptr(\ell)$ to that location. Routines that only operate on specific concrete locations are almost useless. If, for example, the dereference function could only operate on a single concrete location ℓ, we would have to implement a different dereference function for every location we allocate in the store! By introducing *location polymorphism*, it is possible to abstract away from the concrete location ℓ using a variable location ρ, but retain the necessary dependencies. We use the meta-variable η to refer to locations generically (either concrete or variable).

Store Polymorphism. Any specific routine only operates over a portion of the store. In order to use that routine in multiple contexts, we abstract irrelevant portions of the store using *store polymorphism.* A store described by the constraints $\epsilon \otimes \{\eta \mapsto \tau\}$ contains some store of unknown size and shape ϵ as well as a location η containing objects with type τ.

[1] We cannot represent a store containing a pointer into the middle of a memory block.

Unions. Unlike polymorphic types, unions provide users with the abstraction of one of a finite number of choices. A memory block that holds either an integer or a pointer may be encoded using the type $\langle int\rangle \cup \langle ptr(\eta)\rangle$. However, in order to use the contents of the block safely, there must be some way to detect which element of the union the underlying value actually belongs to. There are several ways to perform this test: through a pointer equality test with an object of known type, by descriminating between small integers (including null/0) and pointers, or by distinguishing between components using explicit tags. All of these options will be useful in an implementation, but here we concentrate on the third option (see Sect. 6.1 for further discussion). Hence, the alternatives above will be encoded using the type $\langle \mathcal{S}(1), int\rangle \cup \langle \mathcal{S}(2), ptr(\eta)\rangle$ where $\mathcal{S}(i)$ is another form of singleton type — the type containing only the integer i.

Recursion. As yet, we have defined no mechanism for describing regular repeated structure in the store. We use standard recursive types of the form $\mu\alpha.\tau$ to capture this notion. However, recursion by itself is not enough. Consider an attempt to represent a store containing a linked list in the obvious way: $\{\eta \mapsto \mu\alpha.\langle \mathcal{S}(1)\rangle \cup \langle \mathcal{S}(2), \alpha\rangle\}$.[2] An unfolding of this definition results in the type $\{\eta \mapsto \langle \mathcal{S}(1)\rangle \cup \langle \mathcal{S}(2), \langle \mathcal{S}(1)\rangle \cup \langle \mathcal{S}(2), List\rangle\rangle\}$, rather than the type $\{\eta \mapsto \langle \mathcal{S}(1)\rangle \cup \langle \mathcal{S}(2), ptr(\eta')\rangle, \eta' \mapsto \langle \mathcal{S}(1)\rangle \cup \langle \mathcal{S}(2), List\rangle\}$. The former type describes a number of memory blocks flattened into the same location whereas the latter type describes a linked collection of disjoint nodes.

Encapsulation. In order to represent linked recursive structures properly, each unfolding must encapsulate its own portion of the store. We use an existential type for this purpose. Hence, a sensible representation for linked lists is

$$\mu\alpha.\langle \mathcal{S}(1)\rangle \cup \exists[\rho{:}\mathsf{Loc} \mid \{\rho \mapsto \alpha\}].\langle \mathcal{S}(2), ptr(\rho)\rangle$$

The existential $\exists[\rho{:}\mathsf{Loc} \mid \{\rho \mapsto \tau_1\}].\tau_2$ may be read "there exists some location ρ, different from all others in the program, such that ρ contains an object of type τ_1, and the value contained in this data structure has type τ_2. More generally, an existential has the form $\exists[\Delta \mid C].\tau$. It abstracts a sequence of type, location and store variables with their kinds, Δ, and encapsulates a store fragment described by C. In our examples, we will omit the kinds from the sequence Δ as they are clear from context. A similar definition gives rise to trees:

$$\begin{aligned}\mu\alpha.\langle \mathcal{S}(1)\rangle \cup \exists[\rho_1, \rho_2 \mid \{\rho_1 \mapsto \alpha, \rho_2 \mapsto \alpha\}].\\ \langle \mathcal{S}(2), ptr(\rho_1), ptr(\rho_2)\rangle\end{aligned}$$

Notice that the existential abstracts a pair of locations and that both locations are bound in the store. From this definition, we can infer that the two subtrees are disjoint. For the sake of contrast, a DAG in which every node has a pair of pointers to a single successor is coded as follows. Here, reuse of the same location variable ρ indicates aliasing.

$$\mu\alpha.\langle \mathcal{S}(1)\rangle \cup \exists[\rho \mid \{\rho \mapsto \alpha\}].\langle \mathcal{S}(2), ptr(\rho), ptr(\rho)\rangle$$

[2] Throughout we use the convention that union binds tighter than the recursion operator.

Lists where the terminal node points back to the head and trees where the leaves that point back to their roots can be encoded as follows.

$$
\begin{array}{l}
\mathit{CircularList} = \\
\quad \{\rho_1 \mapsto \mu\alpha.\langle \mathcal{S}(1), \mathit{ptr}(\rho_1)\rangle \cup \exists[\rho_2 \mid \{\rho_2 \mapsto \alpha\}].\langle \mathcal{S}(2), \mathit{ptr}(\rho_2)\rangle\}
\end{array}
$$

$$
\begin{array}{l}
\mathit{CircularTree} = \\
\quad \{\rho_1 \mapsto \mu\alpha.\langle \mathcal{S}(1), \mathit{ptr}(\rho_1)\rangle \cup \\
\qquad\qquad\qquad \exists[\rho_2, \rho_3 \mid \{\rho_2 \mapsto \alpha, \rho_3 \mapsto \alpha\}].\langle \mathcal{S}(2), \mathit{ptr}(\rho_2), \mathit{ptr}(\rho_3)\rangle\}
\end{array}
$$

Parameterized Recursive Types. One common data structure we are unable to encode with the types described so far is the doubly-linked list. Recursive types only "unfold" in one direction, making it easy to represent pointers from a parent "down" to its children, or all the way back up to the top-level store, but much more difficult to represent pointers that point back up from children to their parents, which is the case for doubly-linked lists or trees with pointers back to their parent nodes. Our solution to this problem is to use parameterized recursive types to pass a parent location down to its children. In general, a parameterized recursive type has the form $\texttt{rec}\,\alpha\,(\beta_1{:}\kappa_1, \ldots, \beta_n{:}\kappa_n).\tau$ and has kind $(\kappa_1, \ldots, \kappa_n) \to \texttt{Type}$. We will continue to use unparameterized recursive types $\mu\alpha.\tau$ in examples and consider them to be an abbreviation for $\texttt{rec}\,\alpha\,().\tau[\alpha\,()/\alpha]$. Once again, kinds will be omitted when they are clear from the context. Trees in which each node has a pointer to its parent may be encoded as follows.

$$
\begin{array}{l}
\{\rho_{root} \mapsto \langle \mathcal{S}(2), \mathit{ptr}(\rho_L), \mathit{ptr}(\rho_R)\rangle\} \otimes \\
\qquad\qquad \{\rho_L \mapsto \mathit{REC}\,(\rho_{root}, \rho_L)\} \otimes \{\rho_R \mapsto \mathit{REC}\,(\rho_{root}, \rho_R)\}
\end{array}
$$

where

$$
\begin{array}{l}
\mathit{REC} = \\
\quad \texttt{rec}\,\alpha\,(\rho_{prt}, \rho_{curr}). \\
\qquad \langle \mathcal{S}(1), \mathit{ptr}(\rho_{prt})\rangle \cup \\
\qquad \exists[\rho_L, \rho_R \mid \{\rho_L \mapsto \alpha\,(\rho_{curr}, \rho_L)\} \otimes \\
\qquad\qquad\qquad\quad \{\rho_R \mapsto \alpha\,(\rho_{curr}, \rho_R)\}]. \\
\qquad\qquad\qquad\qquad \langle \mathcal{S}(2), \mathit{ptr}(\rho_L), \mathit{ptr}(\rho_R), \mathit{ptr}(\rho_{prt})\rangle
\end{array}
$$

The tree has a root node in location ρ_{root} that points to a pair of children in locations ρ_L and ρ_R, each of which are defined by the recursive type REC. REC has two arguments, one for the location of its immediate parent ρ_{prt} and one for the location of the current node ρ_{curr}. Either the current node is a leaf, in which case it points back to its immediate parent, or it is an interior node, in which case it contains pointers to its two children ρ_L and ρ_R as well as a pointer to its parent. The children are defined recursively by providing the location of the current node (ρ_{curr}) for the parent parameter and the location of the respective child (ρ_L or ρ_R) for the current pointer.

Function Types. Functions are polymorphic with type arguments Δ and they express the shape of the store (C) required by the function: $\forall[\Delta \mid C].(\tau_1, \ldots, \tau_n) \to \mathbf{0}$. The underlying term language will be written in continuation-passing style and therefore functions never return, but instead call another function (the function's continuation). We use the notation "$\rightarrow \mathbf{0}$" to indicate this fact. Continuation-passing style is extremely convenient in this setting because it makes the flow of control explicit in the language and the store shape varies from one control-flow point to the next.

2.2 Summary of Type Structure

Figure 1 defines the formal syntax for the type constructor language. We use β to range over type constructor variables generically. When we want to be more precise, we use ρ, ϵ and α to range over location, store and type variables. A type context Δ is a sequence of bindings of the form $\beta_1{:}\kappa_1, \ldots, \beta_n{:}\kappa_n$ where none of the β_i are repeated. The domain of Δ, denoted $Dom(\Delta)$, is the sequence $\beta_1, \ldots, \beta_n$. The type constructor language itself contains all the types discussed in the previous subsection and one other, the *junk* type. Objects of type *junk* are unuseable and arise during the initialization of data structures. Section 3 contains further explanation.

A judgement $\Delta \vdash c : \kappa$ states that under type context Δ, the type constructor c is well-formed and has kind κ. Locations have kind `Loc`, aliasing constraints have kind `Store`, and types have kind `Type`. Recursive types have arrow kinds that can be eliminated through constructor application $c\,(c_1, \ldots, c_n)$. The judgement $\Delta \vdash c_1 = c_2 : \kappa$ states that type constructors c_1 and c_2 are equivalent and well-formed with kind κ. Types are considered equivalent up to alpha-conversion of bound variables and constraints are considered equivalent up to reordering of the elements in the sequence. A recursive type is not considered equal to its unfolding. The formal rules for these judgements are straightforward and they appear in Appendix A.

We use the notation $A[X/x]$ to denote the capture-avoiding substitution of X for a variable x in A. Occasionally, we use the notation $X[c_1, \ldots, c_n/\Delta]$ to denote capture-avoiding substitution of constructors $c_1, \ldots, c_n$ for the corresponding type variables in $Dom(\Delta)$. Substitution is defined in the stardard way in all cases except for the substitution of constraints in constraints. Substitution of C'

kinds	$\kappa ::= \texttt{Loc} \mid \texttt{Store} \mid \texttt{Type} \mid (\kappa_1, \ldots, \kappa_n) \rightarrow \texttt{Type}$
constructor vars	$\beta ::= \rho \mid \epsilon \mid \alpha$
constructor ctxts	$\Delta ::= \cdot \mid \Delta, \beta{:}\kappa$
con's	$c ::= \eta \mid C \mid \tau$
locations	$\eta ::= \rho \mid \ell$
store types	$C ::= \emptyset \mid C \otimes \{\eta \mapsto \tau\} \mid C \otimes \epsilon$
types	$\tau ::= \alpha \mid \mathit{junk} \mid \mathit{int} \mid \mathcal{S}(i) \mid \mathit{ptr}(\eta) \mid \langle \tau_1, \ldots, \tau_n \rangle \mid \tau_1 \cup \tau_2 \mid$
	$\forall[\Delta \mid C].(\tau_1, \ldots, \tau_n) \rightarrow \mathbf{0} \mid \exists[\Delta \mid C].\tau \mid$
	$\mathtt{rec}\,\alpha\,(\Delta).\tau \mid c\,(c_1, \ldots, c_n)$

Fig. 1. Type Structure: Syntax

for a constraint variable ϵ in C appends the list C' to the list C. We use the notation $C'@C$ to denote the result of appending C to C' (notice that $C \otimes C'$ is not syntactically well-formed). For example,

$$(\emptyset \otimes a_1 \otimes \cdots \otimes a_m)@(\emptyset \otimes a'_1 \otimes \cdots \otimes a'_n) = \\ \emptyset \otimes a_1 \otimes \cdots \otimes a_m \otimes a'_1 \otimes \cdots \otimes a'_n$$

Formally, substitution for constraints is defined as follows.

$$(C \otimes \epsilon)[C'/\epsilon] = (C[C'/\epsilon])@C'$$

We will continue to omit the initial "$\emptyset$" when a constraint is non-empty. For example, we write $\{\eta \mapsto \tau\}$ instead of $\emptyset \otimes \{\eta \mapsto \tau\}$.

3 Term Structure

The term structure is split into three classes: small values, instructions, and coercions. Figure 2 describes the syntax of the language.

small values	$v ::= x \mid i \mid \mathcal{S}(i) \mid v[c] \mid \texttt{fix}\,f[\Delta \mid C](x_1{:}\tau_1, \ldots, x_n{:}\tau_n).\iota$
instructions	$\iota ::= \texttt{new}\ \rho, x, i; \iota \mid \texttt{free}\ v; \iota \mid \texttt{let}\ x = v.i; \iota \mid v_1.i := v_2; \iota \mid$ $\texttt{case}\ v\,(\texttt{inl} \Rightarrow \iota_1 \mid \texttt{inr} \Rightarrow \iota_2) \mid v(v_1, \ldots, v_n) \mid \texttt{halt}\ v \mid$ $\texttt{coerce}(\gamma); \iota$
coercions	$\gamma ::= \texttt{union}_{\tau_1 \cup \tau_2}(\eta) \mid \texttt{roll}_{\texttt{rec}\,\alpha\,(\Delta).\tau\,(c_1,\ldots,c_n)}(\eta) \mid$ $\texttt{unroll}(\eta) \mid \texttt{pack}_{[c_1,\ldots,c_n \mid C]\,\texttt{as}\,\exists[\Delta \mid C].\tau}(\eta) \mid \texttt{unpack}\ \Delta\,(\eta)$

Fig. 2. Term Structure: Syntax

3.1 Small Values

Small values include integers (i) and singleton integers $\mathcal{S}(i)$. These two different sorts of integer can be implemented using the same representation. The annotation $\mathcal{S}(\cdot)$ is present only to guide the type checker. Plain integers are given the general type *int* and singletons are given the specific type $\mathcal{S}(i)$.

Functions are considered small for the purposes of this paper; we will not concern ourselves with the problem of collecting function closures here.[3] Functions may be recursive and contain a specification of the polymorphic variables Δ, the requirements on the store C and the types of the parameters. These preconditions are used to type the instruction sequence that forms the body of

[3] Programmers may explicitly construct their own closures using the existential types we provide to hide the type of the closure environment [25,29]. We do not closure convert our code here as it would serve only to complicate the discussion.

$$\boxed{\Delta; \Gamma \vdash v : \tau}$$

$$\frac{}{\Delta; \Gamma \vdash x : \Gamma(x)} \qquad \frac{}{\Delta; \Gamma \vdash i : int} \qquad \frac{}{\Delta; \Gamma \vdash \mathcal{S}(i) : \mathcal{S}(i)}$$

$$\frac{\Delta \vdash \forall[\Delta' \mid C'].(\tau_1, \ldots, \tau_n) \rightarrow \mathbf{0} = \tau_f : \mathtt{Type} \quad \Delta\Delta'; C'; \Gamma, f{:}\tau_f, x_1{:}\tau_1, \ldots, x_n{:}\tau_n \vdash \iota}{\Delta; \Gamma \vdash \mathtt{fix} f[\Delta' \mid C'](x_1{:}\tau_1, \ldots, x_n{:}\tau_n).\iota : \tau_f}$$

$$\frac{\Delta; \Gamma \vdash v : \forall[\beta{:}\kappa, \Delta' \mid C'].(\tau_1, \ldots, \tau_n) \rightarrow \mathbf{0} \quad \Delta \vdash c : \kappa}{\Delta; \Gamma \vdash v[c] : (\forall[\Delta' \mid C'].(\tau_1, \ldots, \tau_n) \rightarrow \mathbf{0})[c/\beta]}$$

$$\frac{\Delta; \Gamma \vdash v : \tau' \quad \Delta \vdash \tau' = \tau : \mathtt{Type}}{\Delta; \Gamma \vdash v : \tau}$$

Fig. 3. Static Semantics: Values

the function. The value $v[c]$ denotes type application of the polymorphic function v to type constructor c. We often abbreviate successive type applications $v[c_1] \cdots [c_n]$ by $v[c_1, \ldots, c_n]$. Later, when we give an operational semantics for the language (Sect. 5), we will add other small values, including pointers, but these objects are not manipulated by programmers—they only appear during run time evaluation of programs—and so we omit them for now.

The typing judgements for small values have the form $\Delta; \Gamma \vdash v : \tau$ where Γ is a finite partial map from value variables to small types. The rules are mostly standard and are presented in Fig. 3.

3.2 Instructions

Figure 4 presents the typing rules for the instructions. The judgement $\Delta; C; \Gamma \vdash \iota$ states that in type context Δ, a store described by C and value context Γ, the instruction sequence ι is well-formed.

Memory Management Instructions. The principle interest of the language is the typing of memory management instructions. Operationally, the `new` ρ, x, i instruction allocates a memory block of size i at a fresh location and substitutes the location for ρ and a pointer to that location for x in the remaining instructions.[4] This operation is modeled in the type system by extending the store description with a memory type of length i. Initially, the fields of the memory block are filled with uninitialized junk. Once a block has been allocated, it may be operated on by accessor functions `let` $x = v_1.i$ and $v_1.i := v_2$, which project from or store into the ith field of v_1. The projection operation is well-formed if v_1 is a pointer to some location η and that location contains a object with

[4] For the purposes of alpha-conversion, ρ and x are considered bound by this instruction.

$$\boxed{\Delta; C; \Gamma \vdash \iota}$$

$$\frac{\Delta, \rho{:}\texttt{Loc}; C \otimes \{\rho \mapsto \overbrace{\langle junk, \ldots, junk\rangle}^{i}\}; \Gamma, x{:}ptr(\rho) \vdash \iota}{\Delta; C; \Gamma \vdash \texttt{new}\ \rho, x, i; \iota}\ (x \notin Dom(\Gamma), \rho \notin Dom(\Delta))$$

$$\frac{\Delta; \Gamma \vdash v : ptr(\eta) \quad \Delta \vdash C = C' \otimes \{\eta \mapsto \langle \tau_1, \ldots, \tau_n\rangle\} : \texttt{Store} \quad \Delta; C'; \Gamma \vdash \iota}{\Delta; C; \Gamma \vdash \texttt{free}\ v; \iota}$$

$$\frac{\begin{array}{c}\Delta; \Gamma \vdash v : ptr(\eta) \\ \Delta \vdash C = C' \otimes \{\eta \mapsto \langle \tau_1, \ldots, \tau_n\rangle\} : \texttt{Store} \qquad \Delta; C; \Gamma, x{:}\tau_i \vdash \iota\end{array}}{\Delta; C; \Gamma \vdash \texttt{let}\ x = v.i; \iota}\ \begin{pmatrix}1 \leq i \leq n \\ x \notin Dom(\Gamma)\end{pmatrix}$$

$$\frac{\begin{array}{cc}\Delta; \Gamma \vdash v_1 : ptr(\eta) & \Delta \vdash C = C' \otimes \{\eta \mapsto \langle \tau_1, \ldots, \tau_i, \ldots, \tau_n\rangle\} : \texttt{Store} \\ \Delta; \Gamma \vdash v_2 : \tau & \Delta; C' \otimes \{\eta \mapsto \langle \tau_1, \ldots, \tau, \ldots, \tau_n\rangle\}; \Gamma \vdash \iota\end{array}}{\Delta; C; \Gamma \vdash v_1.i := v_2; \iota}\ (1 \leq i \leq n)$$

$$\frac{\begin{array}{c}\Delta; \Gamma \vdash v : ptr(\eta) \qquad \Delta \vdash C = C' \otimes \{\eta \mapsto \tau_1 \cup \tau_2\} : \texttt{Store} \\ \Delta \vdash \tau_1 = \exists[\Delta'_1 \mid C'_1]. \cdots \exists[\Delta'_j \mid C'_j].\langle \mathcal{S}(1), \tau'_1, \ldots, \tau'_k\rangle : \texttt{Type} \\ \Delta \vdash \tau_2 = \exists[\Delta''_1 \mid C''_1]. \cdots \exists[\Delta''_m \mid C''_m].\langle \mathcal{S}(2), \tau''_1, \ldots, \tau''_n\rangle : \texttt{Type} \\ \Delta; C' \otimes \{\eta \mapsto \tau_1\}; \Gamma \vdash \iota_1 \qquad \Delta; C' \otimes \{\eta \mapsto \tau_2\}; \Gamma \vdash \iota_2\end{array}}{\Delta; C; \Gamma \vdash \texttt{case}\ v\,(\texttt{inl} \Rightarrow \iota_1 \mid \texttt{inr} \Rightarrow \iota_2)}$$

$$\frac{\Delta; \Gamma \vdash v : \forall[\cdot \mid C].(\tau_1, \ldots, \tau_n) \rightarrow \mathbf{0} \qquad \Delta; \Gamma \vdash v_1 : \tau_1 \qquad \cdots \qquad \Delta; \Gamma \vdash v_n : \tau_n}{\Delta; C; \Gamma \vdash v(v_1, \ldots, v_n)}$$

$$\frac{\Delta; \Gamma \vdash v : int}{\Delta; C; \Gamma \vdash \texttt{halt}\ v} \qquad \frac{\Delta; C \vdash \gamma \Longrightarrow \Delta'; C' \quad \Delta'; C'; \Gamma \vdash \iota}{\Delta; C; \Gamma \vdash \texttt{coerce}(\gamma); \iota}$$

Fig. 4. Static Semantics: Instructions

type $\langle \tau_1, \ldots, \tau_n\rangle$ (where i is less than n). In this case, the remaining instructions ι must be well-formed given the additional assumption that x has type τ_i. The update operation is similar in that v_1 must be a pointer to a location containing a memory block. However, the remaining instructions are verified in a context where the type of the memory block has changed: The ith field has type τ where τ is the type of the object being stored into that location, but is otherwise unconstrained. Although surprising at first, this rule is sound because the constraints behave linearly. Despite the fact that the type of a memory block at a location changes, each location can only appear once in the domain of a store type and therefore there is no opportunity to introduce inconsistencies. Constraints such as $\{\eta \mapsto \tau\} \otimes \{\eta \mapsto \tau'\}$ will never describe a well-formed store. The instruction `free` v deallocates the memory block pointed to by v. This effect

$$\boxed{\Delta; C \vdash \gamma \Longrightarrow \Delta'; C'}$$

$$\frac{\Delta \vdash C = C' \otimes \{\eta \mapsto \tau_i\} : \texttt{Store} \qquad \Delta \vdash \tau_1 : \texttt{Type} \qquad \Delta \vdash \tau_2 : \texttt{Type}}{\Delta; C \vdash \texttt{union}_{\tau_1 \cup \tau_2}(\eta) \Longrightarrow \Delta; C' \otimes \{\eta \mapsto \tau_1 \cup \tau_2\}} \ (\text{for } i = 1 \text{ or } 2)$$

$$\frac{\begin{array}{c}\Delta \vdash \tau = (\texttt{rec}\,\alpha\,(\Delta').\tau')\,(c_1, \ldots, c_n) : \texttt{Type} \\ \Delta \vdash C = C' \otimes \{\eta \mapsto \tau'[\texttt{rec}\,\alpha\,(\Delta').\tau'/\alpha][c_1, \ldots, c_n/\Delta']\} : \texttt{Store}\end{array}}{\Delta; C \vdash \texttt{roll}_\tau(\eta) \Longrightarrow \Delta; C' \otimes \{\eta \mapsto \tau\}}$$

$$\frac{\Delta \vdash C = C' \otimes \{\eta \mapsto \tau\} : \texttt{Store} \qquad \Delta \vdash \tau = (\texttt{rec}\,\alpha\,(\Delta').\tau')\,(c_1, \ldots, c_n) : \texttt{Type}}{\Delta; C \vdash \texttt{unroll}(\eta) \Longrightarrow \Delta; C' \otimes \{\eta \mapsto \tau'[\texttt{rec}\,\alpha\,(\Delta').\tau'/\alpha][c_1, \ldots, c_n/\Delta']\}}$$

$$\frac{\begin{array}{c}\Delta' = \beta_1{:}\kappa_1, \ldots, \beta_n{:}\kappa_n \qquad \cdot \vdash c_i : \kappa_i \quad (\text{for } 1 \le i \le n) \\ \Delta \vdash C = C'' \otimes \{\eta \mapsto \tau[c_1, \ldots, c_n/\Delta']\} \otimes C'[c_1, \ldots, c_n/\Delta'] : \texttt{Store}\end{array}}{\Delta; C \vdash \texttt{pack}_{[c_1, \ldots, c_n | C'[c_1, \ldots, c_n/\Delta']] \texttt{as } \exists[\Delta' | C'].\tau}(\eta) \Longrightarrow \Delta; C'' \otimes \{\eta \mapsto \exists[\Delta' \mid C'].\tau\}}$$

$$\frac{\Delta \vdash C = C'' \otimes \{\eta \mapsto \exists[\Delta' \mid C'].\tau\} : \texttt{Store}}{\Delta; C \vdash \texttt{unpack}\,\Delta'\,(\eta) \Longrightarrow \Delta, \Delta'; C'' \otimes \{\eta \mapsto \tau\} \,@\, C'}$$

Fig. 5. Static Semantics: Coercions

is reflected in the typing rule for free by requiring that the remaining instructions be well-formed in a context C' that does not include the location η.

As a warm-up example, consider the process of allocating and initializing a pair of pairs, where the deeper pair is aliased. The comments on the right-hand side present a portion of the type checking context after each program point.

$$\begin{array}{ll}
\texttt{new}\ \rho_x, x, 2; & \%\ x{:}ptr(\rho_x) \\
 & \%\ \{\rho_x \mapsto \langle junk, junk\rangle\} \\
 & \\
\texttt{new}\ \rho_y, y, 2; & \%\ x{:}ptr(\rho_x), y{:}ptr(\rho_y) \\
 & \%\ \{\rho_x \mapsto \langle junk, junk\rangle\}\otimes \\
 & \%\ \{\rho_y \mapsto \langle junk, junk\rangle\} \\
 & \\
x.1 := y; & \%\ x{:}ptr(\rho_x), y{:}ptr(\rho_y) \\
 & \%\ \{\rho_x \mapsto \langle ptr(\rho_y), junk\rangle\}\otimes \\
 & \%\ \{\rho_y \mapsto \langle junk, junk\rangle\} \\
 & \\
x.2 := y; & \%\ x{:}ptr(\rho_x), y{:}ptr(\rho_y) \\
 & \%\ \{\rho_x \mapsto \langle ptr(\rho_y), ptr(\rho_y)\rangle\}\otimes \\
 & \%\ \{\rho_y \mapsto \langle junk, junk\rangle\} \\
 & \\
\vdots &
\end{array}$$

At each update operation, the type checker verifies that x has a pointer type and modifies the type of x's memory block accordingly. The interesting aspect of this example is that after the fourth instruction in the sequence, there are three aliases to the second memory block: the variable y and the two components of x. We can see this is true, simply by counting the number of occurences of $ptr(\rho_y)$ in the type checking context. Each occurence must alias the others. All three aliases are accurately tracked in the type system and any of them may be used. When we are finished with the data structure, we may deallocate it:

$$\texttt{free}\ y;\ \%\ x{:}ptr(\rho_x), y{:}ptr(\rho_y)$$
$$\%\ \{\rho_x \mapsto \langle ptr(\rho_y), ptr(\rho_y)\rangle\}$$

$$\texttt{free}\ x;\ \%\ x{:}ptr(\rho_x), y{:}ptr(\rho_y)$$
$$\%\ \emptyset$$

After deallocation, we are left with two dangling pointers, one to the deallocated location ρ_x and a second to the deallocated location ρ_y. Fortunately, the type checker prevents these pointers from being derefenced. For example, if the next instruction in the sequence was the projection $\texttt{let}\ z = x.1$, it will fail since there is no constraint C' such that $\emptyset = C' \otimes \{\rho_x \mapsto \langle \tau_1, \ldots, \tau_n\rangle\}$.

Control-flow Instructions. The typing of the case expression is somewhat unusual. Operationally, case checks the first field of the memory block in the location pointed to by a value v. If the first field is a 1, execution continues with the first instruction sequence, and if it is a 2, execution continues with the second instruction sequence. However the memory type constructor $\langle\cdots\rangle$ will not be the top-most type constructor (otherwise, the case would be unnecessary). The type system expects a union type to be top-most and each alternative may contain some number (possibly zero) of existential quantifiers to abstract the store encapsulated in that alternative. The underlying memory value must have either tag 1 or tag 2 in its first field.

Because the language has been defined in continuation-passing style, all instruction sequences are either terminated by a function call $v(v_1, \ldots, v_n)$ or a call to the terminal continuation `halt`, which requires an integer argument. Function calls are well-formed if the polymorphic function v has been fully instantiated, the constraints in the current context equal the constraints required by the function, and the argument types match the types of the function parameters.

3.3 Coercions

The last instruction $\texttt{coerce}(\gamma)$ applies a typing coercion to the store. Coercions, unlike the other instructions are for type-checking purposes only. Intuitively, coercions may be erased before executing a program and the run-time behaviour will not be affected. The judgement form $\Delta; C \vdash \gamma \Longrightarrow \Delta'; C'$ indicates that a coercion is well-formed, extends the type context to Δ', and produces new store constraints C'. These judgements are presented in Fig. 5.

Each coercion operates on a particular object *in place* at a location η. The `union` coercion lifts the object at η into a union type and the `roll`/`unroll` coercions witness the isomorphism between a recursive type and its unfolding. The coercion $\texttt{pack}_{[c_1,\ldots,c_n|C'[c_1,\ldots,c_n/\Delta']]\texttt{as}\,\exists[\Delta'|C'].\tau}(\eta)$ introduces an existential type by hiding the type constructors $c_1,\ldots,c_n$ and encapsulating the store described by $C'[c_1,\ldots,c_n/\Delta']$. The `unpack` coercion eliminates an existential type, binds the variables in the context Δ' (so these variables may be used in the following instructions) and augments the current constraints with the encapsulated C'.

4 Applications

In this section, we show how our language can be used to encode two common programming patterns, the destination-passing style pattern, which constructs data structures efficiently and the Deutsch-Schorr-Waite or "link-reversal" patterns, which traverse data structures using minimal additional space.

4.1 Destination-Passing Style

The *destination-passing style* (DPS) transformation detects a certain form of "almost-tail-recursive" function and automatically transforms it into an efficient properly tail-recursive function. The transformation improves many functional programs significantly, leading a number researchers to study the problem in depth [41,22,7,24]. Our contribution is to provide a type system that can be used in a type-preserving compiler and is capable of verifying that the code resulting from the transformation is safe.

Append is the canonical example of a function suitable for DPS:

```
fun append (xs,ys) =
  case xs of
    [] -> ys
  | hd :: tl -> hd :: append (tl,ys)
```

Here, the second-last operation in the second arm of the case is a function call and the last operation constructs a cons cell. If the two operations were inverted, we would have an efficient tail-recursive function. In DPS, the function allocates a cons cell before the recursive call and passes the partially uninitialized value to the function, which computes its result and fills in the uninitialized part of the data structure. If the input list `xs` is linear, it will not be used in the future. In this case, it is possible to further optimize the program by reusing the input list cells for the output list. Our example performs both of these optimizations.

Before presenting the code for the optimized function, we will need to define a number of abbreviations. Such abbreviations not only aid readability, but also help compress typing information in a compiler [14]. First, recall the type of integer lists *List* and their unrolling *List'*:

$$\begin{aligned} \mathit{List} &= \mu\alpha.\langle\mathcal{S}(1)\rangle \cup \exists[\rho \mid \{\rho \mapsto \alpha\}].\langle\mathcal{S}(2), \mathit{int}, \mathit{ptr}(\rho)\rangle \\ \mathit{List}' &= \langle\mathcal{S}(1)\rangle \cup \exists[\rho \mid \{\rho \mapsto \mathit{List}\}].\langle\mathcal{S}(2), \mathit{int}, \mathit{ptr}(\rho)\rangle \end{aligned}$$

Given these list definitions, it will be useful to define the following composite coercion.

$$\begin{array}{l} \texttt{rollList}\,\rho_1\,\texttt{packing}\,\rho_2 = \\ \quad \texttt{pack}_{[\rho_2|\{\rho_2 \mapsto List\}]\texttt{as}\,\exists[\rho_2|\{\rho_2 \mapsto List\}].\langle \mathcal{S}(2), int, ptr(\rho_2)\rangle}(\rho_1); \\ \quad \texttt{union}_{List'}(\rho_1); \\ \quad \texttt{roll}_{List}(\rho_1) \end{array}$$

This coercion operates on a portion of the store with shape

$$\{\rho_1 \mapsto \langle \mathcal{S}(2), int, ptr(\rho_2)\rangle\} \otimes \{\rho_2 \mapsto List\}.$$

It packs up ρ_2 into an existential around ρ_1, lifts the resultant object up to a union type and finally rolls it up, producing a store with the shape $\{\rho_1 \mapsto List\}$.

The function *append'*, presented in Fig. 6, implements the inner loop of the optimized append function. A wrapper function must check for the case that the input list is empty. If not, it passes two pointers to the beginning of the first list (aliases of one another) to *append'* for parameters *prev* and *start*. It also passes a pointer to the second element in that list for parameter xs and a pointer to the second list for parameter ys. Notice that the contents of location ρ_s are not described by the aliasing constraints. On the first iteration of the loop ρ_s is an alias of ρ_p and on successive iterations, it abstracted by ϵ. However, these facts are not explicit in the type structure and therefore ρ_s cannot be used during any iteration of the loop (*cont* will be aware that ρ_s equals ρ_p and may use the resultant list).

The first place to look to understand this code is at the aliasing constraints, which act as a loop invariant. Reading the constraints in the type from left to right reveals that the function expects a store with some unknown part (ϵ) as well as a known part. The known part contains a cons cell at location ρ_p that is linked to a *List* in location ρ_{xs}. Independent of either of these objects is a third location, ρ_{ys}, which also contains a *List*.

The first instruction in the function unrolls the recursive type of the object at ρ_{xs} to reveal that it is a union and can be eliminated by a case statement. In the first branch of the case, xs must point to null. The code frees the null cell, resulting in a store at program point 1 that can be described by the constraints $\epsilon \otimes \{\rho_p \mapsto \langle \mathcal{S}(2), int, ptr(\rho_{xs})\rangle\} \otimes \{\rho_{ys} \mapsto List\}$. Observe that the cons cell at ρ_p contains a dangling pointer to memory location ρ_{xs}, the location that has just been freed and no longer appears in the constraints. Despite the dangling pointer, the code is perfectly safe: The typing rules prevent the pointer from being used.

Next, the second list ys is banged into the cons cell at ρ_p. Hence, at program point 2, the store has a shape described by $\epsilon \otimes \{\rho_p \mapsto \langle \mathcal{S}(2), int, ptr(\rho_{ys})\rangle\} \otimes \{\rho_{ys} \mapsto List\}$. The type of the cons cell at ρ_p is different here than at 1, reflecting the new link structure of store. The tail of the cell no longer points to location ρ_{xs}, but to ρ_{ys} instead. After packing and rolling using the composite coercion, the store can be described by $\epsilon \otimes \{\rho_p \mapsto List\}$. This shape equals the shape expected by the continuation (see the definition of τ_c), so the function call is valid.

```
fix append′ [ε, ρ_xs, ρ_ys, ρ_p, ρ_s |
  ε ⊗ {ρ_p ↦ ⟨S(2), int, ptr(ρ_xs)⟩, ρ_xs ↦ List, ρ_ys ↦ List}].
  (xs : ptr(ρ_xs), ys : ptr(ρ_ys), prev : ptr(ρ_p), start : ptr(ρ_s),
    cont : τ_c[ε, ρ_p, ρ_s]) .
  unroll(ρ_xs);
  case xs
   ( inl ⟹
        free xs;                      % 1.
        prev.3 := ys;                 % 2.
        rollList ρ_p packing ρ_ys;    % 3.
        cont(start)
   | inr ⟹
        unpack ρ_tl (ρ_xs);           % 4.
        let tl = xs.3;                % 5.
        append′
          [ε ⊗ {ρ_p ↦ ⟨S(2), int, ptr(ρ_xs)⟩}, ρ_tl, ρ_ys, ρ_xs, ρ_s]
          (tl, ys, xs, start, cont′))

where τ_c[ε, ρ_p, ρ_s] = ∀[· | ε ⊗ {ρ_p ↦ List}].(ptr(ρ_s)) → 0
```

Fig. 6. Optimized Append

In the second branch of the case, xs must point to a cons cell. The existential containing the tail of the list is unpacked and at program point 4, the store has shape $\epsilon \otimes \{\rho_p \mapsto \langle \mathcal{S}(2), int, ptr(\rho_{xs})\rangle\} \otimes \{\rho_{xs} \mapsto \langle \mathcal{S}(2), int, ptr(\rho_{tl})\rangle\} \otimes \{\rho_{tl} \mapsto List\} \otimes \{\rho_{ys} \mapsto List\}$. It is now possible to project the tail of xs. To complete the loop, the code uses polymorphic recursion. At the end of the second branch, the constraint variable ϵ for the next iteration of the loop is instantiated with the current ϵ and the contents of location ρ_p, hiding the previous node in the list. The location variables ρ_{xs} and ρ_p are instantiated to reflect the shift to the next node in the list. The locations ρ_{ys} and ρ_s are invariant around the loop and therefore are instantiated with themselves.

The last problem is how to define the continuation $cont'$ for the next iteration. The function should be tail-recursive, so we would like to use the continuation $cont$. However, close inspection reveals that the next iteration of append requires a continuation with type $\tau_c[\epsilon \otimes \{\rho_p \mapsto \langle \mathcal{S}(2), int, ptr(\rho_{xs})\rangle\}, \rho_{xs}, \rho_s]$ but that the continuation $cont$ has type $\tau_c[\epsilon, \rho_p, \rho_s]$. The problem is that this iteration of the recursion has unrolled and unpacked the recursive data structure pointed to by xs, but before "returning" by calling the continuation, the list must be packed and rolled back up again. Therefore, the appropriate definition of $cont'$ is $cont \circ (\texttt{rollList}\ \rho_p\ \texttt{packing}\ \rho_{xs})$. Once the continuation packs ρ_{xs} and rolls the contents of location ρ_p into a $List$, the constraints satisfy the requirements of the continuation $cont$. Semantically, $cont'$ is equivalent to the following function.

$$\begin{array}{l} \texttt{fix}\_[\cdot \mid \epsilon \otimes \{\rho_p \mapsto \langle \mathcal{S}(2), int, ptr(\rho_{xs})\rangle\}\{\rho_{xs} \mapsto List\}] \\ \quad (start{:}ptr(\rho_s)). \\ \quad \texttt{rollList}\ \rho_p\ \texttt{packing}\ \rho_{xs}; \\ \quad cont(start) \end{array}$$

However, because coercions can be erased before running a program, it is simple to arrange for $cont'$ to be implemented by $cont$.

4.2 Deutsch-Schorr-Waite Algorithms

Deutsch-Schorr-Waite or "link reversal" algorithms, are well-known algorithms for traversing data structures while incurring minimal additional space overhead. These algorithms were first developed for executing the mark phase of a garbage collector [35]. During garbage collection, there is little or no extra space available for storing control information, so minimizing the overhead of the traversal is a must. Recent work by Sobel and Friedman [37] has shown how to automatically transform certain continuation-passing style programs, those generated by *anamorphisms* [23], into link-reversal algorithms. Here we give an example how to encode a link-reversal algorithm in our calculus.

For this application, we will use the definition of trees from Sect. 2.

$$\begin{array}{l} Tree = \\ \quad \mu\alpha.\langle \mathcal{S}(1)\rangle \cup \exists[\rho_L, \rho_R \mid \{\rho_L \mapsto \alpha, \rho_R \mapsto \alpha\}].\langle \mathcal{S}(2), ptr(\rho_L), ptr(\rho_R)\rangle \end{array}$$

$$\begin{array}{l} Tree' = \\ \quad \langle \mathcal{S}(1)\rangle \cup \exists[\rho_L, \rho_R \mid \{\rho_L \mapsto Tree, \rho_R \mapsto Tree\}].\langle \mathcal{S}(2), ptr(\rho_L), ptr(\rho_R)\rangle \end{array}$$

The code for the algorithm appears in Fig. 7. The trick to the algorithm is that when recursing into the left subtree, it uses space normally reserved for a pointer to that subtree to point back to the parent node. Similarly, when recursing into the right subtree, it uses the space for the right pointer. In both cases, it uses the tag field of the data structure to store a continuation that knows what to do next (recurse into right subtree or follow the parent pointers back up the tree). Before ascending back up out of the tree, the algorithm restores the link structure to a proper tree shape and the type system checks this is done properly. Notice that all of the functions and continuations are closed, so there is no stack hiding in the closures.

5 Operational Semantics and Type Soundness

In this section, we define the syntax and static semantics of the values manipulated at run-time, including pointers, memory blocks and the store and give an operational semantics for the language. The type system is sound with respect to this semantics.

$$
\begin{array}{l}
\texttt{letrec}\ walk[\epsilon,\rho_1,\rho_2 \mid \epsilon \otimes \{\rho_1 \mapsto Tree\}] \qquad \texttt{\% Traverse a tree node}\\
\qquad (t : ptr(\rho_1), up : ptr(\rho_2), cont : \tau_c[\epsilon,\rho_1,\rho_2]).\\
\quad \texttt{unroll}(\rho_1);\\
\quad \texttt{case}\ t\ \texttt{of}\\
\qquad (\ \texttt{inl} \Longrightarrow\\
\qquad\quad \texttt{union}_{Tree'}(\rho_1); \texttt{roll}_{Tree}(\rho_1); cont(t, up)\\
\qquad \mid \texttt{inr} \Longrightarrow\\
\qquad\quad \texttt{unpack}\ \rho_L, \rho_R\ (\rho_1);\\
\qquad\quad t.1 := cont; \qquad \texttt{\% store } cont \texttt{ in tag position}\\
\qquad\quad \texttt{let}\ left = t.2;\\
\qquad\quad t.2 := up; \qquad \texttt{\% store parent pointer as left subtree}\\
\qquad\quad walk[\epsilon\otimes\\
\qquad\qquad \{\rho_1 \mapsto \langle \tau_c[\epsilon,\rho_1,\rho_2], ptr(\rho_2), ptr(\rho_R)\rangle\}\otimes\\
\qquad\qquad \{\rho_R \mapsto Tree\}, \rho_L, \rho_1]\\
\qquad\quad (left, t, rwalk[\epsilon,\rho_1,\rho_2,\rho_L,\rho_R]))\\
\\
\texttt{and}\ rwalk[\epsilon,\rho_1,\rho_2,\rho_L,\rho_R \mid \epsilon\otimes \qquad \texttt{\% Walk the right-hand subtree}\\
\qquad \{\rho_1 \mapsto \langle \tau_c[\epsilon,\rho_1,\rho_2], ptr(\rho_2), ptr(\rho_R)\rangle\}\otimes\\
\qquad \{\rho_L \mapsto Tree\}\otimes\\
\qquad \{\rho_R \mapsto Tree\}]\\
\qquad (left : ptr(\rho_L), t : ptr(\rho_1)).\\
\quad \texttt{let}\ up = t.2;\\
\quad t.2 := left; \qquad \texttt{\% restore left subtree}\\
\quad \texttt{let}\ right = t.3;\\
\quad t.3 := up; \qquad \texttt{\% store parent pointer as right subtree}\\
\quad walk[\epsilon\otimes\\
\qquad \{\rho_1 \mapsto \langle \tau_c[\epsilon,\rho_1,\rho_2], ptr(\rho_L), ptr(\rho_2)\rangle\}\otimes\\
\qquad \{\rho_L \mapsto Tree\}, \rho_R, \rho_1]\\
\quad (right, t, finish[\epsilon,\rho_1,\rho_2,\rho_L,\rho_R])\\
\\
\texttt{and}\ finish[\epsilon,\rho_1,\rho_2,\rho_L,\rho_R \mid \epsilon\otimes\\
\qquad \{\rho_1 \mapsto \langle \tau_c[\epsilon,\rho_1,\rho_2], ptr(\rho_L), ptr(\rho_2)\rangle\}\otimes \qquad \texttt{\% Reconstruct tree node and return}\\
\qquad \{\rho_L \mapsto Tree\}\otimes\\
\qquad \{\rho_R \mapsto Tree\}]\\
\qquad (right : ptr(\rho_R), t : ptr(\rho_1)).\\
\quad \texttt{let}\ up = t.3;\\
\quad t.3 := right; \qquad \texttt{\% restore right subtree}\\
\quad \texttt{let}\ cont = t.1;\\
\quad t.1 := \mathcal{S}(2); \qquad \texttt{\% restore tag}\\
\quad \texttt{pack}_{\rho_L,\rho_R}(\rho_1); \texttt{union}_{Tree'}(\rho_1); \texttt{roll}_{Tree}(\rho_1); cont(t, up)\\
\\
\text{where } \tau_c[\epsilon,\rho_1,\rho_2] =\\
\quad \forall[\cdot \mid \epsilon\otimes\{\rho_1 \mapsto Tree\}].(ptr(\rho_1), ptr(\rho_2)) \to \mathbf{0}
\end{array}
$$

Fig. 7. Deutsch-Schorr-Waite tree traversal with constant space overhead

5.1 Run-Time Values

First, we extend the class of small values to include the junk object junk and pointers $\mathtt{ptr}(\ell)$. Next, we define a class of stored values (s) that include memory blocks $\langle v_1, \ldots, v_n \rangle$ and witnessed values $\varsigma(s)$. Witnessed values are introduced by coercions. There is one witness for each of the roll, $\cup$ and pack coercions.

$$
\begin{array}{lll}
\textit{small values} & v ::= \cdots \mid \mathtt{junk} \mid \mathtt{ptr}(\ell) \\
\textit{stored values} & s ::= \langle v_1, \ldots, v_n \rangle \mid \varsigma(s) \\
\textit{witnesses} & \varsigma ::= \mathtt{union}_{\tau_1 \cup \tau_2} \mid \mathtt{pack}_{[c_1,\ldots,c_n \mid S] \mathtt{as} \exists[\Delta \mid C].\tau} \mid \\
& \qquad \mathtt{roll}_{(\mathtt{rec}\, \alpha\, (\Delta).\tau)\,(c_1,\ldots,c_n)}
\end{array}
$$

The well-formedness of junk and pointers is established using the same judgement form as other values. Stored values use the judgement $\vdash s : \tau$. Since stored values only appear at run time, when type and value variables have been substituted away, they are always checked in an empty context. Figure 8 formalizes these two judgements.

$\boxed{\Delta; \Gamma \vdash v : \tau}$

$$
\frac{}{\Delta; \Gamma \vdash \mathtt{ptr}(\ell) : \mathit{ptr}(\ell)} \qquad \frac{}{\Delta; \Gamma \vdash \mathtt{junk} : \mathit{junk}}
$$

$\boxed{\vdash s : \tau}$

$$
\frac{\cdot; \cdot \vdash v_1 : \tau_1 \quad \cdots \quad \cdot; \cdot \vdash v_n : \tau_n}{\vdash \langle v_1, \ldots, v_n \rangle : \langle \tau_1, \ldots, \tau_n \rangle}
$$

$$
\frac{\cdot \vdash \tau_1 \cup \tau_2 : \mathsf{Type} \qquad \vdash s : \tau_1 \quad \text{or} \quad \vdash s : \tau_2}{\vdash \mathtt{union}_{\tau_1 \cup \tau_2}(s) : \tau_1 \cup \tau_2}
$$

$$
\frac{\begin{array}{c}\cdot \vdash \tau = (\mathtt{rec}\, \alpha\, (\Delta).\tau')\,(c_1, \ldots, c_n) : \mathsf{Type} \\ \vdash s : \tau'[\mathtt{rec}\, \alpha\, (\Delta).\tau'/\alpha][c_1, \ldots, c_n/\Delta]\end{array}}{\vdash \mathtt{roll}_{\tau}(s) : \tau}
$$

$$
\frac{\begin{array}{cc}\Delta = \beta_1{:}\kappa_1, \ldots, \beta_n{:}\kappa_n & \cdot \vdash c_i : \kappa_i \quad (\text{for } 1 \le i \le n) \\ \vdash S : C[c_1, \ldots, c_n/\Delta] & \vdash s : \tau[c_1, \ldots, c_n/\Delta]\end{array}}{\vdash \mathtt{pack}_{[c_1,\ldots,c_n \mid S] \mathtt{as} \exists[\Delta \mid C].\tau}(s) : \exists[\Delta \mid C].\tau}
$$

Fig. 8. Static Semantics: Run-time Values

5.2 Store and Program Typing

The pack coercion encapsulates a portion of the store, S, which is a finite partial mapping from concrete locations to stored values. We treat stores equivalent

$$\boxed{(S, \iota) \longmapsto_P (S, \iota)}$$

$$(S, \texttt{new}\ \rho, x, i; \iota) \longmapsto_P (S\{\ell \mapsto s\}, \iota[\ell/\rho][\texttt{ptr}(\ell)/x])$$
$$\text{where } \ell \notin S, \iota \text{ and } s = \langle\overbrace{\texttt{junk}, \ldots, \texttt{junk}}^{i}\rangle$$

$$(S\{\ell \mapsto \langle v_1, \ldots, v_n\rangle\}, \texttt{free ptr}(\ell); \iota) \longmapsto_P (S, \iota)$$

$$(S\{\ell \mapsto \langle v_1, \ldots, v_n\rangle\}, \texttt{let}\ x = \texttt{ptr}(\ell).i; \iota) \longmapsto_P (S\{\ell \mapsto \langle v_1, \ldots, v_n\rangle\}, \iota[v_i/x])$$
$$\text{where } 1 \leq i \leq n$$

$$(S\{\ell \mapsto \langle v_1, \ldots, v_i, \ldots, v_n\rangle\}, \texttt{ptr}(\ell).i := v'; \iota) \longmapsto_P (S\{\ell \mapsto \langle v_1, \ldots, v', \ldots, v_n\rangle\}, \iota)$$
$$\text{where } 1 \leq i \leq n$$

$$(S\{\ell \mapsto s\}, \texttt{case ptr}(\ell)\,(\texttt{inl} \Rightarrow \iota_1 \mid \texttt{inr} \Rightarrow \iota_2)) \longmapsto_P (S\{\ell \mapsto s'\}, \iota_i)$$
$$\begin{array}{rl} & i = 1 \text{ or } 2 \\ \text{where } & s = \texttt{union}_{\tau_1 \cup \tau_2}(\varsigma_1(\cdots \varsigma_m(\langle \mathcal{S}(i), v_1, \ldots, v_n\rangle)\cdots)) \\ & s' = \varsigma_1(\cdots \varsigma_m(\langle \mathcal{S}(i), v_1, \ldots, v_n\rangle)\cdots) \end{array}$$

$$(S, v(v_1, \ldots, v_n)) \longmapsto_P (S, \theta(\iota))$$
$$\begin{array}{rl} & v = v'[c_1, \ldots, c_m] \\ \text{where } & v' = \texttt{fix} f[\Delta \mid C](x_1{:}\tau_1, \ldots, x_n{:}\tau_n).\iota \\ & \theta = [c_1, \ldots, c_m/\Delta][v'/f][v_1, \ldots, v_n/x_1, \ldots, x_n] \end{array}$$

$$(S, \texttt{coerce}(\gamma); \iota) \longmapsto_P (S', \theta(\iota))$$
$$\text{where } \gamma(S) \longmapsto_\gamma S', \theta$$

Fig. 9. Operational Semantics: Programs

up to reordering of their elements and use the notation $S\{\ell \mapsto s\}$ to denote the extension of S with the mapping $\{\ell \mapsto s\}$. The notation is undefined if $\ell \in Dom(S)$. The store well-formedness judgement is written $\vdash S : C$ and is given below.

$$\frac{S = \{\ell_1 \mapsto s_1, \ldots, \ell_n \mapsto s_n\} \qquad \cdot \vdash C = \{\ell_1 \mapsto \tau_1, \ldots, \ell_n \mapsto \tau_n\} : \texttt{Store} \qquad \vdash s_1 : \tau_1 \quad \cdots \quad \vdash s_n : \tau_n}{\vdash S : C}$$

To prove that execution of our abstract machine cannot get stuck, we must know that there can be no duplication of locations in the domain of the store or in any encapsulated store.[5] We call this property *Global Uniqueness* and it depends upon an auxiliary definition of the *Global Store Locations*.

[5] Alternatively, we could have allowed locations in the store to alpha-convert. We did not choose this route because we wanted to show that our operational semantics does not implicitly copy portions of the store. Alpha-conversion would have obscured this fact since accidental copying of an existential value would have implicitly allocated additional store locations. As it stands, accidental copying of existentials would create duplicate store locations, which Global Uniqueness asserts never happens.

Definition 1 (Global Store Locations). $\mathtt{L}(S)$ *is the multi-set given by the following definition.*

$$\mathtt{L}(\{\ell_1 \mapsto s_1, \ldots, \ell_n \mapsto s_n\}) = \{\ell_1, \ldots, \ell_n\} \uplus \mathtt{L}(s_1) \uplus \cdots \uplus \mathtt{L}(s_n)$$

$$\mathtt{L}(\mathtt{pack}_{[c_1,\ldots,c_n|S]\mathtt{as}\,\tau}(s)) = \mathtt{L}(S) \uplus \mathtt{L}(s)$$

$$\mathtt{L}(x) = \mathtt{L}(x_1) \uplus \cdots \uplus \mathtt{L}(x_n)$$

for any other term construct x
where $x_1, \ldots, x_n$ *are the subcomponents of* x.

Definition 2 (Global Uniqueness). $\mathtt{GU}(S)$ *if and only if there are no duplicate locations in* $\mathtt{L}(S)$.

A program is a store paired with an instruction stream. A program is well-formed, written $\vdash (S, \iota)$, under the following circumstances.

Definition 3 (Well-formed Program). $\vdash (S, \iota)$ *iff*

1. *The store adheres to global uniqueness* $\mathtt{GU}(S)$.
2. *There exists constraints* C *such that* $\vdash S : C$.
3. *The instructions are well-formed with the given constraints:* $\cdot; C; \cdot \vdash \iota$.

5.3 Operational Semantics

The small-step operational semantics for the language is given by a function $P \longmapsto_P P'$. The majority of the operational rules are entirely standard and formalize the intuitive rules described earlier in the paper. The operational rule for the coerce instruction depends upon a separate semantics for coercions that has the form $S \longmapsto_\gamma S', \theta$ where θ is a substitution of type constructors for type constructors variables. Inspection of these rules reveals that coercions do not alter the association between locations and memory blocks; they simply insert witnesses that alter the typing derivation so that it is possible to prove a type soundness result. The rules for program and coercion operational semantics may be found in Figures 9 and 10.

5.4 Type Soundness

We now have all the pieces necessary to state and prove that execution of a program in our language "can't get stuck." A *stuck program* is a program that is not in the terminal configuration $\mathtt{halt}\,i$ and for which no operational rule applies.

Theorem 1 (Type Soundness).
If $\vdash (S, \iota)$ *and* $(S, \iota) \longmapsto_P^* (S', \iota')$ *then* (S', ι') *is not stuck.*

The proof itself uses standard Subject Reduction and Progress lemmas in the style popularized by Wright and Felleisen [44] and is mostly mechanical. Due to space limitations, it has not been included. See Walker's thesis [43] for details.

$\boxed{\gamma(S) \longmapsto_\gamma S', \theta}$

$$\texttt{union}_{\tau_1 \cup \tau_2}(\ell)(S\{\ell \mapsto s\}) \longmapsto_\gamma S\{\ell \mapsto \texttt{union}_{\tau_1 \cup \tau_2}(s)\}, []$$

$$\texttt{roll}_\tau(\ell)(S\{\ell \mapsto s\}) \longmapsto_\gamma S\{\ell \mapsto \texttt{roll}_\tau(s)\}, []$$

$$\texttt{unroll}(\ell)(S\{\ell \mapsto \texttt{roll}_\tau(s)\}) \longmapsto_\gamma S\{\ell \mapsto s\}, []$$

$$\texttt{pack}_{[c_1,\ldots,c_n|C]\texttt{as}\,\tau}(\ell)(S\{\ell \mapsto s\}S') \longmapsto_\gamma S\{\ell \mapsto \texttt{pack}_{[c_1,\ldots,c_n|S']\texttt{as}\,\tau}(s)\}, []$$
$$\text{where } C = \{\ell_1 \mapsto \tau_1, \ldots, \ell_m \mapsto \tau_m\} \text{ and } S' = \{\ell_1 \mapsto s_1, \ldots, \ell_m \mapsto s_m\}$$

$$\texttt{unpack}\;\Delta\;(\ell)(S\{\ell \mapsto \texttt{pack}_{[c_1,\ldots,c_n|S']\texttt{as}\exists[\Delta|C].\tau}(s)\}) \longmapsto_\gamma SS'\{\ell \mapsto s\}, [c_1, \ldots, c_n/\Delta]$$

Fig. 10. Operational Semantics: Coercions

6 Discussion

Our alias type system has intermediate expressiveness when compared with other frameworks for reasoning about aliasing. It is more powerful than simple k-limiting approaches [18] as it provides the ability to represent recursive data structures, but much less powerful than recent approaches based on Hoare logic [32,17]. In the following sections we explain some of the limitations of this work and discuss related research in more depth.

6.1 Limitations

There are at least four significant limitations of the work described in this paper:

1. A lack of *may-alias* constraints.
2. Limited support for union types.
3. Limited logic (no implication, disjunction, negation or equality predicates) for compile-time reasoning about store shapes.
4. Limited coercions.

The first limitation refers to the fact that no element in a store type may alias any other element of the store type. This property is what makes deallocation safe, but it also prevents us from writing many useful functions. For example, it is impossible to write a function of two or more arguments where each argument may or may not alias the others. It is also not possible to write a general graph or DAG in this language. In earlier work with Fred Smith [36], we describe how to add may-alias constraints to a simpler language and we have done this in our Typed Assembly Language implementation [38]. The disadvantage of these may-alias constraints is that destructive object manipulation, including deallocation, is disallowed.

The second limitation refers to the fact that the introduction and elimination rules for union types limit a programmer's choice of data layout. Unions always have the form:

$$\exists[\Delta_1 \mid C_1]. \cdots \exists[\Delta_j \mid C_j].\langle \mathcal{S}(1), \tau_1, \ldots, \tau_k \rangle$$
$$\cup$$
$$\exists[\Delta'_1 \mid C'_1]. \cdots \exists[\Delta'_l \mid C'_l].\langle \mathcal{S}(2), \tau'_1, \ldots, \tau'_m \rangle$$

The only way to eliminate a union is to case on the first component of the memory block. There are many other ways to represent sum types: We may want to separate the union tag from the data structure itself or we may not want a tag at all, relying instead on pointer equality tests or the ability to differentiate between nil and a pointer. In general, to separate the tag from the union type requires more dependency mechanisms than we have in this language. However, we can accomodate some additional data type representations by simply adding a new introduction and elimination forms—the type structure need not change at all. For instance an option type that is either a nil object or reference to τ may be encoded as $\mathcal{S}(0) \cup \langle \tau \rangle$. A test for zero eliminates this form of union. Regardless of which additional choices we make here, we cannot represent completely undescriminated unions; we must use some dynamic test to determine which element of a union a value inhabits before using that value.

The third limitation provides some interesting possibilities for future research. In this work, we have developed a very simple, special-purpose logic for reasoning about the store. Because our logic is so weak (it contains no implication, negation or quantifiers among other possibilities), there are many properties of the store, such as the property of being a "balanced tree," that we cannot express. One avenue for improving the expressive power of our type system is to follow the path laid out by Xi and Pfenning's DML [46,45]. They augment a functional programming language with a general-purpose logic for specifying program properties. The disadvantage of such an approach is that we would have to integrate a theorem prover into our language in order to decide the validity of the logical formulae.

Finally, the coercions we provide (*e.g.*, fold and unfold) are sufficient to do some programming tasks, but are by no means complete.

6.2 Related Work

Our type system builds upon foundational work by other groups on syntactic control of interference [31], linear logic [13] and linear type systems in functional programming languages [20,42,1,15,3,8,40].

Our research also has much in common with efforts to define program logics for reasoning about aliasing [6,9,26,32,17]. In particular, if we view propositions as types, there are striking similarities with recent work by Reynolds [32] who builds on earlier research by Burstall [6]. Reynolds' logic employs a "spatial conjunction," which, like our $\otimes$ operator, joins two operands that depend upon disjoint portions of the store. Updating a single memory cell can alter at most one of the propositions joined by Reynolds' conjunction, making it possible to state simple Hoare-logic rules for memory allocation, dereference and update.

Ishtiaq and O'Hearn [17] have further analyzed Reynolds' rules in the context of the logic of bunched implications. They give a slightly different set of Hoare rules and are able to prove that their rules generate weakest preconditions. They also introduce an operation for safe object deallocation. As mentioned earlier, one practical difference between these program logics and our type system is that for our system there is no need to implement a theorem prover to check the safety of programs. Consequently, we have found it straightforward to integrate alias types with our Typed Assembly Language implementation [38].

There are also similarities between our research and work on alias analysis techniques for imperative languages [18,21,11,12,33]. Our type system appears most closely related to the shape analysis developed by Sagiv, Reps, and Wilhelm (SRW) [33], which has also been used to develop sophisticated pointer logics [34, 4]. Although the precise relationship is currently unknown to us, it is clear that several of the key features that make SRW shape analysis more effective than similar alias analyses can be expressed in our type system. More specifically:

1. Unlike some other analyses, SRW shape nodes do not contain information about concrete locations or the site where the node was allocated. Our type system drops information about concrete locations using location polymorphism.
2. SRW shape nodes are named with the set of program variables that point to that node. Our type system can only label a node with a single name, but we are able to express the fact that a set of program variables point to that node using the same singleton type for each program variable in the set.
3. SRW shape nodes may be flagged as unshared. Linear types account for unshared shape nodes.
4. A single SRW summary node describes many memory blocks, but through the process of *materialization* a summary node may split off a new, separate shape node. At least some summary nodes may be represented as recursive types in our framework and materialization can be explained by the process of unrolling and unpacking a recursive and existential type.

One of the advantages to our approach is that our language makes it straightforward to create dependencies between functions and data using store or location polymorphism. For example, in our implementation of the Deutsch-Schorr-Waite algorithm, we manipulate continuations that know how to reconstruct a well-formed tree from the current heap structure and we are able to express this dependence in the type system. Explicit manipulation of continuations is necessary in sufficiently low-level typed languages such as Typed Assembly Language [27].

Several other authors have considered alternatives to pure linear type systems that increase their flexibility. For example, Kobayashi [19] extends standard linear types with data-flow information and Minamide [24] uses a linear type discipline to allow programmers to manipulate "data structures with a hole." Minamide's language allows users to write programs that are compiled into destination-passing style. However, Minamide's language is still quite high-level; he does not show how to verify explicit pointer manipulation. Moreover, neither of these type systems provide the ability to represent cyclic data structures.

Tofte, Talpin, and others [39,5,2] have explored the use of region-based memory management. In their work, objects are allocated into one of several *regions* of memory. When a region is deallocated, all the objects in that region are deallocated too. Region-based memory management performs extremely well in many circumstances, but unlike systems based on linear types, space is not, in general, reused on a per-object basis. Moreover, regions cannot be encapsulated inside recursive data structures. Recently, Crary, Walker and Morrisett [10] investigated an alternative region type system that reasons about aliasing between regions using similar technology as we use here to reason about aliasing between individual objects. We believe that some of the techniques developed in this paper will make it possible to capture regions in recursive data structures and we are eager to investigate a combined region-alias type framework that can take advantage of both forms of typed memory management.

Acknowledgements. Fred Smith worked with us on the predecessor to this research and the many stimulating discussions we had together contributed to the current paper. Neal Glew and the anonymous reviewers for TIC'00 made many helpful comments on an earlier draft of this paper.

References

1. Samson Abramsky. Computational interpretations of linear logic. *Theoretical Computer Science*, 111:3–57, 1993.
2. Alexander Aiken, Manuel Fähndrich, and Raph Levien. Better static memory management: Improving region-based analysis of higher-order languages. In *ACM Conference on Programming Language Design and Implementation*, pages 174–185, La Jolla, California, 1995.
3. Erik Barendsen and Sjaak Smetsers. Conventional and uniqueness typing in graph rewrite systems (extended abstract). In *Thirteenth Conference on the Foundations of Software Technology and Theoretical Computer Science*, pages 41–51, Bombay, 1993. In Shyamasundar, ed., Springer-Verlag, LNCS 761.
4. Michael Benedikt, Thomas Reps, and Mooly Sagiv. A decidable logic for describing linked data structures. In *European Symposium on Programming*, pages 2–19, Amsterdam, March 1999.
5. Lars Birkedal, Mads Tofte, and Magnus Vejlstrup. From region inference to von Neumann machines via region representation inference. In *Twenty-Third ACM Symposium on Principles of Programming Languages*, pages 171–183, St. Petersburg, January 1996.
6. Rodney M. Burstall. Some techniques for proving correctness of programs which alter data structures. In Bernard Meltzer and Donald Michie, editors, *Machine Intelligence*, pages 23–50, Edinburgh, 1972. Edinburgh University Press.
7. Perry Cheng and Chris Okasaki. Destination-passing style and generational garbage collection. Unpublished., November 1996.
8. Jawahar Chirimar, Carl A. Gunter, and Jon G. Riecke. Reference counting as a computational interpretation of linear logic. *Journal of Functional Programming*, 6(2):195–244, March 1996.

9. Stephen Cook and Derek Oppen. An assertion language for data structures. In *Second ACM Symposium on Principles of Programming Languages*, pages 160–166, New York, 1975. ACM Press.
10. Karl Crary, David Walker, and Greg Morrisett. Typed memory management in a calculus of capabilities. In *Twenty-Sixth ACM Symposium on Principles of Programming Languages*, pages 262–275, San Antonio, January 1999.
11. Alain Deutsch. Interprocedural may-alias analysis for pointers: Beyond k-limiting. In *ACM Conference on Programming Language Design and Implementation*, pages 230–241, Orlando, June 1994.
12. Rakesh Ghiya and Laurie J. Hendren. Is it a tree, a DAG, or a cyclic graph? A shape analysis for heap-directed pointers in C. In *Twenty-Third ACM Symposium on Principles of Programming Languages*, pages 1–15, St. Petersburg Beach, Florida, January 1996.
13. Jean-Yves Girard. Linear logic. *Theoretical Computer Science*, 50:1–102, 1987.
14. Dan Grossman and Greg Morrisett. Scalable certification for typed assembly language. In *ACM SIGPLAN Workshop on Types in Compilation*, Montreal, September 2000.
15. Juan C. Guzmán and Paul Hudak. Single-threaded polymorphic lambda calculus. In *Symposium on Logic in Computer Science*, pages 333–343, Philadelphia, June 1990. IEEE Computer Society Press.
16. Robert Harper. A simplified account of polymorphic references. *Information Processing Letters*, 51(4):201–206, August 1994.
17. Samin Ishtiaq and Peter O'Hearn. BI as an assertion language for mutable data structures. In *Twenty-Eighth ACM Symposium on Principles of Programming Languages*, pages 14–26, January 2001.
18. Neil D. Jones and Steven Muchnick, editors. *Flow analysis and optimization of Lisp-like structures.* Prentice-Hall, 1981.
19. Naoki Kobayashi. Quasi-linear types. In *Twenty-Sixth ACM Symposium on Principles of Programming Languages*, pages 29–42, San Antonio, January 1999.
20. Yves Lafont. The linear abstract machine. *Theoretical Computer Science*, 59:157–180, 1988.
21. James R. Larus and Paul N. Hilfinger. Detecting conflicts between structure accesses. In *ACM Conference on Programming Language Design and Implementation*, pages 24–31, June 1988.
22. James Richard Larus. *Restructuring Symbolic Programs for Concurrent Execution on Multiprocessors.* PhD thesis, University of California at Berkeley, May 1989. Available as Berkeley technical report UCB/CSD 89/502.
23. Erik Meijer, Maarten Fokkinga, and Ross Paterson. Functional programming with bananas, lenses, envelopes, and barbed wire. In *ACM Conference on Functional Programming and Computer Architecture*, volume 523 of *Lecture Notes in Computer Science*, Berlin, 1991. Springer-Verlag.
24. Y. Minamide. A functional representation of data structures with a hole. In *Twenty-Fifth ACM Symposium on Principles of Programming Languages*, pages 75–84, San Diego, January 1998.
25. Y. Minamide, G. Morrisett, and R. Harper. Typed closure conversion. In *Twenty-Third ACM Symposium on Principles of Programming Languages*, pages 271–283, St. Petersburg, January 1996.
26. Bernhard Möller. Towards pointer algebra. *Science of Computer Programming*, 21:57–90, 1993.

27. Greg Morrisett, Karl Crary, Neal Glew, and David Walker. Stack-based Typed Assembly Language. In Xavier Leroy and Atsushi Ohori, editors, *Second International Workshop on Types in Compilation*, volume 1473 of *Lecture Notes in Computer Science*, pages 28–52, Kyoto, March 1998. Springer-Verlag.
28. Greg Morrisett, David Walker, Karl Crary, and Neal Glew. From System F to Typed Assembly Language. In *Twenty-Fifth ACM Symposium on Principles of Programming Languages*, pages 85–97, San Diego, January 1998.
29. Greg Morrisett, David Walker, Karl Crary, and Neal Glew. From System F to Typed Assembly Language. *ACM Transactions on Programming Languages and Systems*, 3(21):528–569, May 1999.
30. George Necula and Peter Lee. The design and implementation of a certifying compiler. In *ACM Conference on Programming Language Design and Implementation*, pages 333 – 344, Montreal, June 1998.
31. John C. Reynolds. Syntactic control of interference. In *Fifth ACM Symposium on Principles of Programming Languages*, pages 39–46, Tucson, 1978.
32. John C. Reynolds. Intuitionistic reasoning about shared mutable data structure. In *Millennial Perspectives in Computer Science*, Palgrove, 2000.
33. Mooly Sagiv, Thomas Reps, and Reinhard Wilhelm. Solving shape-analysis problems in languages with destructive updating. *ACM Transactions on Programming Languages and Systems*, 20(1):1–50, January 1998.
34. Mooly Sagiv, Thomas Reps, and Reinhard Wilhelm. Parametric shape analysis via 3-valued logic. In *Twenty-Sixth ACM Symposium on Principles of Programming Languages*, pages 105–118, San Antonio, January 1999.
35. H. Schorr and W. M. Waite. An efficient machine-independent procedure for garbage collection in various list structures. *Communications of the ACM*, 10(8):501–506, August 1967.
36. Frederick Smith, David Walker, and Greg Morrisett. Alias types. In *European Symposium on Programming*, volume 1782 of *Lecture Notes in Computer Science*, pages 366–381, Berlin, March 2000. Springer-Verlag.
37. Johnathan Sobel and Daniel Friedman. Recycling continuations. In *ACM International Conference on Functional Programming*, pages 251–260, Baltimore, September 1998.
38. TALx86. See http://www.cs.cornell.edu/talc for an implementation of Typed Assembly Language based on Intel's IA32 architecture.
39. Mads Tofte and Jean-Pierre Talpin. Implementation of the typed call-by-value λ-calculus using a stack of regions. In *Twenty-First ACM Symposium on Principles of Programming Languages*, pages 188–201, Portland, Oregon, January 1994.
40. David N. Turner, Philip Wadler, and Christian Mossin. Once upon a type. In *ACM International Conference on Functional Programming and Computer Architecture*, San Diego, CA, June 1995.
41. Philip Wadler. *Listlessness is Better than Laziness.* PhD thesis, Carnegie Mellon University, August 1985. Available as Carnegie Mellon University technical report CMU-CS-85-171.
42. Philip Wadler. Linear types can change the world! In M. Broy and C. Jones, editors, *Programming Concepts and Methods*, Sea of Galilee, Israel, April 1990. North Holland. IFIP TC 2 Working Conference.
43. David Walker. *Typed Memory Management.* PhD thesis, Cornell University, January 2001. To appear.
44. Andrew K. Wright and Matthias Felleisen. A syntactic approach to type soundness. *Information and Computation*, 115(1):38–94, 1994.

45. Hongwei Xi. *Dependent Types in Practical Programming.* PhD thesis, Carnegie Mellon University, 1999.
46. Hongwei Xi and Frank Pfenning. Dependent types in practical programming. In *Twenty-Sixth ACM Symposium on Principles of Programming Languages*, pages 214–227, San Antonio, TX, January 1999.

A Type Well-Formedness and Equality

$\boxed{\Delta \vdash c : \kappa}$

$$\frac{}{\Delta \vdash \beta : \Delta(\beta)} \qquad \frac{}{\Delta \vdash \ell : \texttt{Loc}} \qquad \frac{}{\Delta \vdash \emptyset : \texttt{Store}}$$

$$\frac{\Delta \vdash C : \texttt{Store} \quad \Delta \vdash \eta : \texttt{Loc} \quad \Delta \vdash \tau : \texttt{Type}}{\Delta \vdash C \otimes \{\eta \mapsto \tau\} : \texttt{Store}}$$

$$\frac{\Delta \vdash C : \texttt{Store} \quad \Delta \vdash \epsilon : \texttt{Store}}{\Delta \vdash C \otimes \epsilon : \texttt{Store}}$$

$$\frac{}{\Delta \vdash \mathit{junk} : \texttt{Type}} \qquad \frac{}{\Delta \vdash \mathit{int} : \texttt{Type}} \qquad \frac{}{\Delta \vdash \mathcal{S}(i) : \texttt{Type}}$$

$$\frac{\Delta \vdash \eta : \texttt{Loc}}{\Delta \vdash \mathit{ptr}(\eta) : \texttt{Type}} \qquad \frac{\Delta \vdash \tau_1 : \texttt{Type} \quad \cdots \quad \Delta \vdash \tau_n : \texttt{Type}}{\Delta \vdash \langle \tau_1, \ldots, \tau_n \rangle : \texttt{Type}}$$

$$\frac{\Delta \vdash \tau_1 : \texttt{Type} \quad \Delta \vdash \tau_2 : \texttt{Type}}{\Delta \vdash \tau_1 \cup \tau_2 : \texttt{Type}}$$

$$\frac{\begin{array}{c}\Delta, \Delta' \vdash C : \texttt{Store} \\ \Delta, \Delta' \vdash \tau_1 : \texttt{Type} \quad \cdots \quad \Delta, \Delta' \vdash \tau_n : \texttt{Type} \\ (\mathit{Dom}(\Delta) \cap \mathit{Dom}(\Delta') = \emptyset)\end{array}}{\Delta \vdash \forall[\Delta' \mid C].(\tau_1, \ldots, \tau_n) \rightarrow \mathbf{0} : \texttt{Type}}$$

$$\frac{\begin{array}{c}\Delta, \Delta' \vdash C : \texttt{Store} \qquad \Delta, \Delta' \vdash \tau : \texttt{Type} \\ (\mathit{Dom}(\Delta) \cap \mathit{Dom}(\Delta') = \emptyset)\end{array}}{\Delta \vdash \exists[\Delta' \mid C].\tau : \texttt{Type}}$$

$$\frac{\begin{array}{c}\Delta, \alpha{:}(\mathit{Dom}(\Delta')) \rightarrow \texttt{Type}, \Delta' \vdash \tau : \texttt{Type} \\ (\mathit{Dom}(\Delta) \cap \mathit{Dom}(\Delta') = \emptyset)\end{array}}{\Delta \vdash \texttt{rec}\,\alpha\,(\Delta').\tau : (\mathit{Dom}(\Delta')) \rightarrow \texttt{Type}}$$

$$\frac{\Delta \vdash c : (\kappa_1, \ldots, \kappa_n) \to \mathtt{Type} \quad \Delta \vdash c_1 : \kappa_1 \quad \cdots \quad \Delta \vdash c_n : \kappa_n}{\Delta \vdash c\,(c_1, \ldots, c_n) : \mathtt{Type}}$$

$$\boxed{\Delta \vdash a_1 = a_2 : \mathtt{Atom}}$$

$$\frac{\Delta \vdash \eta : \mathtt{Loc} \quad \Delta \vdash \tau = \tau' : \mathtt{Type}}{\Delta \vdash \{\eta \mapsto \tau\} = \{\eta \mapsto \tau'\} : \mathtt{Atom}} \qquad \frac{\Delta \vdash \epsilon : \mathtt{Store}}{\Delta \vdash \epsilon = \epsilon : \mathtt{Atom}}$$

$$\boxed{\Delta \vdash c_1 = c_2 : \kappa}$$

$$\frac{\Delta \vdash c : \kappa}{\Delta \vdash c = c : \kappa} \qquad \frac{\Delta \vdash c_2 = c_1 : \kappa}{\Delta \vdash c_1 = c_2 : \kappa}$$

$$\frac{\Delta \vdash c_1 = c_2 : \kappa \quad \Delta \vdash c_2 = c_3 : \kappa}{\Delta \vdash c_1 = c_3 : \kappa}$$

$$\frac{\begin{array}{c}\Delta \vdash a_1 = a_1'' : \mathtt{Atom} \qquad \cdots \qquad \Delta \vdash a_n = a_n'' : \mathtt{Atom} \\ a_1', \ldots, a_n' \text{ is a permutation of } a_1'', \ldots, a_n''\end{array}}{\Delta \vdash \emptyset \otimes a_1 \otimes \cdots \otimes a_n = \emptyset \otimes a_1' \otimes \cdots \otimes a_n' : \mathtt{Store}}$$

$$\frac{\Delta \vdash \tau_1 = \tau_1' : \mathtt{Type} \quad \cdots \quad \Delta \vdash \tau_n = \tau_n' : \mathtt{Type}}{\Delta \vdash \langle \tau_1, \ldots, \tau_n \rangle = \langle \tau_1', \ldots, \tau_n' \rangle : \mathtt{Type}}$$

$$\frac{\Delta \vdash \tau_1 = \tau_1' : \mathtt{Type} \quad \Delta \vdash \tau_2 = \tau_2' : \mathtt{Type}}{\Delta \vdash \tau_1 \cup \tau_2 = \tau_1' \cup \tau_2' : \mathtt{Type}}$$

$$\frac{\begin{array}{c}\Delta, \Delta' \vdash C = C' : \mathtt{Store} \\ \Delta, \Delta' \vdash \tau_1 = \tau_1' : \mathtt{Type} \\ \vdots \\ \Delta, \Delta' \vdash \tau_n = \tau_n' : \mathtt{Type} \\ (Dom(\Delta) \cap Dom(\Delta') = \emptyset)\end{array}}{\begin{array}{l}\Delta \vdash \forall[\Delta' \mid C].(\tau_1, \ldots, \tau_n) \to \mathbf{0} = \\ \qquad \forall[\Delta' \mid C'].(\tau_1', \ldots, \tau_n') \to \mathbf{0} : \mathtt{Type}\end{array}}$$

$$\frac{\begin{array}{c}\Delta, \Delta' \vdash C = C' : \mathtt{Store} \qquad \Delta, \Delta' \vdash \tau = \tau' : \mathtt{Type} \\ (Dom(\Delta) \cap Dom(\Delta') = \emptyset)\end{array}}{\Delta \vdash \exists[\Delta' \mid C].\tau = \exists[\Delta' \mid C'].\tau' : \mathtt{Type}}$$

$$\frac{\Delta, \alpha{:}(Dom(\Delta')) \to \mathtt{Type}, \Delta' \vdash \tau = \tau' : \mathtt{Type} \quad (Dom(\Delta) \cap (\{\alpha\} \cup Dom(\Delta')) = \emptyset)}{\Delta \vdash \mathtt{rec}\,\alpha\,(\Delta').\tau = \mathtt{rec}\,\alpha\,(\Delta').\tau' : (Dom(\Delta')) \to \mathtt{Type}}$$

$$\frac{\Delta \vdash c = c' : (\kappa_1, \ldots, \kappa_n) \to \mathtt{Type} \quad \Delta \vdash c_1 = c_1' : \kappa_1 \quad \cdots \quad \Delta \vdash c_n = c_n' : \kappa_n}{\Delta \vdash c\,(c_1, \ldots, c_n) = c'\,(c_1', \ldots, c_n') : \mathtt{Type}}$$

Author Index

Lecture Notes in Computer Science

For information about Vols. 1–1998
please contact your bookseller or Springer-Verlag

Vol. 1999: W. Emmerich, S. Tai (Eds.), Engineering Distributed Objects. Proceedings, 2000. VIII, 271 pages. 2001.

Vol. 2000: R. Wilhelm (Ed.), Informatics: 10 Years Back, 10 Years Ahead. IX, 369 pages. 2001.

Vol. 2001: G.A. Agha, F. De Cindio, G. Rozenberg (Eds.), Concurrent Object-Oriented Programming and Petri Nets. VIII, 539 pages. 2001.

Vol. 2002: H. Comon, C. Marché, R. Treinen (Eds.), Constraints in Computational Logics. Proceedings, 1999. XII, 309 pages. 2001.

Vol. 2003: F. Dignum, U. Cortés (Eds.), Agent Mediated Electronic Commerce III. XII, 193 pages. 2001. (Subseries LNAI).

Vol. 2004: A. Gelbukh (Ed.), Computational Linguistics and Intelligent Text Processing. Proceedings, 2001. XII, 528 pages. 2001.

Vol. 2006: R. Dunke, A. Abran (Eds.), New Approaches in Software Measurement. Proceedings, 2000. VIII, 245 pages. 2001.

Vol. 2007: J.F. Roddick, K. Hornsby (Eds.), Temporal, Spatial, and Spatio-Temporal Data Mining. Proceedings, 2000. VII, 165 pages. 2001. (Subseries LNAI).

Vol. 2009: H. Federrath (Ed.), Designing Privacy Enhancing Technologies. Proceedings, 2000. X, 231 pages. 2001.

Vol. 2010: A. Ferreira, H. Reichel (Eds.), STACS 2001. Proceedings, 2001. XV, 576 pages. 2001.

Vol. 2011: M. Mohnen, P. Koopman (Eds.), Implementation of Functional Languages. Proceedings, 2000. VIII, 267 pages. 2001.

Vol. 2012: D.R. Stinson, S. Tavares (Eds.), Selected Areas in Cryptography. Proceedings, 2000. IX, 339 pages. 2001.

Vol. 2013: S. Singh, N. Murshed, W. Kropatsch (Eds.), Advances in Pattern Recognition – ICAPR 2001. Proceedings, 2001. XIV, 476 pages. 2001.

Vol. 2014: M. Moortgat (Ed.), Logical Aspects of Computational Linguistics. Proceedings, 1998. X, 287 pages. 2001. (Subseries LNAI).

Vol. 2015: D. Won (Ed.), Information Security and Cryptology – ICISC 2000. Proceedings, 2000. X, 261 pages. 2001.

Vol. 2016: S. Murugesan, Y. Deshpande (Eds.), Web Engineering. IX, 357 pages. 2001.

Vol. 2018: M. Pollefeys, L. Van Gool, A. Zisserman, A. Fitzgibbon (Eds.), 3D Structure from Images – SMILE 2000. Proceedings, 2000. X, 243 pages. 2001.

Vol. 2019: P. Stone, T. Balch, G. Kraetzschmar (Eds.), RoboCup 2000: Robot Soccer World Cup IV. XVII, 658 pages. 2001. (Subseries LNAI).

Vol. 2020: D. Naccache (Ed.), Topics in Cryptology – CT-RSA 2001. Proceedings, 2001. XII, 473 pages. 2001

Vol. 2021: J. N. Oliveira, P. Zave (Eds.), FME 2001: Formal Methods for Increasing Software Productivity. Proceedings, 2001. XIII, 629 pages. 2001.

Vol. 2022: A. Romanovsky, C. Dony, J. Lindskov Knudsen, A. Tripathi (Eds.), Advances in Exception Handling Techniques. XII, 289 pages. 2001

Vol. 2024: H. Kuchen, K. Ueda (Eds.), Functional and Logic Programming. Proceedings, 2001. X, 391 pages. 2001.

Vol. 2025: M. Kaufmann, D. Wagner (Eds.), Drawing Graphs. XIV, 312 pages. 2001.

Vol. 2026: F. Müller (Ed.), High-Level Parallel Programming Models and Supportive Environments. Proceedings, 2001. IX, 137 pages. 2001.

Vol. 2027: R. Wilhelm (Ed.), Compiler Construction. Proceedings, 2001. XI, 371 pages. 2001.

Vol. 2028: D. Sands (Ed.), Programming Languages and Systems. Proceedings, 2001. XIII, 433 pages. 2001.

Vol. 2029: H. Hussmann (Ed.), Fundamental Approaches to Software Engineering. Proceedings, 2001. XIII, 349 pages. 2001.

Vol. 2030: F. Honsell, M. Miculan (Eds.), Foundations of Software Science and Computation Structures. Proceedings, 2001. XII, 413 pages. 2001.

Vol. 2031: T. Margaria, W. Yi (Eds.), Tools and Algorithms for the Construction and Analysis of Systems. Proceedings, 2001. XIV, 588 pages. 2001.

Vol. 2032: R. Klette, T. Huang, G. Gimel'farb (Eds.), Multi-Image Analysis. Proceedings, 2000. VIII, 289 pages. 2001.

Vol. 2033: J. Liu, Y. Ye (Eds.), E-Commerce Agents. VI, 347 pages. 2001. (Subseries LNAI).

Vol. 2034: M.D. Di Benedetto, A. Sangiovanni-Vincentelli (Eds.), Hybrid Systems: Computation and Control. Proceedings, 2001. XIV, 516 pages. 2001.

Vol. 2035: D. Cheung, G.J. Williams, Q. Li (Eds.), Advances in Knowledge Discovery and Data Mining – PAKDD 2001. Proceedings, 2001. XVIII, 596 pages. 2001. (Subseries LNAI).

Vol. 2037: E.J.W. Boers et al. (Eds.), Applications of Evolutionary Computing. Proceedings, 2001. XIII, 516 pages. 2001.

Vol. 2038: J. Miller, M. Tomassini, P.L. Lanzi, C. Ryan, A.G.B. Tettamanzi, W.B. Langdon (Eds.), Genetic Programming. Proceedings, 2001. XI, 384 pages. 2001.

Vol. 2039: M. Schumacher, Objective Coordination in Multi-Agent System Engineering. XIV, 149 pages. 2001. (Subseries LNAI).

Vol. 2040: W. Kou, Y. Yesha, C.J. Tan (Eds.), Electronic Commerce Technologies. Proceedings, 2001. X, 187 pages. 2001.

Vol. 2041: I. Attali, T. Jensen (Eds.), Java on Smart Cards: Programming and Security. Proceedings, 2000. X, 163 pages. 2001.

Vol. 2042: K.-K. Lau (Ed.), Logic Based Program Synthesis and Transformation. Proceedings, 2000. VIII, 183 pages. 2001.

Vol. 2043: D. Craeynest, A. Strohmeier (Eds.), Reliable Software Technologies – Ada-Europe 2001. Proceedings, 2001. XV, 405 pages. 2001.

Vol. 2044: S. Abramsky (Ed.), Typed Lambda Calculi and Applications. Proceedings, 2001. XI, 431 pages. 2001.

Vol. 2045: B. Pfitzmann (Ed.), Advances in Cryptology – EUROCRYPT 2001. Proceedings, 2001. XII, 545 pages. 2001.

Vol. 2047: R. Dumke, C. Rautenstrauch, A. Schmietendorf, A. Scholz (Eds.), Performance Engineering. XIV, 349 pages. 2001.

Vol. 2048: J. Pauli, Learning Based Robot Vision. IX, 288 pages. 2001.

Vol. 2051: A. Middeldorp (Ed.), Rewriting Techniques and Applications. Proceedings, 2001. XII, 363 pages. 2001.

Vol. 2052: V.I. Gorodetski, V.A. Skormin, L.J. Popyack (Eds.), Information Assurance in Computer Networks. Proceedings, 2001. XIII, 313 pages. 2001.

Vol. 2053: O. Danvy, A. Filinski (Eds.), Programs as Data Objects. Proceedings, 2001. VIII, 279 pages. 2001.

Vol. 2054: A. Condon, G. Rozenberg (Eds.), DNA Computing. Proceedings, 2000. X, 271 pages. 2001.

Vol. 2055: M. Margenstern, Y. Rogozhin (Eds.), Machines, Computations, and Universality. Proceedings, 2001. VIII, 321 pages. 2001.

Vol. 2056: E. Stroulia, S. Matwin (Eds.), Advances in Artificial Intelligence. Proceedings, 2001. XII, 366 pages. 2001. (Subseries LNAI).

Vol. 2057: M. Dwyer (Ed.), Model Checking Software. Proceedings, 2001. X, 313 pages. 2001.

Vol. 2059: C. Arcelli, L.P. Cordella, G. Sanniti di Baja (Eds.), Visual Form 2001. Proceedings, 2001. XIV, 799 pages. 2001.

Vol. 2060: T. Böhme, H. Unger (Eds.), Innovative Internet Computing Systems. Proceedings, 2001. VIII, 183 pages. 2001.

Vol. 2062: A. Nareyek, Constraint-Based Agents. XIV, 178 pages. 2001. (Subseries LNAI).

Vol. 2064: J. Blanck, V. Brattka, P. Hertling (Eds.), Computability and Complexity in Analysis. Proceedings, 2000. VIII, 395 pages. 2001.

Vol. 2065: H. Balster, B. de Brock, S. Conrad (Eds.), Database Schema Evolution and Meta-Modeling. Proceedings, 2000. X, 245 pages. 2001.

Vol. 2066: O. Gascuel, M.-F. Sagot (Eds.), Computational Biology. Proceedings, 2000. X, 165 pages. 2001.

Vol. 2068: K.R. Dittrich, A. Geppert, M.C. Norrie (Eds.), Advanced Information Systems Engineering. Proceedings, 2001. XII, 484 pages. 2001.

Vol. 2070: L. Monostori, J. Váncza, M. Ali (Eds.), Engineering of Intelligent Systems. Proceedings, 2001. XVIII, 951 pages. 2001. (Subseries LNAI).

Vol. 2071: R. Harper (Ed.), Types in Compilation. Proceedings, 2000. IX, 207 pages. 2001.

Vol. 2072: J. Lindskov Knudsen (Ed.), ECOOP 2001 – Object-Oriented Programming. Proceedings, 2001. XIII, 429 pages. 2001.

Vol. 2073: V.N. Alexandrov, J.J. Dongarra, B.A. Juliano, R.S. Renner, C.J.K. Tan (Eds.), Computational Science – ICCS 2001. Part I. Proceedings, 2001. XXVIII, 1306 pages. 2001.

Vol. 2074: V.N. Alexandrov, J.J. Dongarra, B.A. Juliano, R.S. Renner, C.J.K. Tan (Eds.), Computational Science – ICCS 2001. Part II. Proceedings, 2001. XXVIII, 1076 pages. 2001.

Vol. 2075: J.-M. Colom, M. Koutny (Eds.), Applications and Theory of Petri Nets 2001. Proceedings, 2001. XII, 403 pages. 2001.

Vol. 2077: V. Ambriola (Ed.), Software Process Technology. Proceedings, 2001. VIII, 247 pages. 2001.

Vol. 2078: R. Reed, J. Reed (Eds.), SDL 2001: Meeting UML. Proceedings, 2001. XI, 439 pages. 2001.

Vol. 2081: K. Aardal, B. Gerards (Eds.), Integer Programming and Combinatorial Optimization. Proceedings, 2001. XI, 423 pages. 2001.

Vol. 2082: M.F. Insana, R.M. Leahy (Eds.), Information Processing in Medical Imaging. Proceedings, 2001. XVI, 537 pages. 2001.

Vol. 2083: R. Goré, A. Leitsch, T. Nipkow (Eds.), Automated Reasoning. Proceedings, 2001. XV, 708 pages. 2001. (Subseries LNAI).

Vol. 2084: J. Mira, A. Prieto (Eds.), Connectionist Models of Neurons, Learning Processes, and Artificial Intelligence. Proceedings, 2001. Part I. XXVII, 836 pages. 2001.

Vol. 2085: J. Mira, A. Prieto (Eds.), Bio-Inspired Applications of Connectionism. Proceedings, 2001. Part II. XXVII, 848 pages. 2001.

Vol. 2089: A. Amir, G.M. Landau (Eds.), Combinatorial Pattern Matching. Proceedings, 2001. VIII, 273 pages. 2001.

Vol. 2091: J. Bigun, F. Smeraldi (Eds.), Audio- and Video-Based Biometric Person Authentication. Proceedings, 2001. XIII, 374 pages. 2001.

Vol. 2092: L. Wolf, D. Hutchison, R. Steinmetz (Eds.), Quality of Service – IWQoS 2001. Proceedings, 2001. XII, 435 pages. 2001.

Vol. 2096: J. Kittler, F. Roli (Eds.), Multiple Classifier Systems. Proceedings, 2001. XII, 456 pages. 2001.

Vol. 2097: B. Read (Ed.), Advances in Databases. Proceedings, 2001. X, 219 pages. 2001.

Vol. 2099: P. de Groote, G. Morrill, C. Retoré (Eds.), Logical Aspects of Computational Linguistics. Proceedings, 2001. VIII, 311 pages. 2001. (Subseries LNAI).

Vol. 2110: B. Hertzberger, A. Hoekstra, R. Williams (Eds.), High-Performance Computing and Networking. Proceedings, 2001. XVII, 733 pages. 2001.